Romans: Finding the Faith

Bradley W. Maston

DEDICATION

This study is a product of several years of weekly studies. Within the first year of my pastorate the Lord provided an amazing group of students from Colorado State University. These students were excited to learn, understand and apply the word of God. I have kept in touch with many of them and some are still involved with our local church body today. These studies are, naturally, inextricable from the countless joyous nights of delving into God's word together and sharing sweet fellowship in Him. This collection of studies is dedicated to those students.

CONTENTS

ACKNOWLEDGMENTS

So many people have given so much to make this volume possible. There have been those who have read it, those who went through the various studies and generations out of which it came. The saints of Fort Collins Bible Church have been the willing victims of so very much of this books development. There are far too many people to mention but thanks to all, and particularly to those who were willing to read this study again and again, and provide the helpful insight and encouragement that was needed to see it through to this stage..

INTRODUCTION – WHY ROMANS?

There is always the possibility of doing something and not knowing exactly why we did it. This moment strikes us when someone asks us why we did that thing and we stand dumbfounded for a moment before we are able to even piece together a guess at what motivated us. In Bible study, that answer seems easier to find, yet we get the most out of a study if we have a specific goal. As we come to the introduction of this amazing book, it is valuable to take a moment and consider the great and exciting journey upon which we are about to embark.

Some Interesting Facts about Romans

Augustine came to the Lord reading this book.

Martin Luther identified this book as pivotal in his coming to know the Lord: "I greatly longed to understand Paul's Epistle to the Romans, and nothing stood in the way but that one expression, 'the righteousness of God,' because I took it to mean that righteousness whereby God is righteous and deals righteously in punishing the unrighteous … Night and day I pondered until … I grasped the truth that the righteousness of God is that righteousness whereby, through grace and sheer mercy, He justifies us by faith. Thereupon I felt myself to be reborn and to have gone through open doors into paradise. The whole of Scripture took on a new meaning, and whereas before 'the righteousness of God' had filled me with hate, now it became to me inexpressibly sweet in greater love. This passage of Paul became to me a gateway to heaven."

Luther wrote in the preface to his commentary on this epistle: ""This Epistle is the chief book of the New Testament, the purest gospel. It deserves not only to be known word for word by every Christian, but to be the subject of his meditation day by day, the daily bread of his soul … The more time one spends in it, the more precious it becomes and the better it appears.""

John Wesley wrote that he "… went very unwillingly to a society in Aldersgate Street, where one was reading Luther's Preface to the Epistle to the Romans … About a quarter before nine while he was describing the change which God works in the heart through faith in Christ, I felt my heart strangely warmed. I felt I did trust in Christ, Christ alone, for my salvation; and an assurance was given me that He had taken my sins away, even mine; and saved me from the law of sin and death"

Throughout Church History people have been finding that this book of the Bible can only be described in superlatives. The impact of the Holy Spirit through the writing of this book would be impossible to measure. Barth, a more recent commentator, compared this book to a bomb being dropped on the theological playground. What makes this book so powerful, and important? Do we know what we are getting into?

Who wrote this book?

The fact that Paul wrote this book is beyond question (though it was actually penned by Tertius – Romans 16:22). Internally, Paul claims to have written it, greets people that Paul would have known, and writes like Paul writes in his other known letters. Externally, it has been the uniform testimony of the early church that Paul was the person who wrote it.

But who was Paul?

The fact that Paul wrote this book only gives us a name. What do we know about Paul? The first question that we must answer is: "Why is it important to know who wrote this book?"

There are a number of reasons, but one very important one is this – when taking advice about what pills you should take you want to be sure that the person telling you to take them is qualified to give advice. Advice on why people should avoid addiction is often most powerful when it comes from an ex-addict. Paul's life has many interesting twists and turns that especially qualify him to be the tool that God used to write this magnificent book.

Early Life

Paul grew up with the Hebrew name Saul and the Roman name Paul. Many people of this time would have a name that they would use for dealings with their own people and one that they would use for their official and governmental interactions. He was well versed in Jewish, Roman and Greek cultures. Paul inherited Roman Citizenship – This was a large perk and shows that he very likely came from an influential family.

Religious Training

He was a Pharisee – Acts confirms this as well as Paul's own writing. The Pharisees were people who took God's word very seriously. They were especially legalistic and even went to the trouble of setting "hedges" around the laws of scripture to make sure nobody would break a law. For example, the Old Testament law said that people could not be whipped more than 40 times. So, the Pharisees cut it off at 39, just in case count was lost or mistaken. He studied under Gamaliel (Acts 22:3) a very important rabbi. He was an ambitious man who was coming up the ranks of the sect of the Pharisees quickly. He actively persecuted the early church (Acts 22:4-5) and would vote for the death of Christians every chance he got.

Salvation

Acts 9 gives the account of how Paul met the Lord. As he was on the road to Damascus to persecute Christians there, Jesus miraculously stepped in and blinded Paul. After the experiences surrounding this miracle Paul was changed. Before he had been the most legalistic man he could be, and now he would become the apostle who used the word "grace" more than any of the others. Before this, he had gone after the death of everyone who followed Jesus, now he himself would put his life on the line daily for that very Name. Paul believed deeply, and experientially, what he wrote in 2 Corinthians 5:17 "Therefore, if anyone [is] in Christ, [he is] a new creation; old things have passed away; behold, all things have become new." (NKJV) How powerful did Paul believe this message is?

Who Got the Message?

The Church in Rome was a young Church. We know that there were Jews and Gentiles there, and it is very likely that no Apostle had been out there to help establish the church, as we will see in our study of chapter one. Rome was the center of the world at this time. In all likelihood, this church may have been started by Jewish people who had heard Peter's sermon at Pentecost (Acts 2) and then had to return home. There were also evangelists who were not apostles such as Priscilla and Aquila who may have played a part in the beginning of this church. The reality that Rome is a very important city affects much of the language that Paul will use when writing to these people (by the power of the Holy Spirit). Paul is a master of using just the right phrase to speak to just the right audience. He uses language with laser line accuracy to get his point across in a way that his readers would understand. We will have the opportunity to look more deeply into the historical and cultural background and see more clearly than ever before what Paul was telling the church at Rome and us today.

ROMANS 1

ROMANS 1:1-7

Starting Off Right

This is the opening salutation of this great book of Scripture. In keeping with the ancient custom of addressing letters, Paul describes who he is, to whom he is writing, and the occasion of his writing this letter. While it can be easy to blow by this introduction there is much meat in the very opening of this letter. We find that the Lord reveals some amazing and important core truth about what He has done in and for the believer and the position that we have before Him.

Romans 1:1-4

[1]Paul, a bond-servant of Christ Jesus, called as an apostle, set apart
for the gospel of God, [2]which He promised beforehand through His
prophets in the holy Scriptures, [3]concerning His Son, who was born
of a descendant of David according to the flesh, [4]who was declared
the Son of God with power by the resurrection from the dead,
according to the Spirit of holiness, Jesus Christ our Lord,

Who is Paul?

Some of Paul's remarkable history with the Lord was covered in the introduction, however, it bears repeating. Paul was a violent persecutor of the church, even seeking the death of Christians. The Lord appeared to him miraculously and blinded him, changing the entire course of his life on the road to Damascus. Paul wrote of the incredible power of the Gospel because he had personally experienced it. It turned him from being a hateful persecutor of the church to being one of the major tools that God used to grow the early church as well as give us a large part of the New Testament. Paul's life is a testimony to the power of God's amazing grace. Thus, Paul writes with immense confidence and hope because he knows, personally, the power of God to change even the darkest of hearts. Paul gives three descriptions of himself:

Bond-servant – Paul here views himself as a slave of Jesus Christ. The Romans would have understood what Paul meant in calling himself a slave of Jesus because slavery was an important part of the Roman economy. By the time of Paul writing this there were countless slaves in the Roman Empire. Slaves could be purchased, inherited, sold into slavery because of debts, born into slavery, sell themselves into slavery voluntarily, or be captured in a battle with Rome. There were also many classes of slaves, and we have several examples where there were slaves who owned slaves themselves. Paul was writing as one who was "bought with a price" the price with which he was purchased from sin was the shed blood of Jesus Christ. In pronouncing himself a slave he was communicating the reality that his entire will was subjected to his Master's will. The will of God is revealed in Scripture and in studying scripture we learn what it means to submit our will to the will of God. We will discuss this at greater length when we get to Romans 12:1-2

Called and Apostle – This phrase involves two issues of confusion in the modern church. The first is the issue of "calling." It is quite common to confuse the word calling with Salvation. This Paul does not do. The other common error is to confuse calling with the idea of someone going into full time vocational ministry. However, calling does not have to do with that either. Every believer is called and has been given gifts by the Holy Spirit (more on this in Romans 12). Regardless of what a person does to support themselves they are called to live the life of Christ and use the gifts which He has given.

Apostleship is another idea that has received much abuse throughout church history. An Apostle, in the secular sense, was a messenger who was given the authority to see that his message was carried out. Paul, and the other Apostles, did exactly this. They were given the ability to do signs miracles and wonders to validate their wonderful message of the Lord Jesus Christ. Another thing that Apostles were given authority to do is to write scripture. The requirements for an Apostle are laid out in 1 Corinthians 9 and this office is not subject to human appointment (as with the only existing church offices today of elder and deacon), they were a special class of people for the New Testament church from which the entire church continues to benefit.

Set Apart – This concept describes the fancy theological word *sanctification.* The reality is that every believer is set apart unto God. God has set Paul apart for the specific purpose of spreading and recording the Gospel, and this is exactly what Paul does. Paul is going to spend this letter spelling out what the Gospel is and what it means. Nowhere is Paul more concise in his description of the Gospel (literally – "The Good News") than in 1 Corinthians 15:3-5:

> 3For I delivered to you as of first importance what I also
> received, that Christ died for our sins according to the
> Scriptures, 4and that He was buried, and that He was raised on
> the third day according to the Scriptures, 5and that He appeared
> to Cephas, then to the twelve.

The simple information of the Gospel, the simple message a person must trust to be saved is found here: Trust in Jesus Christ as the sacrifice for our sin, and His literal bodily resurrection. This is great news indeed! Compared to the "work for it" message of manmade religion, the Bible reveals the reality that we could never work for, or earn, the miraculous and amazing gift of Salvation, it had to be given to us by God. There is no way in which a man can come to God.

Promised before hand

This was not a surprise to those who were familiar with the Old Testament. As early as Genesis 3:15 God had already promised that HE would provide a way of salvation through the coming *seed* of the woman. That promise of God is fulfilled in Jesus Christ and no other. God promised these things in the Torah as well as in the Prophets and all the wonderful promises of Psalm 22, Isaiah 53 and the rest of the Old Testament are fulfilled in the Person and work of Jesus Christ. This was why Paul could always go to the synagogues and point to Jesus, because the Old Testament is filled with promise after promise of the coming Messiah!

Physical Requirement - A Descendant of David

As the Lord continued to unfold His plan of sending the Savior He continued to give information about through whom that promised Seed would come. God promised Adam and Eve that the Savior would come through their linage. Then, later, we find that Abraham was promised that the Seed would come through his line (Genesis 12:1-3). When Jacob is blessing his twelve sons who were the federal heads of the 12 tribes of Israel he told Judah:

"The scepter shall not depart from Judah, Nor the ruler's staff from between his feet, Until Shiloh (lit. "He to whom it belongs") comes, And to him shall be the obedience of the peoples." - Genesis 49:10 NASB

The Messiah, who will rule over Jerusalem in the millennial Kingdom, was foretold to come through the line of Judah. This was affirmed in God's covenant with David:

12"When your days are complete and you lie down with your fathers,

I will raise up your descendant after you, who will come forth from you, and I will establish His kingdom. [13]"He shall build a house for My name, and I will establish the throne of His kingdom forever. – 2 Samuel 7:12-13

Thus, when Christ comes the importance of His tracing back to the Tribe of Judah in both the line of Mary and Joseph (as His adoptive earthly father) is of the utmost importance, and thus the genealogies of Matthew and Luke are of such great importance.

Heavenly Requirements – Declared by the Resurrection
Jesus is not only qualified in view of the earthly requirements, but also the Heavenly requirements. The truth and reality of Jesus Christ's death on the cross and resurrection are of the utmost importance. It is remarkably upsetting to see more and more people try to present a "cross-less gospel" or try to downplay Christ's death, burial and resurrection, because without this key fact there can be no salvation for man. It is of the utmost importance that we understand this in our own lives as we trust in the salvation He provides as well as in sharing it with others! Christ is qualified, in every way, to be the Savior!

Romans 1:5-7
[5]through whom we have received grace and apostleship to bring about the obedience of faith among all the Gentiles for His name's sake, [6]among whom you also are the called of Jesus Christ; [7]to all who are beloved of God in Rome, called as saints: Grace to you and peace from God our Father and the Lord Jesus Christ.

Through Jesus
Jesus is the source of all the wonderful blessings that are ours in Christ (Ephesians 1:3-14). There is no other name by which we may be saved. He is the source of our salvation, in the past (Justification), present (Sanctification) and future (Glorification). More on those as the study continues, however each provision is a provision of God's amazing grace for the believer.

Grace

This is the first mention of the most important concept to understand in the entirety of the book of Romans: Grace. Grace is a free, or unmerited gift. When we think of a gift we must understand most clearly what a gift is. If someone gives you something, and then charges you for it, that is not a gift. If someone gives you something and then expects some favor in return that is also not a free gift. God's grace is a free unearned gift. It cannot be earned, it cannot be paid back, it cannot be diminished when we don't live up to it, nor taken away when it is unmerited (because it was never merited). Understanding how full and wonderful God's grace is stands as one of the greatest challenges in the church today. If we truly understood how amazing God's grace is we would never trade it for the petty legalisms and license of man-made religion. This is the point of this epistle: our relationship with Christ is entirely by His free, unmerited, unearned gift of Grace!

Obedience of Faith

This is the most important obedience that we need to keep before us. The word "obedience" here has the sense of "listening under." The obedience of faith differs from the idea of obedience to the law. We have been won to obedience to trust in the revealed truth of Jesus Christ and grow in our relationship with Him, as the epistle to the Romans clearly displays.

For His Name's Sake

This gets to the very core of why everything exists. In theological circles, it is often said that God's purpose in everything is *doxological*, which is a fancy word for glorification. God's purpose in everything is to magnify and glorify Himself! Believers are rightly amazed at this wonderful salvation that God has set out for us in Jesus Christ, and often wonder: "Why did He do that?" The core reason? It glorifies Him! He is glorified by saving Adam's fallen race. By His grace alone will this world be restored and healed during the millennial reign of Christ and it will all be for His glory and the sake of His Marvelous

NAME!

Called as Saints

Every believer is set apart from the world, and that is what the word "saint" means. God has set us apart in His Son, Jesus Christ. While the term "saint" has been confused throughout church history the Biblical use of the word is always consistent: A saint is anyone who places their faith in Jesus Christ and is thus separated from the earth and its destiny. Every believer can trust and rest in the reality that they are a saint. It is not something earned, nor is it some "next level" designation for very best believers. Far from it! We are saints because of what Christ has done, and that is the focus: JESUS made us saints.

Grace and Peace

The idea of God giving unmerited favor (a free gift) would be shocking to the first century reader. The Greek and Roman gods operated on a strictly selfish level. They did for those who did for them. God on the other hand gives His unlimited, unmerited favor through Jesus Christ to anyone who will believe. Paul is tweaking the typical Roman greeting here in a way that would shock and amaze the Roman readers. "Peace" was the typical Hebrew greeting and meant, not just absence of conflict, but rather fullness, wholeness and completeness. These are available only through God.

ROMANS 1:8-12

<u>Romans 1:8</u>

First, I thank my God through Jesus Christ for you all, that your faith is spoken of throughout the whole world.

Beginning with Gratitude

After the marvelous and lengthy Salutation that we studied last week we find that Paul spends the next 10 verses introducing his content matter, but he starts with gratitude. Thankfulness is something that characterized Paul's writing and letters, and it is something that characterizes the Christian life. We find the word for "thank" is very closely related to the word "grace" that we studied earlier. This makes a lot of sense given the reality that the only proper response to a gift freely given is to say "thank you".

Paul is thankful for the believers in Rome, but it is impressive how this works. Paul's thankfulness is to God (e.g. God the Father) through Jesus Christ. This teaches us something interesting about our thankfulness and prayers: they are directed to God the Father through the agency of Jesus Christ.

Faith that is a Testimony

Paul points out that their "faith is spoken of throughout the whole world." It is a fantastic reality that the faithful in Rome were a testimony to the entire ancient world. What made this so remarkable? What made their faith so special? The faith is the content of what they believed and the very fact that they did believe it. It wasn't magic, but Paul was thankful to God that the gospel had reached so far so quickly.

<u>Romans 1:9-10</u>

□ For □God is my witness, □□whom I serve □with my spirit in
the gospel of His Son, that □without ceasing I make mention of you
always in my prayers, □10□ making request if, by some means, now at
last I may find a way in the will of God to come to you.

Putting it together

Greek is often difficult to bring into English. The sentence structure and grammar of the Greek language allows for things that we find a bit confusing in English. For example Ephesians 1:3-14 is all one long sentence, which would be bad grammar in English but is acceptable in Greek. As we look at the parts of this big phrase we don't want to lose the main point. The main clause of the statement could be condensed to : "For God is my witness, I have been praying for a way in the will of God to come to you." So as we dig out the other nuggets of truth we must first be mindful of the fact that the context of this statement is that Paul longs to come and spend some time with these believers.

Can I get a witness?

Paul wants these people to know that he is not just being polite. Some may say, "Paul, if you really wanted to get to Rome you would just go." But Paul wants them to understand that he earnestly and sincerely longs to be with these Roman believers. To claim that God is his witness is a statement of utmost depth and one that couldn't be made if there were even a shade of doubt. God especially has to be his witness because his struggle to reach them has been primarily in prayer.

Service with a smile

Paul's service to God is "with my spirit." The Spirit is the part of man that gives him God consciousness. The spirit of the unsaved person is said to be "dead", that is, separated from God (Eph. 2:1-3). The believer in Christ is given a "reborn" spirit that is now "alive", knowing/connected to God (John 17:3). The concept of "spirituality" is not usually used biblically by Christians. The world often times uses the idea of "spirituality" to communicate anything beyond what our eyes can see. New Age practice, eastern meditation and other things all fall into the general category of spirituality. The Bible talks about spirituality in a restrictive sense. The one who is spiritual is the one who is in fellowship with, or abiding in, Christ (John 15; 1 Cor. 2:15, 3:1; Gal. 5:16; etc.).

Without ceasing

Paul's prayer life is a subject of amazing power and interest to each of us. The word translated here "without ceasing" is a word that means without intermission. Clearly this does not mean that Paul doesn't eat or sleep or talk to people because he is always tied up with the task of praying for the church at Rome. Paul is saying that when he prays he prays for them regularly. It is a marvelous study to look at Paul's prayer list as mentioned in his letters. Paul proves himself to be a man of prayer, constantly before the Lord with the needs and spiritual wellbeing of the body of Christ. Paul believed in the power of prayer and actively walked in that belief.

Find a way in the will of God

Here is something that is difficult to understand for most of us. We are always wondering what the will of God is and how do we figure it out. This is a large study and far too great to cover in its entirety here and now. However, we can, as always, hit the high points. God's will can be divided into three major categories: Sovereign, Moral, and Individual. His sovereign will is fixed, eternal and perfect. Your position in Him and security of salvation is because we are saved as a matter of His sovereign will. When we put our faith in Jesus God the Father identifies us with Christ as a sovereign act, this means that it cannot be undone, changed or affected. Other aspects of God's sovereign will are God's declaration of the future, and the final judgment of all evil.

The next circle in is God's Moral will. This is revealed to us in scripture. These are the things that we know from scripture are clearly right or wrong. There is no need to ask if it is okay to lie in this or that situation because that is ruled on as a part of God's moral will. Where God's sovereign will cannot be broken His moral will can be broken, as we prove out whenever we walk in sin. When a believer sins he is said to be out of fellowship with

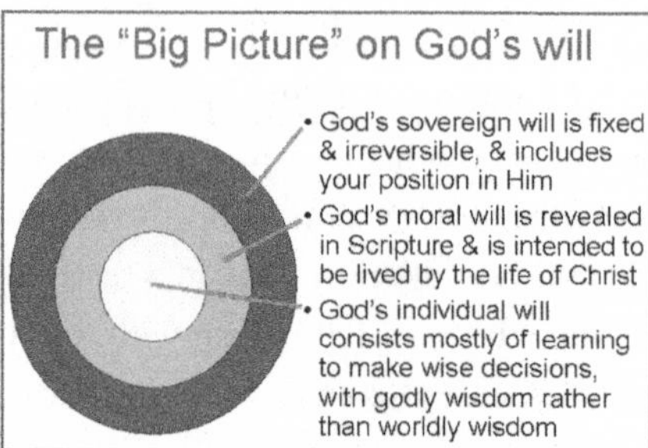

God (though still within the ring of God's sovereign will, which is where

salvation lies). The way back into the moral will is by confession and repentance. Life in this circle is meant to be lived by abiding in Christ, and His power lived out in our lives. We live here by His provision, not by our own abilities.

Finally, the individual will. God's will for the individual is where things get a bit less clear. We find the pattern and teaching of scripture is that God's will to each individual will be revealed as they walk with Christ one day at a time and attempt to make decisions based on godly wisdom and constant submission to Him. God does not intend for us to spend our lives wondering what we are to do. Generally, we can make choices based on the direction of Scripture and the wisdom and guidance of the Holy Spirit. Where we can't see clearly which road is best for us to take we can make the choice that seems like the best to us and prayerfully trust that He will watch over us and direct our steps. God's primary concern seems to be more for the fact that whatever we do, we do it to His glory, than what we do with our lives.

Back to our passage today Paul is praying to find a way, as he rests in Christ and walks in the Spirit to come to Rome and be with the saints there.

ROMANS 1:11-17

Romans 1:11-12

For I long to see you, that □I may impart to you some spiritual gift, so that you may be established— that is, that I may be encouraged together with you by □the mutual faith both of you and me.

Paul's longing

Paul here reiterates his great desire to see them. He then gives the reason for this. Paul wants to give them a Spiritual Gift. This differs from a physical gift. He does not want to give them a Christmas ham, or a million dollars, but he wants to impart on them some spiritual gift. He then tells more about this spiritual gift by saying that it would be one that would help establish them. It may be that he is talking about his gift of apostleship. Apostles were the tool of God to set the foundation of the church (Eph. 2:20) and it could be that Paul wanted to come and visit them to make sure that they believed the truth of the Gospel and had not perverted it with legalism or license so that he could certify to the world that the believers there were "in the faith", that is to say, believed correctly.

Mutual Encouragement

Paul further explains his statement of this spiritual gift by the mutual encouragement of faith. We know that the meeting together of believers is of vital importance. When we spend time together in prayer, worship and study we are reminded that Christ is the focus of our lives. Similarly, we can be easily distracted from the joyful mature lives that God wants for us if we are out of fellowship with others. (John 17: 20-23; Hebrews 10:24-25; 1 John 1:3). Additionally, we find ourselves being encouraged when we use our gifts. Everybody is grown and edified as they are able to use their gifts and be blessed by the gifts of others in community.

A Word on "The Faith"

It is important to note here that "the faith" does not simply mean the fact that we all believe in SOMETHING as the world often uses the word. "The faith" is a technical term in scripture (when it is paired with the definite article "the") to mean the specific teachings of the Bible. Paul is praying for the mutual encouragement of each other and the assumption that they will agree about what it is to believe in Christ.

<u>Romans 1:13-15</u>

13Now I do not want you to be unaware, brethren, that I often planned to
come to you (but was hindered until now), that I might have some fruit
among you also, just as among the other Gentiles. 14I am a debtor both to
Greeks and to barbarians, both to wise and to unwise. 15So, as much as is
in me, I am ready to preach the gospel to you who are in Rome also.

Not Unaware

As a general rule, when Paul says that he does not want people to be unaware, or ignorant the assumption is that they are. Thus, he is assuring his brothers in Christ that he had made plans to come to them many times before. However, each time he has been hindered. We can only speculate what kept Paul back from completing his trip to Rome in the past, but we can sense a measure of Paul's peace in resting in Christ and trusting in God's will throughout his frustrated desire to come to Rome. There is an application for each of us to maintain this same level of trust as we move forward towards the things we desire, even when that desire is frustrated, we must always keep our eyes on the facts of God's will and strength in spite of our feelings.

Gathering Fruit

Paul says that he hopes to have some fruit among them. All too often we in the evangelical world have taken fruit to mean success in evangelism. This does not fit either the context or the rest of the Biblical thought surrounding the term. For certain evangelism is a piece of this, but the passage so far has examined what he hopes to give them, and what he hopes to receive from them. It is probably more prudent to understand this fruit as referring to everything of spiritual benefit, rather than limiting it to success in evangelism.

Why a Debtor?

Other translations prefer the term under obligation, and both carry the context well. Paul is in a special sense under obligation as God's chosen representative to the Gentiles. Paul takes this obligation very seriously and has proven it out. Paul gave us a great portion of the New Testament. He also organized information in a way that would be more clearly comprehended by Gentiles. The life that he led was proof positive of his amazing, God given, desire to see more gentiles receive the gospel.

Greeks and Barbarians
The Greeks cared more about being wise than anything else. The pursuit of wisdom was their primary goal and something that gave them the most pleasure. As a result they characterized other peoples by their lack of wisdom. Barbarians is a word which comes directly from the Greek word. The Greeks characterized the people who surrounded them as sounding like they always said "bar-bar-bar" thus they called them "Barbarians" and we adopted the word into English.

As much as is in me
Paul's whole being is excited to go to Rome and share the good news of God's grace there. He is very serious. His passion to preach the gospel is tireless. In the following verses Paul gives us some great insight into why he is so passionate about the spread of the gospel.

Romans 1:16-17
16For I am not ashamed of the gospel of Christ, for it is the power of God
to salvation for everyone who believes, for the Jew first and also for the
Greek. 17For in it the righteousness of God is revealed from faith to faith;
as it is written, "The just shall live by faith."

The Theme Verse
This is it! Here we have the theme verse of the entire book. Here we have the entire purpose of the book summed up in a few concise sentences, and the rest of the book will be spent explaining and adding depth to these two verses.

What a Shame!
What reason is there to be ashamed? This is probably different than it is in our context. In our context we may be ashamed because there have been societal dictates that we should never talk about "religion and politics." We may be ashamed because our faith is often wrongly characterized as being in opposition to all of the intelligence and wisdom of "true science." The

things that would have tempted Paul to be ashamed would probably not have been these. Rather, both Jew and Gentile had connected the idea of religion to the idea of wealth and material success. The thrust of this argument goes, "I am more successful than you. Furthermore, Paul, you are having a really rough time. Chains, stoning, being chased from town to town. My religion must be right and yours must be foolishness." Paul knows the truth of the gospel flies in the face of all of these human, legalistic ideas. Paul is not ashamed because, no matter what the culture says, the gospel saves.

The Gospel of Christ

As we noted in previous studies, the word "gospel" simply means "good news." It is surprising to most Christians that there are a number of gospels in the Bible and there is the Gospel of the Kingdom (Matt. 4:23; 9:35; 24:13), there is the gospel of the legalists which Paul tells us in Galatians "is not gospel at all" (Gal. 1:6-7). The Gospel must be understood by every believer. One of the simplest passages that summarize the Gospel is found in 1 Corinthians 15:1-5:

"Moreover, brethren, I declare to you the gospel which I preached to you, which also you received and in which you stand, by which also you are saved, if you hold fast that word which I preached to you--unless you believed in vain. For I delivered to you first of all that which I also received: that Christ died for our sins according to the Scriptures, and that He was buried, and that He rose again the third day according to the Scriptures, and that He was seen by Cephas, then by the twelve."

It is putting our faith in this simple fact that saves, and then Paul gives us some more insight.

The Power of God for Salvation

The word translated "power" here is *dunamis* which is, of course, where we get our English word dynamite. This has led some to teach that the gospel is explosive power, or something to that effect. However, dynamite wasn't invented until years later and the Greek word has no real sense of that. The focus of this word is capability, or potential power. The potential power contained in the gospel is enough to save anyone. It can save all (1 John 2:1) however it is conditioned on belief, and only on belief. Notice that it is not here conditioned on belief and water baptism, or belief and a series of good works, simply belief.

Belief

The word "believe" here translates the Greek word *pistis* has the idea of faith, belief and trust all wrapped into one. While we give these three words separate nuances the Greek word holds all three together. So the belief we place in the gospel is not just a mental assent to a series of facts, but rather a trust placed into the truth of the gospel. We aren't just agreeing that Christ died on the cross and rose again, but accepting that death as having satisfied God's righteousness and having saved us.

First for the Jew…

There are a number of ways that this has been interpreted over the years. The Greek is transparent and leaves the same questions as the English. Is it chronological; is it something about God's favor for the nation of Israel, something else? There is something to be said for the fact that the gospel came first to the Jews. It was offered to the Jews first. The gospel of the kingdom was offered first to the Jews, and then, in Acts 2, the gospel of Christ comes to the forefront. From that point until Acts 10 it was only Jews, proselytes (Jewish converts), and Samaritans (half-Jews), that had found salvation. Acts 10, when Peter is called to go to the house of Cornelius, is where that all changes. So in this respect the Jew was first.

Additionally, we see in Paul's ministry a pattern of going to the Jew first and then to the gentile, even as the apostle to the gentiles. Usually this meant going to the Synagogue. However, in towns where there was no synagogue (as in Philippi) Paul went to a body of water on the Sabbath, which was the traditional meeting place of Jews of the Diaspora who did not yet have a synagogue. When the Jews rejected Paul's teaching at Antioch Paul and Barnabas responded by saying, "It was necessary that the word of God should be spoken to you first; but since you reject it, and judge yourselves unworthy of everlasting life, behold, we turn to the Gentiles." (Acts 13:46) We can observe this pattern in Acts 13:5; 13:4-52; Acts 14:1; 16:11-13; 17:1; 17:10; 17:17; 18:4; etc.)

The Righteousness of God

This is the phrase the caused Martin Luther such great pain. He knew that whatever he did he could never match up to the "righteousness of God." As we consider the righteousness of God we must look upon His righteousness as being full, 100% all the time perfection. This is a powerful reality to imagine. If God's righteousness is so great, and so perfect there is no person alive who can attain to it. Luther saw this, and saw the religious people of his day trying to pretend to have attained it, but he knew that the accounts weren't adding up. He didn't see a place in scripture where you could buy righteousness. Until he understood the Gospel and what God has done on our behalf he was in terror and hatred of a God who would demand the impossible of humanity. As we study through the early chapters of this book we will see that there are no new tricks. The same mistakes people were making then are the same ones they are making now. These mistakes are all operating under false assumptions of how great this "righteousness of God" really is.

from faith to faith;
The righteousness of God is here revealed, meaning to uncover something not previously seen. "From faith" here denotes source. This righteousness is attained by faith. It is not something that the believer works for, or attains to, or struggles against. It is, rather, only attainable by faith and through faith.

as it is written, "The just shall live by faith."
This is a quotation from Habakkuk 2:4 and reveals something very pivotal: THIS IS NOT NEW INFORMATION! We will see throughout this study (and we also see it in Galatians) that the Old Testament was filled with the reality that the righteousness of God can only be attained by grace through faith. As we will see, this does not mean that the Church has replaced Israel, but it is the reality that salvation has always been about a person's faith in what God has done, never our own works. And that is VERY GOOD NEWS!

ROMANS 1:18-20

A New Section

Having finished his greeting, and set out his purpose for writing this letter Paul moves onto the beginning of his formal argument. This section (Romans 1:18-32) of Scripture is of immense value to us as we come to understand what the Gospel is, why Jesus Christ came and died, and why the world continues to discount and ignore the God of the universe. We may often think in terms of our time, or our country and wonder how things got so bad. The Holy Spirit, writing through Paul, gives us a perfect concise summary of the position of man before God, and what God holds man accountable to seeing and perceiving. These verses describe completely the God rejecting mind, and succeeding darkness that comes upon man's understanding as he continues to shut his eyes to the light of God's revelation and love.

The Wrath of God

The wrath of God is a topic that gathers a great amount of tension. After any given major disaster someone is bound to stand up and say "This is the wrath of God against us." Additionally, there are many cases when a person will experience difficulty in their lives and wonder if that is God's wrath upon them for one thing or another which they feel guilty about. There is much that could be said about the wrath of God, however, Scripture must be our guide in how we interpret and understand what is and what isn't the wrath of God, and what that concept means in the context which it is used. When we truly understand the wrath of God we will not use the words lightly, because we understand the incredible gravity of what it means to have incurred the wrath of the one true God.

Why does God have wrath against sin?

We may be tempted to wonder why God cannot simply "overlook" sin. Why must it incur His anger and negative reaction? Why are the terms so very strong when the Bible talks about God's view of sin? These are important questions that will come up repeatedly throughout the book of Romans. However, the central reason why God abhors sin so strongly is because of His essential character – Who God IS! While a study of God's wonderful and amazing character will (and should) be the focus of the entire lifetime of the believer, this study will focus on a simple view of God's character.

God is Righteous

Scripture is God's fullest revelation of Himself to mankind. One of the most common ways that God describes Himself to us is "righteous". Other aspects of His character confirm this. God describes himself with other words like "holy", "just", "perfect", "pure" and the like. These words are describing a reality that, apart from God, simply make no sense at all. That is the idea that there is an objective morality that exists outside of mankind and his perspective. Terms like "good", "bad", "evil" and the like are all rooted in the idea that there is some objective and perfect standard that exists, even if we are not directly familiar with what that standard may be. Things that violate this aspect of God's character bring about destruction, pain and death in our regular day to day lives. God, being righteous, cannot tolerate, or share anything in common, with that which is not wholly and perfectly righteous. Any perversion of the good thing that He has created must ultimately be judged and destroyed. While this may sound harsh to the post-modernist mind we can illustrate this reality quite simply. If a person were to wholeheartedly support a massive ethnic or racial cleansing of some kind we could never call that person righteous. For God not to oppose sin in the most extreme possible terms would finally leave the world in a place of having to say that massive genocides and the most horrible realities of planet earth are "okay". However, we know that this is foolishness. Even the atheist would agree that genocides are wrong, yet he has no basis for doing so. God must ultimately render judgment upon all unrighteousness or else He is either: 1) Not righteous, or 2) Not God. This is why ignoring God's wrath against sin always leads to futility in thought and understanding of the world around, as well as draining life of all of its meaning, not to mention removing any importance of and need for Jesus Christ.

The Wrath Revealed

There is no question that God's wrath is being revealed. The sense of the Greek here is that the Wrath of God is currently being revealed. God's wrath upon sin is an existing reality, and that reality is being made known before men. Cultures the world over have been able to discern very clearly that there is a God and that He must be displeased with what is going on right now. This understanding has led to numerous attempts on the part of man to satisfy or appease God. However, all of man's efforts fall terribly short. God's hatred of sin and the rejection of Him is revealed in the consequences of Sin which led to the curse of Genesis 3. These effects – death, decay, destruction, pain, toil, etc – show us that God is not content to live with sin.

Revealed against whom?

The Bible is very plain here that the wrath is directed at ALL ungodliness and unrighteousness of men who suppress the truth. The truth is suppressed by those who reject God. This may take on the academic garments of the Atheist, or the gross actions of false gods, idols and manmade religion. The image is that of men who are holding down the truth. Trying to hide, cover up, or pervert the truth for their own ends – that is to hide from God. It is important to note that this can be either in rejecting the Truth outright, or in perverting the Truth in any and every way.

Evident

The question: "Does God exist?" is a fan favorite in debates on every level from the most academic to the most humble minds. Many interesting and exciting arguments have been made for the existence of God. Interestingly, one could have as much fun proving whether they actually exist themselves with very similar outcomes. Most of the debates over the existence of God, however, end up being rather unprofitable indeed. This is because God does not exist within our system, He is the CREATOR of the system. Because He supersedes the system entirely proving Him within it would be impossible. However, it is even more comical to think how much must be borrowed from God in order to try to refute or disprove His existence. Things like "logic", "reason" and "truth" are terms that can only exist if Someone creates them. Apart from God's existence the idea of an intellect being able to discern what is true and what is false truly makes no sense at all. The point? Everyone knows God exists, it is evident to them at their very core. All the process of argument can do is remove the twisted logic that a person has built up to defend the reality that he or she longs to deny.

How has He made it evident?

God has made the inescapable fact of His existence evident to man in numerous ways. Paul gives a short list in verse 20.

The Creation – All of the silliness of some of the most brilliant human minds of the last hundred years have been bent and twisted and wrapped around trying to answer the obvious problem of how this massive, ordered, and beautiful universe could have come into existence without God creating it. Whether justified by degrees, or math, or anything else the end of the argument is – "Even though I have never seen it happen, and have no reason to think it ever could *nothing* somehow became *everything*." Others have gone so far as to embrace to ancient Greek teaching that the world is eternal and that the physical universe is eternal. Both of these vain imaginations of mankind leave a person in the painful position of having no reason to believe what they believe and no ability to defend it based on what they know to be true now.

His Attributes

There is much that a person can know about God from creation. We can know that God exists. We know that God is powerful beyond our wildest imagination. We can know that God is a God of order and structure as we see the delicate structure of a blade of grass as well as the order of the cosmos. We can know that God is moral – as all humans seem to have some sense of morality that is rooted in a standard that is not kept perfectly by any, nor internally located and defined by any one individual. All of these observations have been termed "General Revelation" in the chart below.

General revelation, however, tells us little if anything about God's love and grace. For that we must look to the special revelation of how God has revealed himself to mankind through the Scripture and through Jesus Christ. General revelation is not enough to save a person, but

God's revelations to mankind

	God is revealed by	Scripture
General	nature	Psalm 19:1-6 Romans 1:18-20
	providence (guidance)	Matthew 5:44-45 Acts 14:15-17;17:24-28a
	conscience	Romans 2:14,15
Special	Scripture	2 Timothy 3:16,17 2 Peter 1:21
	Jesus Christ	2 Corinthians 4:4 Colossians 1:15

only enough to leave man without the excuse that "I can't know God exists."

ROMANS 1:21-23

One Verse in Review and a Pattern of Wills

Though we studied verse 20 in the last session it is included here because it is vital to the course of reasoning given here. This section traces the fall of mankind from knowing God to being unable to know Him. As we trace the movement of mankind we will see that there are both individual and corporate applications. This section begins Paul's explanation of the condemnation of the gentiles. The Jews will be dealt with in subsequent chapters. The Holy Spirit's purpose here is to explain how what is so plain to all of humanity came to be hidden from pagan eyes. There is also a deep nugget of application for each of us as we realize that God is not deterministically controlling our wills, but repeated misuse of the will causes us to be unable to use it properly. Before we begin to look at the verses individually, let's look at the progression of what Paul says has happened:

Man is without excuse (v. 20) -> Did not glorify Him as God (v. 21) -> Became futile in their thoughts (v. 21) -> Foolish hearts darkened (v. 21) -> Claiming to be wise, became fools (v. 22) -> Began worshiping men, rather than God (v. 23) -> Worshiped the creation (v. 23) -> God gave them over to uncleanness (v. 24-25) -> they continued to ignore the little light they had and grew more and more vile and sinful (v. 26-32)

Or if you like we can display this graphically:

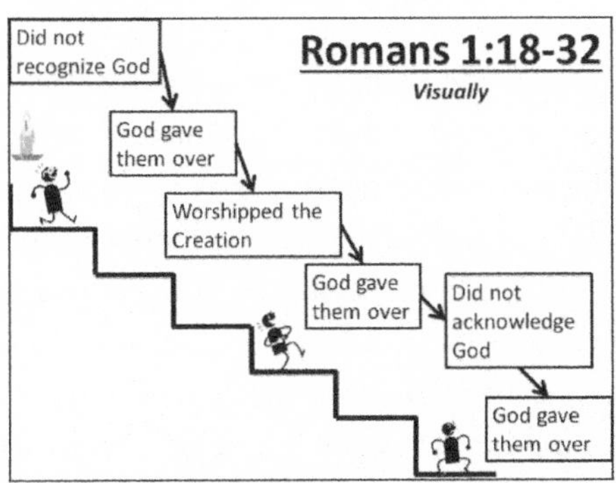

The Issue of Will

There is a great deal of arguing amongst believers regarding whether or not a person has a will that they can exercise in any measure of freedom at all. Some suggest that fallen man has no will except choosing which sin that they commit, thus they hang everything on the sovereignty of God. Others will say that man's will is the sovereign force and claims that God cannot be called just if man is not given a choice. As usual, both sides of the debate can produce a handful of scriptures to support their case, and then are put in the position of arguing why their favorite verses are more important, valid, or true than their opponents. However, the reality is that there are clear verses on both sides and this passage offers some light on how the two viewpoints can be harmonized if we are not too dogmatic.

The Darkening

When examining the pagan cultures and societies of old Paul looks at these steps, one built upon the other. The first steps down are made by man, it is not until the last two that it says "God gave them over…" and even that has the idea of releasing involved. But here is the point: Every time man takes a step away from the knowledge of the one true God he has to take a step back UP to get back. Stepping down, of course, is much easier than a step up. Furthermore, every step down makes it more difficult to see the light from above. The will is still there, the will is still free, but every wrong choice makes it more and more difficult to move back towards the truth. This process is clearly displayed in any addiction:

At first the person exercises their will to do something. As the action is repeated it may be taken or left, however as the action is hardened into a habit it becomes more difficult to stop. The will is weakened by unthinkingly accepting whatever the call of the habit asks for. The habit is then hardened into an addiction where the addict is wondering why it is so difficult to stop doing this simple thing. As the habit takes over the will is weakened, as the will is weakened it becomes harder to break out of the addiction. This is a similar process with the unbeliever and God. Some may have made more steps away than others, but everyone needs to be drawn at some level because of our sin sick wills (John 6:44); Christ also promised that when lifted up He would draw all men to himself (John 12:32). Thus, when we are spreading the gospel, prayer becomes one of the most key steps. This is because only God can affect the heart and call the will back up the steps.

The Context

We must remember that this is not prescriptive. In this passage the Holy Spirit is addressing the specific history of the Gentile religions as they stepped further and further from God corporately. A given society since then may or may not be exactly here, but this is also the general trend of human reasoning and the general movement of society away from God and His standards. It also shows us why so much of the evil that is in the world happens. Surely, original sin is to blame (and act of the will of man) however, we see that each continued step has consequences. If God were to interfere He could only take away the consequences or the will, neither of which is He willing to do.

Romans 1:21
Because, although they knew God, they did not glorify Him as God, nor were thankful, but became futile in their thoughts, and their foolish hearts were darkened.

Where we been
Remember, the previous verse concerned the reality that the existence and order of nature proves the existence of God. It is an act of willful blindness on the part of man that denies this fact. Natural (or General) Revelation, as we studied in the last lesson, leaves man wholly without excuse.

They Knew God
Wait! They KNEW God? This is the amazing step of audacity. They knew God. They knew that He was God and they knew that He created them. They knew that He had the authority. The first step here is not denying the fact that He is God, but just as in the garden of Eden it is a step away from acknowledging and giving Him his due glory honor and praise. We saw this happen in the garden as Adam and Eve knew God and yet were willing to accept the serpent questioning His very character, and chose to disobey Him.

Not thankful
This is an interesting point, worth some attention. Being unthankful was in the early steps. It shows a lack of appreciation for who God is. God deserves all glory and honor and praise and because of His magnificent and glorious character we can be thankful for all that He is. He created humanity, He continued humanity's existence, and man has no appropriate response but thankfulness. It is amazing to realize that thanklessness is among the first steps away from God.

Life point

While the direct meaning and interpretation of this passage is limited to the movement of the unbeliever away from God, there is a principle here that we can observe. As believers in Christ we are saved by grace alone and the only appropriate response for us is the same: thankfulness. If we find that our hearts are ever unthankful towards God for His great character and provision we can guarantee that we are on a path, or a line of thinking that is taking us away from growing in Christ. If we are not constantly absorbed in an attitude of gratitude we need to be asking ourselves, "why?"

Became futile in their thoughts
Here is an important step. We see in the proverbs:

The fear of the LORD is the beginning of wisdom, And the knowledge of the Holy One is understanding. (Proverbs 9:10)

This fear of the Lord is not quaking, trembling fear, but awe-filled reverent respect. The point is that wisdom and reason can only be as good as the foundation on which they are built. Like a building that is built on the sand. Perfect reasoning, built on a wrong assumption is bound to topple. Alternatively a long division problem cannot be answered correctly if the very first calculation is wrong, no matter how perfect the reasoning, starting in the wrong place guarantees that we will end in the wrong place. This is perfectly exemplified by the excellent reasoning of many atheists today. They can reason beautifully, and their arguments seem foolproof, but it all comes to futility because they are starting in the wrong place.

Futility here translates a Greek word that means "vain, empty, and foolish." The end of their reasoning always comes to emptiness, vanity and foolishness. It is also notable that this is found in the passive voice. Just as in English we find both active and passive voices (Active – the subject does the action "the boy hit the ball"; Passive – the subject receives the action "the boy was hit by the ball") When humanity refuses to glorify God as God, and becomes unthankful, their thinking becomes futile by necessity.

Foolish hearts were darkened

Here the hearts of the people is called "foolish." They are the perfect examples of the biblical definition of a fool. Psalm 14:1 and 53:1 both define the fool as the one who says in his heart, "There is no God"; this being the opposite of the definition of wisdom that we saw above. The heart is a metaphorical term. Just as we often use the illustration of the heart as standing in for some immaterial part of us, so was the pattern of scripture. The heart is the seat of the affection, thoughts, desire and will. There is a modern tendency to try to set the heart against the mind as opposites; however, this was not the NT understanding. The idea of mind and heart were not seen as dissimilar by any means. And scripture often talks about the "thoughts of the heart."

"Darkened" here is another passive. Their whole mentality and center of affection, desire and thought was darkened by their continuing pattern of not acknowledging God. The physical picture is clear, working in the dark is challenging. The darker it gets the more difficult it becomes to do the necessary tasks. As the light fades the possibility of being in any way productive is siphoned away and the opportunity is increasingly lost. The final state is a person fumbling around trying to operate by feeling alone. This is not an encouraging picture.

Romans 1:22-23

Professing to be wise, they became fools, and changed the glory of the incorruptible God into an image made like corruptible man – and birds and four-footed animals and creeping things.

Professing. They became…

Here we see the essential nature of the arrogance of mankind. As they grow darker in their hearts, and foolish in their thinking they claim to be wise. We notice that this claim is not rooted in anything but pride. We find these people claiming this wisdom, but in actuality they are fools.

We see this pattern in society today. Those who claim to be wise with their weighty degrees and the recognition of themselves and even other foolish humans claiming that anyone who would dare disagree with them must be the fool. However, the reality is that they are foolish and empty no matter what they say. Evolutionary scientists, philosophers, successful businessmen, and others will all claim the Bible to be false, and Christianity foolishness, but the reality is that they have no basis for their thinking this.

A Significant Change

Here we see the big change. The movement here is from the glory of God to the glory of man. In the ancient Greek and Roman cultures we saw this in terms of the system of god's and goddesses that were essentially just normal men and women endowed with super powers. We can even see this pattern today with films that glorify "the indomitable spirit of man" or the hero worship of politicians, actors, singers, and others. We may think of this as being something that can only happen in the most gross terms, but the reality is that it can happen in a simple relationship between a boyfriend and girlfriend if one is looking to the other for things that only God is capable of providing.

Even Animals!

The progression in the ancient world even continued to worshiping animals as somehow having power over certain forces or events. Man's need to worship something, once confused, will seek satisfaction in any way, regardless of how silly or inappropriate. Whether a government, a marijuana leaf, a movement, or a creeping beetle, man will inevitably worship something that is unworthy of his worship once he has moved away from worshiping the one true God.

Onward and Downward!

We are stopping in the middle of the progression here, however, it is clear to see where we are heading. The core reality is that man is designed to live in a relationship with God. Outside of this relationship man can do nothing but decay. Without the core need of man for God being filled there is no direction for him to go but down towards destruction of himself and others. This is the reality, we find that man uses his will to move farther away from God paralyzing his ability to do anything but destroy everything around him. The important thing for us to note as we move into the physical results and repercussions of this is that those who are ensnared, entrapped and/or destroyed by the sins that follow do not need to be cured of those sins. The core issue is that they need to be restored to a relationship with God. When we see an unbeliever struggling with how they are hurting themselves, or how they are hurt by others let us never forget, the only thing that we should offer them is the only thing that will really help: a relationship with the Living God through faith in His Son, Jesus Christ.

ROMANS 1:24-25

Picking up midstream

We are now looking at another step in the history that Paul is giving us of the gentile's progression down the path away from God. In the last study we saw how this whole process began by the gentiles rejecting what they knew of God and becoming darkened in their understanding. Their wisdom became folly and they began to worship the images of man and then the images even of the creeping beasts whom they were meant to have dominion over. It is interesting that nothing so far extends beyond the sphere of their spiritual awareness. It is all internal at this point.

The verses here begin to discuss the practical actions that they undertook as a result of abandoning the knowledge and worship of the one true God. One thing we can immediately see here in the progression that the Holy Spirit relates through Paul: what we think and believe REALLY MATTERS. We live in a world that affirms the idea that what we believe doesn't matter, only the actions that come from it. Machiavelli gave us the idea that "the end justifies the means." The world has adopted this idea that "as long as you don't hurt anyone else it doesn't matter what you believe." The Bible, however gives us the truth, what we believe REALLY matters, and always translates itself to action eventually. This is one reason why evolutionary thought is so very destructive. It has been the core belief behind countless schemes of euthanasia, mass murder, cruel experimentation, and meaninglessness of life.

<u>**Romans 1:24-25**</u>

[24] Therefore God also gave them up to uncleanness, in the lusts of their
hearts, to dishonor their bodies among themselves, [25] who exchanged the
truth of God for the lie, and worshiped and served the creature rather than
the Creator, who is blessed forever. Amen.

The Logical Connection

This verse starts with a "therefore" which talks about a continued argument. It is building on the basis of what preceded it. Often times this statement looks back on the content of the entire book (as we will see in Romans 12:1). In this specific instance, however, the "therefore" seems to be looking back on the description that preceded it. What follows is based on the gentiles' refusal to acknowledge, and worship God as He is due. The Bible repeatedly affirms that "the fear of the Lord is the beginning of all wisdom" (Ps. 111:10, Proverbs 9:10) and we see that this principle is also given in the negative "the fool says in his heart there is no God" (Psalm 14:1; 53:1). This is the outplay of that foolishness.

Gave them up

This is a Greek word that means that God released them. God did not cause them to sin as a punishment, but rather gave them over to their uncleanness. This is quite important. We often think of God as punishing acts of unrighteousness, but often times the negative results of sin are simply God releasing man to the natural consequences of his actions. God did not want them to fall into their sin, but allowed them to as part of giving man a free will. In this "present evil age" God allows the rebellion of man to continue and all that we see following is the natural result of man's abandoning God. God could have, in His sovereignty, forbidden them to go, but this would not have been concordant with His desire for His creation. He could also have destroyed mankind and judged sin immediately (as we saw in the flood) however, He is patient with mankind, waiting for more to return to Him (2 Peter 3:9).

Uncleanness, the lusts of their hearts

The first word that Paul uses here is "uncleanness" and then the rest of our passage elaborates on that. Paul, in fact, uses a Hebrew poetry pattern here that could be displayed in this way:

24Therefore God also gave them up to uncleanness,

In the lusts of their hearts,

To dishonor their bodies among themselves

25who exchanged the truth of God for a lie

And worshiped the creature rather than the Creator

Who is blessed forever. Amen.

26For this reason God gave them up to vile passions.

For even their women exchanged the natural use for what is against nature.

Likewise also the men, leaving natural use of the women burned in their lust for one another, men with men committing what is shameful,

And receiving for themselves the penalty of their error which was due.

There is more repetition yet to come in this section and we may wonder why? In the writing of the time there was no underlining, bolding, italics, or other form of emphasis. So the way to get something important across was repetition. Paul continually attaches the sins to the rejection of God. Here Paul focuses on their sexual sins, but others are to follow.

We must not think that Paul's condemnation of deviant sexual practices would have been received any differently today than in the ancient world. Homosexuality was the norm for most of the pagan cultures. So then, just as now, people may be tempted to say, "What's wrong with men having sex with men?" Paul doesn't apologize for the fact that both male and female homosexuality is destructive and unnatural. This may be why he goes to such lengths regarding sexual issues, simply because the culture wouldn't immediately accept the idea that such practices are sinful and powerfully destructive.

Uncleanness

This word could be translated "impurity""; it carries the idea of something being blemished and ruined. This is further explained by the phrase "the lusts of their hearts". The heart is a figurative term for the seat and center of all physical and spiritual life. The heart is a term that is also used interchangeably with the idea of the mind and is the seat of the will, emotions and affections. It is often a word used for the whole immaterial part of man. Notice, the uncleanness, and the lusts, are from man. They are not from God, nor is Satan given credit here. The result of our fallen state is that the affections and the desires of the heart (or mind) are unclean and impure. To reject God is to embrace what our own spiritual life has to offer, which is only impure, lustful, and destructive.

Dishonor

Further explanation of this comes in the phrase that they "dishonor their bodies among themselves." The word dishonor here is interesting. The world has continued in the idea that a person's body is their own and therefore, they should be able to do whatever they want with it. This idea has been used to promote the legalization of abortion and many other destructive practices. The reality is that "The earth is the LORD's, and all its fullness, The world and those who dwell therein." (Psalm 24:1) The reality is that God created all matter. He designed the human body and thus it has an inherent honor, glory or purpose. To use the body for ungodly purposes, or to destroy it through these sinful practices, is a direct affront against God, even if the person refuses to acknowledge it.

A really bad deal

Verse 25 reiterates the fact that this occurred among those who left God and didn't recognize Him as God. The word "exchanged" is used. The idea can be made of a trade, or of changing one thing into something else. The truth of God here was changed for the lie. It is important to realize what has occurred. There can be only one truth, yet any number of variations that can only be called lies. However, here the definite article is in front of the word "lie" so it is "the LIE" the specific Lie that God is not God is in view.

Creation or Creator?

Because man is made up of both immaterial and material it can be difficult for us to see past the physical. These people, just as people today, have rejected the spiritual reality and worshipped what they can see. The idea that the physical world is eternal was the standing philosophical theory of the day, just as it is now. We know from the Bible that the Spiritual world existed first and will exist eternally and the physical universe had a beginning and will have an end. This however is not the accepted view of the world system. Then it was accepted that the physical world was forever and will be, now the belief that a "big bang" occurred causing things to happen as they did is just another way to "worship the creation" so as to avoid the truth of the Creator to whom all people and things are ultimately accountable.

Blessed forever. Amen.

There are several words that are translated "blessed" in Scripture. This specific word is only ever used of God and does not mean "blessed" in the sense of given something, but it combines the word for "good" and the word for "message" and has the idea of praise. He alone is praised forever and ever. Men may sing their own praises, honoring one another for a time, but each dies and his praises fade away. Even demonic powers can elicit temporary praise, but all of those praises will be destroyed and the only words of praise that will ring throughout eternity will be the praise and worship of our God!

"Amen" is a word of Hebrew origin and affirms the finality and truth of a statement. God's praise is the end of everything. Even the darkest things, and the most grimy sinful man, or angel will be forced to bow before Him and recognize Him as God. (Philippians 2:9-11) We have the opportunity to be preoccupied with eternity each day and recognize the Amen, Jesus Christ (Revelation 3:14), with rejoicing praise for His character and actions! Amen!

ROMANS 1:26-27

The Giving Over Continues

Throughout this section of scripture Paul has described how man rejects God and God gives them over to the results of their choices. This pattern of man rejecting and God giving over began with rejecting Him as God – which is a choice that chiefly affect a person's thinking. However, results of this rejection of God in the thought life of people finally results in man being given over to the most base and destructive immorality possible. The result of rejecting God and the order which He put into place ultimately ends in man losing his very Humanity – that which separates us from the animals. This is exactly what the world system is after to this day: the attempt to define man as "just another animal" with no responsibility or position differing from any of the animals on the planet. The final result of rejecting God is a loss of humanity.

Degrading Passions

This is a hot topic in society. Many attempts have been made to eliminate or marginalize these simple and plain verses because the thought that homosexuality is a sin is abhorrent to the modern sensibility. This is fascinating because the debate over these verses provides clear evidence that what the Holy Spirit is saying through Paul here is absolutely true. It is the only possible logical result that as mankind rejects God, God's standards must also be rejected. Attempts to justify homosexuality have been made in trying to claim that Paul was only talking about certain expressions of homosexuality, or that he was culturally bigoted and therefore these words can be ignored. All of these attempts to tap dance around what God's word clearly says are, in effect, proving that the beginning of this process has already taken place in the hearts of those who are making them. In essence, what these arguments presume is that WE are the ones who make the ultimate decision about what is right and what is wrong. We will agree with God so long as He agrees with us first. This is, in effect, putting man in the position of God, and demanding that God acquiesce to our moral standard rather than the other way around.

Females and Males

Paul uses very specific language here. Words for men and women are words that we could well bring across as "male" and "female" speaking of the basic distinction between human males and females in regard to sexual identity and function. God created mankind to reproduce in a very special way. Angels do not reproduce, and neither does God. However, God created mankind by creating one man (Adam) and one woman (Eve) to come together in the beautiful way of a loving, bonded, sexuality. God made this wonderful process to be pleasurable and productive. As a result of this, before the fall, there was no pain associated with birth or child rearing. The product of this congress is that another human is conceived, carried and born. This order was created by God before the fall and is a part of God's revealing His plan for all of humanity. In this way God created the natural order of things. The result of rejecting God was that man would also, ultimately, reject the wonderful gift of sexual relationships by abusing it and using others simply for the physical pleasure that they can provide.

Just another sin?

Much of the greatest ugliness has come forth from Christians and non-Christians alike regarding this issue. Some have suggested that homosexuality is a sin that is somehow greater, or worse, than other sins. Much media coverage has been given to those reprehensible liars who would try to claim that "God hates homosexuals" however, nothing could be further from the truth. Sin is sin. Sin separates us from God. Regardless of what specific sin is at play we are not given spiritual directive to go about weighing the value of one sin over another. Sin, however, always bears repercussions. Rejecting God's created order for marriage results necessarily in an inability to enjoy life as it was meant to be lived. The reason why Paul mentions this particular sin here seems quite clearly to be the fact that rejecting God will ultimately result in making choices that draw us further from Him, and falling far short of the great pleasure and happiness which we were meant to have. The sin of homosexuality is, however, no more difficult for God to forgive at the cross than any other. The person and work of Jesus Christ paid for this sin, too. God's desire is not to destroy sinners, but to save them. His motivation is not hatred, but of love.

Hate Speech

Increasingly the world attempts to define the Bible's clear teaching that homosexuality is a sin as "hate speech". Sadly, many calling themselves Christians have given legitimacy to this claim. However, the believer's attitude towards homosexuality should be one of love, grace, and a desire for the best good of those who are practicing this sin. Far from hatred, the Biblical attitude towards this (or any) sin should be the same: desiring the very best for those who are enslaved to sin. It is the most loving thing a person could do to tell someone that they are driving towards a cliff. It is the most loving thing a person could do to tell the drug addict that drugs are ruining his or her life. This message may be received or rejected but it is never a loving act to allow a loved one to destroy themselves.

Dealing with THE ISSUE

From my personal point of view, the homosexuality issue is a trap of the world to keep people from looking to Jesus Christ. If believers are entangled in a battle over whether or not homosexuality is a sin (which it clearly is in the Bible) then the issue of man's need for Jesus Christ can be pushed to the wayside. It is my personal practice, whenever this issue comes up in talking to a non-believer, to direct the conversation to man's need for God's provision of salvation in Jesus Christ. Harping on this one issue is usually just a way for people to avoid the real issue: man is in need of the Savior, Jesus Christ the Righteous.

Starting with the issue of Homosexuality in a discussion about the Lord is like reading a book backwards. Starting from the end, and not finding out what is really important until we get to the beginning. Not only is it not productive, it is frustrating to everyone involved. Rather than beginning with the end, direct these conversations back to beginning. Individual sins are merely a result of having rejected God as God (Romans 1:18-20). Rather than blustering on about what is or isn't a sin, the conversation must be returned to focusing on what has gone wrong to lead to the sinful behaviors. We must never "give-in" on God's word, but arguing over the conclusions is meaningless without looking at the presuppositions that bring us to that point.

ROMANS 1:28-32

The Pattern

Here we see Paul's continued pattern in this chapter which he emphasizes by continued repetition. The pattern continues to repeat the idea that man rejected God, and God gave man over to the consequences of rejecting Him. We could illustrate this pattern in a chart:

Assigned to Man	**Assigned to God**	**Logical Consequence**
Suppress the truth (v. 18)	Wrath revealed (v.18)	
Evident to them (v. 19)	God made it evident to them (v. 19)	
Without excuse (v. 20)	Power and nature clearly seen (v. 20)	
Knew God, did not honor Him as God (v. 21)		Became futile in their thoughts (v. 21)
Professing to be wise (v. 22)		Became fools (v. 22)
Exchanged God for images and things (v. 23)	Gave them over to the lusts of their hearts, dishonor their bodies (v. 24)	
Exchanged truth of God for a lie,	Blessed forever	

worshiped creature (v. 25)	and ever (v. 25)	
Women and men became perverted (v. 26-27)	Gave them over to degrading passions; (v. 26)	Man received the due penalty of his actions (v. 27)
Did not see fit to acknowledge God any longer (v. 28)	Gave them over to a depraved mind (v. 28)	Man filled with all unrighteousness (v. 29-31)
Though they know it is wrong they continue, approve others in wickedness (v.32)		**FINAL JUDGMENT:** Man worthy of death.

Here we see an amazing picture of the guilt of mankind. Man rejected God, who displayed Himself clearly to them. Continued rejection resulted in continued movement down this path of rejection. In the final analysis man is worthy of one thing: death.

Romans 1:28

And just as they did not see fit to acknowledge God any longer,
God gave them over to a depraved mind, to do those things which are not proper,

They did not see fit

This phrase translates the word *dokimatzo* which means to test or approve. So the idea is that mankind, based on their wrong assessment of God, thought the best thing was not to acknowledge God any longer. Atheists the world over continue to make this bad assessment again and again. Famous writers, celebrities and scholars go through this bad calculation in loud voices and public venues. They think about it and volitionally choose that it would be better for them not to acknowledge God. This is exactly what Adam and Eve did in the garden of Eden. Being deceived by the serpent they decided that it would be better to try to be gods unto themselves. This bad decision is repeated daily, both privately and publicly, by the mass of humanity.

Acknowledge

There is another progression we can observe in man's behavior. As we look at the left side of the chart above we see that man moved from suppression of the truth to not honoring God, from not honoring Him they moved to exchanging Him for the creation, from that point they moved further to not even acknowledging Him. In man's self-delusion he pushes the Truth further and further away so that ultimately he can ignore God completely and go about his merry sinful way to his own destruction. The KJV translates this phrase this way: "they did not like to retain God in their knowledge." So from this point they tried to ignore or forget about God altogether. And the results are tragic.

Depraved Mind

In the third "God gave them over" statement God gives them over to a depraved mind. Previously he had given them over to the lusts of their hearts, and then to degrading passions, but here he gives them over to a fully depraved mind. The word "depraved" here is based on the same root word that we saw above in the statement "did not see fit", but here it has a negative particle on it. Their very minds became undiscerning, unfit for proper function; they lost the ability to reason correctly. Often times when we share the gospel with the unsaved we may feel like we are talking good sense and they just can't see it! They may use reason, but reason is only a tool. Like a car, no matter how good the car is it simply will not run on orange juice! The car is made to burn gasoline, and reason is only a valuable tool if it is built on the correct presuppositions. The depraved mind of man can come up with theories like "evolution" or "the big bang" or any number others, and even work hard to defend it convincingly, but at the end of the day we must realize that they are standing on the core base presuppositions that they have adopted against all of the knowledge and evidence that God has put in and around them so that they can continue down the path that they want to go: rejecting God. The reason for all of these mental jumping jacks is so that "they can do those things which are not proper"

Romans 1:29-31

29 being filled with all unrighteousness, wickedness, greed, evil; full of envy,
murder, strife, deceit, malice; they are gossips, 30 slanderers, haters of God,
insolent, arrogant, boastful, inventors of evil, disobedient to parents, 31
without understanding, untrustworthy, unloving, unmerciful;

The "Dirty 21"

In this passage we have one of the big "sin lists" of the New Testament. These occur in a number of passages, where the Holy Spirit, through the biblical writer rattles off a list of sins that is amazingly daunting! Some have attached catchy names to these lists "the dirty dozen" or "the sinful seven" and the like. Often times these passages are referred to in order to put the believer under some form of law. While these lists do indeed show us a number of things that displease God we must always remember to take them in context. The purpose of this list of horrible things is to show the continued degeneration of man once he has rejected God as God. These are the natural result and outplay of man's rejection of God. This is not a check list to put on the fridge and look at each morning and evening and rate our level of sinfulness, this is the natural outplay of rejecting a right relationship with the Living God revealed to us in the Bible. The purpose of this passage is not: "God would have been fine with anything if it didn't come to all of these bad things." Rather, that these are the outcome of not having a relationship with God – the answer is to have a relationship with Him, as we will see in the chapters to come.

Filled with

Here we see the term "filled with" which has the idea of being full. That sounds simple, but if a cup is full, how much more fits in it? This is what the unbeliever is filled with:

all unrighteousness – The opposite of what is right, correct, or should be.

Wickedness – Evil nature, delighting in evil

Greed – a ceaseless desire for more possessions and the desire to always have the bigger portion, always wanting more

Evil – generally involving every form of evil, or badness

full of envy – jealousy over another person's works, character, possessions or abilities.

Murder – unlawful killing of another person

Strife – rivalry, contention, being quarrelsome

Deceit – bait; adulterating the truth to confuse or entrap or catch others

Malice – depravity of heart and life; lit. "ill-natured"; taking everything with an evil connotation

they are gossips – lit. a whisperer; has the idea of slandering, backbiting, gossip

slanderers – one who speaks falsehoods against others

haters of God – hating God as a part of their character and worldview

insolent – one who outrageously insults others, spiteful

arrogant – proud, unduly putting themselves above others, snotty

boastful – one who falsely claims ability, or honor. A quack.

inventors of evil – create new ways of doing evil, not just doing bad things, but finding new and more effective ways to do evil

disobedient to parents – refusing obedience to parents, as God's created authority figure that is due honor simply in respect of the position of parenthood, we take this lightly in our culture today, but it is clear by the other items on this list that not honoring parents is something God takes very seriously.

without understanding – devoid of understanding, unable to listen and apprehend truth

untrustworthy – covenant breaker, promise breaker, faithless, dishonest

unloving – devoid of even the natural love, affection and care that even animals display towards their young. Complete handicap in this area of love and practical affection

unmerciful – lacking in compassion, not seeing the need and pain of others and desiring to help

Romans 1:32

and although they know the ordinance of God, that those who practice such things are worthy of death, they not only do the same, but also give hearty approval to those who practice them.

Really Know it

The word translated "know" in the first phrase here is *epignosko* which combines the word for "to know" and a prefix that intensifies the verb. They REALLY did know the ordinance of God. They knew it right down to the core of them, yet, as we have seen, they chose not to heed it.

Worthy of Death

We see here the result of sin – death. Sin has created death since the very beginning. Death, in Scripture, always means separation. Physical death is the separation of the immaterial from the material part of man. The death that is more often in view is spiritual death, which is defined as separation from God (John 17:3 gives us the reverse statement that "life" is defined as knowing God). Man is finite, however, being made by God, will never be annihilated or obliterated. Every person will enter into eternity; either an eternity of life (relationship with God – heaven) or an eternity of death (separation from God – hell). When God condemns man to an eternity apart from him (death) He is only giving man what he is worthy of, it is a perfectly just act. This is the position that the heathen is left in at this point in the epistle, he is getting exactly what he wanted, and exactly what he deserves by spending an eternity apart from God.

They didn't just do it…

The final statement is the saddest state of affairs. Mankind not only did all of these evil things, but they approved them in others whole-heartedly. This is a tragedy beyond measure. No longer hiding their sins, or maintaining the sense of shame that is rightly attached to it, they lifted each other up and glorified the wrong doing as something that was laudable. This approval of wrong turns all of reality on its head, and it is tragic. Once what is wrong is approved, what is right becomes even more difficult to discern.

ROMANS 2

ROMANS 2:1-4

Judgmental Religious People

One of the most common complaints about Christians (or "religious people" at large) is the issue of being judgmental, or self-righteous. At all times and in all ages the world has been plagued with religious people who use religion as a tool to judge others and try to feel superior to others. Inevitably someone sets up a very subjective set of standards so that they can judge the sin of others with great exacting self-righteousness and yet overlook all of their own sin in the process. Often times the very act of judging someone else can help alleviate our own feelings of guilt in knowing that we are guilty of the same things. This attitude is abhorrent to the Lord. It is destructive in the greatest degree! This all comes from the assumption that salvation can be earned, and that God just wants us to be better than the next person. Nothing could be further from the truth! God's standard is the absolute righteousness and perfection of Christ, and Paul, writing under the inspiration of the Holy Spirit, turns his attention to this religious attitude in humanity. This is vital to understand as the person who seeks to judge others in order to make himself appear more righteous is easily as far from God as the most ungodly person on the planet!

Romans 2:1

1Therefore you have no excuse, everyone of you who passes judgment, for in that which you judge another, you condemn yourself; for you who judge practice the same things.

No excuse…again!

Paul has used this phrase, "no excuse" before, in chapter 1 it was the person who wanted to pretend like God doesn't exist. The witness of nature, providence and conscience leaves man without excuse before the living God who created him. There is another group here that is without excuse. This is the person who would presume to pass judgment upon others. This is the religious person who claims that he is innocent while everyone else is guilty. This spiritual far-sightedness when we come to evaluating sin in other's lives and overlook sin in our own lives doesn't solve the problem at all! Paul opens up in this assault on the religious mindset by letting the reader know that judging sin in others will never erase sin in our own lives!

Everyone of You

Again, Paul is using inclusive language. This isn't directed only at those people who are obviously hypocrites. A person may be able to put on a quite convincing show and fool much of the world into thinking that he really is without sin. However, God is in no way deceived. Anyone who would attempt to approach God on the basis of self-righteousness, or the idea that: "At least I was better than that other person!" is equally without excuse. There is nothing that can be said in their defense.

Judging and Condemning

The reason why the religious person condemns himself with those he judges is that he is not innocent. Most commonly the sins a religious person denounces most vehemently are the ones of which he himself is guilty. However, there is a further reality that makes this so important for every person to understand. James tells us: "For whoever keeps the whole law and yet stumbles in one point, he has become guilty of all." (James 2:10) Righteousness, with God, is an all or nothing affair. While we have a tendency to want to assign sins different "weights" or grade them as "worse" sins or "better" sins there is no difference before God, because in God there is room for NO unrighteousness at all! So the person who defends their "little" sins by pointing to the person who is committing "big" sins has missed the point altogether! In judging any unrighteousness in someone else we only accentuate the judgment of our own unrighteousness!

Romans 2:2-4

[2]And we know that the judgment of God rightly falls upon those who
practice such things. [3]But do you suppose this, O man, when you pass
judgment on those who practice such things and do the same yourself, that
you will escape the judgment of God? [4]Or do you think lightly of the riches
of His kindness and tolerance and patience, not knowing that the kindness
of God leads you to repentance?

We know

We know from scripture, as well as from observation, that Sin always brings about pain, loss and judgment. Some of these come as a natural course of action, other judgments (like the plagues upon Egypt, or the Babylonian Captivity of Judah) are brought about by the direct action of God. Sin will be judged in this same way during the Tribulation period. Finally, every person who has not trusted Christ will stand before the great white throne judgment and bear the guilt for all their sin. This is why Paul is leading so conclusively and thoroughly to the need of man to trust in Another to pay the penalty of our sins. For anyone who trusts Jesus for salvation, their sin was judged at the cross of Jesus Christ. But that is getting ahead of things.

Rightly

Paul points out another fact that is common knowledge. That is that God's judgment of Sin is right, righteous or correct. No one is able to stand before God and "explain away" their sin. There are no excuses that will be good enough, and no argument strong enough. God's judgment of sin is absolutely correct and justified.

Interesting Psychology

It is a strange reality of man's psychology that we would ever dream that by pointing out and judging sin in others that ours would be somehow overlooked. It would be akin to a student who was caught cheating on a test thinking that by turning other cheaters in his guilt may be overlooked or forgotten. As silly as this sounds, this is exactly what we do when we seek to point out guilt in others to draw attention away from our own guilt.

While it makes no logical sense it is still common to every person. Paul wants to call this religious attitude out on the carpet and let us know that we cannot escape from our own unrighteousness simply by pointing it out in others.

Asking Questions

Paul asks two rhetorical questions that are both meant to imply the answer "NO!" First is the question that we may actually be deceived into thinking that by judging others God will overlook our sin. This is both a logical inconsistency as well as being spiritually untrue. It betrays man's flawed view of God's character and righteousness. In our humanity we have a tendency to try to assume that God is just like us, only bigger. This however, is not in any way the case. God's righteousness is not partial, nor is it sometimes righteous and sometimes fuzzy. It is 100%, all the time, perfect righteousness. No trick of argumentation or comparison will erase the unrighteousness in our own lives.

The second question Paul asks is if we think lightly of His kindness, tolerance and patience. Each of these words describe God's attitude in allowing mankind time on this earth to recognize our sin, recognize our own need for the Lord. The religious person is always ready call down the judgment of God upon another person. Yet the very reason that God is waiting until later on the timeline to make His final judgment is so that man has time to repent! God waits because of His kindness – His desire to see everyone come to a place wherein they recognize their need for Him. Scripture is clear that not everyone is willing to come, to recognize their need, yet God's patience is one of the amazing and nearly incomprehensible things about His character. Peter writes:

The Lord is not slow about His promise, as some count slowness, but is patient toward you, not wishing for any to perish but for all to come to repentance. (2 Peter 3:9)

ROMANS 2:5-11

Guess who is Guilty?

In this section Paul is dealing with the guilt of the Jewish person, or we may also indirectly apply this statement of guilt to whom we might call "the moralist." First of all, however, we must find out why Paul is so serious about making sure everyone acknowledges their guilt. As we are going to see the understanding of one's own inability to have a righteousness of their own before God is a primary step in understanding our need for God's grace. This is obviously important enough to Paul to spend the bulk of the first 4 chapters of this letter to it. As Paul will say in Galatians 2:21: "I do not nullify the grace of God; for if righteousness comes through the Law, then Christ died needlessly." So, we find that if there was the slightest ability of man to produce righteousness in and of himself then the Christ's work on the cross would have been pointless. Jesus didn't come and die on the cross just because mankind were slackers, and too lazy to do right. He did it because we were utterly dead in our transgressions and sins, lost in all things, unable to restore ourselves to God (Ephesians 2:1-3).

The Jewish people had an even greater difficulty in understanding this. There were those among the Jews who believed that just by being born Jewish a person was saved. There was even a Jewish myth that Abraham sat on the gates of Hell to assure no circumcised person went in by accident! This is why Paul has to be so sure, as he explains the whole gospel from start to finish. He wants to be fully sure that none of the people in the Church at Rome think that they got themselves some of the way there, and then Christ made up the difference. That is why he is taking so much time to fight this seemingly redundant battle.

We may or may not know a Jewish person when we share the faith, however, we will meet many moralists who claim that they are "good enough" or "better than average." The reality of this confusion could very well keep them from looking to Christ and Christ alone for salvation, and that is unacceptable. It's not that we need to be the "guilt police" but the reality that when we share the gospel we need to realize that anyone who thinks that they are "good enough" is thoroughly indoctrinated against understanding their need for the gospel.

With this in mind we begin this week's verses:

Romans 2:5

But because of your stubbornness and unrepentant heart you are storing up wrath for yourself in the day of wrath and revelation of the righteous judgment of God,

Looking Back

Remember where the previous verses left us in this argument that the Holy Spirit is making through Paul. Having anticipated the Jews response to his assessment that the pagans are condemned he started in on them. He knew that they would say "I've never worshiped an idol, I've never engaged in sinful sexual practices" and so forth. His response is to tell them that they also are without excuse. Because they practice the same things! He reminded them that their judging others will not cause God to overlook their sins, especially when they so often consist of the very same sins for which they judge others. He then criticizes them for their harsh judgmentalism in verse 4 that seems to rejoice in the destruction of others rather than rejoicing in the reality that there is still time for repentance.

stubbornness and unrepentant heart

Here Paul gets at the root of the issue. We remember when we saw all of the horrid sins of the gentiles (Romans 1:29-31) it was because they repeatedly rejected the proper worship of and knowledge of God (Romans 1:18-21, 25, 32). The sinful behaviors flowed from the wrong attitude and understanding of God. Here the judgmental moralist, or in this case the Jew, shows the true motivation for his judgmental heart. Paul uses two words to describe them:

Stubbornness – This word is translated more literally by the King James Version as "hardness." It is an image of hardness that comes from dryness. Though their own Scripture stated that the Lord is pleased with a contrite heart (Psalm 51:17; Isaiah 57:15) they had developed hearts that were like hard, dry, soil. We find that this hard dry soil is the natural outflow of their legalism. Though the Lord had called the Jews into relationship with Him they had hardened their hearts through legalism and their supposed ability to keep the Law.

Unrepentant heart – Again, this speaks to the same problem. These are people who are so convinced of their own righteousness that they can't see that they are sinful. Literally this is a dedication to not change one's mind. This is the same attitude when we see non-believers repeatedly affirming "I'm a good person" though their acts contradict it fully.

storing up wrath

What is the result of this hardness of heart? Is God fooled by their stubborn self-deception? Not for one moment. They are said to be storing up (*thēsaurizō*), even treasuring, this wrath for themselves. Now the question is what day will all accounts be settled? This "day of wrath" is the day of reckoning that will be held before the Great White Throne Judgment described in Revelation 20:11-15. Every unbeliever who rejected God's grace throughout all of human history will stand before Christ on that day and be judged on the basis of their works and assigned their personal eternal punishment in the Lake of Fire. All of this will occur because they would not look at the humbling truth that they, too, are sinners in need of God's grace provided at the cross.

God's Judgement

God's judgment is described here as righteous, or we might say correct. The person who wants pure justice will get it, but not one of them will be happy once they have seen all of the facts laid before them. Not one will be shown to be righteous as they thought they would have been. Every person has the choice to accept Christ's perfect payment for sin at the cross, or supply their own payment by an eternity in the Lake of Fire. This is why this message is so incredibly important for us to communicate clearly whenever we get the chance!

<u>Romans 2:6-8</u>

[6] who WILL RENDER TO EACH PERSON ACCORDING TO
HIS DEEDS: [7] to those who by perseverance in doing good seek for
glory and honor and immortality, eternal life; [8] but to those who are
selfishly ambitious and do not obey the truth, but
obey unrighteousness, wrath and indignation.

Seems difficult…

These verses may be difficult for us to understand as they would seem at the first reading to mean that if someone kept the law perfectly then they could possibly seek to earn their salvation. We know by the context of the book of Romans and the testimony of the rest of the Bible that this simply could not be the case. However, there are those who persevered in doing good in the Old Testament. Some examples of this would be Noah, Abraham, Moses, and David. These men understood their need for God's grace and love. As they continued in their reliance upon His grace they were able to do good things that resulted in the reward of "glory and honor and immortality, eternal life." Each, however, sinned. Each was forced to take the gift of God's gracious provision of salvation in order to receive his gift of eternal life, thus they were rewarded. They were, as verse 8 speaks to in the negative, obedient to the truth.

The other side of the coin

Paul's purpose here is pointing the moralist, the one who was so convinced of his own righteousness that they are actually described by the second half of this statement. They are "selfishly ambitious and do not obey the truth." This continues the idea that the person who is trying to "earn salvation" only succeeds in being selfish, ambitious, and heaps up wrath and anger upon themselves.

Romans 2:9-11

[9] *There will be* tribulation and distress for every soul of man who does evil, of the Jew first and also of the Greek, [10] but glory and honor and peace to everyone who does good, to the Jew first and also to the Greek. [11] For there is no partiality with God.

Getting to the Point

Here Paul gets right down to the point. To the Jew who believed that just being born Jewish might save, Paul reminds them that God's justice is complete, and perfect and doesn't place one people group above another. Every soul who does evil receives tribulation – which is crushing pressure from all sides. Eternal pressure that is crushing as the result of continued evil behavior. Additionally the word translated "distress" could be brought across with the word anguish. There is no hope of life and peace if a perfect record cannot be presented to God.

First for the Jew

Here Paul clarifies what he said earlier. Because the Jew has more information than the Gentile, and could conceivably have known and understood, he receives judgment first. Having had the Law of Moses, and the whole of Scripture, he should have been aware of his need for grace, not puffing himself up with the feeling that he is so good that he can judge others.

The Good Stuff

On top of the good things mentioned in verse 7 peace is added to this list. We can clearly see the structural parallelism between verses 7-8 and 9-10. We may display it graphically this way:

> 7 to those who by perseverance in doing good seek for glory and honor and immortality, eternal life;
>
> 8 but to those who are selfishly ambitious and do not obey the truth, but obey unrighteousness, wrath and indignation.
>
> 9 *There will be* tribulation and distress for every soul of man who does evil, of the Jew first and also of the Greek,
>
> 10 but glory and honor and peace to everyone who does good, to the Jew first and also to the Greek.

The focus of this structure is on the negative aspects of judgment. He is telling the Jew, and the moralist, that if they seek a fair trial before God they will get one, however they should know that a perfect record is what is needed. He is challenging them to think and evaluate very honestly whether or not they will really come out blameless before God.

But don't forget…

Verse 11 hammers Paul's point home. While verses 9 and 10 include the Jew in judgment and the gentile in having the same potential for reward he then reminds them that just because they were born Jewish doesn't mean that they will get an easier standard to be judged against. Their ethnicity is meaningless before the Great White Throne.

Take Home

It is the Holy Spirit's job to convict the non-believer of his sin (John 16:8). However, it is vital for us, as we share the gospel with an unbelieving world, that we inform them that God's judgment is perfect, and complete. If anyone operates under the delusion that they will be put on a scale and hope the good outweighs the bad we must correct them. This isn't a 51% will do it issue. God requires absolute perfection, not even 99.9% will get the job done as sin requires a payment and there is no chance that God will let even the smallest thing go in His perfect justice. This is a vital message that we must share so that people can understand their need for the work of Jesus Christ.

ROMANS 2:12-14

Getting Everyone in the Same Boat

The purpose of these early chapters of Romans is very clear. The Holy Spirit is revealing that every single person is in the same boat. Every single person is in a place of absolute need. While every individual on earth hides away a hidden hope that their one little pet idea or practice makes them better than everyone else we find that none of these things meet God's standard. Whether we seek to become fit for God by our good works, or by our honest viewpoint, or any other self-imposed standard, the result is the same. Every person stands in the same place of need. This can be an uncomfortable reality for humanity. So much of a person's identity is derived from how a person defines themselves against those others who surround them. Here we see that when it comes to our position before the Lord we all share a place of need, and all of our best or worst performances can do nothing to change that reality.

Romans 2:12-13 (NASB)

12For all who have sinned without the Law will also perish without the Law, and all who have sinned under the Law will be judged by the Law; 13for *it is* not the hearers of the Law *who* are just before God, but the doers of the Law will be justified.

Sinning without the Law

This is important! In America there is constitutional protection against being convicted for breaking a law before that law was in place. In other words: you cannot be convicted for jaywalking in 1988 if jaywalking were not made illegal until 2002. So we come to the very difficult issue: How can God convict humanity of sin if they did not know His Law?

This is very important: The Law of Moses is NOT God's ultimate standard. Something is not sin because it violates the Law of Moses. God's perfect and holy character is the ultimate standard. The Law has a specific use in human history, but we can come into all sorts of problems when we try to root God's righteousness anywhere but in Himself. In other words – life is not a game. It isn't as if God handed out the rules to everyone on earth and blew off the starter pistol and waited to see who could make it to the end of the race without being disqualified.

When Adam and Eve sinned the relationship with God was broken and that changed everything. No amount of rule following can change that situation. The Law of Moses was a helpful tool for the children of Israel for a number of reasons. In certain places it revealed His moral standard to them. In other places it told them how to remain distinct from their neighbors so that the Messianic line would be protected. The Law most often reminded them about the loving and gracious character of a God who can forgive based upon the promise of a Redeemer. However, obedience to those rules could never bring a person to spiritual salvation. That had to come through faith alone. Whether a person lived under the Law or never knew the Law the problem was not their relationship to the Law as a Law breaker – it was that they were not in line with the character of God.

Doers only

While the Law could never make an unrighteous person righteous before God, those who had that revelation would be judged by it. Just as the person without the Law would be judged guilty even by their own seared conscience so the person with the Law would have the additional testimony that they had failed to live up perfectly to the Law and commandments of God. This was important for the Jewish person of Paul's day, and it is just as important for any manner of legalist today.

Humans are great at self-deception. It has well been said that we look at our own sin though a microscope and other's sins through a telescope. It is a funny picture, but it is true. The person who believes that they are earning or improving their position before God by their good behavior must do this in order not to fall into complete despair. It starts by minimizing or legitimizing our failures and then spending a great deal of time focusing on the failures of others and trying to proclaim that we would *never* do such a terrible thing.

It is much like a person who shows up at a dinner party and finds that they have a small stain on their shirt. In an embarrassed panic this person picks up a cup of spaghetti sauce and lobs it at the person across the table. While someone else at "the party" may have a "bigger stain" no amount of focus on them will clean the first person's shirt. This is precisely what the legalist does, and in so doing he renders the Law of Moses utterly useless. It was never meant to be used for that purpose – it was always meant to draw each individual to his *own* need for God's gracious and merciful provision for us in Christ Jesus.

<u>Romans 2:14-16</u>

14For when Gentiles who do not have the Law do instinctively the things of
the Law, these, not having the Law, are a law to themselves 15in that they
show the work of the Law written in their hearts, their conscience bearing
witness and their thoughts alternately accusing or else defending them, 16on
the day when, according to my gospel, God will judge the secrets of men
through Christ Jesus.

The Power of Conscience

Mankind is made in the image of God. Thus, even with the fall, there is residual evidence of the Image in which we have been created. Thus there are countless pagans who are extraordinarily moral. How can this be if they do not have the Law? It is quite plain, while they do not have the Law they do have access to the greater standard and that is the intuitive knowledge of man of God's righteous standard and character. God does not hide His righteousness, and the Holy Spirit now convicts the world of sin. Thus the person who may never have known God's revelation can seek to ease the burn of conscience by trying to strive all the harder to satisfy that longing for righteousness.

The Law Written on their Hearts

This differs entirely from the promise that God made to Israel that the Messianic kingdom will be characterized by Israel having the Law written on their hearts. You can see Jeremiah 31:33 for this promise which is a commitment that God will supernaturally endow Israel with the ability to keep His Law during the kingdom. In this verse, however, Paul is simply making it clear that these pagans who seek to keep a moral standard are proving that they retain this standard from the character of God.

Same place

This "noble savage" however is no better off than the person who has the Law. He is also in a place of being constantly either affirmed or condemned even by his own corrupted standard of righteousness. This is the major point of Paul's argument in these chapters. Even those who may try and define their own standard are condemned by their inability to maintain even that standard. Thus, the most moral of sinners often drive themselves mad with their inability to maintain even their most simple of rules. This has been seen in some of the greatest lives of men who sought to achieve their own moral perfection. Eventually they had to cry out for mercy, or they broke completely in the trying.

The Secrets of Men

It is very common for religious leaders to maintain a level of distance from their congregations. This is often because they don't want their secrets getting out. The secret? They are still not perfect. The only way a person can remain perfect in the view of another is to maintain a great distance. A person may look lovely from the distance of a football field and be shown to be an unkempt mess from a few yards. These tricks of perspective mean nothing before the righteousness of God. Fooling every person in the world into thinking that you are perfect will mean nothing before God. Even if every sin is hidden from view and no one could ever know – God knows all of the secrets. Again we must say – God's standard is HIS righteousness! God is not "grading on the curve" because, apart from absolute perfection, mankind is unfitted for eternal life with Him. Just like a chair with a mostly broken leg will eventually give out, so the person with any sliver of sin in their life will ultimately be destroyed. The need of all men is the same: The need for the person and work of the Savior – Jesus Christ.

ROMANS 2:17-29

Who's in View?

Here Paul continues his vehement argument concerning the guilt of the Jews. He is telling them about their high calling and special place in the plan of God, and then shows them that they have not, for all of their advantages, represented God accurately to the unbelieving world. Every Jew knew, correctly, that they were a chosen people. God was quite explicit in the "how and why" of this choosing of national Israel. Deuteronomy 7:6-8 reads:

> *For you are a holy people to the LORD your God; the LORD your God has chosen you to be a people for His own possession out of all the peoples who are on the face of the earth. For you are a holy people to the LORD your God; the LORD your God has chosen you to be a people for His own possession out of all the peoples who are on the face of the earth. but because the LORD loved you and kept the oath which He swore to your forefathers, the LORD brought you out by a mighty hand and redeemed you from the house of slavery, from the hand of Pharaoh king of Egypt.*

The Jew must be cognizant of the fact that God's choice of them is not based on their own greatness, righteousness, or ability, but because of His faithfulness. Not just to them, but to the covenant that He made with Abraham in which He promised that "through you all nations will be blessed" (Genesis 26:4)

Looking at the Structure

Paul then goes into a very structured argument that may be put forth by the Jew who is trying to claim that he would be saved just by his being born a Jew. There are a handful of things that could rightly be claimed special to the Jewish nation, so these are not all false claims. In fact, Paul's ultimate condemnation of them doesn't rest on the truths of these statements but on the failures of the Jews as individuals. Let's look at the structure of verses 17-20:

17 But if you bear the name "Jew"

and rely upon the Law and boast in God,

18 and know *His* will and approve the things that are essential,

being instructed out of the Law,

19 and are confident that you yourself are a guide to the blind,

a light to those who are in darkness,

20 a corrector of the foolish,

a teacher of the immature,

having in the Law the embodiment of knowledge and of the truth,

The first thing we may notice is the repetition of the phrase "the Law." Here, "the Law" means, not simply the Law as the list of commands to obey, but the whole of Old Testament Scripture. He is drawing into the forefront the chief advantage that the Jews had: the fact that they were the possessors of divine revelation. The Jews had the only real revelation of the person and character of God. They had every opportunity, including the very prophecies that reveal the fact that Christ is the Messiah of the Old Testament. The Jews were the keepers of God's truth, and there were many non-Jews who came to salvation, knowing and serving the One true God of Scripture through their witness (Ruth, Uriah the Hittite, the Ethiopian Eunuch and others). It was God's intention that people would draw near to Israel to know Him.

Bear the Name

The first statement that Paul here makes is interesting. He doesn't just say, "you who are a Jew" but rather, "You who bear the name 'Jew'". This is significant as it is moving towards the argument that he will draw to conclusion in verses 28-29. He is beginning to question the legitimacy of the thought of the day that just being Jewish was enough to please God. But, as we will see, God has no grandchildren, and just being born into a Jewish family (just as being born into a Christian family) is by no means enough.

rely upon the Law and boast in God

Here we see the Jew is resting in the Law. The trouble is that the Law provides no rest for man. As James point out, "For whoever keeps the whole law and yet stumbles in one *point,* he has become guilty of all." (James 2:10) Having the Law is an advantage; we will see proved again in this epistle. However, it is not something that a person can rest in, it must be perfectly obeyed in order to provide any rest.

Boasting in God is another interesting accusation to level upon the Jew. They were proud of their place in God's plan, but for all the wrong reasons. They would boast and brag about their special place before God forgetting that it was because of His grace and action that they were chosen, not their faithfulness by any means! Paul, being a Jew would later say of boasting, "But may it never be that I would **boast**, except in the cross of our Lord Jesus Christ, through which the world has been crucified to me, and I to the world." Galatians 6:14

know *His* will and approve the things that are essential

The Jew was unique in the fact that he did know the will of God. All of the other pagan myths that had cropped up since man abandoned the true knowledge of God conflicted with the truth revealed in Scripture. The Jew knew that God was the creator of all things. The Jew knew that the standard of right and wrong under which he should be operating was given by God and not a subjective standard of righteousness.

We will see that this claim is also empty, although they did possess the Law they did not understand God's heart for the gentiles (which is revealed, among other places, in Jonah) they did not understand that God wanted them to have a contrite and humble heart before Him (Psalm 51:17; Isaiah 66:2; Jeremiah 44:10). They should have known what the Lord had for them, but they did not understand. This was clearly displayed when Jesus spoke with Nicodemus in John 3. He says to Nicodemus: "Are you the teacher of Israel and do not understand these things?" (v. 10) It is clear that the Jews of the day, though they were passionate about God's word, had missed the key points.

being instructed out of the Law
This is another thing that the Jew would have been extraordinarily proud of: Every Jewish boy would be sent to Hebrew school to learn the Torah. Literacy was expected in the Jewish community. Every young boy received a relatively high level of teaching as to the Law and traditions of the Jews. Young men who showed an exceptional talent were then able to continue in their studies and would ultimately be most proud if they were able to qualify to study under a great rabbi, as Paul studied under Gamaliel.

confident that you yourself are a guide to the blind
Notice where their confidence is placed: themselves. The Greek is emphatic "you yourself." The Jews were convinced that they were going to be a guide to the blind by themselves, the focus again is on the person, not on God. This is the malady that Christ spoke of frequently, when the Pharisees picked up on the implication that they were blind and took offense Jesus responded by saying, "If you were blind, you would have no sin; but since you say, 'We see,' your sin remains." (John 9:41) Christ's assessment agrees with Paul's assessment: "Let them alone; they are blind guides of the blind. And if a blind man guides a blind man, both will fall into a pit." (Matthew 15:14).

Light…corrector…teacher
Here Paul continues to use the Hebrew pattern of repetition to accurately describe how the Jew might have felt about himself. However, the reality is that the Jews were achieving none of these purposes anyway. Because of their extreme separatism they were not compassionately sharing the light and the law to help people see correctly. Rather they were totally turned in upon themselves. By no means showing the Lord to the sin darkened world.

having in the Law the embodiment of knowledge and of the truth
Here Paul is not speaking in any way sarcastically. In the Old Testament we see knowledge and truth that the world had rejected. The Scriptures of the Jews was the truth and was able to make them wise to salvation. As we will see, even salvation by faith through grace are not solely New Testament concepts. Abraham had no righteousness of his own but God accounted

his faith as righteousness (Genesis 15:6) and, as Paul noted in Romans 1:17, Habbakuk 2:4 says, "the righteous shall live by faith."

Romans 2:21-24

21 you, therefore, who teach another, do you not teach yourself? You
who preach that one shall not steal, do you steal? 22 You who say that one
should not commit adultery, do you commit adultery? You who
abhor idols, do you rob temples? 23 You who boast in the
Law, through your breaking the Law, do you dishonor God? 24 For "THE
NAME OF GOD IS BLASPHEMED AMONG THE
GENTILES BECAUSE OF YOU," just as it is written.

The Turning Point

Remember, in the context, the Jew may have been saying to himself "Yes, I am those things…that describes me perfectly." But here Paul pulls the plug on their pride. He starts with more than a touch of sarcasm, asking those who claim to be teachers, do they teach themselves?" This would have been a stinging moment if a non-believing Jew were to read it. While it would be unlikely that the reader was expecting a pat on the back, undoubtedly the previous verses would have touched on one or many points that they had put some confidence in. As Paul turns the corner here this is a dramatic way of saying, "Not so fast!"

Stealing, Adultery, Robbing temples

Sadly, as we will see, the Jews were viewed by Greco-Roman culture as being a less than wonderful people. Stealing here could refer to charging one another interest (which was prohibited by the law). However, taking anything, no matter how small, that didn't belong to them was stealing and the honest person would have to admit if they had done it. We see frequently in humanity those who condemn loudly and publicly that which they are guilty of in private, hoping to deter people from imagining that they could be as guilty as those whom they judge. Paul highlights the 7th commandment against adultery and it would not be surprising at all to imagine with the variety and accessibility of prostitution that a Jew might go to the synagogue and then slip off to visit a prostitute of some kind. The idea of robbing temples may be even more close to them. Part of the worship of a given god would involve a free or cheap meal. Paul is asking them if they were compromising with the world and going in for free meals and "worship." Furthermore, every devout Jew would make a trip to Jerusalem if at all possible and would have beheld the same "den of robbers" that desecrated their own temple, by turning the outer court into a marketplace.

Boasting and Breaking

Here Paul brings the bitter reality of boasting in one's own righteousness to light. Though many would like to be recognized for their own righteousness, an honest consideration of one's own conduct will always bring a reality check upon the legalist. Paul is eluding the incredible arrogance of the Jewish mindset here and asking them honestly if they think that they are honoring God with their conduct. It is simply not so. They pronounce and preach the righteousness of the law, and the darkened state of the gentiles, but then go and live like gentiles themselves. The point is clear: God is not honored by man's hypocrisy.

The Name of God is blasphemed

Here Paul draws from Isaiah 52:5 and Ezekiel 36:22 to convey the sad reality. The fact that this statement was taken from the Old Testament would have been a stinging rebuke for the Jews. This had happened before and was happening then, and the Jews are once again judged by their own law. William Barclay writes extensively about the general feelings of the Gentiles concerning the Jews, and it isn't good. He writes, in part:

They regarded Judaism as a "barbarous superstition" and the Jews as "the most disgusting of races," and as "a most contemptible company of slaves." The origins of Jewish religion were twisted with a malicious ignorance. It was said that Jews had originally been a company of lepers who had been sent by the king of Egypt to work in the sand quarries; and that Moses had rallied this band of leprous slaves and led them through the desert to Palestine. It was said that they worshipped an ass's head, because in the wilderness a herd of wild asses had led them to water when they were perishing with thirst. It was said that they abstained from swine's flesh because the pig is specially liable to a skin disease called the itch, and it was that skin disease that the Jews had suffered from in Egypt.[1]

This same author goes on to tell about how: "Juvenal declared that if a Jew was asked the way to any place, he refused to give any information except to another Jew, and that if anyone was looking for a well from which to drink, he would not lead him to it unless he was circumcised."[2] Undoubtedly, much of this was exaggeration and slander (as the story of the origin of the Jews clearly was just slander). However, often times when a stereotype is made there is a kernel of truth at the core of it, and Paul wanted these Jews to be honest about the public perception of them by the Greeks and Romans. This is not to condone anti-Semitism, but rather to accentuate the truth that the Jews were not presenting such a flawless witness that the world was getting an accurate representation of the character of God.

Romans 2:25-29

25For indeed circumcision is of value if you practice the Law; but if you are
a transgressor of the Law, your circumcision has become uncircumcision. 26
So if the uncircumcised man keeps the requirements of the Law, will not his
uncircumcision be regarded as circumcision? 27 And he who is
physically uncircumcised, if he keeps the Law, will he not judge you
who though having the letter *of the Law* and circumcision are a
transgressor of the Law? 28For he is not a Jew who is one outwardly, nor is
circumcision that which is outward in the flesh. 29But he is a Jew who is one
inwardly; and circumcision is that which is of the heart, by the Spirit, not by
the letter; and his praise is not from men, but from God.

True or False?

Now, having established the guilt and hypocrisy of the Jewish person, Paul goes right to the heart of the issue and establishes what really makes someone a Jew in the way that matters before God. Paul is asking for something that is terrifying to most every person alive: honesty. When we really look at ourselves we have to admit that we are not as impressive as we would have hoped, not as good as we would have expected, and we don't even meet our own flawed standard.

We must keep in mind that Paul isn't "picking on" the Jews. He himself

---

[1] Barclay, Wm. The Daily Bible Study Series: Romans. Pg. 48.

[2] Ibid. p. 50.

was Jewish and it was quite likely that he had to make all of these realizations himself. He would most likely have affirmed each of the previous statements before he trusted in the Lord. He is being hard on the Jews here because he loves them so much, and doesn't want any one of them to miss the ultimate reality that there is no salvation through the Law as none can keep it perfectly. But his point here is that no one even comes close! This all may seem rather harsh, but he doesn't want them thinking that they could have done it. He will not allow anyone to think, "I could have been saved by the law, but it was nice of God to give us Jesus to make it easier." Nor does he want anyone to think that they go 75% of the way on their own and Jesus makes up the last 25%. He wants the Jew, just like the pagan before, to see that they need a Savior – they need Him 100% and have nothing to contribute at all.

Circumcision

This word is very culturally important. To the Jew circumcision was the sign that they wore on their body, proving that they were a "good Jew." It was a certification that they would see several times a day certifying who they were, and what people group they belonged to. To them this was the ordinance that mattered most of all. Even to the point it was taught that Abraham sat on the gates of hell to be sure that no circumcised person went in by accident. Paul's point here is that they would not be saved by this observance alone.

The Way the Law Works

The Law is a fairly simple concept: If you break the law you are a transgressor and have earned condemnation. If you obey the law you are not punished. The law of our own land gives us an easy way to understand this reality. Imagine a man on trial for murder. When he is asked to give an account for what he did, imagine he were to say, "Well, yes, I did murder that person, BUT look at all of the laws I haven't broken! I haven't broken the speed limit this week, nor have I stolen anything that didn't belong to me, nor have I…" It seems silly to think of that even occurring, however, that is exactly what the Jew looks like when he looks at the face of his own sinful transgression and says, "Well, I am circumcised, so I'm sure it's okay." It is the nature of the Law that if you only keep part of it you may as well have kept none of it, because guilty is guilty. How a person is guilty, or why, is of little importance in light of the reality that a transgressor is a transgressor and the standard of God is perfection.

The Switch-a-roo

Here Paul turns the argument around for them. He tells them that not only does their physical circumcision not matter if they break the law, but also to tell them that if a person were to keep the Law perfectly, though they were uncircumcised, they would be viewed as circumcised. This would have been the ultimate affront to the Jew. To think that they would be judged by a pagan if he were to keep the Law would have been repugnant. Yet, as we saw previously, the Gentiles didn't have a positive view of the Jews. They saw in them basic flaws and shortcomings of love for all mankind, and that testimony was fatal. But even more to the point, God would not be unjust in regarding a person as being "circumcised" if that were the only thing standing between Him and the Lord. Imagine that! It is as if Paul is tearing away from them any idea that they may have had regarding their advantage of being a Jew. Chapter 3 outlines the true advantages that the Jews had, but Paul is trying to make ultimately quite clear that the advantage of being a Jew is not what they may have come to believe.

Who's a Jew?

Verses 28 and 29 require some very serious and very careful attention. These verses have been misread and misinterpreted for many years in the church to very destructive ends. We want to be quite careful about what these verses say and what they don't say.

28For he is not a Jew who is one outwardly,
nor is circumcision that which is outward in the flesh.
29But he is a Jew who is one inwardly;
and circumcision is that which is of the heart, by the Spirit, not by the letter;
and his praise is not from men, but from God.

Keep in mind that Paul is addressing the Jews here. The very clear statement leads back to verse 17 where he addressed the one who is "called 'a Jew'". As we noted Paul is drawing a contrast here, but not the contrast we may think at first glance, nor the contrast many interpreters have taken him to be making. In the first statement Paul tells that being a Jew outwardly isn't enough. Even though the physical signs may be there, it cannot be taken for granted that that person is a true Jew. Paul highlights the reality that the circumcision is outward in the flesh.

The second statement that he is a Jew who is one inwardly. The logical trap that people have fallen into is the mistaken conclusion that anyone who believes is, therefore, a Jew. This is not the correct understanding, and clearly not what is being addressed even in the translation to English. Paul is saying that being a Jew is not just a physical matter of being born into the right lineage, but also a choice of faith, it is a reality of something inward and real. So it is important to get to Paul's conclusion: not that everyone is a Jew who believes, but that the only Jews that are true Jews are those who are Jews inwardly and outwardly…believing Jews. Paul is referencing a repeated Biblical pattern:

So circumcise your heart, and stiffen your neck no longer. Deuteronomy 10:16

Moreover the LORD your God will circumcise your heart and the heart of your descendants, to love the LORD your God with all your heart and with all your soul, so that you may live. Deuteronomy 30:6

Circumcise yourselves to the LORD And remove the foreskins of your heart, Men of Judah and inhabitants of Jerusalem, Or else My wrath will go forth like fire And burn with none to quench it, Because of the evil of your deeds. Jeremiah 4:4

Conclusion

Paul closes with one final stinging remark. He tells them that the true Jew's praise is from God and not from men. He brings to the forefront one of the issues that Jesus had to deal with concerning the rulers of national Israel, and her religious folks as well. They were all parading their holiness before men. They didn't much care for God's approval, they wanted man's approval. They didn't want only to please God, but had an ulterior motive – to gain praise from other men. Paul lets them know that this is unacceptable. This is not the goal at all, but the true Jew would be humble and contrite of heart before God. The mark of his faith being seen in his character as being like God's for the glory of God alone. It is only to serve Him, and the Jews, like the rest of humanity, come up short. So we see that the Jew, like the gentile, needs the Messiah. Praise the Lord, He has been provided!

ROMANS 3

ROMANS 3:1-4

What is the point?

The last chapter soundly placed the Jew in the same place before God as the gentile. For all of the advantage of being God's chosen people, and for all of the advantage of having the Law they still needed a Savior. This would have been shocking to many of Paul's Jewish recipients. Some were even taught that just being born a Jew and being circumcised (for the boys) was enough to guarantee salvation! There is even one myth that Abraham sat on the gates of Hades and made sure that no circumcised man ever went to the place of torment.

With this as their background, it is understandable why they may say, "What is the point of being Jewish! I thought we were a shoe-in to salvation." Paul has to reset their understanding. It wasn't enough to be only ethnically Jewish, but it had to be combined with a trust in God and His provision. The fact that they were Jewish didn't make any difference in the whole sin problem. However, was there any advantage in being Jewish? Oh yes! And here Paul tells us about that great advantage.

Great in Every Respect

This is the starting place. The Jews had a remarkable advantage over the rest of the world. While every gentile was raised in a world of strange mythologies and confused philosophies the Jew was raised in a culture that at least pointed to the one true God. Before we look at these advantages it seems prudent to take an aside.

It has become very popular in Christianity today to have a very dramatic conversion story. As if somehow a person's conversion is all the better for coming from the darkest depths of drug addiction and despair. These are wonderful stories of God's grace and faithfulness, and I hope they are told until the Lord returns. These stories, however, often have a sad effect on those who are raised in Christian homes. I have seen far too many believers tell their story of coming to trust Christ having been raised in a Christ-honoring Church going family almost apologetically, as if their testimony was too easy. This is foolishness. These believers have been given a legacy! A legacy and an advantage of having been loved and seen Christ in their very own homes and the lives of their families. These testimonies have no shame, but only strength. It is my prayer that rather than telling a bashful, apologetic tale, the third and fourth generation Christian would declare their spiritual heritage with both thankfulness and joy. I hope to hear more and more of *these* testimonies, for they ring of God's amazing faithfulness.

Trusted with the Oracles of God

It must be pointed out: the Jews foremost advantage is that they were trusted with the Oracles of God. Read here: the Holy Scripture. The written word is how God designed to communicate Himself to humanity, and Israel had the blessed advantage of having, guarding and applying those Sacred documents. This is a marked advantage. When a Jewish person comes to Christ they have the advantage of seeing that they knew Him all along because it is His character and the hope of His coming that are the consistent promise of the Old Testament. To grow up knowing the story of Creation – knowing the moral character of God. To be raised in the regular hearing of the accounts of Adam and Eve, Cain and Abel, Abraham, Moses, Joseph, Elijah and the other wonderful accounts of the Old Testament was an advantage that could not be fully understood by those who would grow up in the pagan confusion of the Greco-Roman world. When we consider this advantage it becomes absurd how much access we have to Scripture now, and how frequently Christians' Bibles simply go unread.

Yet some didn't get it…

Something very important is being pointed out here. A story will help to illustrate. A man gets a new immersion blender and soon calls and complains to the friend who gave it to him:

"Thanks for the gift, but it doesn't work. Mess everywhere, and really nothing productive I can see. Just a bunch of dog hair all over!"

Of course the friend stops at the last comment and asks how dog hair may have entered into the equation…

"Well, that's what I was trying to use it for – grooming the dog! Isn't that what an immersion blender is for?"

Clearly the giver of the gift could not be blamed for the recipient's misunderstanding and misuse of the gift. This is Paul's point. Just because some of the Jews had not taken the slow time to understand and apply their own precious gift of the Oracles of God did not draw God's faithfulness into question by even the smallest measure.

The Choice

It seems that humans very frequently want to be treated like children. A child will very often suffer with freedom, and then blame the adult for the trouble that their limited freedom has brought to them. This is the point: Just as a good parent will hold their child accountable for their decisions and not take responsibility for their errors, so God is not responsible for the sinful and rebellious choices of mankind. This simple fact is vital to understand because many even today would like to draw a world where a person's choice for or against Christ today makes no eternal impact.

These moments matter. They will be the difference between eternity with Christ and eternal damnation…all for this one important choice.

ROMANS 3:5-8

Following the Argument

Paul here continues his argument that shows the Jewish people to be guilty of faithlessness before God. In the last four verses Paul gave us a clear view of the advantage that the Jew had. While he has no advantage in regards to righteousness, and has not righteousness of his own, he does have the advantage of having had the Scriptures. This advantage should have been proof to him of a couple major things. The Scriptures should have proved to him that no one can attain to the righteousness of God. They also proved that Jesus Christ is the Messiah, the promised one, the savior! The scripture also revealed the eternal and everlasting character of God. In the Old Testament we see no less clearly God's sovereignty, grace, love, kindness, mercy and compassion for fallen mankind. This was all a significant advantage. Not the sort of advantage that would enable him to earn his salvation, but the sort of advantage should have helped the Jews realize that they needed the Savior, God in His mercy was sending the Savior, and they should have embraced Jesus as the Messiah when He came.

What advantage to children in a Christian home have?

There are many in the world today, especially in the so called "Christian Nations" who "were raised Christian" or claim to have "always been a Christian." As if by being born into a Christian family salvation is theirs by inheritance. In many ways their situation is similar to the Jew that Paul is addressing. While they have every advantage and opportunity to understand and put their faith in the Gospel, they must actually trust in Jesus personally for salvation, not just assume that, as they were raised in the right home, go to church and don't do bad things that God is pleased with them. Our indirect application of this argument can be made towards those who are "cultural Christians" and have never actually believed the Gospel.

The Great Debator

The stakes are high here. Paul is writing to convince these people (Gentiles, Moralists, Jews, et al) that they need the Savior. They are wholly unable to help themselves, that they can only rest on the saving work of Christ Jesus. In order to do this, Paul makes his arguments clear as crystal. Even to the point of anticipating objections, questions and accusations and answering them before they are actually raised. Paul is not going to leave any stone unturned. As we will see the argument he addresses doesn't hold water, and is filled with slander and bad thinking, yet he addresses it anyhow. Why? Because Paul isn't afraid to ruffle some feathers to be clear.

Romans 3:5

But if our unrighteousness demonstrates the righteousness of God, what shall we say? The God who inflicts wrath is not unrighteous, is He? (I am speaking in human terms.)

Posing the Question

It is important to realize that Paul is not making his own argument but rather he is making a human argument. We will look at the nature of this claim at the end of this verse, however, this illustrates the great importance to always take Scripture in context, and hold others accountable to do the same. If we were to take this verse out on its own it could be misinterpreted and someone could say, "See, the Bible says that your God is unrighteous and condemns people without cause!" But they would be wrong. This is an important point in biblical interpretation as well as whenever someone is presenting something that seems weird, foreign or unorthodox to you. They may rattle off verse references like honey rolling off their tongue and is always a good idea to say, "Wait a moment, let's look at those verses in context and decide if they are really saying what you claim." Nevertheless, Paul here anticipates the Jew's rebuttal to his previous arguments.

Our unrighteousness

Here Paul talks about the unrighteousness of the previous verse. We saw in verse 3 that the unrighteousness of the Jews was their faithlessness. Paul suggested in verse 5 that God is proven all the more truthful by the proven fact that every man is a liar. Then he slows down and says, "I know where your dirty little mind is going next." The Jew is ready to give his defense through an argument that doesn't hold water, but one that does fit with some of the other slanderous accusations that were floating around in the ancient world.

Demonstrates

This Greek word could also be brought across as "commends." The idea is much like the girl who wants her friends to choose an ugly dress so hers will look that much more alluring. The fallacious argument is that the worse I am, the better God will look. That by being as bad as I can be I can make the goodness of God look somehow better by comparison, as if my D- makes God's resounding 100% more conspicuous.

The Unjust God

Here's where the argument that Paul is anticipating really hits its peak. J.B. Phillips paraphrases this verse as: "But if our wickedness advertises the goodness of God, do we feel that God is being unfair to punish us in return? (I'm using a human tit-for-tat argument.)" The idea is that someone might accuse God of being a bit unfair since He comes out looking better next to our failures. The chief problem with this argument is found immediately following this phrase.

Speaking in Human Terms

Paul issues here a disclaimer saying that these are not his words, this is not his argument, but rather he is making a human argument. The Greek phrase here is three words long *kata anthropon lego*. In order it would literally translate as "according to mankind I speak." Here we see the essential problem of the human viewpoint. God doesn't need anyone to advertise His goodness, it is only humans that need that assurance because we are essentially evil! It is only us that would dare to try to be glorified by standing next to someone worse off than we, but for God nothing can make His righteousness any greater. His condemnation of this argument really begins here, in a sense, as he is issuing a "this is what the stupid human viewpoint on the thing may be" disclaimer. Imagine that!

<u>Romans 3:6</u>

May it never be! For otherwise, how will God judge the world?

May it never be!

A person doesn't need to know Greek to behold the Lord through His word. However, there are a couple of Greek words that would benefit every Christian to be aware of because they are so radically bigger than the words that we use to translate them. Words like *charis* (grace), *agape* (Love, often God's unique kind of unconditional love), *hagios* (saint, which is used to describe every single person who has placed faith in Christ). For the purposes of the study of Romans we must add one more Greek phrase to this list – *me genoito*. *Me* is a particle that means "not" or negates what it is grammatically attached to; while *genoito* is related to the word for "become, or be birthed" so the idea is "Don't even imagine it!" Translators grasp at straws trying to translate this phrase as extremely as they can. We have already seen it once (in verse 4) and will yet see it again. Some have brought this across as "God forbid!" others as "Perish the Thought!" even as "No way!" And they all get the idea across. It is an extreme statement that implies the absolute absurdity of the argument!

How will God Judge the world?

Paul is drawing on what people far and wide know and have known forever. That there will be a judgment, a summing up, a time where the accounts are all reckoned. We see that God's judgment is poured out in the Bible and throughout history. Paul is essentially extending the argument to the point of absurdity. Having started down that logical track you can only wind up in one logical place, "Let's call it quits, do whatever you want, God's hands are tied!" And it is clearly unreasonable as we know that God will judge the world as we even dare to judge situations by an objective standard or righteousness, and don't praise the bank robber for making us feel better about the fact that we have never done anything so bad as that. The logical end of this way of thinking is, there is just no such thing as right and wrong. Note, again, this confusion comes from the human viewpoint. If we are ever going to make sense of this world only God's viewpoint, as He has revealed to us in His word, will profit us anything.

Romans 3:7-8

[7]But if through my lie the truth of God abounded to His glory, why am I
also still being judged as a sinner? [8]And why not *say* (as we are
slanderously reported and as some claim that we say), "Let us do evil that
good may come"? Their condemnation is just.

Repetition, repetition, repetition!

Here the rebuttal to the short address of this argument in the last verse is to repeat the argument in a slightly different manner. Rather than "unrighteousness" and "righteousness" which have a moral character to them the change of focus is to the individual deception as it relates to actual states of affairs. Once again the argument sounds almost silly as it comes across, but that doesn't mean that there aren't those making this argument…even today! Imagine two children standing in a room with a broken vase. It is clear from the circumstances and guilty expressions that they have broken the vase. When asked one says: "No, we didn't." and the other says: "Yes, we did it." The child who lied is just twice proved a liar (once by circumstance and once by testimony of his friend). It doesn't make the truth telling child look any more righteous, it only shows that the truth telling child is taking responsibility.

To His glory

Here we see an intrinsic misunderstanding in the character and nature of God. To be sure, God will be glorified in the judgment and defeat of Satan, the Liar (Revelation 20:10) as well as by the judgment of all who have rejected Him (Revelation 20:15), however that is not the way that God wants to be glorified. He wants to be glorified by the salvation of unworthy sinners who have placed faith in His Son (Ephesians 1:3-14, note "to the praise of the glory of His grace"), but He will be glorified either way. However, one way He cannot be glorified is by letting sin go unpunished because "it makes Him look better."

The Slander

When we come into contact with the true doctrine of grace we will always see people begin to slander those who are preaching or teaching it. The slander that was going around is that Paul was teaching justification by grace through faith and not by law (Chapter 5), sanctification by grace through faith and not through law (Chapter 6-7) and glorification by faith through grace and not by law (Chapter 8). And people take that and say, "If we take away the law then people will just do whatever they want!" "If we take away the fear of punishment then people will go crazy and become licentious sinners!" Even in dealing with these verses Christian publications show their legalistic colors and betray their own lack of understanding of grace. One example is from the *NIV Archaeological Study Bible* which reads in its note on this verse:

"Antinomianism is the view that the oral law does not apply to Christians, who are instead under the law of grace. Because salvation does not come through works but through grace, it is held, moral effort can be discounted. Paul found that this kind of heresy had crept into the church (1 Cor. 5-6). Others had chosen to misrepresent Paul's teaching on grace (as in this verse), and Paul pointed out the absurdity of the charge (Ro 6:1, 15). From the first century to our own day, some individuals or groups have sought to combine the spiritual life with moral license, but Scripture leaves no doubt that the new life in Christ means death to the old, evil desires (Gal. 5:24)." Archaeology Study Bible Page, pg. 183)

Notice the logical flaw here. They are making the exact mistake that the slanderers were making! The logical fallacy is a forced "either/or" statement and ignoring the third option which is actually the biblical reality. The argument goes, "If you don't put people under the law they will become licentious." However, this is manifest nonsense. As Paul will point out in Chapter 6 the Christian who continues to live in sin doesn't need "a little bit of law" they need a better understanding of grace, and law just brings the man to an understanding of his own inability and wretchedness (Romans 7). Paul's judgment remains – "their condemnation is just."

ROMANS 3:9-18

Passing Judgment

This has taken quite a bit of time. No one could say that this conclusion was drawn hastily. Quite to the contrary all of the possible players have been examined and all of the positions put forward. When Paul finally comes to the biblical diagnosis of the position of mankind under sin we find that the experience has already very much proven that position to be the case. Everyone is born under sin. We may find these words of the Old Testament to induce despair. And it is right that they do so, for until we understand our complete inability before the Lord we have not the faintest hope of understanding the Salvation which He has provided for us. Not understanding the salvation we have been given is the most central reason that most believers don't grow as they ought to grow.

None Righteous

The first clear statement is that there is not a single righteous person. Righteous translates the Greek word *dikiasune* meaning "to be in right standing." There is not one person who is in right standing. It is important that the primary focus is on what humanity *is*, while what humanity *does* simply flows naturally forth from the statement of being. This is the core issue that every unbeliever has to deal with. This is the core condition of the human soul apart from Christ's saving work.

Understanding and Seeking

Because of that first natural starting place it makes perfect sense that there is also not one person who understands. The English word "understanding" translates the word *sunion* which means to draw all of the facts together in a meaningful way. This is a perfect description of the state of the person who is trying to figure out why things are how they are apart from the revelation of God. This explains the tremendous amount of confusion that exists in the world today. People try to find any other explanation for the corruption and difficulty in the world apart from God's clearly revealed truth and the end is a totally hopeless confusion. This is because they refuse the clear truth that only comes from seeking God's revelation. But why? All of the other methods for trying to draw together the facts attempt to retain some hope for humanity apart from God. They are united in finding some other solution that does not put man in the position of having hope in God's grace and provision alone.

Turning aside and doing good…

The reality is that once man has turned aside from seeking the only true basis for knowledge and understanding there is no hope that the works that would flow forth from that basis would be worthy of being called "good". Thus we see that the truth of the word of God is clear. What a person does flows forth from what they are. Because of the arrogant unwillingness to accept the humiliation of man's fallen provision event the works that would appear "good" can only be shadows and imitations of goodness at best. Just as a mime can only give a good illusion but never show the reality of what they would act like if they were really trapped in an invisible box, so a person who has placed himself outside of the truth of God's revelation can only come up with a semi-convincing display of what true goodness ought to look like.

The Mouth

The mouth is the next logically affected organ. Having deception and confusion as a starting point nothing that comes forth can be good. We see this in every political race. People attempt to look good, but wind up simply slandering and cursing. The sorry state of man goes forth into the very words that are spoken. Even the good things ring with divisive cursing and hatred. There is nothing that can flow out of this corrupted spring. As Jesus perfectly expressed: "But the things that proceed out of the mouth come from the heart, and those defile the man." (Matthew 15:18). There is nothing pure that can come from the corrupted well of the heart that refuses to acknowledge the Lord.

The Feet

Sadly, corruption does not stop at the mouth. It moves out into the feet and hands. Those very ideas that attempt to look so pretty and helpful result in the worst kind of destructive and hateful action. George Orwell's book Animal Farm clearly displays the reality that the most compassionate talk of man only results in more evil slave masters, and greater destruction. Every promise of secular thinking always results in more murderous and destructive action and intention. While it looks like some sort of good, it always winds up in action that is ultimately repulsive. It is repulsive even to the God rejecting world.

The Eyes

This is ultimately because there is no understanding of God or man. There can be no right way to fit all of the pieces together and no way of coming up with any other solution apart from God. It is hard for humanity to deal with the reality that the road to hell is often paved with the very best of intentions. When humanity abandons God and still hopes to attain a good and pleasant end there is nothing but pain and loss awaiting. The Savior, Jesus Christ, is the only answer to the problems and desires of the world. Scripture does not leave us with any second best or second option. We are left to seek Christ and Christ alone.

ROMANS 3:19-26

[21]But now apart from the Law *the* righteousness of God has been
manifested, being witnessed by the Law and the Prophets,
[22]even *the* righteousness of God through faith in Jesus Christ for all those
who believe; for there is no distinction; [23]for all have sinned and fall short
of the glory of God, [24]being justified as a gift by His grace through the
redemption which is in Christ Jesus; [25]whom God displayed publicly as a
propitiation in His blood through faith. *This was* to demonstrate His
righteousness, because in the forbearance of God He passed over the sins
previously committed; [26]for the demonstration, *I say,* of His righteousness at
the present time, so that He would be just and the justifier of the one who
has faith in Jesus.

Getting to the Gospel

Glimpses have been given along the way, however, this detailed study has been moving towards this week when the gospel is finally made clear! It may seem amazing to think that Paul has taken this much ink to get to the good news, but there is a reason: it is VITAL to understand the great and complete need of man for the gospel, or else we cannot understand the gospel. It is pivotal that we don't lose sight of the fact that the Gospel is not God's "plan B". This is the only plan that God ever made for salvation. It had to be clear that the Jew and the gentile alike understood that there is no option two. The Gospel is not the way that God gave us to earn our salvation, or a bit of help along the way. The Gospel is the only way that a man can get to God. As Jesus Christ said, "…no one can come to the Father except by me." (John 14:6) Misunderstanding this is a fatal flaw.

<u>Romans 3:19-20</u>

[19]Now we know that whatever the Law says, it speaks to those who are
under the Law, so that every mouth may be closed and all the world may
become accountable to God; [20]because by the works of the Law no flesh
will be justified in His sight; for through the Law *comes* the knowledge of
sin.

Who's in view?

Paul just finished a powerful section demonstrating by sewing together scripture after scripture, verse after verse to prove that all of mankind, Jews and Gentiles alike followed the path that begins with turning from God and ends with destruction. Paul draws the point to a close by reminding them that these verses of universal condemnation were written to the Jews and it must therefore apply to them as well, as they are not exempted in the passages themselves. The Jews are being addressed and thus they cannot claim that they are not under this universal condemnation of sinfulness. The Holy Spirit guided Paul here to show them that their behavior, their reputation and their own Scriptures all testify together with great unanimity – all are fully sinful!

Why?

Paul uses the language of a trial to finish his case against humanity. The purpose of the Law is here given. It is a tool that every person should be silenced when they stand before God. When we watch court programs on television there always seems to be an excuse, a rebuttal, something left to say. When the world stands before God in judgment there will be no excuse, no rebuttal, no cries of "it's not fair." Every mouth will be shut before Him. There will be nothing left to say and no word in man's defense. That is why Paul had been so very emphatic about the great need and universal guilt of mankind, if we can do it on our own then Christ died for nothing.

Becoming Accountable

The purpose of the law, then is for the purpose of showing man something that He should have known anyway. Everyone had to be shown to be guilty before God. Here is the courtroom imagery, and mankind in the place of the accused. Many try to throw off their responsibility toward God, trying to claim that they are not accountable to Him. This is, of course, ridiculous. This is proven by the amount of gymnastics that they will go through to escape from Him. The big bang, evolution, and other ridiculous theories that defy any observable basis or scientific confirmation (not to mention being counter-intuitive) are simply theories that flow and hide behind the erratic preconceived notion that "there is no God." The Law is simply a tool to show mankind that there is no escape from the guilt and sinfulness of our humanity. We need help!

Justified

This is the clear need of man – Justification. This is a 10 point theological word that every Christian should know. It is another court room word – the image given is that of a person sitting in the accused stand waiting for the verdict. Justification is when the accused is declared righteous. It is more than just a forgiveness or pardon from sin, but also a positive declaration of righteousness. This is something that the law is simply unable to do in the life of a sinful humanity.

The Clear Statement

Verse 20 gives us the clear statement. It is shocking how many people miss this simple statement. The works of the Law justify no single person, ever. Works cannot save under any circumstances. This is in direct contradiction to the Mormon and Catholic cultic doctrines of "faith AND works" no man can ever be justified by his own works. The purpose of the law is again given: "…the knowledge of sin." The Law proves one thing and only to the person honest enough to see it: mankind needs a Savior.

Romans 3:21-24

21But now apart from the Law *the* righteousness of God has been
manifested, being witnessed by the Law and the Prophets,
22even *the* righteousness of God through faith in Jesus Christ for all those
who believe; for there is no distinction; 23for all have sinned and fall short
of the glory of God, 24being justified as a gift by His grace through the
redemption which is in Christ Jesus;

A Really BIG "BUT"

This is a fantastic little word. This expression in Greek is *nuni de*, and it is most always translated "but now". This phrase is a beautiful picture for what God is doing, what He has done. We have been looking for weeks at the incredibly bleak picture of humanity. Humanities efforts end with the final judgment that everyone is condemned, unrighteous and have no hope of justification by our own means. The tragic news all ends with this great "but now…"

Apart from the Law

This is another blessed revelation. This new righteousness of God comes fully apart from the law. We are going to see that at every phase of our salvation someone is going to try to place works of the law back into the equation. Paul is very careful not to allow it at any point. The law is not useful for any of the three phases of salvation, and it is important to realize that all of the righteousness in the Christian life comes from the Source, from Christ, not from the works of the Law. We will see continually that it is His life, His righteousness and His glory that are in view.

Righteousness of God

The definite article "the" is missing from the original Greek here. When the definite article is missing from the Greek text we find the character of the thing is in view. In distinction from the righteousness that we cannot earn for ourselves by the law, God has revealed a righteousness that is of Himself in bold counter-distinction to this. This is the real deal. This is mankind's only hope as we clearly could offer nothing of our own. Furthermore, in keeping with his theme, Paul highlights the fact that this was witnessed by the Law and the Prophets. This is a Hebrew pattern of speech referring to the entire Old Testament. A short list of these passages would include Genesis 3; Deuteronomy 18:15; Psalm 22; Isaiah 53 and Daniel 9. However, Christ was promised as the Messiah, and the witness of the Old Testament is still a powerful tool in showing the reality that all of humanity only has any hope in the righteousness of God.

Further explanation

Paul again works in this Hebrew parallelism explaining what he said before in different words. The righteousness that has been revealed apart from the law is appropriated through faith in Jesus Christ through all who believe. There are some important points to be made about these statements. First of all the word "through" is the Greek word *dia* which when paired with the genitive (as this construction is) means instrumentality. The instrument by which this righteousness is appropriated or received is faith.

Faith is a word that is not well understood in our times. The Greek word here is *pistis* and it is translated faith, believe and trust in various places throughout the New Testament. It is a Greek word that carries all three contexts in it. In modern English language the word "faith" differs from its Biblical usage. We might say, "I believe there is a gas station up here on the right." What we mean by *believe* in that instance is that there may be a gas station, but there may not. We have turned the idea of faith into a weaker form of the verb *to know*. I am told that in the Air Force Academy if a person uses the word believe in the sense mentioned above they are asked "What do you believe?" To which the appropriate answer is: "I believe in God and country. I *think* that…" This is a clear attempt to keep this word from being perverted to mean something it doesn't. If the culture can convince us that our faith is something somehow less than trust in the facts of revealed Scripture than we can surely be persuaded to leave it, as nobody would bother dying for something they aren't sure about.

So the picture here is that faith (belief, trust) is the operation by which a person appropriates, or receives the gift of God's righteousness. It is important that we understand something right up front. Paul has just finished saying that there are none righteous and he is going to reiterate it in the very next phrase. There have been some confused thinkers throughout church history who want to claim that faith must be a gift, because putting one's faith in the right place is in some way meritorious (or we would get some credit for it). This is ridiculous, and counterintuitive. The faith is clearly the property and action of the person, and there is no imaginary process alluded to here involving God "giving the faith" to people. As far as faith being meritorious we can dismiss this idea simply. If I put my faith in the chair and the chair holds me up I can take no credit for it holding me up. The chair gets the credit, whether I believed it would hold me or not. Additionally, if you give me a hamburger and I take it, trusting that you didn't put something poisonous on it I don't credit my faith in your friendship for feeding me…I credit you! This is the same situation. By faith we trust in the salvation that God has provided for us in Christ, it doesn't mean that we deserve it, or earned it, or deserve a pat on the back, it just means we dared to put our faith in the correct place. This is a key error in interpretation that must be avoided.

In what? For Who?

The interesting thing about the word "faith" today is that people will often talk about "people of faith" meaning that people who believe in some deity as opposed to atheists. This is a ridiculous assumption. Firstly, the atheist must have as much or more faith in his preconceived notions, and perceptiveness than any other adherent to a different religion. Secondly, faith itself isn't a virtue at all. The power is in WHAT is believed not how much it is believed or by whom it is believed. You might believe that you can live a long and happy life eating only marshmallows and soda, but no matter how much you believe it you will soon become sick and die. Similarly, the faith must be placed in the person and work of Jesus Christ.

Who is this available to? Some have made the preposterous assumption that Christ only died for those whom He predestined to believe. This is of course, ridiculous. The salvation that Christ offers is available to everyone who believes. Anyone who puts their trust in Christ Jesus for salvation is given this same free salvation. It is free to all who believe, not just to some particular group. In the context, of course, Paul is addressing Jews who believed themselves to be the only ones for whom salvation was available. However, this passage is equally in contradiction with the theology of the Neo-Calvinist who would claim that God makes some for salvation and others to be damned eternally, just for fun. These problems come from a slavish obedience to an extra biblical system which stems from the unbiblical assumption that "we can get this all figured out" and thus they hang everything on God's sovereignty forcing them to marginalize all of the passages that would suggest that man has a will. Those on the other side, who share the same assumptions (we can figure it all out) but decide to hang everything on man's will or God's justice will have to marginalize everything that speaks about God's sovereignty. Fortunately, we need not be fooled into any "either/or" thinking and are free to admit that God's ways are admittedly higher than ours, and that we can't fit everything into our system and thus we can just read the Bible for what it says, even when there is a gap in our understanding.

All have sinned

We see here the out-play of what has already been clearly displayed in the previous chapters. There is not one person who could dare to claim a perfect track record. Every single person is stained with imperfection and short coming. The word "sin" here is *hamartia* which means to miss the mark, to swerve, to err, and thus to sin. There is not one person who has lived a perfect life, and we all know that those sins must be dealt with. Most of secular psychology seeks to deal with this very problem of guilt. We have been hurt, and hurt others. What are we to do? Psychology may suggest just forgetting about it, if possible, or blaming someone else for our shortcomings. This is why many psychologists are so obsessed with asking and talking about a person's upbringing as if, given a perfect upbringing a child will somehow become perfect, which is manifest non-sense as neither term has any real meaning in the scientific sense.

The Real Problem

The real problem with sin is made plain. The real shortcoming is that we fall short of being a part of the glory of God. The glory of God can be defined as "the radiant essence of who He is." His glory is the chief concern of everything in creation, seen or unseen. We were made to bring Him glory and we have failed to do that. Having failed to fulfill our very purpose we cannot maintain communion with the perfect and holy God. His perfect glory would destroy us in our imperfection. This is why it is so important to Paul to make sure that Jews and gentiles alike see that they have all fallen short, because there is no "faking it" or "half way measures" that are going to get the job done.

Verse 24

Verse 24 is filled with 10 point words that all need to be defined and understood biblically.

Justified – This word has been encountered before. It was observed that no one could be justified through the works of the law. Remember the meaning is not just absolved from guilt, but declared righteous. This is about our standing in Christ. This is a once and for all judgment that is made from the throne of eternity. The person who puts their trust in Christ and His work on the cross is then declared to be righteous. Not just forgiven but given a positive account balance of righteousness in the same measure as Christ's righteousness, that is perfect. Justification is the first phase of our salvation in Christ. Justification is the freedom from the penalty of sin. We need never fear that we must pay the price, on the eternal scale, for our sinfulness. We are forever justified before God because of our association with Christ by accepting His perfect sacrifice in faith. Phase 2 of salvation will be discussed in Chapter 6 which is sanctification, and phase three, glorification, will be discussed in chapter 8. Justification is step one. It is an external ruling that we did not deserve. It is the declaration of an unrighteous one that we are righteous.

Grace – Grace is defined, as we have already gone to great lengths to define in previous studies: The unlimited and unmerited blessing and favor of God given to us freely by the work of Christ Jesus. We discussed at great length grace must not expect to be paid back, or it is not grace, nor demand a payment up front. It cannot be revoked under conditions bad, nor can it be increased under conditions good. God's grace is something that is totally free of our meriting or potential for earning. Paul sees fit to draw this point home even more clearly by saying that Justification is a gift of God's grace. This phrase is even a bit redundant because Paul wants to make it crystal clear that God's salvation is exactly what we need – totally free. Were there any merit on human side, to earn or to keep, it could not be called "grace."

Redemption – This is another huge theological word. It has meaning and imagery that is powerful and poignant. The Greek word is *apolutrosis* which is a compound word. The root word *lutron* is a word meaning a ransom is paid and the party is bought back. The word that is used here gives the image of a kidnapping. The idea being that we were kidnapped by sin, and held hostage. The only way out for us was to be redeemed from that predicament by Christ. This word *lutron* is then modified by the prefix *apo* meaning "out or away" thus intensifying its meaning. We are forever, eternally and perfectly ransomed and redeemed out of that situation of our slavery to sin and the penalty of our sins (being eternal separation from God) by our faith in Christ Jesus and what He has done. This Redemption is found in Christ Jesus. This is all of grace. It is God who justifies and He who redeems, it is all about Jesus Christ and what He has done.

Romans 3:25-26

25whom God displayed publicly as a propitiation in His blood through
faith. *This was* to demonstrate His righteousness, because in the forbearance
of God He passed over the sins previously committed; 26for the
demonstration, *I say,* of His righteousness at the present time, so that He
would be just and the justifier of the one who has faith in Jesus.

Public Displays of Affection

Here we see that the "whom" refers to Jesus Christ in the previous verse. This was a public display by God of His love for us. This is the actual moment in history that we can look back upon and say that it happened in the presence of many witnesses. There were many in the crowd who knew that Jesus was who He claimed, and many who were convinced then, or shortly thereafter. This was a public record that everyone could appeal to. The resurrection was witnessed by many and the point is clear: God did what He said He was going to do and accomplished what He set out to accomplish in Jesus Christ. This public display leads us to another big theological word:

Propitiation – While justification and redemption refer to the sinner (us). Propitiation has God specifically in view. The idea that should stick in your mind is "satisfaction." In the sacrifice of Jesus Christ, God the Father was satisfied. His righteous wrath was appeased. This is where we get to the point that Chafer makes in his work on grace that may seem confusing. Grace is not immediately involved in the way God deals with sins. God in His righteousness and justice must see sin punished. He must be appeased. We might view it like a math problem. Every sin or crime must be paid for. There may be an abatement of sentence but the equation must balance in the end. That is why God made a perfect and full payment for sin in the work of His Son at the cross. On the part of man sin was paid for, and the sinner declared righteous. On the part of God His wrath and justice were satisfied for anyone who would accept the payment that His Son made on the cross. Oh how great a salvation is this!

Just and the Justifier

This is how God can be righteous and still save us. We were helpless and hopeless, we deserved only death. God loved us and cared for us and did not want to see us perish, even though it was perfectly righteous to let us do so. God's solution? He balanced the account by allowing the full amount of punishment fall on His Son. It may be an oversimplification, but the idea that a finite sinner (us) can suffer for an infinite period of time to pay the price for sin. The equation will also balance if an infinite person (Jesus Christ) suffers for a finite period of time (at the cross). This is the reality, and anyone who accepts His sacrifice is covered in His blood and by His work. This is amazing! This is how God can be absolutely just and yet absolutely loving and gracious. He shows himself to be totally just and yet still be the justifier of anyone who accepts the free gift of salvation given to anyone who puts their faith in Jesus Christ for salvation.

This is why John can say in 1 John 1:9: "If we confess our sins He is faithful *and just* to forgive us our sins and purify us from all unrighteousness." He is just because all of the sins have been paid for at the cross. They are already forgiven, the price paid and now the sinful imperfection of man no longer presents an impossible barrier between man and God. God overcame the barrier at the expense of His own Son, at the Cross, 2,000 years ago. Praise the Lord!

ROMANS 3:27-31

Getting Ready to Boast

The word translated "boasting" is a word that means to glory in something. When we think about glory we may think of winning a great victory in a war or in a sporting event. We think of being remembered on into the future for some great deed, work or accomplishment. This is the great difficulty of the world with biblical Christianity. The Bible has a clear message: there is no place for man to glory in his own works or words. To do so misses the point of our very creation. We were created with the simple purpose to know and bring glory to our Creator. Yet this is exactly what our forefather Adam rejected. Just as he sought his own glory in response to the enemies false promise ("Ye shall be as gods.") so the world seeks after that same promise today. Any system is palatable to the world except one that robs man of his glory and gives it to God and God alone.

Boasting by the Law?

The legalist still seeks this venue for his own glory today. Proudly flaunting his own perceived righteousness before men he rejoices in what he does or does not do in order to try to retain or maintain some glory above all other people. Yet, as this message has made so clear, there is no place of boasting. Even if all sin and shortcoming can be held secret it is not a secret from God. There is no place for boasting by the works of man. There is no hope of a person having a truly perfect track record and we are again left at the feet of God seeking his mercy.

Man is Justified by Faith

Justification is one of the most important concepts in the first half of the book of Romans. To be justified means simply to be declared righteous. It is a word that is most comfortably found in the courtroom. Often humans imagine themselves on trial, and long to have someone before whom to state their case. Yet the word is clear, and the Apostles maintained uniformly, that there would be no way for a man to be declared righteous apart from simply trusting in the provision of God. Humanity was made by God's gracious desire to express His glory and man is saved by the same means. All by God's perfect effort and provision for us in the life, death, burial and resurrection of Jesus Christ.

God of the Jews only?

This statement cuts to the core of the misunderstanding of some Jews. The idea is simple: that God exists simply to save and provide for us. There was, among many, a complete lack of compassion and desire for the rest of the world. In fact there were some who wrote that God created gentiles for the sole purpose of fueling the fires of Hell.

This tragic sentiment is sadly not absent from Christianity today. There are many who would seek to claim that God only desires to save a certain number of those they call the elect. The others, they would be forced to claim, were made only to glorify God through their eternal punishment. It is a sad reality that there will be many who are punished for all eternity because they refused to accept His perfect provision of salvation. Yet this does not mean that God created them just for this purpose. Far to the contrary there is nothing that keeps a person apart from God save their dedicated desire to be god of their own little universe. God is the God of all, and He longs for the salvation of every person (2 Peter 2:9).

By Faith

This gift is free and available to all who would receive it by faith. By simply trusting in the character of the Giver to the ultimate end that He would be glorified in all things and at all times an in all places. This is the purpose of the entire history of the planet earth. Angels will look in wonder at the amazing provision of God and redemptive work on behalf of mankind and they will respond. They will not respond by extolling the greatness of mankind, but the greatness of the merciful and loving Lord who saved those who were willing to come to Him and trust in the provision which He made for them in Jesus Christ.

Nullifying the Law

Then next question is that of somehow nullifying the Law of Moses? We must again refer to the book of Galatians, and chapter 3 in particular, to understand the purpose of the Law. This does not nullify the Law, but rather shows the full purpose of the Law! The Law existed to prove that even the simple standard of the law could not be met by sinful humanity and that God alone could provide the solution to our great and hopeless problem of sin. This very thing God did on our behalf through Jesus Christ. The question before every single person is the same: will we take His gracious and loving gift, or rot in our own pride and inability?

ROMANS 4

ROMANS 4:1-4

An Example From History

This chapter begins a new section in our study of Romans. Having established the guilt of gentile and Jew, then the fact that the need of man is salvation by grace through faith Paul wants to show the Jews that this is nothing new. Having proved beyond question that the law cannot serve the purpose of making a person righteous, Paul goes back to the Old Testament to show the Jews and Gentiles alike that this is how salvation ALWAYS worked, there was never anyone saved by the law, but always by grace through faith. It was always by trusting in God and His provision.

Why Abraham?

The previous may be all well and good, but then the question comes as to why Paul would specifically choose Abraham? Why not Jacob? Why not Joseph? Why not David? There are two major reasons: first of all, the Jewish person derives much of their identity from their relationship to Abraham. The first sign of what it is to be a Jew (circumcision) came through Abraham. So to prove the doctrine of salvation by faith through grace by connecting it to the person to whom circumcision was given would be powerful indeed.

There is, however, one more reason why Abraham is an important person to plug the Church into. Just being a descendant of Abraham did not make one a Jew. In order to be a proper Jew one had to be not just a descendant of Abraham but also of Isaac (as opposed to Ishmael). Not only that but one also had to be a descendant of Jacob (as opposed to Esau). So by referencing Abraham Paul efficiently sets up for the church which will not be Israel, but will be rather connected to Abraham and His faith, rather than the Jews who are identified by descending from Jacob and their relationship to the Law of Moses. Paul's use of Abraham would give the Jew the understanding that this doctrine was not novel while protecting the church from being mistakenly identified with Israel (or as replacing Israel, as modern heretics falsely assert).

Romans 4:1

What then shall we say that Abraham, our forefather according to the flesh, has found?

New Questions

In the previous section Paul concluded quite forcefully that there is no place for boasting if Justification is only to be found through faith. It may be difficult for us to understand the veneration given to Abraham and Moses in the Jewish mindset. It would be a bit too far to compare their emphasis on Abraham and Moses to the Christian's relationship to Jesus Christ, however, there are compelling similarities. While the Jew did not view Abraham as divine, there was a similar sense of identification found there. The Jews took great pride in saying that they were "sons of Abraham" (Matthew 3:9; Luke 1:73; Luke 3:8; John 8:39). This veneration had raised itself to a dangerous level and Paul here sets out to straighten the record on WHY Abraham was so very special and so very important.

Our forefather according to the flesh

This phrase makes it clear that Paul is still targeting the Jew in his discourse here. As we noted earlier it was not relation to Abraham that made one a Jew (as Arabs and Edomites were also descended from Abraham and were not Jews), however he was the first step in God calling out a peculiar people to Himself. Furthermore, the covenant made with Abraham is the abiding and controlling covenant directing all of the future of Israel in regards to Land, Seed and Blessing. (Genesis 12:1-3; Genesis 15; Genesis 17:19-22).

Regarding the phrase "in the flesh", it must be noted that the word "flesh" is a perfect example in Scripture of a word with multiple meanings. The flesh can mean the Sin Nature that remains with the believer even after they are a new believer. This use of the flesh is quite common (Gal. 5:17). This, however, is not the use of this word here. This word can refer simply to the physical body of a man or animal. In this case it is used as a sort of metaphor for the reality that the Jew's relationship to Abraham is not necessarily spiritual, it is primarily physical in their thinking. The Jews were very serious about genealogy and a significant portion of the Temple compound (Herod's temple – the temple of Jesus and the Apostles day) was dedicated to the keeping of in-depth genealogical records so that everyone could be kept straight as to tribe and heritage. There was a very high likelihood that any Jewish person reading this letter from Paul could say exactly and specifically the nature of his or her relationship to Abraham.

Romans 4:2

For if Abraham was justified by works, he has something to boast about, but not before God.

If…

Paul sets his argument out on the line here. The purpose of this section is to check and see on what basis God deals with mankind. While the Jewish people are defined by a few more genealogical steps (Isaac, Jacob, their tribal head) and additionally identified with the Law of Moses, Abraham was the first step in the establishment of their nation. If something was true of him, and for him then it would be true for those who follow as his descendants.

Justified

Here is that ever important word "Justified" again. Justification means "declared righteous" and as we have seen there are two ways a person can be justified. One could be declared righteous based on their own works, or based on faith as the previous chapter explained. So the query that Paul sets out to answer here is whether Abraham was declared righteous as a result of his own works.

Bragging rights

The word boast here means "glorying in one's own self or ability." Paul puts the point rather straightforwardly and takes one of the strongest characters in The Old Testament. The Old Testament did a magnificent job of recording the faults and flaws of its heroes. The sins of Adam, Noah, Saul, David, Solomon and Abraham are all recorded right alongside their positive accomplishments. For an Old Testament character Abraham does make an excellent showing. Perhaps someone could level an accusation of dishonesty at him regarding his choice to continually take a less than straightforward approach to introducing his wife, but Abraham comes off looking pretty good in the Old and New Testaments alike.

But not before God
Even if someone can be shown to be righteous in relationship to other humans, they can still only fulfill God's expectation for them, and not exceed it. As has been previously established, even the greatest righteousness that man has to offer is nothing in comparison to the righteousness of God. (Isaiah 64:6)

Romans 4:3
For what does the Scripture say? "ABRAHAM BELIEVED GOD, AND IT WAS CREDITED TO HIM AS RIGHTEOUSNESS."

A Great Question!
Paul now brings about another great question. He appeals to the authority of Scripture. This is exactly what Jesus was doing when He used the phrase "you have heard it said…but I say unto you" in the Sermon on the Mount. The Jews had built up a tradition and a set of commentaries that they respected far beyond their worth in comparison to the word of God. So here we see Paul pointing the Jews back to Scripture as the most valid and important witness of truth.

On a side light, this is the same question that we need to be asking constantly. We are presented with new and strange ideas every day in books, on television, from movies and billboards. Our focus needs to constantly return to the vital question: "what does the Scripture say?" as it is the deciding factor in what is true and/or false.

The Quote
Here Paul quotes Genesis 15:6. The subjects, verbs and objects are vital to understand here. Abraham is the subject of the sentence. The first verb is

believed. The object (the One he believed) is God. The result of this belief was that it was credited to Abraham as righteousness.

Credited – This Greek word is *logizomai* and is an incredibly important word for our study. This word is an accounting term. It gives the picture of an accountant keeping his books of accounts and moving righteousness from one account to another. The reason for the transfer? Faith. The reality is that whether the money is moved from one account to the other because it was "earned" or because it was a "gift" doesn't change the reality that the account is full. This is the nature of this transaction. Abraham is only said to have believed, and because of that faith God credited Him (reckoned him, as a matter of divinely dictated fact) righteous.

Righteousness
This is, once again, the theme of the letter. The perfect, objective righteousness of God to which man cannot attain. Martin Luther was noted for saying that the phrase "the righteousness of God" terrorized him because it so clearly exposed man's complete inability to reach God by any means of His own. He understood God's righteousness very well. He saw it clearly, what really changed his life was when he beheld God's grace more clearly.

Romans 4:4
Now to the one who works, his wage is not credited as a favor, but as what is due.

Works and Faith
It is important here to notice something. Reformed believers have wrongly assumed that believing in God would be something that man could boast of, implying or claiming that faith is a good work and therefore God must give the faith for one to believe in order for the believer to have no boast before God. This is all because their thinking is controlled by the humanistic system of thought, and therefore their interpretation of everything else is dictated by obedience to an unbiblical system. Here the faith is accredited to Abraham, no system of "Prevenient grace" is referenced, because such a step does not exist. Here the faith is held in stark opposition to "works" thus placing faith is something that cannot be classified as a work, and in this passage, provides the person no reason to boast (glory in self). This "meritorious faith" is an unbiblical invention of

Reformed theology to defend their flawed system of thought.

Favor

This word, here translated "favor" is the Greek word *charis* – grace. Paul draws an important distinction here. The righteousness that Abraham received was not given according to his works. If it were given according to his works, even the smallest one, it could not be called "grace." However, we see here, that God credited Abraham righteousness entirely on the basis of Grace. Abraham's faith did not "earn" it, it was the vehicle by which he accepted the grace gift of righteousness. Being unable to earn righteousness God gave it for free based on the one thing that Abraham could do of his own free will – trust God. If faith is a work, as reformed theologians sometimes claim, this verse would be interpreted as meaning the exact opposite of what it clearly means. If faith is a work, then Abraham DID earn righteousness here, as the passage says nothing besides the fact that Abraham believed, not that "he was given faith."

Even Abe

It is clear here that even Abraham, that giant figure of the Old Testament, had to throw himself whole heartedly, without reserve, on the grace of God. He, just like everyone who followed after Adam, had no hope of saving himself. Salvation was always by grace through faith, as man could never earn righteousness for himself.

ROMANS 4:5-8

Nothing like a hard day's work!
The reality of God's salvation is more shocking the more that it is considered. There is something very basic and central in every person that longs to see people get what they deserve, or get the thing for which they have worked. We like the idea of just rewards and just desserts and part of us always cheers at the end of film when the bad guy gets what is coming to him. This is built into the human mindset and it is confirmed and conditioned into us by human society. This is what makes the salvation of God so amazing and glorious to those who receive it, and also so offensive to those who do not receive it. In considering these verses, it can be easy to not adjust our mindset to understand what is being revealed. We see and know so little real grace and love in the world that the level of God's grace can blow out the contrast on our spiritual circuitry. Much like looking into a flash of bright light can overwhelm our ability to see correctly for a time so these glimpses of God's grace are so unlike what we are used to seeing that we can forget to let the light of this revelation into every aspect of our lives.

Not working
When considering what it takes to achieve salvation the world comes up with one standard and rule after the next. The idea of living a life that is basically pleasing to God, based upon what *we* think He values and desires, is a total illusion. It must be understood with the simplest clarity. The person who works for their salvation is the one to whom God can give *none* of His salvation. God cannot justify (declare righteous) the person who seeks to be declared righteous because of their own thoughts, words and actions. Whether a person is successful and appearing righteous before others or not the simple fact remains: Trying to work for the kind and level of righteousness which I can produce makes it impossible for me to receive by God's grace gift the quality and quantity of righteousness which God needs in order to share eternity in unity with His creatures.

It can be shocking and even offensive to us. Especially when we think about this reality in totally natural terms. We are prone to think of a person who is really working their hardest to please a father who simply cannot be satisfied with the sub-par work of his children. A boss who will not be pleased with his employee, regardless of how hard and well he works, would seem quite a tyrant indeed. This is what the world often imagines the Biblical message of Salvation by grace alone, through faith alone, in Christ alone is all about. It makes sense that they find it offensive…they may have worked very hard to feel like they could give themselves a title "good person". However, the story told from the perspective of the child of the dissatisfied father and the story told from the perspective of the father himself looks quite different.

From the son's perspective: "I tried to make my father the best brownies he had ever had for his birthday. I worked hard to put them together and even used my creativity to invent my own recipe. After a whole day of work, he wouldn't even try the brownies I made! He couldn't even pretend to like them…what a tyrant!"

From the father's perspective: "My son knew it was my birthday and presented me with brownies. The trouble is that my son does not bake, nor does he know how. It was evident from the brownies that were presented, as well as from the hole in the backyard, that these brownies were made from the dirt in the area where we keep the dog's feces. Not only could I not try them, I couldn't even pretend to be pleased that my 18-year-old son would bring me plate filled with dried mud and refuse and then be surprised when I would not eat it. It shows that he doesn't understand in the slightest who I am and what standards I have for our family."

The illustration is not perfect, but it gives us a graphic picture of what our righteousness is like when we bring it before God. The dilemma becomes even more clear when see that God has provided the perfect gift of salvation in the righteous and priceless work of Jesus Christ on the cross. Offering to try to earn salvation at the cost of our good works is to completely devalue and misunderstand the nature of the sacrifice which Christ made on our behalf. The one who tries to work to be in God's favor is the one who doesn't understand the value of God's favor, grace and salvation.

But to the believing one…

Now the contrast is made. The repeated issue of faith (or believing) cannot be overlooked. This is the condition that is set forth, and no other. This salvation is received by faith alone. Trusting in this reality has quite a bit implied within it. It implies very strongly that the person trusting in God's gift of salvation understands that they couldn't do it upon their own. It implies an understanding that God's standard is immeasurably higher than our standards of what is right and good. It implies that God is loving and gracious in His character and is willing to provide the justification which man needs to be brought back into a relationship with Him. It also implies trust in the fact that God is powerful to do what He claims in the Gospel of Salvation. It is not that these things must all be understood in order to trust in the simple gospel (that Christ died for our sins and was risen again on the third day) but that simple humility before God is a vital piece in understanding our salvation.

Righteousness

Just as it was with Abraham, so it is with the believer today. The gift of righteousness was credited on the basis of having trusted in God's provision. The word "credit" here is accounting language. God gives this grace gift of the quality of righteousness which He needs us to have in order to share eternity with us on the basis of our willingness to trust that He is Who He claims to be and that He provides this salvation for us in the person and work of Jesus Christ.

Does anybody else have anything to say about this?

As it turns out this is a common message in the Bible. It is not as if God *became* gracious after Christ came and fulfilled His mission. God's character was, is and always will be perfectly gracious in every way. The Old Testament is a constant record of the gracious and forgiving faithfulness of God who loves and gives man every opportunity to come to Him. The next heavy hitter whom Paul sites is King David.

It may be easy to think of how different historical figures are important to a society. Americans may look to George Washington. The British may look to Winston Churchill. These figures may give a slight picture of the importance of David in Hebrew culture – but the comparison falls horribly short. David was shown to be God's chosen man to rule Israel. God preserved David and spoke though him as a prophet. Furthermore, the hope for the Messiah was also promised to David and through his line. David's word on the matter, especially as guided by the Holy Spirit, have a great depth of importance in the issue of salvation.

Sing a Sad Psalm

One of the penitential Psalms is here quoted (Psalm 32). Psalms 6, 32, 38, 51, 102, 130, and 143 are all psalms that deal with guilt before God, and approach him in pursuit of undeserved and unearned forgiveness. These vital psalms show the great consistency of God's character throughout the biblical revelation. God is willing and able to forgive those who would come before him in the act of confession. Because God has already punished Christ (the Perfect sacrifice) for sin He is able to account that sin as paid for and no longer associate that sin with the person who did it. This is the only source of hope for mankind. If God had not provided this way for man to be saved from His sin there would be no chance for mankind, and thus it is the central reason for the believer's happiness, peace and joy.

Near Death Experience

Often times a person who survives a brush with death finds their perspective on life radically changed. Some people stop being bothered by the "small stuff". Others change their priorities to match how they would have wished that they had lived thus far. A small revelation of our own mortality can cause us to appreciate being alive more than ever before. However, if we were to understand what life is given to us in Jesus Christ then our outlook upon every moment is changed. When we understand the punishment which we have been spared by the work of Christ we can look at every situation and have the confident and joyful heart of one who knows that nothing could be as bad as that from which we have been spared, and nothing can take away the greatest things which we have gained: a permanent and eternal relationship with God.

ROMANS 4:9-12

Faith Plus What?

Here Paul has lain out that salvation is by faith, and demonstrated it from the life of Abraham. However, he wants to be fully clear. We know that there were people following behind Paul in his missionary journeys who would demand that people come under the law and become circumcised. Paul anticipates this error and deals with both circumcision and law-keeping in this section of Scripture. But it answers one key and abiding question for us: Faith plus what equals salvation?

Our world is filled with lies and deceit, especially concerning the gospel. "Faith-plus" Christianity dominates many churches today, and while it may look radically different from church to church or speaker to speaker it is the same. Here are some popular examples:

Faith + Discipline
Faith + Works
Faith + Helping the poor
Faith + an experience of some kind
Faith + being nice
Faith + giving money
Faith + baptism
Faith + Joining a certain Church
Faith + resultant fruitfulness
Faith + church attendance
Faith + service

The point is plain. You can hear this message on television and in pulpits and bible studies around the globe. It is often couched in statements like, "If you don't have such and such…you just might not be saved…" or "I don't know if you can be saved without…" We must stand vigilant, watch as those who take the Bible at what it says, and not allow this heresy to enter in.

Abraham and Circumcision

Circumcision was a distinctive mark of the Jew. Circumcision actually came apart from the giving of the Law of Moses, and thus it may have been viewed differently by the Jews. It was a symbol of identification, and it was a symbol that would be noticed by others. Attitudes towards nudity were somewhat different in the ancient world. The public restrooms didn't have private stalls but were holes in a bench. This would mean that a person's circumcision would be plain to the rest of the world. Additionally, many athletic events were played in the nude, so there would be no question that the Jew would stand out. This would be a part of his identity and also something that he may think others should have as well. But God's word, written here by Paul, is quite clear regarding the nature and meaning of circumcision and what its purpose was.

<u>Romans 4:9-12</u>

9 Is this blessing then on the circumcised, or on the uncircumcised also? For
we say, FAITH WAS CREDITED TO ABRAHAM AS
RIGHTEOUSNESS." 10 How then was it credited? While he was
circumcised, or uncircumcised? Not while circumcised, but while
uncircumcised; 11 and he received the sign of circumcision, a seal of the
righteousness of the faith which he had while uncircumcised, so that he
might be the father of all who believe without being circumcised, that
righteousness might be credited to them, 12 and the father of circumcision to
those who not only are of the circumcision, but who also follow in the
steps of the faith of our father Abraham which he had while uncircumcised.

It's all part of the plan

There is something to be noticed here. Paul doesn't simply know Scripture, but he knows the chronology of Scripture, he knows the way things fit together. Notice also that it becomes clear that this was also done by God's planning. God knew when to declare Abraham righteous and on what account. This is not something Paul is "cooking up" but Paul is relating the clear teaching of Scripture here. It brings us to an interesting realization: chronology is important. While God dwells outside of time, and is not limited by it, time is His creation in which we dwell. Therefore the order in which things occur really does matter.

Our philosophy of history is something that needs to be examined. The academic world has drifted largely to an eastern view of time. This view of time assumes that matter is eternal, and that history is a constant cycle of repetitions. The idea of time being cyclical then colors their whole perspective on time. However, the Biblical view of time is different. The Biblical view of time is linear. It started with a garden and the first man and woman. After they sinned it has been a progression of God continually dealing with fallen mankind and displaying His love for fallen mankind through words, events and circumstances. Time will be consummated when the Lord Jesus Christ comes to reign on the earth for 1,000 years after a 7 year tribulation period in which the church will not participate having been removed by the rapture. God has a purpose and a goal for History. He has a direction and it is to His glory, thus the order of events is important.

How was it credited?

Paul repeats the phrase yet again that Abraham's faith was credited to him as righteousness. This phrase is the theme that Paul is working from here, and also the theme that He is defending. So, as other elements of Abraham's life were revealed it becomes pivotal to understand what came first? If righteousness comes through circumcision then Abraham couldn't have been declared righteous before he was circumcised. If the first declaration of righteousness occurred after circumcision it could be said that the act of becoming circumcised was a necessary demonstration of saving faith. This however, becomes a moot point. Verses 9-10 clearly and correctly point out that in the Genesis account Abraham was declared righteous on the basis of his faith long before he received the symbol of circumcision.

Woodrow Kroll points out:

> The facts are these. (1) Genesis 15:6 records the event of Abraham receiving righteousness from God. (2) Sometime after that, Abraham had a son by Hagar when he was eighty-six years old (Gen. 16:16-17). (3)At least one year had to elapse between the Genesis 15:6 and the conception and birth of Hagar's son so that the outside Abraham was eighty-five years old when righteousness was imputed to him. (4) Ishmael was thirteen years old when both he and Abraham were circumcised (Gen. 17:25-26). (5) Abraham had righteousness imputed

to him at least fourteen years before he was circumcised. Paul concludes that circumcision had nothing whatever to do with the imputation of righteousness to Abraham.[3]

So what was Circumcision?

Having revealed the reality that Abraham's being declared righteous had nothing to do with circumcision, Paul then turns to the purpose and meaning of circumcision. The next question on the Jewish mind would obviously be much like the question before. When Paul explained that the Jew has no ethnic corner on salvation he knew that they would then ask what advantage that they had, or if there was any. Paul tells them that their advantage was great. They have the Scriptures! They have proof that they had held onto for generation after generation that attested to the truth of Jesus Christ and the unchanging, perfect, eternal and amazing character of God.

This situation is similar. Having shown that circumcision was by no means a method, means or part of salvation for Abraham the question comes to what is the real meaning of it? Paul takes verse 11 to explain. Circumcision was in fact a *sign*. Let's look at this word. It can be defined as: "a sign, a signal; an ensign, a standard; a sign by which anything is designated, distinguished, or known; hence, used of the miracles of Christ as being the signs by which He might be known as the Christ of God: a sign authenticating His mission; a sign with reference to what it demonstrates."[4]

This same Greek word is used by John to describe the miracles that Jesus performed. The miracles were to prove, show (as a sign) that Jesus was who He said He was. The miracles didn't make Him God, He was God whether or not He chose to prove it. Similarly, here, the circumcision is a sign that he received by God. He would have a daily reminder, in his flesh, that God had declared him righteous based on his faith.

The circumcision also served as a *seal*. The concept of sealing something in the ancient world is key to understanding this. Some things were sealed to keep them from spoiling (like we seal containers of cheese and meat),

[3] Kroll, Woodrow. The Book of Romans: Righteousness in Christ. AMG Publishers, Chattanooga, Tennessee. 2002.

[4] www.greattreasures.org

documents were sealed for protection and authenticity. So this mark that was on Abraham's flesh, and the flesh of his physical descendants was something that displayed the nature of faith in God. Once someone has trusted Christ for salvation the very nature of it is in permanence and security. This is "a seal of the righteousness of faith, which he had while uncircumcised." The "which" in that statement refers back to the righteousness of faith. So we see again circumcision didn't GIVE Abraham righteousness, it was a picture of it.

Father Abraham had many sons…(v. 11b-12)

Here the fatherhood of Abraham is very important. The Jewish people claimed this as their specific right, however we find that this title was not exclusively theirs. In verse 11b Paul explains how the uncircumcised gentile believes and is accounted righteous, and is thus associated as a child of Abraham. So the gentile can know with utter certainty that justification (the righteousness of God) can come to the uncircumcised and that person shares an identity with Abraham who was justified by grace through faith.

The Jew, however, is not totally disenfranchised. Verse 12 shows clearly how Abraham is also the father of circumcision. However, there is a qualifier here: "but who also follow in the steps of the faith of our father Abraham…" So we see again physical relationship (being a descendant of Abraham) is not the key distinction. The key distinction is faith. This is very similar to something Jesus said in John 8:39: "They answered and said to Him, 'Abraham is our father.' Jesus said to them, 'If you were Abraham's children, you would do the works of Abraham.'"

While uncircumcised…

Paul, while still including the Jews, does not want to open even the slightest door for this circumcision legalism to inch back in, and closes this four verse discourse on the place and part that circumcision has in justification by reminding them that Abraham really was declared righteous before he was circumcised.

ROMANS 4:13-17

A Promise is a Promise

We very rarely have encounters with true grace. It is alien to our existence, and to our natural way of thinking. However, when it comes to considering the promises of God we find that God makes unconditional promises to Abraham. Not based upon his action or inaction. Simply a statement of what God would do for Abraham. Abraham received this promise of God by trusting, or believing, in the Giver. This is an important point for us to notice because it is by this same faith in the Giver that we exercise in laying hold of the Salvation which Christ won for us.

God's Promise

[4] *Then behold, the word of the LORD came to him, saying, "This man will not be your heir; but one who will come forth from your own body, he shall be your heir."* [5] *And He took him outside and said, "Now look toward the heavens, and count the stars, if you are able to count them." And He said to him, "So shall your descendants be."* [6] *Then he believed in the LORD; and He reckoned it to him as righteousness.* Genesis 15:4-6 (NASB)

Some valuable things to note: God promised the heir to Abraham unconditionally and reminds him that even though the fulfillment of God's promise to Abraham wasn't in sight; the promise was not in question. Note that all important phrase in verse six. Abraham believed God. God *reckoned* it to him as righteousness. As we have in seen the previous chapters of this book man has a BIG righteousness problem. God must *reckon* (or account) His righteousness to Abraham on the basis of belief because belief is wholly non-meritorious. In other words believing is not an act that DESERVES any reward. The reality is that just as a person whose eyes are opened will be looking upon something so the faith faculty of man will always be in use. Abraham's choice to trust in God and His promise did not ENTITLE Him to any righteousness, but that was the gift of God's grace. Accounting His kind of righteousness upon Abraham on the basis of his faith.

Later Additions

We see that the Law of Moses was added later on. That Law was added with a very specific purpose in the context of the nation of Israel. That purpose was never meant to abrogate or replace the promise that God made to Abraham and which was given to Him on the basis of faith alone. If we were to hear about a person who made an unconditional promise to someone to provide a service and then some time later changed his mind about what payment he wished to receive we would justly call that person dishonest.

But there is another sense in which adding the law would void the promise. If the system changed and the promise was now to be received through righteous works then not one person would be able to receive it. Even Abraham himself would have been disqualified! For not even he could keep the law perfectly.

The Law and Accounting

Verse 16 may seem a bit confusing, but the meaning is perfectly plain. The ultimate standard of wrong and right are eternally unchanging because they are rooted in the unchanging character of God. However, there is a difference between transgression and sin. Sin conflicts with all that God is and therefore brings the ultimate result of death. Transgression is violating a specific commandment of God. For instance, there are many things that are immoral, and yet not illegal under the American penal code. Thus, there are plenty of things that a person can do that are not "right" but are also not punishable under law because there is no specific commandment surrounding that action. Douglas J. Moo writes: "Violation of law turns 'sin' into the more serious offense of 'transgression,' meriting God's wrath. God gave the law to the Jews. The Jews have transgressed the law. The law brought wrath to the Jews...Paul, then, is not claiming that there is no 'sin' where there is no law, but, in almost a 'truism,' that there is no deliberate disobedience of positive commands where there is no positive command to disobey."

Faith in Accordance with Grace

It would be easy to overlook this simple statement, but we must not. There are those who would try to add the Law into the Christian faith or life at any given point. They will suggest that the believer is saved by grace initially but must then rely upon Law to grow (these believers must read Paul's epistle to the Galatian church). There are others that want to add some split of law and works – such as baptism or church membership – to be saved. However, this statement reveals much. It is faith alone that is in accordance with the principle of Grace. Far from being another work, or the right kind of work we find that the only way to receive grace is by faith. There is simply no other manner in which a person can receive grace. Add anything on and it is no longer grace…it may be very nice, but if anything is added to the simple condition of receiving the free gift by faith in the Giver then the principle of grace is violated and it is no longer grace, it is now some system of law and merit.

Even God

Abraham's faith was in God. It was a belief in His ability to give what was promised. Abraham got to exercise this faith on a number of public instances. He exercised regarding the reality that Sarah and he could still have a child, though they were well past their years of reproductive ability. This natural condition, by the way, is also called a type of death in scripture. Going beyond this Abraham also believed that God was able to raise the dead and thus was willing to offer up his son Isaac – the child of the promise – in sacrifice; knowing that God could raise Isaac from the dead in order to keep His faithful promise. It also is an interesting parallel to note that Abraham believed that Isaac could be raised from the dead, where Christ ultimately *would* be raised from the dead. It is remarkable to note how much Abraham and the patriarchs likely knew about the promised Messiah, and expected Him at any time!

ROMANS 4:17-25

Abraham's Story

As we conclude the study of chapter 4 by wrapping up Abraham's story. Abraham has been a biblical example of the truths of our salvation by faith through grace. The reality is that salvation was never found any other way, and this thorough account of Abraham (along with the testimony of David) proves this beyond a shadow of a doubt. It is so vitally important to realize this fact that Paul takes a great deal of time to defend it. There are many who have attended church their entire lives and have never understood this message. It is vital, because anything that is added to this is not the gospel, and no "Faith *plus*" formula can save, from the biblical perspective.

Romans 4:16-18

[16]For this reason *it is* by faith, in order that *it may be* in accordance with
grace, so that the promise will be guaranteed to all the descendants, not
only to those who are of the Law, but also to those who are of the faith of
Abraham, who is the father of us all, [17](as it is written, "A FATHER OF
MANY NATIONS HAVE I MADE YOU") in the presence of Him
whom he believed, *even* God, who gives life to the dead and calls into
being that which does not exist. [18]In hope against hope he believed, so that
he might become a father of many nations according to that which had
been spoken, "SO SHALL YOUR DESCENDANTS BE."

The quote

Paul here quotes from Genesis 17:5. It is quite important to notice the tense of the verbs. God tells Abraham that He has already made him the father of many nations. At this point Isaac had not been born, and Sarah wasn't even pregnant at this point. Only God can speak this way. Knowing the end from the beginning God can say what He is going to do as if it is already done. No one else has that ability, every human must confess that there is always some possibility that they may be inhibited from doing something until it is already done. This outlines the reality that God is able to speak authoritatively on everything. He knows all things and no one can withstand His sovereign will.

The father of many nations

This promise was realized to Abraham in bigger and deeper ways than he could ever have imagined. He is the father of the Arabs, as well as the Edomites, and, of course, of Israel by way of physical descent. However, as we see here, He is also called "father" of everyone who believes and is saved by faith through grace. This is complicated for those who don't read well. The assumption is that because people were saved by grace through faith in the Old Testament and we are saved by faith through grace in the Church we must be the same. This is a logical fallacy. Similarity does not mean that two things are identical. Just because two people share parents does not mean that they are the same person. They may go by similar names, same last names, have similar features and traits, but one cannot conclude that the two brothers are the same person without having made a grievous logical error.

In the presence of God

Genesis 17 records a conversation that Abraham had with God. In receiving the promise that God would be good to His word Abraham was actually standing in the physical presence of God in a special way. Notice the object of Abraham's faith: God. He has a set of physical circumstances before him; he has a promise that challenges those circumstances. The text here doesn't say that Abraham believed the promise, it says he believed HIM! Abraham's faith was in God, not just simply in this singular promise. He believed in God's character. Why did he believe God?

life to the dead

Abraham knew that God brings life to the dead. This phrase can be understood in two ways. In this section of Scripture death is used in a special sense: reproductive death. The three major uses of the word "death" in the Bible are as follows:

1) Physical Death (Genesis 24:67) Separation of the immaterial part of man from the material

2) Spiritual Death (Genesis 2:17; Romans 6; John 17:3) Separation from God

3) Reproductive Death (Romans 4:19; Hebrews 11:11-12) Separation from ability to procreate

So a separation is always in view when the word death is used. This is interesting because God has shown Himself to be the master over all three forms of death. In both Old and New Testaments people were raised from the dead. Christ was raised from the dead in such a way as to never taste death again (and we with Him, by faith). Christ is the giver of spiritual life, and it is only in Him that that death is overcome, and as we see in the account of Abraham, reproductive death is also his to control.

calls into being that which does not exist
This is another phrase that can be understood two ways. In the general sense Abraham was aware that God called everything into being from nothing: speaking things into place. An extension of this recognition of God as the sovereign creator is His ability to call a child into their life that did not exist before. Abraham believed God in both senses and on both counts. This shows, in part, how absolutely important our understanding of God's role as Creator is. If He is not responsible for creating all things (and if the Bible is not accurate in its record of that fact) then how can we trust Him (or the message of the Bible) for salvation?

In hope against hope he believed
This is a figure of speech that essentially means that Abraham's faith in God exceeded all rational and earthly reason. There was no natural reason for Abraham to have faith in God. Anyone giving Abraham advice about his wife, who was barren for nearly a century and was now too old to bear children anyway, would tell him plainly: "Give up. It's hopeless." Yet he did believe with the firmness of biblical hope that is not a probability by a 100 percent guarantee that the Lord would do it.

<u>Romans 4:19-22</u>
19Without becoming weak in faith he contemplated his own body, now as good as dead since he was about a hundred years old, and the deadness of Sarah's womb; 20yet, with respect to the promise of God, he did not waver in unbelief but grew strong in faith, giving glory to God, 21and being fully assured that what God had promised, He was able also to perform.
22Therefore IT WAS ALSO CREDITED TO HIM AS RIGHTEOUSNESS.

Without becoming weak in faith

The strength of Abraham's faith is mentioned here twice (vss. 19 & 20). Notice the information that is given here. Abraham remained believing of God's promises, while he may have questioned how the Lord would complete His promise, he did not waver in his belief. Notice what happens here. In Genesis 17:5 Abraham is being reassured of the promise that God had given him. The first time the promise was given, Abraham believed. However at that time, it would not be surprising to see Sarah conceive as she was not past the age of fertility. Now believing in God meant that he had to trust that God would work this thing by supernatural means. Now Abraham had to believe that God would interfere with the natural order of things on his behalf. The faith is the same, but God waited until there could be no doubt as to how this child came.

Not Blind

The other wonderful thing that this text shows us is that Abraham was not blind, by any means, to reality. He saw clearly that he was not in a place to father a child. He knew beyond a shadow of a doubt that Sarah was barren and had gone through menopause. He didn't deny those facts, or close his eyes to them, he was able to look squarely at them and say, "Those things are true, but God is faithful, and able to perform his promises."

Similarly, we need not be blind. When we see the salvation that has been offered us by faith through grace we will be continually reminded of our inability to earn, maintain, keep, or complete this salvation. We see this in justification, sanctification and glorification. However, our faith is what is to steady us. We are not to waiver in faith, because we know that HE is able, we know that HE is trustworthy, we know that HE has declared us righteous. We don't need to ignore our continuing sin and weakness, we can bring it to God, trusting Him in everything to be faithful to His promise. We need not be blind as Christians, only believing in His power to save through the work of Jesus Christ on the cross. We can frankly admit our inability, and recognize that only He can save us.

Grew Strong in Faith

Remember, Paul is talking about an occurrence that is late in Abraham's life. It is notable that Abraham could still grow in faith. Even at this late time, after all that God had brought him through, he could still grow strong in Faith. Notice what enabled him to grow strong in faith? Believing! Paul will later say: "Faith comes by hearing, and hearing by the word of God." How to grow strong in Faith? Read the Bible, understand it, and believe (trust) in it. The pattern that worked for Abraham, works for everyone whose faith is in the Lord.

Glory to God

God's glory is the sum total and end result of all history. The whole of creation exists to bring God glory, and this is the time that God is said to be brought glory. Not through Abraham's works of righteousness, but through his faith. We think of worship music as being the way that we glorify God. However, the way God is glorified most fully is by our knowing Him, and by our trusting in His character. That is how He is glorified in our lives, not by our own personal holiness, or our self-righteousness, but by our knowing Him, trusting Him, in all things.

Fully Assured

Does this attitude characterize our faith? Reading Christian publications and headlines it would seem that the focus is mostly on us. Most Christian media works to undermine a person's confidence in their salvation rather than promote it. Even Calvinists (who teach unconditional election/predestination) will sometimes say that we aren't to know if we are secure or not because it may cause us to be lazy in our faith. This is a core misunderstanding about the relationship that God wants to have with us. God wants us to be fully assured that He can and will save us, not most sure, not partly sure, not sure that He will do His part if we do ours, God want us to know that we can count on HIS promise because HE made it.

Imagine you are a father of a child. Do you want that child to grow up thinking that you will love and protect them? Do you want your child to wonder if you are able to help him and really are looking out for his best interests? Or do you want him to wake up every morning and try to earn your love and approval? The nature of God's love is clear: unconditional, complete, secure, forever. This is the nature of the relationship that every single person enters into when they place their faith in Christ. It is accepting the gift, entering into the relationship, once we enter, we cannot exit, because He has placed His name on it. He cannot fail.

God is able

The core belief that Abraham exhibits is in God's omnipotence. His character is fully able to do whatever He says that He will do. To question our salvation by faith through grace isn't to question ourselves, it is questioning His ability. We are regenerated after we believe and we continue to be alive as that new creation, the one that is in Christ, the one that can never again know death (separation from God)! This is the only way man can be called righteous by God's standard.

Romans 4:23-25

23Now not for his sake only was it written that it was credited to him, 24but
for our sake also, to whom it will be credited, as those who believe in Him
who raised Jesus our Lord from the dead, 25*He* who was delivered over
because of our transgressions, and was raised because of our justification.

Why write it down?

Paul brings out a point here: this was recorded for a reason. Scripture didn't happen on accident. This very important fact of Abraham's faith being reckoned to him as righteousness wasn't just recorded for his sake. God was laying down the core principle of justification for all time. God's principle goal in humanity was to be glorified by humans in the context of relationship. The way that He brings us back into relationship after the fall is through this process of crediting faith as righteousness. Paul brings about the important point that it is not just for Abraham that this principle is true, it is also for us. Those who would wonder if God had changed from salvation by works to salvation by grace through faith would have to realize that it is the firm and consistent testimony of Scripture that man is only brought back into a relationship with the Living God through belief, trust in His ability to restore us to that relationship.

The Gospel

There are a number of places where one can find the gospel very clearly laid out. This is one of them. When we wonder what it means to be saved we can often be confused by the images and words of Christians that are not from scripture. Some may say, "Ask Jesus into your heart" or "believe and be baptized" or "believe and make a public confession." Yet, here it is very clear what is to be trusted in:

1 - We believe in Him who raised our Lord Jesus from the dead.

2 – Jesus died for our sins (our transgression of God's perfect standard)

3 – He was raised from the dead

These are the exact three elements we find in 1 Corinthians 15:1-5:

> [1]Now I make known to you, brethren, the gospel which I
> preached to you, which also you received, in which also you stand,
> [2]by which also you are saved, if you hold fast the word which I
> preached to you, unless you believed in vain. [3]For I delivered to
> you as of first importance what I also received, that Christ died for
> our sins according to the Scriptures, [4]and that He was buried, and
> that He was raised on the third day according to the Scriptures,
> [5]and that He appeared to Cephas, then to the twelve.

ROMANS 5

ROMANS 5:1-2

Romans 5:1-2 NASB

[1]Therefore, having been justified by faith, we have peace with God through our Lord Jesus Christ, [2]through whom also we have obtained our introduction by faith into this grace in which we stand; and we exult in hope of the glory of God.

Opening a New Chapter

In Romans 5 justification by grace through faith is put forth in resounding clarity and power. This is a powerful reality that defies all human reasoning and destroys any place which we may hope to find for human pride. This is the very simple pure fact of the Gospel: Jesus has done everything because we could do nothing. This chapter speaks with such incredible power and clarity that many would seek to try to "explain away" the clear message because the wild and ferocious grace of God seems too terrifying to deal with. However, the message, no matter how shocking and offensive to our sensibilities and desire to bring something to the table in our salvation, cannot be denied. The complete salvation of God is provided to helpless mankind, is conditioned upon receiving it by faith alone, and it is assured to be brought to full completion because it is Jesus Christ who has done it.

Having Been Justified

The word "therefore" begins this marvelous chapter which indicates that Paul is going to continue this major theme of the believer's justification before God (being declared righteous judicially). This continuation makes an overt statement of the position of the believer in Jesus Christ. The English translates the Greek simply and clearly. Note that the word justified - *dikaioō* in the Greek – means to be declared righteous. This is a legal statement. It doesn't say that the believer becomes righteous or perfect in his or her every thought word or action, but only that God has declared us righteous on the basis of Christ's righteousness. This is an unconditional, undisputable and irreversible fact of God's word. The believer can no more be declared "unjustified" than a day be reversed and done over again. It is the standing judgment of the highest Judge in the land – God the Father.

We have peace

This is a remarkable statement. The believer has peace – the full and complete wholeness that can be given by the Son of God alone. This peace is based upon our justification with God. A human being who is still identified with his sin could only ever be at odds with God, and therefore could only be on the path to eternal destruction. However, because of Christ's work appropriated by faith the believer is now in current and ongoing possession of the peaceful fullness and wholeness of God. The Greek present tense could be translated – "we have and we keep on having peace with God." This is the state of every believer. Whether we "feel" like it or not…we have peace before God based upon God's amazing work.

Through…

The Scripture is so clear! The power and the passage which gives the believer this peace with God is Jesus Chris and Jesus Christ alone. It is important to realize that Jesus is the only possible way for a person to come to God. While we may try to find many ways to satisfy our own desires, or even attain some superficial sense of spirituality the only way to have peace with the Creator God of the universe is to approach Him on the basis of the shed blood of Jesus Christ. This is the central message of Romans and the central message of the Bible. Man has a problem which he could never solve – God has provided the only solution. The trouble with all man made solutions (human religion) is that they do not solve the problem of the offense against the eternal holiness and righteousness of God. An illustration may help explain:

Imagine a man had brutally murdered another. As the murderer takes the stand he declares his guilt and smiles. As the trial continues he maintains confidence and smiles quietly as the proceedings continue and the death penalty is finally reached as the decision of the court. The murderer still maintains absolute confidence. As the trial is drawing to the close he stands up and declares: "I have killed this man, and I am sorry for his family. You may have wondered why these proceedings haven't bothered me at all…it is because I have a secret – I intend to give the family an entire coupon book that I received in the mail earlier this week in exchange for my life. I think that should make us even."

Not only is the offer of a coupon book a meaningless gesture, it also shows a complete lack of understanding for the gravity of the offense. And this is the precise nature of man-made religion before God's holiness.

Obtaining an Introduction

We are familiar with the idea of an introduction. The common saying: "It's not what you know, it's who you know" is an example of this idea. It is not strange to think that a connection could get us tickets to an exclusive event or even access to a job interview that we could not get otherwise. This is related to the biblical idea found in this verse. Then, as now, one would never have access to simply walk into the courtroom of a king or ruler. One must have an appointment and an introduction in order to come before a king or a ruler. It was this lack of introduction that made Queen Esther's approach to Xerxes so courageous. Had he not welcomed her she could have been executed swiftly.

These verses tell us that we not only have peace with God we also have this ready and standing introduction. This is a remarkable privilege that is shared by every single believer. Access to God the Father, the Creator and Ruler of the cosmos, at any and all times and in all situations. We have this access because we have faith in God's provision for us in Jesus Christ.

Into the Grace in which we stand

Grace is the new operating procedure for the believer. Grace is the air that we breathe. It is the way in which we are saved from sin's penalty, the way in which we are being saved from sin's power and the way we will ultimately be saved from sin's presence. It is the grace of God and the grace of God alone that does these things, and thus it is to God's sole glory. This grace is the place of our new standing before God. Where we were once at odds with God and stood in a place only of being able to receive His judgment, we now stand in His grace because of what God has freely done for us in Jesus Christ. This is a statement of our permanent and eternal position before God in Christ. It will be made clear as this letter continues that our entire lives are spent growing in understanding of what God has already given us in Christ Jesus.

Let's Celebrate!

As we grow to understand this grace in which we stand our lives and our hearts will be filled with rejoicing more and more so! The believer finally has a reason to rejoice and exult, praising God for his great and gracious provision for us in Jesus Christ. Nothing else in the world compares to the joy of the position of the believer in Jesus Christ. This is a remarkable and wonderful reality and it is valuable for us to see that we can rejoice in this position because we are restored to our original purpose of knowing and glorifying God with our lives.

The "hope" that believers rejoice in isn't a probability, it isn't that we *might* bring glory to God. Because of what He has done in the believer through the person and work of Christ He *is* glorified. This hope is a sure thing, something that cannot be anything but the ultimate reality. Regardless of what happens in a believer's life once he or she is placed in Christ the entire universe will behold and marvel at God's amazing redemptive power in the life of a believer. He took sin-wrecked people – destined for destruction – and placed them in His Son, restoring us to usefulness by the power of His amazing grace. Men and angels look on in awe and wonder – glorifying God for His endless power, righteousness, and His amazing grace.

Drawing things together…

As a believer in Jesus Christ we are given a remarkable position before God. One that we could never earn and never deserve. We can and will still get confused at times(Romans 6-8 will discuss the present element of our salvation – sanctification) but we can always rely upon these amazing positional gifts which are now ours in Christ Jesus. By Christ's work we are justified. By Christ's work we have continual peace with the God of the universe. By Christ's work we have access to Him. By Christ's work we rejoice in the reality that we now exist as a continual monument of the power, love and character of God. How great a salvation we have in Jesus Christ!

ROMANS 5:3-5

Where we were…

Last week's study delivered the amazing news that tied together Paul's argument that proved that justification (phase 1 of salvation) is by grace, through faith, and that it has always been by faith. We learned through the study of the lives of both Abraham and David that this understanding that we are saved by believing in the salvation and provision of God is not a "new" teaching by any measure. We learned that we have continual peace with God because of what Jesus Christ did on the cross. We saw that we have, in Christ, obtained access to God and that we have an inexhaustible hope in the glory of God. That leads us to the next verses, which may surprise us, but fit perfectly with the argument in Paul's context.

Getting the Full Package

Every year around Christmas time we begin to think about exchanging gifts. As children we may have fond memories of gazing with great longing throughout the month of December at the gifts under the tree. Wondering what is in the boxes and if we got the things we were hoping for. Imagine all of that excitement leading up to Christmas and then only opening a few of the gifts and leaving the rest under the tree. It would seem silly that a child would receive a CD player and leave all of the CD's still wrapped under the tree, yet this is what often happens to believers. We take forgiveness, and miss all of the other amazing gifts that we have been given, and we NEED them, which is why God gave them to us. The gifts that are talked about in verse five are: Justification (being declared righteous), Peace with God (we keep on having this), access to God (continually in the person of Jesus Christ), hope for the future (knowing we will be with Him in Glory forever). But the coming verses add more to this package list, and explain the hope that we have in Christ yet more clearly.

Romans 5:3

And not only this, but we also exult in our tribulations, knowing that tribulation brings about perseverance;

Not only this

This verse is something like the people on television saying, "BUT WAIT, THERE'S MORE!" And there is much more. Often times we get confused about our salvation, thinking that we have simply received "fire insurance" against the possibility of going to Hell. While this is true there is much more. The Holy Spirit, writing through Paul here, reminds us that our walk with Christ is not just for the future, but for today as well. In fact, there is shocking news that connects perfectly to what has already been revealed as a part of the package.

Rejoicing in Tribulations

The word *exult* is the same as the one we studied last week. It means to rejoice. But the last time this word was used (in verse 2) it made a great deal of sense. We can easily understand how we can exult in the hope that we will share God's glory for all of eternity. That is great news! However, here we see this same word 'rejoice' again. The rejoicing is not just in anticipation of what is to come, but also in what the Lord is doing right here and now.

The word "tribulation" translates the Greek word *thlipsis* which has the idea of pressure, external forces that bring forth squeezing difficulty, pain or pressure. On a physical level, we can imagine the terror and pain of being squeezed to the point where breathing becomes difficult. This is an image of the tribulation that we often bear. There is often even greater pain in terms of emotional difficulties and pressures which are also included in the semantic domain of this word. Notice also, the tribulation and difficulty is expected. Paul doesn't say, "if I have tribulations…" it is expected that there are difficulties going on. What does this mean? We will often hear a believer say, "Why is this happening to me? What is going on?" as if they were somehow caught by surprise by the fact that there is suffering involved in the Christian life. Trials are to be expected, anticipated, but they are to be rejoiced in!

The word "in" is another important preposition. We may have the idea that what Paul is talking about is rejoicing "in spite of" these difficulties. While it would be true to say, "I am going through tough times, but I know I have hope at the end of this journey," it is not the appropriate attitude for believers. The rejoicing here is *a result of* the suffering. Imagine someone gives you a million dollars. You don't rejoice *in spite of* the million dollars you have just been given, you rejoice *because of* the million dollars that you have been given. This is the picture that scripture paints. Paul goes on to explain why believers are able to rejoice in suffering, and even why they are logically obliged to rejoice. It must first be noted that the first thing we must understand is the Biblical value system.

Biblical Values

What is most important to you? Is it your job, school, family, hobbies, recreation, food, pleasure, music, church activities? These are all great things, but it must be understood, the true Biblical attitude desires a relationship with God, and growth in that relationship so much more than any of the things of this world that they are nothing by comparison. What on this list could you not live without? What would make you most miserable? What does your life say about your values? How you spend your time and your money? The ability to rejoice in suffering or not will be exactly in relationship to how much we value our relationship with God. Don't be discouraged if you can't answer this question as you should (that just makes you honest) this is what growth in the Christian life is all about. It is a process of learning that everything is about Him and His glory, rather than being about us and our temporary happiness.

What do you know?

Here the rejoicing is based on something that we are to know. The word translated "know" here is a knowledge that is based on observation. It refers to knowing something the way that we know facts. This is a knowledge that we can count on because we perceive its truth, both in because it is revealed in Scripture and because we observe it in our lives, and the lives of other believers.

The word translated as "perseverance" here is a Greek word that literally translates as "to suffer under." The great Greek grammarian William Barclay did a magnificent amount of work on this one word and discovered that this word is not simply a word that means someone who "puts up with anything" but is rather a very courageous word. This is the word for the one who endures the greatest difficulties with grace, confidence and fortitude. The word "endurance" may give us a fuller sense of the concept that is here being described. The first reason the believer can rejoice because of suffering is because it is producing in him the courageous ability to endure any circumstance with fortitude and confidence of one who knows that the ultimate reality of every circumstance, and every possible circumstance, will bring about the outcome that he is drawn closer to the living God.

The word "brings about" is also a colorful word in Greek. This word combines the prefix for "down" and the word from which we get our English words "energy" and "energize". The tribulations in the life of the believer are energizing the production of this courageous perseverance. But there is more said about this process of growth through tribulation and trial.

Romans 5:4-5
4and perseverance, proven character; and proven character, hope; 5and hope
does not disappoint, because the love of God has been poured out within our hearts through the Holy Spirit who was given to us.

Proven Character

The NASB seems to have the best translation available here. The idea is character that is proven in a legal and objective setting. It is interesting to think that the goal that the Lord is growing us towards is a goal of character change. We may be tempted to think in terms of our actions as being what the Lord wants us to focus on, however, the Lord is far more interested in having authentic actions that grow from authentically godly character. How does this proven character come about? Through endurance; which we obtain by way of trials. This is why we rejoice in (because of) our trials. We know every moment that we suffer, struggle or are under pressure that the Lord is creating in us character that we can rely on: the character of Christ in us. It is through trials that we learn that we cannot rely on our own resources, it is through trials that we realize that we must rely on the Holy Spirit moment by moment. And that works to create:

Hope

The next verse goes further in discussing what this hope is: biblical hope. Biblical hope is something that is trustworthy. It is not an "I hope so" hope. It is an assurance that the Word of the Lord is true, that His faithfulness is beyond question or compare. Biblical hope is a hope that trusts in the reality of God's view of things over anything that the world, the flesh or the devil can provide. There is no "maybe" in biblical hope. But how is this hope energized in us? How do we place more and more confidence in this hope? By way of the character that the Lord develops in us through endurance as a result of trials. We see what the Lord does IN us as we are forced to rely on Him through our trials and we become more assured than ever that He is able to do everything that He has promised us in Christ. This is great news.

How can I know?

The next statement addresses the issue of how we can know that this hope does not disappoint. How do we know that we don't simply become "good at suffering"? We know because it is in suffering that we must be consoled only by the love of God. In times of physical blessing we run the risk of becoming attached to the world. In times of abundance we may begin to think that the physical world is all that there is and we need not bother with God. However, in suffering we know that there is no other comfort in life but the comfort of God's love as expressed through His indwelling Spirit within us. In trials we see what is really important, what is really eternal and can no longer be deluded by our imagined physical needs when it is quite clear that nothing on this earth will last, but our relationship with God, and our Spiritual growth are eternal.

Holy Spirit

The Holy Spirit is the expression, the agent, of the love of God towards us. This love is *agape* love. It is the love that always looks out for the best interests of the beloved. This deep, caring, sacrificial love that is provided by the Father here comes through the agency of the Holy Spirit who permanently indwells the believer. This is one of the four ministries of the Holy Spirit that occur instantly (and are not experientially or "felt") upon the moment of belief. These ministries are Regeneration, Indwelling, Baptism and Sealing. Regeneration is the gift of new life, Indwelling is the permanent placement of the Holy Spirit into the believer, Baptism (dry) is the change in identification permanently to be forever associated with Christ's death, burial, resurrection, ascension and seating. Sealing is the ministry by which the believer is permanently claimed as the property of God and forever under His protection, authenticity and care.

Conclusion

The bottom line is that struggles increase our dependence upon the Lord, His comfort and His resources. C.S. Lewis referred to pain as the chisel strikes that knock away the stubble and error revealing the beautiful masterpiece that God has created within us. The choice to rejoice in suffering is a conscious one for the believer. We may choose to embrace God's view on things, and trust that He is writing the prescription on our lives. Or we can wallow in our self-pity and fear. The choice is ours to make every day, in every trouble, trial and difficulty. From a broken shoe lace, to bad news from a doctor, to the loss of a loved one.

ROMANS 5:6-11

SALVATION!

During the course of this study, weeks and weeks were spent studying the absolute inability of man to achieve God's standard. We wallowed in the misery of our own complete inability to do one single thing that would please God and get us our "well done" from Him. Now we see what happened. These verses further explain the hope that is ours in Christ Jesus. As was seen in the previous study, Biblical hope differs from the way the word "hope" is used in our secular context as biblical hope is a sure thing – a 100% guarantee. Paul explains in these verses that the hope is secure because of the character of God, His love, and the completeness of the Cross, along with the guarantee that He will complete it. Having identified our inability to do anything but accept the provision of another, Paul tells us what God did. In verses 6-7 we see the absurdity of dying to save an unrighteous man. It is as if someone was caught as a mass murderer and someone volunteered to be executed in his place. The thought is almost too absurd to imagine! But what we see is that God went way beyond the absurd for the pure and simple reason that He loves us.

Romans 5:6-7

6For while we were still helpless, at the right time Christ died for the
ungodly. 7For one will hardly die for a righteous man; though perhaps for
the good man someone would dare even to die.

Our Place

Our position before God is here reiterated. The place that man has before God is a position of total and complete helplessness. The word translated "helpless" here means "weak, feeble, sickly". The idea is an absolute inability to help ourselves, there is no ability that man can claim or work that he could do to correct the broken relationship between man and God. This is the core misunderstanding of the world religions, they teach that with the right set of rules, the right change in behavior, a person can correct the problem and enter back into a relationship with God. The Bible is clear that if we think we have any strength or ability to save ourselves we are out of line, mistaken about the most important reality of our need for God's salvation and interference.

At the Right Time

This is a wonderful phrase. Often times we forget that God has a perspective that is totally outside of the bounds of human history. Time is not a limiting factor for God. We may wonder why God didn't send Jesus immediately after the fall. Eve believed that both Abel and then Seth may very well be the One who would save. Yet, there were still several thousand years before Jesus would be born. We may ask why? Why not just get it over with? We are often tempted to ask the same question about Christ's return. Why not now? The reality of the matter is that the Lord waited until the perfect time. Man had, by the first century totally displayed his inability to reach God. The Bible documents exactly how man failed using conscience as a guide, government as a guide, the Mosaic Law as a guide, and each time came up empty. God used our history to show humanity that there could be no salvation apart from Him, and no strength that mankind can provide will return man to the place that he had been created for.

The rightness of the timing extends, however, even further than this. Daniel predicted the year that the Messiah would come onto the scene and this is why the Magi may have been looking for the King of Israel to come. They knew from Daniel's prophecy that the time was right and God would be sending the Messiah. The timing was also perfect on the world scene because the Pax Romana (the Peace of Rome) made it safer to travel throughout much of the ancient world. This was further aided by the development of the Roman road system, many of which are still in place today. Additionally, by this point Koine Greek had become the accepted language of the people. Never before in History could a message be written in a language that would be understood so broadly. The reality is that the time was right spiritually, the time was right historically, the time was right linguistically and the time was right culturally.

As we look at this reality, can we not also trust God regarding His choice to wait until the right time to return to Rapture His Church and begin the end-times events that follow?

Christ died for the ungodly

This is what happened at "just the right moment." This is the concept of Substitution, which will be examined in greater depth in the coming verses. But the radical and shocking nature of this must be examined. It is easy enough to let these words become "familiar" to us and thus, less shocking. But realize that this action of God would not have been in keeping with the character of any other man-made deity. All manmade religions fashion God in man's image. They make God act like a man. Sometimes lying, sometimes deceptive, never giving out anything or blessing freely. Man will always invent a new legalism by which he can "earn his way" and feel good about himself in relationship to others.

Biblically however, we know that God is love, that He is always just, that He is always gracious. In order to satisfy His demands He had to do it Himself. Nothing broken, marred or stained could ever meet the standard. In order to save mankind God had to step in and act on man's behalf. Why He would do this is beyond human comprehension. The love that God bears towards rebellious humanity should shock and amaze us, no matter how often we may hear about it.

one will hardly die for a righteous man

History is filled with martyrs who died alone. The crucifixion of Christ proves this to us in spades. Christ in His total righteousness was illegally arrested and tried by the religious leaders of His day. Yet nobody stood up and spoke against it (so far as we know), nobody walked out on the trial saying, "This is just a joke!" Furthermore, Pilate, knowing that Christ had done no wrong thing still condemned him to death. He was not willing to undergo so much as a bit of discomfort to protect a righteous Man from wrongful murder by his jealous compatriots.

Perhaps for a good man…

While examples of either may possibly be found, Paul's purpose is not to say "this never happens" but only to say that it is extraordinarily rare. And while it is most rare for a person to give their life on behalf of someone that is righteous there is a slightly greater chance that someone will give themselves up for a good man. "Good" here is talking about objective goodness. This is someone that is loved by others. This again is displayed clearly in the person and crucifixion of Jesus. Jesus was fiercely loved by

His disciples and they said that they would die with, or for, Him if necessary. But as we see in the Biblical record of the event, all fled from Him when the moment of danger arrived. Only two of the disciples could gather up the courage to do so much as follow at a great distance while the trial and crucifixion took place.

The Point

The point is quite clear: human nature would not do this. Human nature does not understand this kind of love and dedication to what is good and what is righteous. How could we be expected to naturally understand dying for one who is positioned themselves as an enemy before us? This is a wake-up call for us to realize the great power and love of God as expressed in Christ Jesus. If we understand the love of God aright, we will continually be humbled and amazed at what He has done for us. That is striking!

Romans 5:8

But God demonstrates His own love toward us, in that while we were yet sinners, Christ died for us.

But

The purpose of this conjunction is clear. The previous verses told of how no one is jumping up and down to die for an unrighteous person. This verse starts out with a contrast. God went way beyond the example in the previous verses. The focus here is the character of God's love for us.

Demonstrates

Have you ever been lied to about how a person feels toward you? Have you ever wondered what that was all about? A person says they care for you and then they totally undermine those words by their actions. God's love is not just abstract, or arbitrary. God's love is demonstrated. This word for *demonstrates* has the sense of introduction. He introduces His love through this great loving and merciful act. If we ever wonder how much we are loved by God we need look no farther than the cross. It is planted in History as an every day, all the time reminder of the incredible love that He bears towards us. We may be tempted to look for some other explanation, or some other expression of His love, but this neglects the big point that the Lord wants us to see: His love was expressed for us at the Cross forever. It is a final statement of His endless love for us that will never go away and will never change. This is the stake in the earth that allows Paul to later say: "For I am convinced that neither death, nor life, nor angels, nor principalities, nor things present, nor things to come, nor powers, nor height, nor depth, nor any other created thing, will be able to separate us from the love of God, which is in Christ Jesus our Lord." (Romans 8:38-39)

It should be noted that this verb is in present tense. The Greek present tense conveys what we usually use the English present continuous tense to relate. This passage could be translated as "God is continually demonstrating His love for us in this…" The idea is that the cross is a continual witness to the immense love of God. This is also indicative of the fact that when a person placed their faith in Jesus, the Cross is then applied to their lives and they are "crucified with Christ." While the events of the Cross took place in time, the effects of the cross go backwards and forwards such that every person who comes to salvation by grace through faith in all of History is experiencing the demonstrated love of God exercised in the person of Jesus Christ.

Yes, but WHEN

It is important to note that Christ died for us, while we were yet sinners. This shows the lengths of Christ's love. He went to the cross for us long before we were even repentant. He died for us before humanity was even contrite of heart. We were yet fully identified with our sins, yet He came to be the perfect sacrifice and bring us back into a relationship with God. This shows God's amazing love for us. It is beyond even that for a mother who sees that drug addicted, neo-Nazi murderer, and still can see only her son whom she loves, no matter how much she may hate everything that he does and stands for. God's love is the most extreme love the world has ever known.

Christ Died for Us

It may be surprising to us in our modern perspective, but the understanding of Christ's substitutionary death in our place, is not found before around the 11th century with St. Anselm. Imagine that! However, in having the Biblical text before us we see that Christ's death was absolutely in our place. He paid the ultimate penalty where we could not. Being wholly without sin, and a fully infinite Being (God alone is infinite) He alone was able to pay the penalty for sin, propitiate (satisfy) God's righteousness. He replaced our history with His own and we are now found completely in Him. It has been rightly observed that "There is no gospel without substitution." And this is true. Without the payment for sin we are wholly out of luck.

Romans 5:9

Much more then, having now been justified by His blood, we shall be saved from the wrath of God through Him.

Justified by His blood

"His blood" here stands for the violent death of Christ on the cross. The blood is used in Romans as a covering for sins. We have been forever declared righteous in our position in Jesus Christ because of the blood that He shed on the Cross.

Shall be Saved?

Shall be saved? What does this mean? Many have used these future tense salvation verses to try and claim that we may not if we don't make it that far. Or even to suggest that past, perfect and present tenses wherein we are told that we are saved, are nullified by these future tenses. This however, is not at all the case. We find that Scripture talks about 3 tenses of salvation:

1) I was saved. I was saved from Sin's penalty the moment I believed. This is theologically called Justification.

2) I am being saved. I am being saved from sin's power. Theologically this is the process of Sanctification.

3) I will be saved. I will be saved from sin's presence and from the punishment to come on the earth. Theologically this is glorification.

Each of the three tenses of salvation are part of the process of Salvation which is by faith through grace. It is the Lord who will do it and is never intended to cast the slightest doubt upon the nature and permanence of the salvation of anyone who enters into a relationship with Jesus Christ through faith. It is much like getting onto the automated car wash. Once you are on the tracks there is no way of reversing, or turning yourself off until the whole job is done.

The Wrath of God

The wrath of God is something that was very close to the mindset of the person of this time. God's wrath and judgment was often poured out by way of physical judgments. Without the immense super structure that we enjoy today, imagine the position of those who went through the catastrophe of Hurricane Katrina. A swarm of locust (as seen in the book of Joel) could very well mean that a whole village would starve for the year.

The Wrath of God, as it is expressed here is specifically a promise to be preserved from the wrath of God as it will be poured out upon the earth in the Tribulation period. The Wrath of God begins to be poured out with the 6th chapter of Revelation and the seven years that follow contain the most horrific catastrophes and judgments that the world has ever seen, or will ever see. This preservation continues on into the eternal state as we are also preserved, by His work, from the eternal torment and punishment of the Lake of Fire which has been prepared for Satan and the angels that followed him.

Through Him

This is noteworthy indeed. We are preserved from wrath through Jesus Christ. It is through the identification with Him that we are preserved. This is important as many will attempt to try to guilt people into doing something (usually give money) by threatening them that they will be punished, or lose their salvation. The salvation from the wrath of God comes wholly and entirely through the person of Christ and our identification with Him.

Romans 5:10

For if while we were enemies we were reconciled to God through the death of His Son, much more, having been reconciled, we shall be saved by His life.

We were Enemies

Here is the third reiteration of our place. It has been shown in verse 6 that we were helpless and in verse 8 that we were yet sinners (mark missers), here we see that the result of this is that we were enemies of God. The person who tries to "do it on his own" is only shown to be a criminal, a sinner, an enemy of the Living and Righteous God of Creation. We see this reality constantly in the lives of people who continue to reject God. They are at enmity with Him on every point, these are the same people who are passionate to keep Christianity out of schools and government, yet working as hard as they can to get New Age garbage in. These are the people that deny the death penalty (death of the deserving), and promote abortion (murder of the innocent). These are the people who fight for gay marriage, yet fight against the nuclear family. Their mindset is simply against anything that God is or stands for, almost in the game say manner of saying, "What does God say? I hate that!" But here is the point: This is the natural state of man. If we expect otherwise then we don't understand what the Bible says about those who reject God. Furthermore, if we think we are better we must realize that we too were among them, and were only redeemed by the work of Christ (Eph. 2:1-3)

Reconciled

This is another weighty doctrinal word. Often times we use the word reconcile to mean compromise, as two parties "meeting in the middle" in some way. This is not the Biblical doctrine of reconciliation. The word translated "reconciled" here is related to another word which we would translate with the same English word. One Greek word means that one party stayed where they were (was righteous) and the other changed to be reunited, the other related Greek word says that both parties changed (compromised) to be reunited. The Greek word here is the former rather than the latter. God didn't change, or compromise His standard, we were the changed party.

Notice also: this is in the passive voice. We didn't reconcile ourselves; we had to be reconciled by the work of Christ. Reconciliation doesn't just mean admitting you were wrong, but means that you were made right and thus enabled to return to a relationship with the Living God. This was done through the work of Jesus Christ as well. This is a restoration to relationship and fellowship with God. So we weren't simply declared safe from wrath, but we were restored to relationship that God intended man to have with Him.

Through the death of His Son

In an alarming study aired on "The Whitehorse Inn" when at a youth pastor's conference most youth pastors could not correctly identify the Gospel as it exists in the Bible. When asked: "Would you say that the gospel is that Jesus came down to show us how to live?" The majority said: "Yes, that is the gospel." And a few said, "That is part of the gospel." However, that is neither part nor the whole of the gospel! The Gospel is not the gospel without the death of Christ. It wasn't enough that He came. He didn't just come to SHOW the way to God he came AS the way to God, and the only way (John 14:6). His death on the cross was the vehicle, the action by which we are justified and reconciled to God. There is no other way, and no other Gospel. No other "take on Jesus" will do, the death of Christ is central to the Good News, and there is no Good News apart from that death of Christ.

Much more…

Here Paul jumps again (just as in verse 9) to the last phase in our salvation. Paul includes the whole process of salvation because eternal security is in view. Paul wants every believer to know that it is Christ's work all the way that saves us. It has rightly been said that a believer who does not understand the safekeeping of the believer in Christ will never experience substantial spiritual growth. If we think that we contribute to our salvation then we will not be trusting God, and therefore will not understand our most basic need. It is like not eating any food and then going on a weight lifting regiment. If you don't eat, and then try to lift weights you will end up in a bad position, similarly if you try to maintain or perfect the salvation that God has won for you in Jesus Christ you cannot grow.

Verses 9 and 11 both emphasize that the salvation at the end is the same as the salvation at the beginning, it is by faith. All three phases are totally of Christ, and in each phase we are completely helpless, and must rely on His life, His working for anything positive to happen.

Romans 5:11

And not only this, but we also exult in God through our Lord Jesus Christ, through whom we have now received the reconciliation.

And not only this

But wait there's MORE! Paul continues to sing the praises of the salvation that is ours in Christ with the most extreme and amazing terms possible. The next aspect spoken of is the reality that all of the things that were done by Christ at the Cross change us completely! Whereas before we could do nothing but fear and hate God we now exult in Him. We celebrate and rejoice in who He is! This is an amazing reality. The change is complete and plays itself out in our day to day experience!

Celebrate Good Times!

Finally! We are not in a place of being terrified of God. We can come to Him in loving and sure confidence that we are reconciled to Him. Not based on what we have done, but based on what He has done. The works of our hands are at best temporary, the things which we are capable of are here and gone. Our moods, devotion and strength fail every time. It is only because He saved us that we are saved, and because of this we can continually be rejoicing in the wonder of His character and love.

We can praise Him for His love and grace because they were the attributes of His character that saw us in the helpless situation and sent His Son to save us.

We can praise Him in His perfect justice and absolute righteousness because HE has brought us up to the standard. We do not need to be afraid anymore! Praise the Lord!

ROMANS 5:12-17

Two Men

In these verses we see two men contrasted. The first is Adam and the second is Christ. The first thing we must note is that if Adam didn't literally live this passage is meaningless. Paul, along with all of the other Biblical Authors (and Christ Himself), views Adam as a real literal man, who was the first of all men, created by the very hand of God. It may seem like a compromise to suggest the days of creation are "symbolic" or to be interpreted "poetically" but if this is so there is absolutely no theological meaning for what follows hereafter, as we will see. The remainder of this study will take for granted that Adam was a real, physical man and really was the first of all men whom we are all ultimately descended from, not a "symbol" or a "poetic device" or any other allegorical non-sense.

The contrast is between Adam and Christ and will give us an understanding of the two positions that are available to mankind. We can be positioned in Adam, and identified with his sin and our own, or we can be positioned in Christ, and identified with His righteous sacrifice and perfection. This is yet more important information in understanding the character and nature of our salvation, and will be the very important background information as we begin to consider sanctification in the coming chapter.

Romans 5:12-13

Therefore, just as through one man sin entered into the world, and death through sin, and so death spread to all men, because all sinned – for until the Law sin was in the world, but sin is not imputed when there is no law.

Therefore

Having explained the amazing depths of Salvation in the preceding verses, Paul then launches into a theological explanation of what happened, and how this can be so. In doing so Paul goes right back to Genesis, where it all started. Paul is now backing up what he explained in such clear terms in verses 1-11 of this chapter. We were helpless (v. 6), sinners (v. 8) and enemies (v. 10); but we now rejoice in the very character and nature of God

(v. 11). The nature of our salvation is in view here.

Through one man…
This is talking about how Sin entered the world. How sin began. Notice that Satan is not given credit for this, neither is Eve, but Adam as the corporate head is given full credit for introducing sin to this world. We find that Eve was deceived by the Serpent (the Devil) (1 Timothy 2:14); and Adam simply rebelled, knowing full well what he was doing. Through that one act sin (missing the mark) entered into and infected the entire world system. The effects of this action spread to the very ground, to the animals who then began to kill and feed on each other, and of course all human relationships. This is the greatest tragedy in all of History and the earth still waits for its redemption from the curse (Romans 8:18-22).

And Death through one man
Here again, we see the incredible importance of understanding the Genesis account as being literal, correct and true. If we try to allow for the days of Genesis to become ages, or some gap in these days, and thus try to allow for the supposed "great age of the earth" and then try to allow evolution to be "God's tool for creating man" we come to the conclusion that death could not have entered the world through Adam and his sin, as the theory of evolution insists in billions of generations and billions of deaths to come to the "more advanced" life forms. If all of these deaths were occurring leading up to Adam's life and sin then we come to the conclusions that God's word cannot be trusted, that this passage is an out and out lie, that salvation doesn't mean what the Bible says, and that God is not a perfect creator, but rather a cruel child creating and destroying countless generations of life through an inability to "get it right".

The Biblical reality is that the word is in no way unclear: death entered the world because of Adam's sin. There was no death in the garden of Eden. Physical death came as a result of the infection of sin that characterized Adam's being and all of His progeny after him because of sin. We see from the very beginning of time that the result of sin is death. It is separating from the only true and eternal Source of Life and therefore by logical necessity results in death (the absence of life).

Because all sinned
This one may catch us by surprise as modern readers. The idea of being held accountable to the sin or action of our forebears seems strange indeed to us. However, this is the reality, and it is easily understood when viewed from two angles.

Broke makes broke

When thinking of the principle of procreation something can only reproduce after its own kind. Much to the chagrin of those who would fight for the theory of evolution there is not a single fossil example of a dog giving birth to anything but a dog. As much as science-fiction has had fun with the idea of mutation we find that mutation only hurts and never helps (as in the case of Down's syndrome) and never causes a creature that breathed with lungs to be born with gills, or the other way around. What does this mean to us? When Adam sinned he became broken, sinful, and fallen. He was no longer flawless in his innocence and thus could no longer make flawless children. This is why, while Adam and Eve were made "in the image of God" (Genesis 1:27), their children were brought forth "in the likeness of Adam" (Genesis 5:3).

In Adam we did…

The principle of imputation can be a bit confusing to us. There are two types of imputation: actual and judicial. Actual imputation is when you are imputed with the very sin for which you are responsible. While there is not universal agreement about this amongst scholars, it is my position that we are imputed the sin of Adam because we were in his body when he sinned. Every person is stained with their very own sin nature from the very beginning of their natural life, and this is the gift and inheritance of the original father and progenitor of our race – Adam. It was his and it is now ours. The principle of imputation is also displayed in Hebrews 7:9-10 where Levi is give credit as tithing to Melchizedek as he was yet in the loins of Abraham when Abraham paid tithes to Melchizedek.

Until the Law
The period being spoken of here is the space in between Adam and Moses, as will be referenced in the following verse. Sin did not cease to be in the world between the times that Adam sinned and the time the Law was given.

Sin is not imputed
WHAT?! Does this mean that everyone between Adam and Moses was off of the hook? That nobody suffered for their sin because "sin is not imputed when there is no law"? Clearly not. Once again, we need to return to the reality of what sin is. Missing the mark means that the relationship with God is broken. However, without the Law to label it there was no way of holding people accountable to what they may or may not have known. Essentially, if there is no command to be violated then one cannot say that there is a violation of the command. This does not mean that the consequences of sin did not continue to be seen and experienced, it only means that until the Law was given it was impossible for man to fully understand how short he fell of God's perfect standard.

An example of this would be if two people were travelling out in the wilderness where (hypothetically) no government had rule, and one killed the other nobody could say that they broke the law. Surely it would be sin, surely it would be in conflict with the character of God. The effects of it would continue, but it would not be a violation of the law, it would just be sin.

Romans 5:14-15
Nevertheless death reigned from Adam until Moses, even over those who had not sinned in the likeness of the offense of Adam, who is a type of Him who was to come. But the free gift is not like the transgression. For if by the transgression of the one the many died, much more did the grace of God and the gift by the grace by the one Man, Jesus Christ, abound to the many.

Nevertheless death reigned
So here we have the conclusion of the statement just before. While sin was not imputed before the law was put into place, the death continued. So we see that the Law did not cause the death, sin caused the death and it continued whether or not the Law was there to tell what sin was. The reality is that sin, and separation from God, has effects that are going to occur whether or not there is a standard by which to judge it.

The death that was incurred under the sin of Adam was passed down through all of those between Adam and Moses, even though none of them violated the express commandment of God in the way that Adam did. The idea that is being put forth is that sin, whether labeled or unlabeled, brings only death, loss and destruction. Sin always brings death and pain, regardless of "the rules"; anything that is not concordant with God and His character will destroy them. This is lending more credence and understanding to the truth that the Law cannot save, sanctify or bring glory. All it can do is to set clear lines and designations.

Who is a type of the Him who was to come…

We may wonder what this "type" is. The New Testament uses this word "type" to mean an Old Testament picture of Christ before He came. It is a sort of picture of something that helps us understand the person and ministry of Jesus Christ. The way in which Adam is a type is that he is the corporate head of humanity and all who are born are in him. In the same way the person who puts their faith in Christ is forever and permanently identified with Christ, as his new representative Head. This is fantastic news, it tells us that if we put our faith in Christ our association and identification with Adam is broken off and our new identification, our new "family" is found in Christ.

Not like the transgression

The free gift of God is different than the transgression? When Adam sinned he, and everyone after him got exactly what they deserved. Broken imperfection simply cannot last forever, so the transgression caused a natural and just reaction: death. Physical and spiritual death are the natural outplay of sin.

The "Free Gift" explains emphatically the nature of salvation. It can only be received by way of the free bestowal of God. And it is the exact opposite of the transgression. While humanity received exactly and precisely what is due in death, Salvation can only be attained by way of this free gift of God. It is not "earned" nor can it be said to be "deserved". This is yet more reason to understand that it cannot be lost! It is not on the "merit system," thus, it can't be lost because it can't be earned, it is by grace and grace alone, and this is great news!

Abound to the many

Here we see the grace of God abounding to the many. This is not a statement of universalism and by no means can be understood to mean that everyone will be saved. However, it does indicate that the death of the Lord was powerful and complete and this offer of salvation is available and powerful to save any who would come. There is not one who will be turned away who puts their faith on Jesus Christ for salvation.

Romans 5:16-17

[16]The gift is not like that which came through the one who sinned; for on the one hand the judgment arose from one transgression resulting in condemnation, but on the other hand the free gift arose from many transgressions resulting in justification. [17]For if by the transgression of the one death reigned through the one, much more those who receive the abundance of grace and of the gift of righteousness will reign in life through the One, Jesus Christ.

Repetition, repetition, repetition

Here we see that Paul repeats this reality that the gift is not like the transgression. The gift of salvation is not an earned or deserved state, it is by grace alone through Christ alone. Notice also that the sin of Adam is the only one that was imputed to the rest of humanity. While that original sin caused everyone who followed after him to be tainted and born sinful this is not to say that every sin of every father falls on every son. Simply the consequence of the sin nature is given and imputed upon all of Adam's race.

On One Hand

Here Paul continues to weigh the difference between Christ and Adam. The nature of the fall (condemnation) versus the nature of the gift of salvation (justification). While one singular sin of Adam landed us where we are now, we find that the salvation of God arose even though we had added countless sins of our own to the equation. As a result of the sin nature that was inherited by every person after Adam, we continued to sin in practice and we are redeemed out of Adam's sin as well as our own.

Those who receive

Death reigned through Adam, Life reigns in Jesus Christ. But here we see the qualifier. The gift is there, and as we saw in the previous verses is powerful enough, and available to all of humanity. It is only appropriated by "those who receive the abundance of grace…" Righteousness is here reinforced as something that is only attained by the grace giving of Jesus Christ. Do you want to be righteous? The only way to do so is to place faith in Christ, for He alone is our righteousness. We have no merit, no strength of our own to stand on. Righteousness is our need, and righteousness is found in Christ alone, through faith alone, by grace alone. And we can constantly rest in His righteousness, His ability, and His gift of salvation and need never try to "confirm" or "establish" this on our own. To do so invalidates what He has done because if we could have a righteousness of our own then Christ died in vain.

"I have been crucified with Christ; and it is no longer I who live, but Christ lives in me; and the life which I now live in the flesh I live by faith in the Son of God, who loved me and gave Himself up for me. I do not nullify the grace of God, for if righteousness comes through the Law, then Christ died needlessly."

Galatians 2:20-21

ROMANS 5:18-21

Repetition

When something is very important it is normal to see it repeated. When traveling by airplane it is not uncommon to hear important information announced over the loudspeaker, posted in signs, reinforced by pictures and then spoken personally to each person in the terminal by a specific individual. The reason for this is that what is being communicated is of the utmost importance for the safety and convenience of every passenger. This is the nature of Paul explaining this concept in this section of Romans. It is vital for the believer to understand the basic truths of our spiritual re-birth in Christ. Without a solid understanding of what happened at the beginning of this spiritual life it becomes increasingly difficult to grow. If we don't understand that initial forgiveness and justification comes exclusively by God's grace through faith alone in Christ alone then we will have an even more difficult time understanding how we are meant to grow in Christ. This is because we are meant to grow in that same grace and by that same power. Misunderstandings in the most basic things leads to terrible misapplications in all of the things that follow.

Romans 5:18-19

18So then as through one transgression there resulted condemnation to all men, even so through one act of righteousness there resulted justification of
life to all men. 19For as through the one man's disobedience the many were made sinners, even so through the obedience of the One the many will be made righteous.

So then…

In these verses the explanation and defense of God's plan to save humanity through the work of Jesus Christ. The special nature of man as a creature who was created at once by God in our great progenitors Adam and Eve is what makes us savable in this way. Because we were born into the human family and share the guilt and destiny of our human father, Adam, God is able to spiritually move us from that family and account us as being spiritually attached to a new family – the family of Christ by identifying us with Christ in His death, burial, resurrection, ascension and seating. Jesus Christ, the eternal son of God, suffered and died upon the cross and every person who accepts this grace gift of salvation by God shares in that death we can now be freely justified. Having been declared righteous by virtue of our new position in Jesus Christ, the Righteous One.

To all men.

All men, Jew and Gentile alike, are born into the identification and destiny of Adam. The salvation that Christ won for humanity is also available for all men. There is no person who is disqualified, or unsavable before God. The last remaining limitation on the salvation which God has offered is the willingness to receive that salvation. Scripture is clear and very voluminous in the statements that God has presented His salvation, but it is the responsibility of man to respond. When a person trusts in Christ they are no longer associated with their personal guilt, nor the guilt of fallen humanity, but they are now associated with the life and righteousness of Jesus Christ.

Romans 5:20-21

20The Law came in so that the transgression would increase; but where sin
increased, grace abounded all the more, 21so that, as sin reigned in death,
even so grace would reign through righteousness to eternal life through
Jesus Christ our Lord.

Making the transition

In concluding the section on the believer's freedom from Sin's penalty in Christ the next section is being prepared. A believer's growth is dependent upon understanding how extreme and amazing this salvation by grace actually is. The Law became a clear tool to help mankind see the nature of God's character and what it was to be in opposition to His perfect righteousness. Having been given this standard mankind saw an increase in sin. Yet God's grace abounds even more. While the believer will yet deal with Sin, and still have to grow in respect to this salvation it is vital to understand that it is impossible to run out of God's grace. As the old hymn tell us:

> *His love has no limit, His grace has no measure,*
> *His power no boundary known unto men,*
> *For out of His infinite riches in Jesus,*

He giveth and giveth and giveth again.
"He Giveth More Grace" by Annie Johnson Flint

Enjoying the Reign
Every human is born into an oppressive relationship with Sin. Sin rules every human like a brutal tyrant. We see this most clearly displayed in those who struggle with besetting sin. The alcoholic who knows that his addiction is destroying his health, his work and his family. Yet he is ruled by that sin and the results are only death in every sense of the word. The person whose anger, jealousy or bitterness keeps them from every having the meaningful relationships for which they so badly yearn. This is the reign from which the believer has been freed. In Christ Jesus the principle of Grace can now be the reigning principle within the life of the believer. This means that the believer is finally able to choose to humbly submit to God and see His life grow in and through us – freedom and life is now available and the tyrannical reign of sin is forever broken. As the next chapter will display the believer can still submit himself to this deposed tyrant – through legalism or through license – but God will ultimately accomplish His promise in the believer and draw us fully into line with all that He has designed for us in Christ Jesus our Lord.

ROMANS 6

ROMANS 6:1-4

The Beginning of the Middle

Romans 6,7 & 8 are possibly the most important chapters in the Bible when it comes to Christian growth and maturity. It is important to notice that Paul does not even begin to talk about growth until the problem of righteousness and salvation is completely settled. Paul ended chapter 5 explaining that the Law finished its purpose in bringing us to Christ and the believer is now completely under the grace of God. Grace is repeatedly placed in opposition to law in Scripture (John 1:17; Romans 5:20; 6:15; Galatians 2:21; 5:4). What we have to realize is that what Paul puts forth here is radical and amazing. Something never seen before in all of human history. It should be shocking and alarming. It should be surprising to us.

Conversely it should NOT be surprising to us that the world doesn't get it. It should not shock us one bit that the world has perverted this message again and again and again, trying to put the believer back under law. Placing the believer back under the curse of the law (2 Corinthians 3:7; Galatians 3:10), usually for their own selfish gain or power. The Book of Romans brings us to the full and complete understanding that salvation can come one way and one way only: Through the work of Christ on the cross, and no righteousness can be accrued or retained in any other way whatever.

Law keeping is no longer to be the driving force of our existence…a life motivated by fear of punishment is no longer the factor that conducts our lives. God has much more in store for us. All by grace, all in Christ.

Romans 6:1

1What shall we say then? Are we to continue in sin so that grace may increase?

Teaching with Questions

Paul then uses the tool of rhetorical questions to make his point. The use of rhetorical questions is an important teaching tool. They are employed here because Paul wants the readers to interact and take seriously the information that is being given. Additionally, he wants them to know that he has already considered their rebuttal to this amazing thing called grace. Here is the comical thing: When sharing the message of salvation by grace alone, through faith alone, in Christ alone you will still be answering this question all the time.

The Obvious Question

This would almost be comical, if it weren't so sad. Here we have the flagship book in the Bible on what it means to be saved (Romans along with Galatians) and if you go to any random church and say "You are not under Law, but under grace." You will often have half the church down your throat in no time with the same rebuttal, never from the Bible, always, "So you are saying I can do whatever I want? What would keep me from…" The first thing that must be noticed about this argument is that it is totally worldly and human centered. It isn't about the Bible, the Cross or the Holy Spirit; it is an argument that presupposes that if nobody was looking we would do whatever we could get away with. Of the non-believer this may be true. But the normal Christian life is totally different than the unsaved non-believer.

Shall we continue in sin?

- Sin vs. Sins

There is something to be noted first about the word "sin". Until now, Paul has been chiefly concerned with "sins" (plural) meaning the individual acts of unrighteousness by which a person can be condemned apart from Christ. In chapter 6 we see two changes:

First – The plural (sins) is no longer used and the singular (sin) is employed talking about a thing, or a principle rather than many individual things.

Second - the definite article is used. This is no longer talking about "sins" but "the Sin". The definite article in Greek means specificity. The specific "sin" is what is in view. This use of the word "sin" here is the motivating force in the life of any person that we call "the sin nature". Another term used for this is "the flesh." The "sin nature" is the controlling factor before we were in Christ, and it is the only basis for operation that the unbeliever has.

– The issue of sanity

Paul is going to make repeated appeals to this issue of sanity? What have seen to be the natural consequences of sin in the world? The last 5 chapters of Romans have been hammering away the reality that sin and sinning brings nothing but hatred, sadness, death, loss, hopelessness, weakness, separation from others, separation from God, and pain. Forgiven or not the question is: why is this question even being asked? Would you want to continue to live your life at the behest of this master who wants nothing but your own pain and destruction? The person who does so could only be called one thing: *insane.*

Grace may increase

The reasoning behind this false argument is "that grace may abound". Will grace abound? Yes, we know that grace increases all the more whenever sin is present (Romans 5:20). Notice here, that Paul is not taking anything back. He does not retreat one single inch from his position that God's grace increases over all of our sins. There is not a question, but is that any reason to sin more?

Romans 6:2-3

[2]May it never be! How shall we who died to sin still live in it? [3]Or do you not know that all of us who have been baptized into Christ Jesus have been baptized into His death?

Never! Never! NEVER!

This is one of the strongest ways, in Greek, that Paul could forbid something. This could be brought across as: "Don't even conceive of the thought!" or "Don't even think about thinking about it!" It is very extreme and very serious. Paul is saying, "you've got it all wrong!" Paul will come back to this phrase again when exposing erroneous thinking surrounding the gospel, and in so doing he will expose many of the heresies that are STILL GOING ON TODAY. We find that the Devil, the flesh and the world don't stop playing the same old strategies just because they are addressed in the Bible. In a way, that is the safest place for the answer to be, as people who are looking to get away with something, or flee from God's Spirit will rarely care to check His word.

Logic!

C.S. Lewis's *Lion, Witch and the Wardrobe* features a funny old Professor who bemoans the children's lack of critical thinking skills by complaining that Logic is no longer taught in schools. While this is true (and it shows in our society) it is important to note something here. Paul COULD HAVE said, "NO! That's just wrong and that's that!" This would be a dogmatic assertion based on his position and authority as an apostle. That is not what he does. Instead Paul reasons with the reader. The significance? This is not just good doctrine…it is REASONABLE doctrine. The reality is that this is something that isn't just coming from the throne of God, but it also proves out as right and sensible.

Died to

Here we see our continued topic of "death" in the Bible. The issue of the proper biblical definition of the word "death." We see that, biblically, death always involves a separation. Physical death is the separation of the soul and spirit from the body. Spiritual death is separation from God (Gen. 3; John 17:3). Reproductive death is the separation from reproductive ability, functional death in the life of the believer is lack of fellowship with God. Here is the important fact: Death NEVER means annihilation or inability to respond. The unbeliever is dead to God (Ephesians 3:1-3) it does not mean that he cannot respond to God and must therefore receive some pre-grace to respond, it only means that he is separated from God. To define spiritual "death" as "out on a slab, cold, unable to respond" not only makes no sense given the rest of the information about salvation, it also is monstrously bad exegesis to change the word meaning to match your theological presupposition.

What did you die to?
The question is, if we have died to that slave-master Sin, why would we continue to live in obedience to it? What logical reason can we come up with? It is insane to imagine the separation we have from the sin nature and then think that we would ever want to go back under it? The question, of course, exposes the ridiculousness of the assertion that we may want to do go back and be evil "if we knew we could get away with it."

Do you not know?
The issue of knowing is a big issue in the Bible. There are those who can say that we cannot know, or that knowing what the Bible says is secondary or less important than whatever their pet doctrine is about. However, the reality is that, having spoken, God expects us to know and apply the information in His word. This is what He wants: that we would know what the Bible says, and continually believe it (faith, believe, trust). As we will see here, the knowing IS the answer to how we are meant to grow. It is not out of fear of punishment but because we know what we are, what He has made us to be. Consider the following distinction:

The Law -> "What you do is what you are" -> You sin, therefore your are a sinner

Grace -> "What you are dictates what you do" -> You are a saint, who sometimes sins

The point is that God's plan for us in Christ is to make us new creatures, not just polish up the old creature. What He wants us to be is those who freely conform to His will in everything we do. Every thought, every word, every action flowing from the life of Christ within us. This is who we are, when we act otherwise it is because we are not acting like what God declared us to be.

Baptized
The concept of baptism occurs throughout the Bible. Every time baptism is mentioned in Scripture the meaning is identification. There are wet and dry baptisms throughout the Bible, but the imagery is identification. Those who were baptized with John the Baptist's baptism were identified with his movement and identified themselves to follow the coming Messiah. The word "baptism" is a word that carried a great deal of cultural power. It was

used of a sword being tempered. It would first be super-heated and then plunged into cold water, thus hardening the metal and making it useful for battle. This word was also used in dying cloth. White cloth was *baptized* into the red or purple dye and was permanently and irreversibly changed from that point forward.

Birth Order

So here we find the first true step in the biblical order of your birth. You believed and you were Baptized into Christ's death. You died with Him, and your history before you were saved was forever replaced with the history of Christ. At that point you were forever separated from your sin nature. However, your sin nature still lives within you, it was not annihilated it was simply taken out of the driver's seat. Just as you used to be dead, separated from God, though not unable to respond to Him, now you are separated from your sin nature, though you are still able to respond to it.

What's Real

We live in a world that gets confused between the real and the imaginary. The point of this passage is this: This separation, this identification with Christ in His death, was real. We are familiar with tragic situations where people are unable to distinguish reality from fantasy. A person who believes he is Napoleon spends his days in a mental ward wondering why the hordes of France don't flock to his call. This is what we look like when we live in subjection to our sin nature. We are acting like something we are not and operating under the delusion that our sin nature is still our operating nature, but in reality we have died to that and are identified with Christ in His righteousness. So, just as with the first phase of salvation, the issue is not about obeying some rules, it is about believing what God has said over and above our experience.

Romans 6:4

Therefore we have been buried with Him through baptism into death, so that as Christ was raised from the dead through the glory of the Father, so we too might walk in newness of life.

Next step in the Birth order

After dying with Him on the cross we were buried with Him. As Christ was buried physically so we were spiritually. Though we do not remember this experience it is the actual spiritual reality that we are called to live in. The physical death of Christ was confirmed by His three days in the grave. There is no doubt that He physically died, and thus, our separation from Sin, punishment and wrath are permanent and complete.

Raised from the Dead

However, praise the Lord, Christ did not remain in the grave, and neither do we. Our old life done away with we are now raised from the dead with Him. This is exactly what Paul was writing about when he penned Ephesians 1:18-21:

18I pray that the eyes of your heart may be enlightened, so that you will
know what is the hope of His calling, what are the riches of the glory of His
inheritance in the saints, 19and what is the surpassing greatness of His
power toward us who believe. These are in accordance with the working of
the strength of His might 20which He brought about in Christ, when He
raised Him from the dead and seated Him at His right hand in the heavenly
places, 21far above all rule and authority and power and dominion, and
every name that is named, not only in this age but also in the one to come.

He raised us from the dead and ascended us with Jesus and seated us at the right hand of the Father. This is the true "birth order" of the believer that the Bible declares to us.

Walk in newness of life

The word "walk" is another word that had great 1st century meaning. Most people got everywhere by walking. When Paul talks about our walk, he means every aspect of our life, from waking up, to shopping, to school or work, this is what the Christian life is about. We are walking in the life that He won for us. While we rest in what He has done, He lives His life out in us every day, day in and day out here on earth. "Newness" here is not new in chronology, but new in kind. So it is not like "I bought a new car" though I really just mean it is new to me, as I just bought it. It is a whole new manner and type of existence, wholly unseen by the world. Your new life is the life of Christ, as you rest in Him you will be pleasing to the Father. You will do the KINDS of things that please Him, because He is doing them IN you! This exchanged life is the Bible's prescription for our sanctification. It's not just: "Keep trying." It is "Stop trying and trust."

Like anything, doing something successfully means doing it right. Trying harder doesn't mean a thing if you are trying to do something the wrong way. For instance it doesn't matter how hard I TRY my car won't go unless I put the key in. I can say, "But I tried and I tried! I worked the pedals, change the oil, I didn't grind the gears!" Until we walk the way we are meant to we will meet only failure, frustration and defeat.

ROMANS 6:5-6

Romans 6:5-6 (NASB)
[5]For if we have become united with Him in the likeness of His death, certainly we shall also be in the likeness of His resurrection, [6]knowing this, that our old self was crucified with Him, in order that our body of sin might be done away with, so that we would no longer be slaves to sin;

Identity Theft

There is a great deal of information being put out regarding "identity theft." This is when somebody steals another person's financial identity through a credit card or a social security number and then steals massive amounts of money from them. When we look at the case of the believer we see that we have a new identity in Christ. Our old identity is gone forever. However, there is a tragic case of "identity theft" that can still occur. Through misinformation, or a lack of faith in God's word a believer can be convinced that his identity in Christ is not his actual identity. This is the chief aim of the sin nature in the life of the believer. Trying to convince the believer that what God's word says is true of him is not true. The only logical way to strike back is exactly what Paul describes: *knowing* the truth of the word of God and *believing* it. That is what these verses are about…knowing who the believer really is in Christ Jesus all by God's grace…all through faith.

An Origins Issue

The first thing to notice is that Paul uses an important word as the subject of his sentence: WE. This is something that Paul shares with the believers at Rome, and every other believer in this age who places their faith in Jesus Christ. This word is related to the word for "birth" and talks to the origins of a thing. This "becoming" is in the perfect tense. That is, it is something that has been done in the past and has ongoing effects into the present time. A human birth is a great example of this concept. A child is born and that completed past fact is the beginning of their life outside of the womb. This is the way that Paul is talking about what is true of the believer in Jesus Christ.

United

This is one of the key words that shows us our identification with Christ. When two things are united they were separate at one point and then were brought together. Here we are said to have been united with Christ as a past completed fact. But how and when we were united with Him becomes the great issue. The first place that believers were united with Him was in His death. This is something that we don't have a physical recollection of. It was done for us, as a spiritual reality, by God at the moment we placed our faith in Jesus Christ. Because God is outside of time completely He is able to account certain events as happening together. This is what has happened to the believer. When a person places their faith in Christ God takes that person and unites them to the death of His Son Jesus Christ on the Cross. It is because this person is united with Christ in His death that the saint also is united with Christ in His resurrection life. This is the spiritual life that courses through the immaterial portion of the believer.

Resurrection Life!

This resurrection life is the day to day operating life source of the believer. However, there is also a future reality in store for every believer. As we look forward to our final state we find that we will be given a new body, which is like the Resurrection Body of Jesus Christ. Paul writes to the Corinthians:

[42]*So also is the resurrection of the dead. It is sown a perishable body, it is raised an imperishable body;* [43]*it is sown in dishonor, it is raised in glory; it is sown in weakness, it is raised in power;* [44]*it is sown a natural body, it is raised a spiritual body. If there is a natural body, there is also a spiritual body.* 1 Corinthians 15:42-44

John writes about the same reality when He tells us:

[1]*See how great a love the Father has bestowed on us, that we would be called children of God; and such we are. For this reason the world does not know us, because it did not know Him.* [2]*Beloved, now we are children of God, and it has not appeared as yet what we will be. We know that when He appears, we will be like Him, because we will see Him just as He is.* 1 John 3:1-2

For Paul the two realities were inseparable. Our unity with Christ in His crucifixion and resurrection are the source of the believers day to day operating source of control, and it also looks forward to the ultimate fact that we will be glorified with Him, in a body that is like unto His. These two realities could not exist apart from one another.

Knowing

Again, Paul pulls out this very important word: to know. We may well say: "You have to KNOW to GROW." What we know, and believe (trust in) affects the choices that we will make. Often people struggle with controlling their weight. They KNOW what they have to do, but they don't act in accordance with what they know. The knowledge that Paul is talking about is not just intellectual knowledge, but activated, trusted knowledge. For Paul every believer must KNOW the facts in order to act in accordance with that knowledge of the truth of God's word.

What we are to be "knowing"

Every believer is to "know", that is to say, be fully assured of the fact that our "Old Man" (all of who we were in Adam) was crucified with Christ on the cross. It is important to realize that our old self (KJV: "old man") is not the same as our "old nature" or our "sin nature". While the old man (all of who we were "in Adam") was crucified with Christ at the cross our sin nature was merely de-throned there. While the believer can never go back to being "in Adam" or be harassed by our "old man" we can be plagued by obedience to our Sin Nature, which continues on in the believer.

Crucified

This is important: Our entire body of sin was done away with at the Cross. This is going to be a large part of the reasoning for the joyous declaration of Romans 8:1. The sins of the believer (past, present and future) were paid for at the cross. If this is difficult to understand we must remember that in regard to the cross ALL of our sins were yet future. This is the reason that God can now deal with the believer's sins on the basis of legality (the Justification described in Romans 5:1 is complete – the believer is eternally declared righteous). The believer's sins are now a family matter, affecting fellowship not relationship. Therefore 1 John 1:9 becomes the operating basis for the believer's restoration to fellowship when he walks in accordance with his sin nature.

When?

It is important to realize that there is a timing text here. The believer's "old self" (KJV: old man) is crucified *WITH* Christ. To understand this we must look at some examples:

"I went to the zoo with my wife and children."

"Bob was at the concert with Judy."

"Charles ate with Mike last night."

In each of these cases the meaning would be horrible skewed if there were any separation in time or space. One couldn't say that they went to the zoo *with* their wife and children if they went to the zoo on one day, and their wife and kids the next day. It would be equally silly to say that Charles ate *with* Mike if they ate in different places (though at the same time). The point? The believer is said to be crucified *with* Christ. If a person has placed their faith in Jesus Christ then they were unquestionably THERE when Jesus Christ was crucified. They also, were (as a spiritual reality) on that cross with Jesus Christ. Every believer is to view their co-crucifixion with Christ as an accomplished fact.

No Longer a Slave

"Sin" here has the definite article in front of it. It is not just "sin" but rather "*the* sin" or, if it is clearer, the sin principle (or sin nature) within the believer. Before a person comes to know Jesus Christ the sin nature (aka "the flesh") is the only life source that the person has. An unbeliever may do any variety of things, and some of them may even look like "good works" but since they are rooted in the sin nature they are only "filthy rags" before God. Before a someone comes to know Jesus they are in slavery to the sin nature. There is no other choice than to obey the "slave master." The final choice that a person makes, from this perspective, is to trust in Christ. At that point a person is crucified with Christ and no longer a slave to their sin nature. They are FREE! Believers are free forever from the destructive tyrant of the sin nature. As we will see, that sin nature has not been obliterated, or removed from the life of the believer. However, the believer is no longer obligated to obey the sin nature, and operate under its dictates. The believer can now abide in the Spirit and is free to rest in Christ's resurrection life.

ROMANS 6:7-9

Haven't we already looked at this?

You will have noticed that verses five and six have been included. This is not because we are going to go over them again, but rather because they are necessary to understand the logical conclusion that comes in verse seven. That having been said, verses five and six are amazing verses to consider. Paul is telling each and every believer that they have died with Christ, and will share in the likeness of His resurrection. The knowledge of this accomplished fact is the operating basis for the life of believer. We need to be abundantly clear in realizing that we don't ever NEED to walk in sin again. As we have seen the continuing presence of the sin nature can fairly well ensure that we will walk in sin (anytime our eyes are taken off of Christ), but we are no longer under any obligation to sin. The cross is not just freedom from sin's penalty, the only power to live in freedom from that old master of sin also comes at the cross as well.

It furthermore comes in the same way. We had to believe (trust) in the power of the cross for our salvation. For our continuing sanctification there is only one path – continuing to believe that our identification with Him frees us from the power of our old sin nature. We find that the major operating force in the life of the follower of Jesus is FAITH. Not discipline, not hard work, not programs, not rituals, not traditions, nothing but knowing what God's word says is true and believing it. This is the path to growth in Christ prescribed by the Bible, anything else will only have us treading water.

Romans 6:7

for he who has died is freed from sin.

Has died

It is important to realize the tense of this verb. This is about something that has occurred in the past tense. It doesn't say, "he who is in the process of dying…" but rather: "He who HAS DIED". This past tense completed action occurred (as the previous verses showed us) when we were identified with Christ at the cross. It is important to note that there are five steps in our salvation which we have already seen in part. To quote Newell:

There are five parts to our salvation:

> 1. Christ's propitiatory work toward God through His blood: bearing the guilt and condemnation of our sins.
>
> 2. Christ's identification with us as connected with Adam, "becoming sin for us," releasing us from Adam, our federal head: "our old man" being crucified with Christ.
>
> 3. The Holy Spirit's whole work in us, as "the Spirit of grace," involving conviction, regeneration, baptism into Christ's Body; being in us as a "law of life" against indwelling sin, the Witness of our sonship; our Helper, Intercessor, and, finally, the mighty Agent in the Rapture.
>
> 4. Christ's present work in Heaven; leading our worship and praise as our Great High Priest; and protecting us should we sin, as our Advocate with the Father (as against our accuser).
>
> 5. Christ's second coming to redeem our bodies, and receive us to Himself in glory: The Rapture.[5]

What we are studying here is the second point. This is an established fact for every single person who has put their faith in Jesus Christ. This is the basis upon which we move forward. We are not "crucifying ourselves" or "dying daily" by any stretch of the imagination. True growth will come when we realize what we *already are* based on what Christ has *already done.*

Freed from Sin

"Sin" here, again, is "the sin" or "the sin nature" as opposed to the individual sins being in view. This controlling principle, whom we will see is a hateful slave master, is our master no longer. We have been set free

---

[5] Newell, William R. Romans: Verse-by-Verse. http://www.ccel.org/ccel/newell/romans.html, p. 140.

forever. Notice again the tense in which Paul is writing. Not "will eventually be freed" but this is, again, past tense. You are already free from sin! You are no longer the slave of sin, based on the supernatural reality of what Jesus Christ did on the Cross. So why do I still sin? The Devil, the Sin Nature, and the World are all working in perfect concord to try and convince you that this isn't so. Everything is working together to convince you that you do need to continue to live subject to the sin nature, either in a way that is legalism (external rule keeping of any kind) or a way that is licentious (lying, cheating, sexual sin, etc.).

Romans 6:8

Now if we have died with Christ, we believe that we shall also live with Him

"if-fy" topic

Here we have an interesting word. In English the word "if" most always insinuates probability ("maybe you will, maybe you won't"). However, the Greek construction surrounding the word "if" can mean one of three different things. Either that the statement is being assumed true, that is assumed false, or that it may be either way. This case is the first type. Paul is not suggesting that we may or may not have died with Christ; this much is assumed to be true. So the very reality of the grammar in this sentence is that what has already been said ("you were baptized into his death") is being enforced in this statement. Because of this grammatical construction some translate "Now since you have died with Christ…"

A Word on "with"

Here our death is again described as being "with Christ". This is interesting. If I were to tell you: "I went to the store with my wife." You wouldn't assume that I went to the store and then she went to the store five hours later. If that were the case my statement would be a lie. Here Paul tells believers that we died *with* Christ. How can this be so? We carry no recollection of that event, how can we be said to have been crucified "with Him" when we were still many years from even being born? This is the power of our God who is totally outside of time. When we put our faith in Christ, He includes us in the death of Christ which occurred 2000 years ago outside of the city of Jerusalem. So what we see, is while there was only one person on the cross, Golgotha was spiritually a very crowded place. Scripture encourages us to see Christ's death very much as our own. The spiritual reality always supersedes the physical reality in truth and importance. Our death with Christ is no less spiritually real, than His death was physically real.

We believe

The world abuses the concept of "faith" regularly. It is often times presented in the form of a false dichotomy. "Faith" is held in contrast to "facts". Nothing could be further from actual states of affairs. We find that in order to "know" anything requires faith. What we believe will happen when we turn a light switch, or what we believe happened 300 years ago in Europe, what we believe to be a scientific "law" now and whether we believe there is a God who can supersede those observed phenomena, or not, must all be taken on faith. So when Paul says, "We believe we will also live with Him" He is not using the word "believe" as a weaker form of the verb "to know" he is using it as a knowledge that is apprehended by faith and is every bit as valid and trustworthy as anything known by any other human means or method for establishing truth.

We shall live with Him

There is a difficulty of translation here. The English rendering of the Greek here gives the impression that Paul may be looking at our fellowship with Christ, either on this earth, or in the hereafter. While fellowship with Christ is a very important topic, this is another case where there is a slight difference in the Greek language than in the translation tradition. The picture that is painted by the context is far more about instrumentality. In other words, the "living" here isn't just "with" Him, but rather, "by means of Him." This verse is actually saying that, having been crucified with Christ, we live our lives by means of Him and will do so on into eternity future. Wuest translates this passage: "…we shall also live *by means of* Him".

<u>Romans 6:9</u>

Knowing that Christ, having been raised from the dead, is never to die again; death no longer is master over Him.

Knowing…again

Notice that word "knowing" comes up again. The focus of this word is on knowledge that comes by perception. There were indeed several eye witnesses to the resurrected Christ, of whom Paul was one. The fact of Christ's resurrection was not a fact ever questioned by the early church. Those who wrote the New Testament had seen it with their very own eyes. This word knowing, is the counterpart of "believing" in the previous verse. Here we see again, the reality that the Biblical authors did not mean faith was a weaker form of knowing, but rather a trust in what is clearly known and why.

Raised from death

Christ defeated death once and for all. We share in His life, right now. That is a life that will never again be separated from the eternal God who created us. We see that the life within us is no longer subject to death. There is no opportunity for separation from God. Surely we may be out of fellowship, but the reality is that the only reason death ever had any power over Christ was because He had taken on our sin. Having done so, death (eternal separation from God) is no longer available to those who believe.

No longer master

The true fear that physical death holds is in the reality that it means eternal separation from God. However, having conquered death, all that physical death is to the believer is a gateway into the new phase in our union with the Lord. We have nothing to fear in physical death as we know exactly what waits for us on the other side. We know that He has saved us completely, and we know that since it is fully impossible that Jesus Christ would spend eternity apart from the Father, the same is true of all who have placed their faith in Him for salvation.

Just keep believing

Hopefully, the conclusion is clear. We were saved (justified) by placing our faith in Christ. We are being saved (sanctified) by our continued belief in that same fact. We see the power of the cross is the tool that God meant to use in every aspect of our salvation. Many believers waste years and years of their time trying to "perfect themselves" or eliminate sins one bad behavior at a time. Usually this legalism drives the believer into despair as years go by and no progress seems to have been made. In the most frightful and sad cases the person is able to convince themselves that they have succeeded, leading to a life of cold, hard self-deception and hatred of all of the rest of humanity who they perceive as being "far below them." Salvation, in all three phases, is always: by grace alone, through faith alone, in Christ alone.

ROMANS 6:10-11

Included…positioned…identified

Romans chapter 6 is one of the most important chapters in the Bible for the understanding of our identification with Christ, as we have seen. It is crystal clear in Romans 6-8 that our life is in Christ. Every moment of every day is about looking to Jesus, trusting in Him, beholding Him. Jesus didn't just offer "fire insurance" or a "get out of hell free" card. Our faith in, and reliance upon Him is a part of every single aspect of our salvation and day to day life. Scripture repeatedly displays for us the reality that we are to rest in what He has done, and He is to live His life out within us.

Romans 6:10

For the death that He died, He died to sin once for all; but the life that He lives, He lives to God.

The Death He died

Unlike many world religions, our faith in Jesus is rooted in reality. The fact that God has been interacting and involved with human history is vital. If the accounts that are recorded in the Bible are false, then we are to be pitied above all other people. Christianity is rooted in History, and this fact is no more clearly portrayed then at the cross. If Jesus Christ did not die for us, then our entire faith is fully in vain. The nice thoughts, and pretty poems mean nothing if Jesus wasn't actually God in the flesh and if He didn't actually die for our sins.

This historical fact of Christ's claims and death on the cross are beyond question. Besides the New Testament documents (which are substantial) we have the works of Josephus and other ancient historians who confirmed Christ's death and that His disciples believed He had risen again. While the unbelieving world readily denies the resurrection no serious attempt can be made to deny the crucifixion of Christ.

So what?

The question may be asked: Why is the death of Christ so important? We learn here in this chapter that the death of Christ is not merely symbolical, nor is it mythological. The death of Christ on the cross actually occurred and had real consequences for everyone who is in Him. It is important to notice that Paul is emphatically and repeatedly describing Christ's death for the chief and shining purpose of letting believers know that they share this history. When we were placed in Christ at His crucifixion everything that was true of Christ became true of us! When Jesus died, I died. When Jesus died, every believer died with Him. The effects for Him are also the effects for us. What were the effects of Jesus' death on the Cross?

Died to Sin

Jesus was forever separated from the power of sin. The funny thing is that we know that Jesus had no sin nature. There was no sin within Him. He became a curse for us (Gal. 3:13). And died, forever separating us from the power of Sin. The death of Christ to sin is said to have happened "once for all". This is a very special Greek word *hapax* it means something that is once given and perpetually valid. The death that Christ died to sin is not something the He needs to repeat again and again, and thus it is not something the believer needs to repeat again and again. This is something that is clearly shown to be done once and finished. Christ did it once, and He doesn't ever need to repeat it. Thus if we attempt to repeat what Christ has already done, or pray for something that He has already given us we will be continually frustrated.

But the Life…

However, death to sin isn't all that occurred in us at the Cross. It gets better. Christ isn't just the freedom that we needed from sin, but rather the source of our very life! This is the positive side of the coin, and it is very positive indeed! In Christ we are now raised into His life. His life that will never end, eternal connection and relationship to God. We are now able, capable of, having unbroken fellowship with the Father! This is fantastic news! Before the cross we were only able to live by our own means and devices, and now you share HIS life, now HE is the motivator for everything. This is why the believer is not going to continue in Sin, because we live by the life of Jesus within us, and He doesn't sin. So why do we still sin? As we will see, we still have a choice. We can choose to live by our new nature in Jesus Christ or we can choose to live by our old nature (the Sin – or the Sin Nature).

<u>Romans 6:11</u>

Even so consider yourselves to be dead to sin, but alive to God in Christ Jesus.

Even so…

Resting on the reality of the life of Christ and our newfound connection and relationship to God we are to have a choice to make. There are countless books, and methods created every year for dealing with sin in the life of the believer. 12 step programs, video courses and Christian councilors giving new and novel methods to deal with sin in the life of the believer, but this is what the Bible has to say about it. Here it is:

Consider – Reckon – Count it as true

How are we going to have freedom from the sin nature, even though it continues to dwell within us? How are we going to experience victory from that horrible old slave master that only brought death, pain and destruction? The message of this passage is clear:

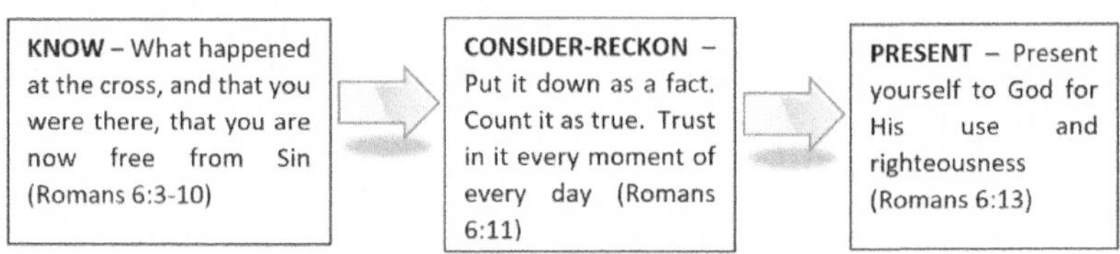

The word translated "consider" here is an accounting term. It means to record something in the books as a fact, an actuality. Paul is essentially saying, "This is true – you have already been given freedom from Sin – trust in it."

Imagine a person jumping out of an airplane. He has a parachute strapped to his back and is jumping with a friend. The friend screams, "Pull your rip cord! Release your chute!" to which the first person says, "I don't trust my parachute!" He then begins furiously flapping his arms like wings, and consequently plummets to his death. This is exactly what Christians do when we try to do battle with sin on our own power or might. We ignore what Christ has already done for us and then wind up as a messy spot on the spiritual pavement.

Not this…but THAT

As we see in Paul's pattern here, we haven't just been getting the negative, but the positive as well. To be dead to God (separated from God) was to be alive to sin (united to sin), but here we see to be dead to sin, is to be alive to God. We are to continue to live trusting in the reality that we are alive to God. The sin nature has no power over us. There is no hopeless moment of doomed despondency. The penalty and sting of sin have been forever dealt with at the cross. The reality of what happened doesn't just separate us from the power of sin, but unites us to the life of God. Faith in Jesus Christ is not just about being saved from the negative, it is mostly about the immense positives of knowing God and living in a vital and active relationship with Him!

But where?

This verse closes with one of the most powerful phrases of Scripture. That phrase is: "in Christ." This is a positional statement that we have already seen outlined. The believer has been identified with Him in His death, burial, resurrection, ascension and seating at the right hand of the Father. All of our life is found, and to be lived, In CHRIST. We are to be constantly trusting Him with every moment, with every trial, with every difficulty, with every relationship. While we live our lives at rest in Him in the heavenly places, He is living our lives out for us here on earth. It is His life, His love, His joy, His peace. We realize that if we try to fake these things, or try to create these outcomes on our own we continually fail, it is in HIM that we have eternal life, it is IN HIM we have victory over sin. It is His life within us that can change our lives and the lives of those around us, and it is our greatest delusion that we thought we could "fake it."

It is worth noting that for as frequently as this all important phrase "in Christ" is applied to the believer, the idea of being "out of Christ" is never once presented in scripture. There is never anyone who is "un-baptized" or "un-seated". Everything that Scripture tells us is that once we put our faith in Jesus Christ a permanent change has occurred that cannot be ruined, destroyed or eliminated.

Conclusion

Just as your justification was by faith in what Jesus has done and is yet powerful to do, so your sanctification will be handled by the very same means – faith in the God who loves you, and has set you apart for His own purpose!

ROMANS 6:12-14

The Power Principle
As we have observed throughout our study of this important chapter, the focus of our life is not to be on the individual sins that we are struggling with. Those are like status updates on what nature we are abiding in. Just as a person with a cold may cough, but the cough isn't what is wrong with them, the cough is a symptom of what is wrong. Treating the cough with a spray or some other medicine may feel good and provide some satisfaction; however, these things don't treat the real problem. This theme and idea persists and repeats itself throughout this passage and throughout the Bible. The pertinent question remains: "Where are you looking, at yourself or at the Lord Jesus Christ?"

Romans 6:12
12Therefore do not let sin reign in your mortal body so that you obey its lusts,

Therefore
What is the "therefore" pointing back to? Clearly it is pointing back to the issues addressed in Romans 6:1-11 which we notice is still answering that all important question, "Are we to continue in sin so that grace may abound?" Paul immediately recoiled at the very idea, but there is more to this story. Paul explains that it isn't just "because Paul says so." There is a perfectly good reason why believers should not continue in sin…that reason? It doesn't make any sense for the believer to continue in sin! It is like a duck driving a car, it isn't safe and it just doesn't make any sense!

Don't let it be your ruler!
This is in the imperative. It is a command. Paul is not mincing words. This word is related to the word for king and kingdom in the Greek. The idea is "do not let the Sin nature be your ruler!" Just as a king demands absolute submission, the sin nature gets our absolute submission when we walk in the flesh. The symptoms of individual sins are the outcome of

letting the Sin nature rule our outlook, our thoughts, our words and our actions. The place of this occurrence is in our mortal flesh. Domain that our sin nature controls is this body and all that it does. The eyes, ears, hands, feet, nose and mouth. When we are abiding in the sin nature the sin nature controls all of these things, and even if they "look good" on the outside, before God they are only sin.

Forward or backward

There is a note to be made about the order here. It is not "don't obey the lusts in your mortal body and you will not be reigned by the Sin nature" it is the opposite. Once again, attempting to control our sin nature by the symptoms is never going to get further than skin deep. Sure we may do more good things, and fewer bad things, by our estimation. But God is after the good that He wants to create in us.

Obey what you want…

So our sins don't matter? Far from it! It is not a question of what our sins mean. Anytime we find ourselves walking in sin we must confess (agree with God that our actions are sinful) as 1 John 1:9 tells us and receive His forgiveness, which occurred at the cross. However, the question is what you are going to do. If a person is coughing wildly and puts a new band-aid on every time they cough will that ever help them get better? Clearly not! Trying to treat a sin, or sin pattern, by the attempt to use discipline or "grit" always ends up with loss and despair. Realizing that you have a sin nature, which is never going to truly change, will bring us to a better place. Confessing that we have been walking in the sin nature and fixing our eyes on Jesus is what will help.

Romans 6:13

And do not go on presenting the members of your body to sin as instruments of unrighteousness; but present yourselves to God as those alive from the dead, and your members as instruments of righteousness to God.

Presently Actively

Here we see the command not to present your members is in the present tense. The idea is that this is a day by day moment by moment possibility.

The reality is that until a person puts their faith in Jesus they could only ever present their members to the sin nature. They could only produce what is, in God's eyes, unrighteousness. Even if what they are doing is most admirable. The very fact that it is connected to the motivation and source of the sin nature makes it unacceptable to God to be called righteous and must therefore be "unrighteous". So this command to stop presenting our bodies to the control of the sin nature is a new prerogative of the Christian. This is a choice that we could never make before we became a believer in Jesus Christ. This is something to keep in mind when we see non-believers going deeper and deeper into sin (whether that sin is self-righteous legalism, or lascivious activity), or when they are not willing to put their faith in Jesus Christ. You must be fully clear on the reality that the idea of another operating system outside of the sin nature is too foreign to imagine for them. Almost like a deep water fish could perhaps conceive of the concept of what it means to be "dry" but only as a distant exercise of imagination.

The Precious "Presenting"

Here we have the idea of offering something, our resources, in service to something else. When a soldier gets into a new town he reports to his commanding officer and says something to the effect of "Private John Doe, reporting for duty" and the commanding officer then gives him his orders, and the soldier obeys. This is exactly what we do on a moment by moment basis. We looked last week at the process of abiding in Christ as Romans 6 presents:

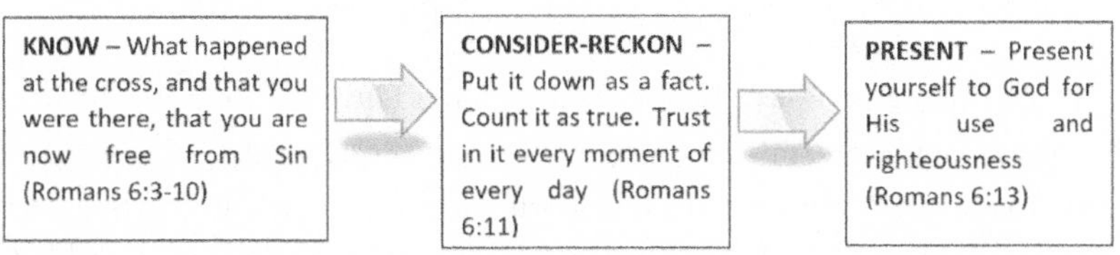

So the first step is knowing what occurred when we put our faith in Jesus Christ. How we were identified with Him fully in His death burial and resurrection (ascension and seating also, though those are not mentioned here). The second step is to put it down as truth. To rely on that fact as a trustworthy statement of reality and realize we are no longer under any relational obligation to the sin nature. It is a deposed dictator and no longer needs any loss. Finally, we stop presenting ourselves to the old dictator for service.

The members of our body (our limbs, our mouths, our minds, our eyes, etc.) are no longer to be in the service of the sin nature. You see, Paul gives the reason for the believer to sin no longer and it is not a law based on fear of punishment but because it is illogical for us. It is silly, crazy, and insane for the believer to live in sin. How many insane believers are there out there today simply because they don't understand the message of Romans 6-8?

Not *this* but *that*

As Paul's pattern has been thus far, he tells them how not to live, and then offers the correction. So we are not to be pawns for the sin nature to the end of unrighteousness, but rather, day by day, moment by moment, be presenting ourselves to the God of the universe. This is an every moment attitude or choice. It is a function of the will by which the believer is now able to be in constant contact and fellowship with the God of the universe. And then we get some exciting news!

Righteousness, REAL Righteousness!

The believer is now able to do something that he or she was never able to do before. When the believer, understanding his co-crucifixion with Christ, and consequent death to the sin nature, believes in His new life in Christ, and presents himself to God He is able to produce real righteousness. The believer is at last able to perform good works that God rewards. This is what Paul was talking about when he penned Ephesians 2:8-10:

> 8For by grace you have been saved through faith; and that not of yourselves, it is the gift of God; 9not as a result of works, so that no one may boast. 10For we are His workmanship, created in Christ Jesus for good works, which God prepared beforehand so that we would walk in them.

Once we understand what has been done, entirely by God's grace, and appropriate it through faith we are able to live out the life of Christ within us. These "good works which God prepared beforehand that we would walk in them" are not like bowling pins set up throughout our day, but is rather the life and character of Christ lived out in us, every single moment of every single day. The believer is, of course, still able to produce works which to the world seem "good" but are totally motivated by the flesh, and those works God cannot reward. He can only reward, and accept the good works that occur as we rest in Him, that come from Him as the source.

Romans 6:14

For sin shall not be master over you, for you are not under law but under grace.

Sin shall not be your master

This is in the future tense. Going forward sin is not to be your master anymore. This word "to master" is related to the word that is often translated "Lord" in the New Testament. This word was used for a slave master. The sin nature is no longer to be the abiding principle, or the controlling force, by which we live our lives. Then Paul says something that much of the Christian world rejects outright.

Back to basics

Paul started chapter 6 anticipating the exasperated legalists question, "If people aren't ruled by law they will do whatever they want and sin all the time!" However, we see why sin shall not be our master is because we are no longer under the law. The law of Moses was a whole life system. It dictated what a person was to do in nearly every situation. How much they were to give, and what times they were supposed to celebrate, what situations that they needed to offer sacrifices, and how to "atone" for those sins through the sacrificial system. We are no longer under this system of law as a principle. Something new has come:

You Are Under Grace

The system that believers in Christ are to live under is the system of Grace. Where the Law said, "Do this and you shall live!" Under grace God says, "I have given you life, now how will you choose to live?" The person under law lives under the constant fear of punishment and denial of blessing. The person under Grace is permanently, infinitely blessed in the Heavenly Places in Christ, in whom we are seated (Ephesians 1:3). Under Law a person is continually focused upon themselves, hoping that they are within the boundaries. Under Grace a person is continually focused upon Christ our Savior and looking to Him every single moment.

Conclusion

In the section that follows Paul spells out again how incredibly important the distinction between Law and Grace is. Paul points out repeatedly how this new life and relationship with God through Jesus Christ is so radically different than any superficial changes that can be made under law. The entire next chapter (Romans 7) describes the frustration of the grace saved believer if he attempts to continue to live under law, rather than abide in Christ by faith through Grace. But the repeated point is the same: God has taken away the hindrances of our sins (acts of unrighteousness) by paying for them at the cross. He took care of our sin nature, by identifying us with Christ at the cross, thereby separating us from the demands of the sin nature. He took care of the Law as a medium of relationship to God and replaced it with the very life of Christ lived out in us. Changing what we do, by changing what we are. And that makes all the difference!

ROMANS 6:15-18

I'm a slave…

Paul now continues with the illustration of slavery which he started working with in verse 12 ("do not let sin *reign* [as a slave master] in your mortal body"). However, some comments need to be made about the Roman institution of Slavery. When Americans read about slavery we immediately think of the kind of slavery that existed in America. While there were certain similarities, there are far more differences. The modern view of slavery and human trafficking isn't the same as the ancient view. First of all, slavery in the Roman world was not tied to any race or class. Any person could become a slave. There were slaves of many kinds and having different skills and abilities. In Hebrew, Greek and Roman cultures there were allowances made for someone who wanted to be a slave permanently in a given household to do so.

People became slaves one of a number of ways. One could become a slave by being unable to pay a debt. One could be born into slavery. One could be sold into slavery by his or her father. Many became slaves because they were conquered in battle. We have records of slaves of every level, and slaves were valued based on the skills that they possessed. We even have records of slaves that owned slaves. In many ways the ancient institution of slavery bore some similarities to our modern system of employment.

There were, however, some striking differences. The will of the slave was totally sold out to the will of their master. The law demanded strict obedience and offered very little protection of the preferences and virtues of the slave. Slaves could certainly be freed, and as in the case of the slave who became one due to indebtedness, would often be once they paid their debt. Slavery was a regular part of Roman life, and there was not the same stigma of shame associated with slavery in that culture. Some have estimated as much as 1/3 of the Roman empire was comprised of slaves at the time of the New Testament.

Paul makes clear in verse 19 that he is borrowing this analogy, though it is imperfect. In Christ we are free, truly free. But we find that the believer can never be free of an operating principle. The picture being painted here is the reality that everyone is a slave to whom they choose to obey and freedom is the ability to choose not to follow the tyrannical dictator of the Sin Nature ("*the* Sin" in Romans 6) and choose the New Nature within us, submitting to its desires that bring life and peace and continued growth in the Lord.

Romans 6:15

What then? Shall we sin because we are not under law but under grace? May it never be!

Coming back to the point

Paul spent the last fourteen verses answering the anticipated question: "If all our sins are and will be forgiven should we not just sin all we want?" Paul began by explaining to them that the reason why we would not live in sin is that it makes no sense for us to do so. Having been totally made anew in Christ it is sheer madness for us to continue to live as if we were still trapped helplessly in our own sin. Now he anticipates a different question: "Since we aren't under law anymore, shall we sin all we want?"

The Evil Legalist

Paul told them that their newfound freedom from the sin nature exists because they are not under law but under grace (Romans 6:14). Paul knows that this attachment to a law is deep seated in the heart of man. We want a standard, we want a set of rules, we want boundaries. We want to be able to put our quarter in and know exactly how many gumballs to expect. But this is not the nature of our new life in Christ. Paul is not yet finished explaining this and will spend the bulk of Chapter 7 specifically dealing with the believer who continues to try and live by the law, though he is under grace.

The legalist's argument, however, never changes: Always assuming that leaving the law will result in absolute license and chaos. As Paul will show this is a ready denial of the power and magnitude of what Christ did at the cross. And to think that we would continue to live in Sin only shows a lack of understanding of what happened to each of us the moment we put our faith in Christ and were identified with Him in His death, burial, resurrection, ascension and seating at the right hand of the Father.

Certainly Not!

Paul responds with his characteristic, "Don't even let the idea be conceived of!" or "Don't even think it!" This is an out and out extreme denial of the very idea. Once again, Paul is taking the argument to an entirely new level. We must understand clearly: the Legalist is undervaluing the very power of God and Christ within us. Paul is not just saying "Nuh-UH!" The reasons he gives are so much greater, and open up a new world of freedom and life that the believer could never know apart from Christ. Paul begins another logical argument based on the power of the Christ-life within us.

Romans 6:16

Do you not know that when you present yourselves to someone as slaves for obedience, you are slaves of the one whom you obey, either of sin resulting in death, or of obedience resulting in righteousness?

Do you not know?

Here again we see Paul appealing to their knowledge. He is suggesting that this is something that should be plain. Again this emphasizes the reality that we can and do know what the Lord is doing in each of us by the Scriptures.

Present yourselves

Here, again, is this concept of presenting ourselves. We show up each day presenting ourselves as a soldier presents himself for duty. We make this presentation each moment of each day, either presenting ourselves to God for His Spirit to work in and through us, or presenting ourselves to our Sin Nature (our old master) to continue to consume us. The idea is plain, and the logic is embarrassingly clear: Paul is saying "whoever you obey is your master." Even if our certificate of freedom says that we are no longer obligated to obey to the sin nature. When we do obey it we are, in actuality, the slave of the sin nature. Your freedom means nothing to you if you continue to live like a slave! Why do we do this? There are probably many reasons, but here are some ideas:

1) **Not knowing we are free.** So many believers think that their job in this life is to do their best at trying to stop sinning. They

play by the sin nature's rules and obey it even while trying to avoid it. They show up for work every morning and continue to present themselves because they don't understand the power of what Christ did.

2) **Preferring the comfort of the rules.** This is related to the last. Because they don't understand the primacy of the relationship into which we have been brought by the precious blood of Christ, they continue to try to operate under a legalistic view of God who will reward them if they follow the rules, and punish them if they break them. Whether this takes the expression of legalism or license the end result is the same: Selfishness.

3) **We forget.** We often let the world, the flesh and the devil deceive us into believing that walking in the sin nature, and doing things its way is the only way to get things done effectively.

4) **We lack faith.** We know the truth, we understand it, and we just don't trust it.

Results

There is an interesting reality that needs to be made clear. The difference must be understood between results, or consequences, and punishment. Punishment is the idea of justice as related to the law. The idea is that God punishes sin, in order to appease His justice. Consequences, or results, are quite different. The punishment for sin was paid fully and completely at the cross forevermore. The penalty was paid and that was the imperative need for understanding of Justification (or Phase 1 of Salvation) that we portrayed in Romans 3-5. However, while there is no punishment left for Sin (Jesus paid it all) there are consequences for choosing to walk in sin. What is the consequence, for the believer, of living by the power of the Sin Nature?

Death

As we have seen repeated in Scripture death always means separation. We have seen the reality that once we have put our faith in Jesus Christ we are unchangeably, fully, and completely saved. We have committed ourselves to Jesus Christ and He cannot fail. Romans 5:1-10 repeatedly emphasized the reality that once a person enters into salvation God takes the responsibility to confirm him or her to the end. The death (separation) being discussed here is a loss of fellowship. When we put our faith in Jesus Christ we are said to be born again. We are adopted and placed, irreversibly as adult sons and daughters into the family of God. That relationship is eternal, just as no matter what you do you will always be the child of your father and mother you are now eternally a "child of God." (John 1:12) However, just as with our physical parents, while we can have periods where we do not have fellowship with them. While walking after the sin nature does not sever the relationship with God, the fellowship is temporarily disconnected. Fellowship is restored by the process of confession (agreeing with God that we were walking in sin) as illustrated in 1 John 1:9.

Obedience Resulting in Righteousness

The other option that is available to the believer is simply unavailable to the non-believer and that is that we can now abide in the new nature and produce, by His power and His life, real actual righteousness. The reality is that we can now live by the power of Christ's life within us and everything we do will be reward-able, every action, every word and ever breath will be the work of Christ within us, and thus be the very thing that He wants to see in us. Far from a "to do list" that we can succeed or fail at. This is a joyous reality that should, logically, characterize every moment of the believer's life.

Romans 6:17-18

17But thanks be to God that though you were slaves of sin, you became
obedient from the heart to that form of teaching to which you were
committed, 18and having been freed from sin, you became slaves of
righteousness.

Thanks be to God

Notice that God is the One who stepped in to correct the situation. Gratitude is the great motivator of the Christian life. Not hard work, not discipline, not practice, but gratitude. If we rightfully understand what God has done we will gladly rest and praise Him. If we are acting out of a secure and firm knowledge of what it is to be in Christ then we will display His life and righteousness as naturally as a healthy apple tree grows fruit. The word "thanks" is intimately related in Greek for the word for "grace" or "free gift." Here again we see man bringing his inability and sin to the table, and God bringing the gift of salvation. And what is the only proper response to a gift? Thanksgiving – Gratitude.

You were

In describing our previous position, we were helplessly beholden to our sin nature. We were slaves to sin with no hope of redemption of our own power or work. Salvation came by way of the gift of God.

You became obedient

Our obedience here is outlined first as being "from the heart" (NIV: "wholeheartedly"). The phrase "the heart" is the most comprehensive term for the immaterial part of a human. It includes the mind, the will, the soul, the personality. It is the seat of the desires and the reasoning center of the human being. This obedience was the response to the gospel message in accepting Christ's payment for us, and the agreement that we were not able to save ourselves. This whole-hearted obedience takes as its object the next phrase.

That form of teaching to which you were committed

The word "form" here translates the Greek word *tupos* which is where we get the English word "type". The picture that it conveys is a sort of stamp that would be set on something and then struck to make the same impression every time. This form of teaching to which we were committed is the teaching of salvation by Grace through faith. As we have seen already in Romans 6:1-14, that Grace is not just our "get out of Hell free" card, it is to be our operating principle of existence for all things thereafter. We began in faith in what Christ has done in the cross, we continue in faith in what God did in resurrecting Him from the dead. At the end of all things we will see that everything that was good or worthwhile in our lives was what we allowed Him to do in and through us, and anytime we tried to get in the way we goofed everything up.

A New Relationship

Having placed our faith in Christ we were forever freed from the demands of the sin nature and given a new basis of operating, which is the Holy Spirit within us. We are now given the option, every moment, to rest and abide in the sin nature or our rightful master – Jesus Christ. Each of these choices, as we have seen, has consequences. The consequences of walking with Jesus are life, peace, joy and the other fruit of the Spirit. The consequences of abiding in our sin nature is broken fellowship with God, selfishness, hurting those we care about and lack of growth in Christ. The choice is ours to make each day.

ROMANS 6:19-23

Freedom!

The ideas of freedom and free will are interesting ideas to understand. We may think of freedom as being free will without any limitation, but this isn't precisely correct. We notice that there are many limitations set on our will that we don't usually consider. For instance, if you will to fly around the room you will find that gravity restricts your will from reality. We may will to jump off of a 50 story building and live, but the reality which we occupy will overcome our will without much of a fight. We have seen an example of the restricted will already in Romans in the first three chapters. Try as we might, outside of Jesus the non-believer cannot will anything that God can reward, or anything that is truly good. The non-believer is unable to be a part of the works of divine good. Our freedom in Christ isn't autonomy; it is freedom to rely on God as we were designed to. We have the freedom to do what we were made to be, which is pleasing to God and to glorify Him.

Romans 6:19

I am speaking in human terms because of the weakness of your flesh. For just as you presented your members as slaves to impurity and to lawlessness, resulting in further lawlessness, so now present your members as slaves to righteousness, resulting in sanctification.

Speaking in human terms

Paul here makes it clear that he is using a human analogy to describe a spiritual reality. The reality is that it is not a perfect parallel and Paul is appealing to his readers to see where the analogy to the social institution of slavery breaks down, and not take it too far. The reason for this human analogy is given "because of the weakness of your flesh." We have already established that life abiding in the Sin Nature is slavery. It only brings the singular outcome of death. Humans often blunder into the wrong idea that if we can just keep some set of rules then we will not be slaves to the Sin, but this is the problem that Paul is warning against, and then he will devote all of chapter seven to that particular error.

Not this…THAT!

Next, we get a clarification of the analogy with another clear, "Don't do this anymore…do that instead." Paul is setting up the dichotomy very clearly. There are certain cases where two things are possible (like walking and chewing gum) and other situations where two things cannot be done simultaneously (like being in Denver and in Fort Collins at the same time). Paul is saying that presenting our members to Sin and presenting our members to God cannot happen at the same time. Here again, the exhortation of Scripture is not simply to "not sin" but rather telling us to put our focus (present our members) toward God rather than the Sin Nature. The two are opposites and we cannot continue to offer ourselves in obedience to the Sin nature and Offer ourselves in Obedience to God through Jesus Christ. It is a one or the other, moment by moment, act of our will.

Romans 6:20

For when you were slaves of sin, you were free in regard to righteousness.

Free…but from what?

As a citizen of the United States a person is free from civic responsibility to England. A citizen of the US, living in the US, need not concern himself with the taxes that he owes to the Commonwealth of England. Similarly the non-believer is free from any obligation to the standard of God's perfect righteousness. All actions can be evaluated and gauged in relationship to self alone. The idea of "getting away with something" may mean that it was "okay" for the unbeliever. The only thing that may hold them back is the possible consequence of something bothering their own consciousness. Being free of the absolute standard of God's righteous character as a standard outside of themselves, their life and actions become relativistic in its outplay.

A Word on Righteousness

Righteousness is the absolute character of God. A person is "righteous" or "unrighteous" in relationship to Him. For God, however, righteousness is a function of His person and character. He cannot be anything but righteous, all the time. He doesn't uphold a standard, nor cling to a standard, He IS the standard.

"The Rock! His work is perfect, For all His ways are just; A God of faithfulness and without injustice, Righteous and upright is He.
Deuteronomy 32:4

So the princes of Israel and the king humbled themselves and said, "The LORD is righteous."
2 Chronicles 12:6

Romans 6:21
Therefore what benefit were you then deriving from the things of which you are now ashamed? For the outcome of those things is death.

What Benefit?
Often times we think of obedience to the Sin Nature as more expedient, or productive in some way. We are tempted to think that things would somehow be easier or better if we could just do it "the other way". The World System encourages this. When the world system wants to justify ungodliness, pragmatism is usually the top reason it uses. Machiavelli coined the phrase "The end justifies the means." And the world has bought that premise hook, line and sinker.

Ashamed
Undoubtedly, someone would be able to say, "Yes, I was dishonest in that business deal – but look, I made a bunch of money!" however the question then comes down to what is of the greater value. Before a person knows the Lord "getting away with it" may be good enough. However, once we are in a relationship with God He places His Spirit within us. One of the consequences of that indwelling ministry of the Holy Spirit is that He convicts us of sin. This leads us to shame. We then see Christ's words most clearly illustrated in our own lives: "For what will it profit a man if he gains the whole world and forfeits his soul? Or what will a man give in exchange for his soul?" (Matthew 16:26) All of the advantages in the world

are meaningless if we are not in fellowship with God. This plays out differently between the non-believer and the believer:

> **The Non-Believer** – The unbeliever is free from righteousness, and may therefore pursue their own best good in every situation as they perceive it, forsaking all others. However, the end of this road is an eternity separated from God in Hell. And nothing accrued on earth, whether time, money, fame, popularity or influence will bring any comfort.
>
> **The Believer** – The believer cannot ever lose his relationship to God. However, he will fall out of fellowship. The believer who is abiding in his sin nature (called "carnal", "worldly" or "fleshly" in Scripture, see 1 Corinthians 3) is still indwelt by the Holy Spirit, however, he doesn't receive the comfort, peace and joy of that union. The carnal Christian is the most miserable person on earth.

And the Outcome is…

The word "outcome" here is an interesting one. It has the sense of something being brought to maturity, or completed. The idea that abiding in the sin nature somehow fulfills some short term goal, or meets some short term need is always eclipsed by its final and eventual outcome which is always the same thing: Death.

Death

As we have seen death is separation. When we were said to have died to the Sin Nature in 6:1-11 we noted that it does not mean termination, but rather a separation from that Nature. Here the separation is from fellowship with God. We see an interesting principle at play. Often times people's major objection to believing in Jesus is the imperfection of those who believe. Here we see that putting our faith in Christ isn't a "magic perfect pill" that makes the believer never sin again. It may surprise us to see this, but the believer is capable of everything that the nonbeliever is capable of. The non-believer is not a child of God, is not in Christ, and can only walk by the power of the Sin Nature. The believer is a Child of God, is permanently and irreversibly in Christ, but can choose to walk by the power of the sin nature. In either case the sin nature is in no way changed, it produces shame, pain, loss, fear and death. Anything that the unbeliever can do, the believer can do. The believer, however, has the ability to walk in the Spirit, and this whole chapter is an exhortation that every believer should do just that.

Romans 6:22-23
22But now having been freed from sin and enslaved to God, you derive your
benefit, resulting in sanctification, and the outcome, eternal life. 23For the
wages of sin is death, but the free gift of God is eternal life in Christ Jesus
our Lord.

Freed!
Paul repeats his claim again: We are FREED from the Power of the Sin Nature. This repetition should alert us to the incredible importance of this reality. It is a point that needs to be continually repeated because it is of such magnificent power and we so easily are distracted from it. Having been freed from the horrible yoke of the cruel master of the Sin Nature it would be madness to run back to it and abide by it, but sadly we do this often as believers.

Enslaved to God
God is the new master in the life of the believer. There is a reality of care and ownership, as well as accountability at play here. Paul has already noted the shortcoming of the analogy that he is using. We are not only His servants, but also His children (John 1:12), His adopted children (Roman adoption differed from our institution as it was a process by which an adult son was accepted permanently and irreversibly as a member of the family – Ephesians 1:5); the Bride of Christ (Ephesians 5:22-33), and friends (John 15:15).

Derived for your Benefit
Here is a new reality. We are going to serve a master. Either the Sin Nature or God. However, there is a principle difference between the masters. The end of every action, word or deed done by the power of the sin nature is death, pain and loss – short term benefits always lead to long term consequences that are bad for us and others. However, in the service of God we find that our actions, abiding in the Holy Spirit, are always to the best of all. God is glorified by them, and thus He benefits; we are edified, built up, and strengthened. We also receive life and peace because we are

functioning as we were meant. Abiding in the Spirit produces life and peace at every turn (Romans 8:6). We find that our service to the Lord is also the best thing for us at every turn because it is who and what we were designed to be.

Sanctification

This is another 10 point theological word with a simple meaning. Often times this has been described as "holification" or the "Making Holy in our condition". However, while that idea is involved, the perspective needs some addressing. The idea behind the biblical use of this word "sanctification" is the idea of something being set apart and dedicated to God. It was used of priests and even the furniture that were involved in a pagan temple. Everything was "set apart" as being for Zeus or Apollo or some other god. This is the idea present here. When we put our faith in Christ we were positionally and eternally sanctified in Him forever. That is, He set us apart for Him and His glory at that moment. There is an ongoing process of sanctification as well, whereby more and more of our life and conduct (in our daily condition) are also being set apart to Him, by the power of the Life of Christ within us. Paul then discusses the outcome (the coming to maturity) of this action on the part of God, which is vital to us: eternal life.

Eternal life

These words are the bane of the person who would put forth the idea that salvation could be lost. The word "eternal" means beyond time or space. Not subject to it. In the Greek understanding of this word it wasn't just something that lasts forever, but it is something that is not subject to time. This eternal life would not be eternal if it could be lost, stolen, taken or rejected. We may abuse it, we may take it for granted, we may spiritually jump off a cliff, but the eternal life (if it is indeed eternal) cannot be broken or removed. If the Biblical authors wanted to convey "spiritual life" they would have allowed for the possibility of its loss, however the idea that we are given eternal life does not allow for that interpretation at all.

Salvation Verses?

Romans 6:23 is often used as a verse to illustrate the gospel. It is often employed to explain the power of Salvation to unbelievers. However, while the application is correct, that is not the direct context of this verse. The direct context of this verse is talking about the sin nature in the life of the believer. In other words, this verse is talking about Phase 2 of salvation (Sanctification) not phase 1 of Salvation (Justification). This is a verse for every believer every moment of their life on earth.

Wages

When are wages accrued? When a person works. Wages aren't a present or a gift – they are earned. Paul makes a very interesting distinction of language here. When we "work for it" we can only "earn" one thing – Death. Justification (Salvation from sin's penalty) came only through faith in Jesus by Grace. Sanctification (Salvation from sin's power) is exactly the same. It is also a free gift. We see here the reality of grace. If we can work for it, either by earning it, or by paying it back, then it is not grace. If that is our motivation then we don't properly understand the Christian life. The only wages that we are good for is death, and that is what it pays out.

Free Gift

Isn't that redundant? Isn't a gift always "free"? Paul is being specifically and intentionally redundant here to help us to realize that this phase in our salvation, also, is an expression of His grace in Christ Jesus our Lord. We must not fall into the trap of: "Jesus saved you so you could work for it." The reality is that the Lord is turning us into something else, something new, and He is not in the business of "fixing up the old." On the contrary, "the old has gone the new has come!" (2 Corinthians 5:17). And every day we have the choice to either abide in the Sin Nature which will result repeatedly in separation from fellowship with God, or we will abide in Christ and the Gift that He has already given all those who believe, and be motivated totally by gratitude.

ROMANS 7

ROMANS 7:1-6

Where were we?
If there were one rule of understanding the Bible clearly it would be "Context." When a word, phrase, sentence or paragraph is taken out of context it can often lead to disaster. The goal of good Bible study is to find the clear answer to the question: "What does the Bible say?" So, where have we been?

Introduction and Purpose (1:1-17) – Key verses 1:16-17

The state of the heathen (1:18-32)

The state of the 'moral' person (2:1-16)

The state of the Jews (2:17-3:8)

Conclusion: All are in need of a Savior (3:9-20)

Salvation in Christ (Phase 1 - Justification)

Justification by Faith alone in Christ alone explained (3:21-31)

Justification by Faith illustrated (4:1-25)

The implications of Justification in Christ (5:1-11)

The Application of Justification in Christ (5:12-21)

Salvation in Christ (Phase 2 – Sanctification)

Identification with Christ (6:1-14)

Application of our Identification (6:15-23)

Did Paul get confused?
In chapter 6 Paul laid out the path for our sanctification. Having established the fact that we can earn no righteousness of our own he clearly displayed how we must rely on Christ's righteousness. We saw how, just as we cannot be saved through our own works, so we will not be sanctified by our own good works. It is the life of Christ within us, and not adherence to any external law that will sanctify (set us apart in our daily condition). Many interpreters, hoping to keep Christians under the Law, have interpreted chapter 7 as being out of place. Suggesting that it would "fit" better just before chapter 3 when Paul was saying that man could never be saved by the works of the law. They then argue that Paul is here going back to justification, and leaving his discussion of the process of sanctification. However, we believe firmly that ***God does not make mistakes when speaking through His Apostles and Prophets, and the Bible is just as it is supposed to be.***

So, what IS Paul saying?
Paul made the statement in 6:14: "For sin shall not be master over you, for you are not under law but under grace." This statement needs a great deal of explanation because, as it has been said, "Mankind is incurably religious." Mankind is always looking for the rules by which he can make God happy and get what he wants. However, the uniform message of the word is the reality that God doesn't just want robots that do what they are supposed to do. He wants a ***relationship*** with His creatures that He loves (us). This is why the relationship that God desires with man is repeatedly described in the most intimate terms: Shepherd/sheep, Father/children, Friends, Husband/wife, etc. Yet, even understanding this, humans repeatedly fall back into the legalism of "I gave God what He wanted, He has to give me what I want." The Lord wants us to focus on Jesus and what He is doing

in us, not on conformity to some standard that we think is going to make Him happy.

Romans 7:1-3

[1]Or do you not know, brethren (for I am speaking to those who know the
law), that the law has jurisdiction over a person as long as he lives? [2]For the
married woman is bound by law to her husband while he is living; but if her
husband dies, she is released from the law concerning the husband. [3]So
then, if while her husband is living she is joined to another man, she shall
be called an adulteress; but if her husband dies, she is free from the law, so
that she is not an adulteress though she is joined to another man.

Or do you not know

Paul has used this phrase before (Romans 6:3, 16). This question has the sense of "You should know this – this is basic!" As salvation is presented logically there is a high premium placed on knowing what we are supposed to know. Paul emphasizes what we should know in Romans 6:6, 9. The reality is that, as believers, we need to KNOW what the Bible says so that we can trust in it. It is not "what does my pastor say" or "what does this Christian author say?" but what does the Bible say exclusively.

To those who know the law

This is a fascinating point. Paul tells them that he is writing to them and they "know the law." The question is this: "Which law is in view?" Surely the Jews that he was writing to would know the Mosaic Law. However, this isn't exclusively what Paul seems to be getting at. One of the most famous and important contributions that Rome made to western culture is the contribution of law. The Romans used their magnificent legal system to govern the largest empire then in existence. So Paul is recognizing that they know how law works. Law is based on outward behavior. Rewarding one thing, punishing another. They knew this way of thinking and Paul is quite clear in declaring that this, while appropriate for governing a nation, is not the way that the Lord intends to deal with those who have placed their faith in Jesus Christ. However, this is the constant temptation of mankind.

Out of your Jurisdiction

The next point Paul brings up is jurisdiction. Nobody would try to drag a corpse into the defense box and hold a trial for a dead man. Once a person has died they are no longer prosecutable under the legal system. This will be one of the chief metaphors that Paul uses in order to explain the believer's relationship to the Law (whether the law of Moses, or simply the principle of law as an operating procedure). Paul brings this together with a practical example.

The Example of Marriage

In the context of marriage a wife is attached to her husband. If she should seek another sexual relationship outside of marriage she would be committing adultery. She is bound by the law NOT to seek other husbands, or live as if she were the wife of another person. There were, of course, extreme consequences under the Law of Moses for adultery both for the adulteress and for the one who committed adultery with her.

Imagine a woman who was promised from birth to marry a man. This man is a horrible, hard-nosed task master, demanding perfection at every turn and absolute submission to every single whim. However, the woman has known another from her childhood who has loved her unconditionally. Here she is between the husband she hates, but she is obligated to him, and the man who loves her and longs to care for her. If she engages in the relationship with the man who loves her she will be an adulteress, and yet she cannot continue in the relationship with her cruel husband.

Then a miracle happens…the husband dies! She is now free to pursue the marriage with the one who loves her. She is able to marry him and live in that relationship for the rest of her life. Is she then an adulteress? By no means! The law that bound her to her cruel ex-husband is broken with his death, and she is now free to marry the one who loves her.

Romans 7:4-6

[4]Therefore, my brethren, you also were made to die to the Law through the
body of Christ, so that you might be joined to another, to Him who was
raised from the dead, in order that we might bear fruit for God. [5]For while
we were in the flesh, the sinful passions, which were aroused by the Law,
were at work in the members of our body to bear fruit for death. [6]But now
we have been released from the Law, having died to that by which we were
bound, so that we serve in newness of the Spirit and not in oldness of the
letter.

Applying the Story

Verses 4-6 apply the story that Paul just told about the wife who was bound to a husband. Each person who is born into this world is born under the system of law. As one poet put it:

Do this and live, the law commands, but gives me neither feet nor hands.

A better word the gospel brings. It bids me fly and gives me wings.

The relationship of the believer to the law is very well, and very clearly established: death.

Death

As we have seen "death" in scripture means separation. Physical death is separation of the body from the immaterial parts of man. Relational death is separation from another person in relationship. Spiritual death is used to describe separation in our relationship with God. What has the believer died to here? **THE PRINCIPLE OF LAW.** The believer's relationship with God is no longer governed by the principle of Law. Notice that this is passive; we were "made to die to the law" through our association with Jesus Christ. The word used for death here specifically insinuates a violent death – meaning the death of the Lord Jesus Christ on the cross. The Law had one thing to offer man, who is incapable of keeping it: Death. And this is exactly what was accomplished at the cross. He paid the penalty for us, forever freeing us from the demands of the law principle.

So that

This, however, isn't simply a death, we are also united to Someone: Jesus Christ. This word "joined to" has the idea of being recreated in union with another. The KJV translates this as "married to". We must also note that the "might" here is not a contingency. It could be translated as a definite statement – if you have placed faith in Jesus Christ you ARE dead to the law and joined (united, married to) Christ.

Him who was raised from the dead

This is saying, quite clearly, that when Christ was raised from the dead, you were united with Him! You are joined to Him, identified with Him, in that action. When Christ died on the cross, the believer died with Him. When Christ was raised from the dead, you were raised with Him. It is His power,

His life, which is now the operating procedure for your life. Not a list of rules, but a person: God incarnate. It is a relationship.

In order that

Notice all of the logical connections that are being used here. The believer is made dead to the law SO THAT he may be united to Christ IN ORDER THAT fruit may come. Before good works came out of our lives because we felt we should, felt guilty or "wanted to do the right thing." Now the fruit grows naturally in the life of the believer, because we are connected to the source of life. The works that come out of the believer are not because of a rule or law, but because they are sourced in God himself. Just as fruit grows naturally from a healthy tree so the believer who is connected to Jesus Christ in daily relationship will naturally produce the fruit described in Galatians 5:22-23:

But the fruit of the Spirit is love, joy, peace, patience, kindness, goodness, faithfulness, gentleness, self-control; against such things there is no law.

Then and now (verse 5)

Paul refers back to before a person is a believer. The only operating principle for the unbeliever's life is the Sin Nature (the flesh, *the* sin). The person who is not in a relationship with Jesus Christ has only this Sinful Nature to work with. The effect of the Law on that sin nature is only excited by the opportunity of more "rules" to break. The fruit of that relationship only brought forth death. As the sin nature sought repeatedly to disobey the law the results are only pain, hurtfulness, anger, hatred, fear and loss. Yet this is the only principle, and the only relationship that we have apart from entering into a relationship with Jesus Christ.

But now…

Praise the Lord something changed! We have been delivered from the Law! The Greek word used here means to "cut off completely" or "render inoperative". Having died to the principle of Law we are now free! Completely and utterly free to live in the new relationship with Jesus Christ who has made us.

It's a life

Our new "code of conduct" isn't a set of rules that bring punishment for disobedience and reward for obedience. Our new way of life is governed by our being identified with Christ and His power and ability in us. This newness of life is not simply an outward conformity by an inward transformation. It doesn't just involve our outward actions, it involves our attitudes, our thoughts, our words, and our actions. We are now free to be what God intended us to be all along! His beloved children who freely conform to His will for us all by the work, power and life of Jesus Christ. Which He has given us, all by grace, all through faith, all of the time. Amen!

ROMANS 7:7-12

False Dichotomy

A false dichotomy is a situation where something is presented as an "either/or and not both" situation when it is not actually the case. Then Paul anticipates the argument of his readers that they are going to say, "So you are saying that the Law of God (or law in general) is evil? How dare you say that about God's LAW?!" People hearing the clear teaching of the Bible and grace today often fall into the same trap. Because of a lack of understanding of the distinctions in scripture they cannot see how something can be objectively good, but not for us as church age believers. The false dichotomy is "either you say everything applies directly to me, OR you are saying that it is an evil waste of time." Neither being the case we believe, along with Paul: "All Scripture is inspired by God and profitable for teaching, for reproof, for correction, for training in righteousness; so that the man of God may be adequate, equipped for every good work." (2 Timothy 3:16-17) We see the clear reality that God gave the Law of Moses for the children of Israel and not for the church. Just as the promises of the land and physical blessing were made to Israel not the church, we find that we are simply applying the portions of scripture that are directly applicable to us. Going to the beach in your swimsuit is usually appropriate, going to a wedding in your swimsuit usually isn't appropriate. Living life under the law was appropriate for Joshua, David and Solomon. We are to live seated in Christ, beholding Him (as we have already seen in Romans 6) it is not a value judgment on the Law of Moses, it is a recognition that it isn't directly applicable for us.

Romans 7:7-8

7What shall we say then? Is the Law sin? May it never be! On the contrary, I would not have come to know sin except through the Law; for I would not have known about coveting if the Law had not said, "YOU SHALL NOT COVET." 8But sin, taking opportunity through the commandment, produced in me coveting of every kind; for apart from the Law sin is dead.

How to Fail (in one easy step)
Having taken verses 1-6 to describe how the believer in Christ is now out of the Law's "jurisdiction". He goes forward describing what happens if the believer attempts to live his life under the Law system, or any kind of a law system. The result of the believer putting himself under law again is failure. Total and complete failure. Every time. All the time.

Another one of those rhetorical questions
In verse 7 Paul anticipates what his readers are thinking. They may be wondering if Paul is saying by all of this that the Law is somehow evil, or that the Law causes sin. Paul responds with his characteristic, "May it never be!" This, again, in the Greek text is the most extreme way to forbid even the possibility of something. It could be translated as "Perish the thought" or "Don't even let the idea be conceived!"

The Good Thing about the Law
Paul repeatedly claims that the law is righteous. It was given by God. The shortcoming is not in the Law, it is in us! The Law was the tool that showed Paul beyond a shadow of a doubt that he could not claim any righteousness of his own. Because the Law *is* righteous it can show that we are *not* righteous based on our inability to live up to the perfect standard. This mirrors what Paul wrote to Timothy in 1 Timothy 1:8-9:

"[8]But we know that the Law is good, if one uses it lawfully, [9]realizing the fact that law is not made for a righteous person, but for those who are lawless and rebellious, for the ungodly and sinners, for the unholy and profane, for those who kill their fathers or mothers, for murderers."

The law can be useful when talking to an unbeliever to convince them of their need for Christ's righteousness and Christ's payment for their sin on the cross.

What about those Ten?
It is interesting that those who are resistant to the reality that believers are not to live under law are generally quite inconsistent. Very few people would suggest that we are under the dietary laws, and even fewer would suggest that we should continue to observe the sacrificial systems described under the Mosaic Law. The inconsistency comes when they try to root through the law picking choosing which parts of the Law they are willing to

be under. Some (like the Seventh Day Adventists) try to fool themselves into thinking that they are under more of the law than anyone else. Others (like the covenant-reformed camp) try to outline the parts of the moral law that they are still under. People often get really animated when it comes to defending the 10 commandments. However, here Paul uses one of the 10 commandments ("Thou shalt not covet" Exodus 20:17) as the specific example of how life under law is not appropriate, nor profitable, for the believer in Christ today.

Opportunity Knocks

The idea here is not that the law is evil, but that the sin nature uses the commandment as an opportunity. The sin nature is looking for things to disobey, is looking for rules to break. The Law would be helpful, useful, and even easy, if we were perfect. However, in the hands of the sin nature it is just a weapon for greater destruction.

It is like one football team giving their playbook to the opposing football team. Is the playbook good? Yes. However, if the other team knows exactly what you are planning to do then they will also know the most efficient way to undo it.

Or if you wanted to sabotage a piece of electronics the instruction book may be the most helpful thing. It would tell you exactly how to operate it so that you could simply do the opposite to destroy it.

Just like this, the Law is a good thing, it would have caused people to live good and happy lives, but in the hands of the sin nature (which every human possesses) it only gave the sin nature a more direct plan for destroying the person, giving them something to focus on besides the relationship with God.

Sin is Dead

Apart from the Law the Sin Nature has no standard to violate…no "instruction book" to use against the person. This is closely related to Romans 5:13: "for until the Law sin was in the world, but sin is not imputed when there is no law." As chapter 5 demonstrated, even without imputation sin still only yields death, loss, pain and separation. However, facing our sin nature on the battlefield of Law is a war that we can never win.

To illustrate this we may look to another sports analogy. For most of us playing one on one with the greatest living basketball player will result only in loss. No matter how many times we play, no matter if we have a "good game" based on our abilities or a "bad game" the professional player will always defeat us. However, if we weren't playing basketball with him we would never have known how much better he is. This illustration shows the insanity of the Christian attempting to live under law. We can try again and again and again but we will never "beat the champ". Repeatedly doing so only improves our ability to lose.

Romans 7:9-12

[9]I was once alive apart from the Law; but when the commandment came,
sin became alive and I died; [10]and this commandment, which was to result
in life, proved to result in death for me; [11]for sin, taking an opportunity
through the commandment, deceived me and through it killed me. [12]So
then, the Law is holy, and the commandment is holy and righteous and
good.

Once alive

Paul looks back here to chapter 6. When he first put his faith in Jesus Christ he was alive to God. He trusted in Christ's righteousness alone and rejoiced. How many have this exact experience. When they first come to know the grace and love of the Lord they are on fire for Christ. The first days after their conversion they want to tell everyone about Christ's love, grace and provision for them. They are fully satisfied with Christ's sacrifice for Him, having been saved by His grace, and giving Him the glory.

But then…

Sadly the resulting command comes to them after that. Like so many new believers that are desperately in love with Jesus something changes. Someone comes into our life who tells them that they should be obeying these rules. Or our own spiritual pride starts to puff us up and we start to think that we should be accruing our own righteousness by now. Paul is not saying that the commandment MUST come in, but he is saying that it came into his life and caused a very clear result: death.

If we apply this to our previous analogy it may look like this:

Chapter 6 – I finally realized that I could never ever beat the professional basketball player in a game of one on one. I realized that I couldn't win, so I let Christ play the game for me and I found that He already won the game. I trusted in His victory and I enjoyed fellowship with God.

Chapter 7 – After a while I figured that maybe, since I fooled myself into thinking that I am stronger now, I thought I could win the game, so I decided to accept my Sin Nature's challenge and try to win, and I lost again.

Was to be life

Once again, the commandment was supposed to result in life. If I could ever "win" that game then it would result in life. I would have righteousness of my own with which I could approach God. Essentially, the Sin Nature, knowing that it can never win against the perfect and absolute righteousness of Jesus Christ attempts to deceive Paul into another game of one on one.

Deceived me

There is a deception going on here. The deception that is being played by the sin nature is that Christ won the battle of Justification for us (when we were declared righteous by means of our identification with Christ), we are somehow responsible for our own righteousness in our Sanctification (the process by which we are being set apart for God in our daily condition). The Sin Nature knowing it cannot defeat the saint who is resting in Christ's life, power and righteousness attempts to tempt the saint back to the game that it can win – one on one between the saint and the sin nature.

Conclusion

So Paul is being very clear – the Law is not evil. It simply cannot do anything for me. The problem that we have is that we cannot live up to it. When we attempt to do so we inevitably wind up focusing on ourselves, and not on our perfect Savior. We end up trying to come up with some righteousness of our own and wind up back in the place of having to realize our own inability and need to abide constantly in our relationship of relying on Jesus Christ every moment and every day, in the relationship that He won for us on the cross.

ROMANS 7:13-21

What's happening to me?

In the movie Teen Wolf Michael J. Fox plays Scott Howard, a boy who is beset with werewolfism. As the transformation takes place he locks himself in the bathroom and helplessly watches as he turns into something else. His father comes to the door and offers to help, but Scott rejects that help. Finally, once the transformation is complete Scott's father insists on being let it. Scott relents, expecting to scare the socks off of his dad. He opens the door and finds that his father is also a werewolf (as he had also transformed).

Similarly, most Christians go through this experience of wondering what in the world is going on inside of them. They see their desire to do the right thing, and yet they continually make choices that conflict with the true desire within them. Like the "teen wolf" they sit afraid, ashamed and isolated in their bathroom, hoping that nobody finds out what a hypocrite they are. We try to figure out the reasons and come up with crazy suggestions like:

-Did I not believe correctly?

-Did I not "really" put my faith in Jesus?

-Perhaps I don't really *want* it bad enough?

-Perhaps I need an accountability group, or I need to make a new rule to follow?

-Maybe I'm not saved?

Here, however, in the word of God we have an exact description of what is going on inside the saint by the apostle Paul. This is an autobiographical look, he isn't just saying that this may be the case for some of us, but he is saying, "This is what I have struggled with!" Here, again, in the word, we find every provision for our salvation. Past (Justification), present (sanctification) and future (Glorification).

Romans 7:13-14

[13]Therefore did that which is good become a cause of death for me? May it never be! Rather it was sin, in order that it might be shown to be sin by effecting my death through that which is good, so that through the commandment sin would become utterly sinful. [14]For we know that the Law is spiritual, but I am of flesh, sold into bondage to sin.

Therefore

This logical connection links what Paul is about to say with what he has just said. In the previous section Paul made it clear that the law isn't evil, it just has no power to help him. In fact, in the hands of his sin nature the law was a fast track to destruction because the sin nature knows exactly how to destroy him by seeking to break the law constantly.

Pointing fingers

The next question that Paul anticipates is, in essence: "Are you blaming the Law for your failure?" The response is the "May it never be!" that we have grown accustomed to hearing. Paul, and every believer today, ought to have the utmost respect for God's Law as it was revealed to Moses. It is strange what it means to understand and respect the law. Those who seek to be "law keepers" will claim they respect it and are keeping it, when really they ignore most of it, and use it as a basis for their own self-righteousness. However, Paul's point of view here is: "I respect the Law enough to realize that I could NEVER keep it because of the sin principle (the Sin Nature) that lives within me – the only righteousness that will do is found in Christ."

The Sin

The word translated "rather" here denotes a strong contrast or change in direction. Paul is saying, "It's not what I imagine you are going to accuse me of, it's the exact opposite!" Here again we see the phrase "*the* sin". As was the case in chapter six, "the sin" refers to the sin nature within the believer. Notice that Paul continues to deal with the sin nature throughout his description of the process of sanctification. The Law isn't the problem, it is the sin nature within. The law would be a perfect method of managing men, if men were perfect. However, as long as we have our sin nature we find the Law is not the correct tool for reforming men. This can be done by the life of Christ within the believer who is positioned in Him alone.

Why would God do that?

The next question we could ask would be why would God give a standard that man could never truly live up to? In essence the law acts like an indicator to show how hopeless man's situation is apart from Christ. This is the case in our justification, which we saw in Romans 1-5 that we could not earn. This is also the case in our sanctification, which we are seeing that we cannot earn or "work for" either. Attempt to live by the law, or by any governing set of laws only shows us that we cannot be conformed to the image of Christ by the best efforts of our flesh. We are reminded regularly by our lives and our situations how hopeless we are apart from Christ, how much we need Him, and fellowship with Him every moment.

The Problem

In verse 14 Paul gives a clear statement of the problem, and also the value of the Law. The Law is spiritual. The law is given from God and would be perfect for perfect people. But the problem is in himself. Paul knows that He is not spiritual. We have no hope of becoming spiritual through any set of rules, rewards and punishments. It simply cannot be done!

It would be like teaching an earthworm to do archery. No matter how good the instruction book, no matter how great the rewards, and how painful the punishment, the earthworm lacks the necessary apparatus to succeed at archery. You can punish the earthworm when he fails, but the end will never be success.

<u>Romans 7:15-16</u>

15For what I am doing, I do not understand; for I am not practicing what I
would like to do, but I am doing the very thing I hate. 16But if I do the very
thing I do not want to do, I agree with the Law, confessing that the Law is
good.

I don't get it!

This section of scripture can be a bit confusing if we don't read it carefully, but the way it is written helps portray the amount of anxiety that Paul is feeling. He opens by saying that what he is doing (present active indicative) he doesn't "understand" (present active indicative). The word "understand" is a word that means knowledge by experience. The sense here is, "I just don't get it!

"Practice" here is talking about his repeated and continued actions. He is saying, my walk doesn't match my talk. I want to practice the things that I know are good, but I am doing the exact opposite.

And I hate it!
Paul expresses absolute hatred for the actions that are coming out of him. To keep this in perspective this is all present tense. Paul is writing about this in "right now" terms, as a saved person who is trying to live under law. Those things I am doing, I am HATING!

Silver Lining
Paul is able to find the silver lining to the cloud here: even though he is unable to meet the standard he knows is good; he can, at least, affirm that the Lord is good and His standard is right, even if he is unable to meet it in his flesh.

Romans 7:17-21
17So now, no longer am I the one doing it, but sin which dwells in me. 18For
I know that nothing good dwells in me, that is, in my flesh; for the willing is
present in me, but the doing of the good is not. 19For the good that I want,
I do not do, but I practice the very evil that I do not want. 20But if I am
doing the very thing I do not want, I am no longer the one doing it, but sin
which dwells in me. 21I find then the principle that evil is present in me, the
one who wants to do good.

Who's Who?
Paul then comes to an important realization. He knows what HE wants. He wants to keep the Law and do righteous things all of the time. However, he is inhibited from doing so by his sin nature. Does it sound like his sin nature has been obliterated, or removed? Not at all! It is alive and well and able to keep him in the pattern and practice of sinfulness. Furthermore, Paul gives the sin nature a location: "Within me". He finds the sin nature at work in him.

Nothing!

Verse 18 comes to a deeper realization: "NOTHING GOOD DWELLS WITHIN MY FLESH!" This is a huge admission. Paul realized in chapters 1-5 that there was nothing that he could do to earn salvation. Chapter 6 outlines the reality that we will grow in Christ only so long as we are trusting in the spiritual facts of what was accomplished at the cross, but here Paul is brought to a deeper reality. I cannot bring forth any positive, rewardable work from my flesh!

This is a process of years, for many of us, and days for others. Most often we must come to increasing revelations of the reality that we are in absolute need of Jesus Christ every moment. When we first come to the Lord we see that we are helpless to affect our own salvation. Having trusted in the Lord for that we come to see that we are totally hopeless to affect our own sanctification. Increasingly, we realize, more and more with each passing moment that we need Him for every second, every word, and every breath. We begin to grow when we realize, with Paul, that "Nothing good dwells within me."

I didn't do that!

Paul comes to this greater realization: "It is not I that do it...but the sin nature within me!" This may sound like an excuse, but it isn't. Paul isn't saying, "Hey, I'm off the hook, the Sin is doing it within me!" That is not the point at all. Paul is saying that when he tries to please God by keeping the law his sin nature is always the one in charge. In fact, by going to the Law he is proving his point because the result is always more sinful practice and behavior. In essence one way to find out if a believer has slipped back into legalism is to observe their life. Is sin abounding? It may be because the believer is a legalist! To use the illustration from last week this person is getting back onto the basketball court with 1997 Michael Jordan again and again and again and losing every day because he doesn't want to admit that he needs the Savior, Jesus Christ, every single moment.

The Principle

Some translations bring this across as "law" because it is the Greek word *nomos* which is the word translated "law" elsewhere in this chapter. However, just as in English, the word law can mean "a standard of measurement, or a set of rules" or it can mean a principle or an observed pattern, just as we use the term in the phrase "the laws of nature." So here is the principle:

Evil is present within me: This is a present middle passive. Paul is saying that evil (his sin nature) is, and will continue to be, present within him.

Who wants to do good: While he wants to do good he finds that he cannot escape the sin nature. The desire is there but just willing more or "willing harder" is not going to solve the problem. This is quite a conundrum that we all face every time we attempt to live by the principle of law!

ROMANS 7:22-25

Giving up!
These verses continue to document another very important step in the lives of many believers. It is important to note that Romans 7 is prescriptive (it doesn't HAVE to happen), however it is a very common case for many believers just as it was with Paul in his walk with the Lord. Paul finally gets to the point of objective despair. Many legalists live their entire lives trying to maintain the outward image. They think that if they can somehow fool everybody else they must be fooling God as well. They forget that God judges the hearts of men and is never fooled by outward appearance.

But the LORD said to Samuel, "Do not look at his appearance or at the height of his stature, because I have rejected him; for God sees not as man sees, for man looks at the outward appearance, but the LORD looks at the heart." 1 Samuel 16:7

Romans 7:22-23
22For I joyfully concur with the law of God in the inner man, 23but I see a different law in the members of my body, waging war against the law of my mind and making me a prisoner of the law of sin which is in my members.

In Conclusion
These verses form the conclusion of this section. In the prior verses Paul has narrated the reality that he affirms the Law of God to be good. He also has noted very strongly that anytime he tries to go back under that authority of the Law (the "first husband" in verses 1-4) he meets failure and desperation. Furthermore, he has seen very clearly the reality of the sin nature and what the sin nature does with the law when we attempt to keep it of our own flesh. And all this as a believer who has already put his faith in Jesus Christ for Justification.

Delightful

The word rendered "joyfully concur" here (KJV: delight) has the idea of rejoicing, together with something. Paul is saying, very clearly, that he agrees that the law is good. In fact it brings him pleasure and delight. It is as if he can see the beauty and perfection of it and longs to be so perfect. Longs to be what he was intended to be, but is made incapable of by his sin nature.

Inner Man

This "inner man" is a phrase used for the immaterial part of man. It stands for the part of him that longs to be right with God that longs to have righteousness. Surely every believer longs in his spirit to please the Lord and to live according to His ways and His standards. However, there is a pivotal need of understanding. Our desire is often to be able to show God something good of our own making. We may agree that a certain accepted standard of Godly behavior is good, but if we are doing it for our own purposes it becomes worthless. **Wrong motivations ruin "good" actions**. East of Eden by Steinbeck provides a powerful illustration:

Two sons (Aaron and Caleb) of a farmer (Adam) both seek to please their father. The elder Aaron easily receives the approval of Adam because he has known his father, his father's character and his desires. Caleb longs for Adam to approve the results of his actions which are good. However, the types of things he does, and the ways that he does them (while not "wrong") conflict with the character of his godly father Adam. The final chords are struck when Adam has lost money trying to improve the lot of mankind. Caleb, longing to see his father financially restored, engages in planting crops to profit from the war effort (which Adam disagrees with). The final scene occurs when Aaron presents his desire to be married and live a life that is in step with Adam's and Caleb presents the money that Adam lost. Adam accepts the actions of Aaron, but rejects the actions of Caleb because they don't match in spirit to what he is about as a person.

Similarly, when believers try to place themselves back under the law and come before the Lord with a "see what I have done" attitude the Lord only mourns, and no progress is made. As we have seen, the gross reality of it is that the harder we try to keep the law the more pronounced our failures become.

A Different Law

Paul then talks about a different law. "Law" here is not talking about the type of law like the law of Moses (an objective standard) but rather the "natural law" type of law. This is the type of law that says, "It always happens just this way." This is like the law of gravity. Every time I drop something it falls to the ground, without exception.

This different law also has a location: in "the members of my body." Paul here is talking about his flesh. We see, again, the relationship of the sin nature to the physical body. It does not mean that our physical bodies are intrinsically evil by any stretch of the imagination. It does mean that our sin nature is somehow essentially attached to our physical bodies. This is in line with our understanding of when we will finally be rid of the Sin Nature – when we are freed from these "old bodies" and given our "new bodies" which are like Christ's body.

(1 Corinthians 15:47-58) This will occur either at our physical death, or at the rapture.

Making me a Prisoner

Here Paul observes that this law that is at work in his flesh wages a military assault against the Law that he wishes to keep in his mind. The result of this is that he is in bondage once again. Yet we know that "it is for freedom that Christ has made you free." (Galatians 5:1) So how can we, who have been set free then be in bondage? Paul has already discussed one way believers can be in bondage in chapter 6. We can choose directly to be in bondage to the sin nature. Simply obeying the demands of our flesh at all times, that is walking in the sinful desires that the sin nature dictates. However, here we see another potential bondage for the believer. If we attempt to keep the law we will wind up in bondage yet again. The question then is who our "captor" is at that point. We find that it is the same villain as before: Our sin nature! "The Sin" has not just one, but two lethal ways to rule us here! It can rule us by licentious behavior, and it can rule us by legalistic thinking and behavior! Here again we see the simple reality of the Lord's words echoed in the negative:

Jesus said to him, "I am the way, and the truth, and the life; no one comes to the Father but through Me. John 14:6

Our relationship with Jesus is not just a door that we walk through, though Jesus himself is the door we must walk through (John 10:9). He is also the way upon which we tread. Leaving that relationship to err on either side of the difficulty (legalism or license) takes us off the path that we were meant to be on, and we are left in bondage again. Notice: Neither one is preferable to the other!

<u>Romans 7:24-25</u>

[24]Wretched man that I am! Who will set me free from the body of this death? [25]Thanks be to God through Jesus Christ our Lord! So then, on the one hand I myself with my mind am serving the law of God, but on the other, with my flesh the law of sin.

Wretched

Here Paul declares himself absolutely wretched! His state of affairs is simply ghastly. He wants to do what is right so very badly, yet he winds up getting battered and bruised, afflicted and destroyed again and again and again. This is a full realization of his complete inadequacy to do anything. It seemed easier for him to come to this conclusion in Romans 1-3. He could condemn the whole humanity with a pen stroke (and include himself) in describing the need for a savior. Yet on this side of the cross (AFTER he put his faith in Jesus for salvation) he still feels he should be able to offer something to God. He feels, as most believers do in their immaturity, that he SHOULD be able to do something. He can't reconcile the fact that he knows what is right and wants to do it with the fact that he didn't just need a Savior before he knew the Lord – He needs a Savior RIGHT NOW!

FREEDOM!

He longs for freedom. What does he want freedom from? The body of death. Death, again, means separation from God. This is not talking about eternal death (not being saved, or loss of salvation) but of the temporal death that believers can experience by living out of fellowship with God. He identifies his flesh as the causative problem, keeping him from conforming to the outward demands of the law. He even calls this inability a law. Translation: I couldn't keep it before, I can't keep it now, I will never be able to keep the law and satisfy the Lord's righteous demands! And he cries out in despair. How can I be freed? There must be a better way!

Still need a Savior

Paul continues in his acknowledged need of a Savior. The word "set me free" denotes the idea of saving someone. It carries the idea of being snatched out of danger. Like from the jaws of a lion. Note that he doesn't say "What will save me". Paul is not looking for a method, or a practice, or a special magical prayer that will save him from this miserable situation that he is in. So many books that are called "Christian" offer wrong answers to this question that are "What can rescue me". Some of their wrong responses to this pivotal question:

- **Discipline** – Try harder until you get better at it
- **Psychology** – Try to figure out why you are so tempted by it
- **Fear based** – Just get more scared of God's wrath
- **Sloppy Agape** – "Don't worry, God really doesn't care that much anyway."
- **Any Number of Steps** - Progress based "step programs"
- **Any Number of days** – "40 days of this" "30 days to that" etc.

All of these "solutions" do nothing but distract us from our true and genuine need: We need the true grace of God. Our identification with Jesus Christ on the cross and understanding of our need to look to Him and His life at every moment is our only hope.

Closing Conflict

This chapter closes with a repetition of the problem. Paul repeats the reality that he sees in himself. He has given hints and intimations of the joy that is to come in Romans 8, but he wants to make the situation abundantly plain – Justification does not come by the Law (Romans 1-3) and Salvation does not come by the law. Both come the same way – by grace through faith. Not in a contract, or a set of rules – but in a relationship with and faith in our Lord and Savior Jesus Christ.

ROMANS 8

ROMANS 8:1-4

Jesus is still the Answer
Romans 7 described graphically the only thing that the Law can accomplish in the life of the believer: fear, shame, hopelessness and destruction. Paul was left with nothing but "O wretched man that I am." In Romans 8:1 he turns a corner. That change in tone and attitude is based on the realization of the complete sufficiency of the life of Jesus Christ within us. Christ in the believer, and the believer in Christ.

Romans 8:1
Therefore there is now no condemnation for those who are in Christ Jesus

Therefore
"Therefore" is a logical connective. Trying to live under the Law as a believer brought Paul to a place of absolute hopelessness and left him asking who would save him. What follows is the logical need to the fact that we are totally helpless in our struggle against our sin nature. Many believers live their entire lives in struggle to try to prevail against their sin nature and never have a single day of life, peace and joy that they were meant to have in Christ Jesus.

Now

Shockingly, "now" means "now"! Right now. At this very moment this statement of fact is in effect. This is not something that is contingent upon something else. This is not a statement of probability, or a statement of what will be true in the future. This is the present moment.

No condemnation

As a point of interest: the Greek language does not rely on word order to derive meaning. In English we know how a word is functioning in a sentence by where it is place. Our basic structure is <subject> <verb> <object>. So in English the sentences: "The boy hit the ball" and "The ball hit the boy" mean different things. In Greek, however, the information of what is the subject and the object is built into the very conjugation of the word. This allows them to use word order for a different purpose, emphasizing the most important word by placing it first in the sentence. In English we would use italics or underlining to do this type of emphasizing.

The emphasized word in this sentence is the word "no". Paul is especially drawing our attention to the fact that there is absolutely no single word of condemnation for the saint who is in Christ Jesus.

"Condemnation" means a sentence pronounced against someone. It was a word used in the legal realm when a person was declared guilty, they were condemned. Condemnation is the chief ability of the Law. If you keep it you are commended, if you disobey it you are condemned. Paul faced constant condemnation and inability throughout chapter seven as he tried to live up to a righteous external standard and met only with His own failure. His solution is that there is "no condemnation" in Christ Jesus. And that makes all of the difference. Our unrighteousness cannot be accrued to us because we are draped with Christ's perfect and unmarred righteousness.

Who are In Christ Jesus

If there could be two words that are most important in an understanding of our salvation they would be the wonderful words "in Christ." The first question to ask is:

Who is this person who is "in Christ Jesus"? How did they get there?

We see throughout the New Testament how we get to be in Christ Jesus. We are placed in Christ Jesus by the Father when we placed our faith in Jesus Christ.

> [3]Or do you not know that all of us who have been baptized into Christ Jesus have been baptized into His death? [4]Therefore we have been buried with Him through baptism into death, so that as Christ was raised from the dead through the glory of the Father, so we too might walk in newness of life. [5]For if we have become united with Him in the likeness of His death, certainly we shall also be in the likeness of His resurrection, [6]knowing this, that our old self was crucified with Him, in order that our body of sin might be done away with, so that we would no longer be slaves to sin; [7]for he who has died is freed from sin. [8]Now if we have died with Christ, we believe that we shall also live with Him, [9]knowing that Christ, having been raised from the dead, is never to die again; death no longer is master over Him. [10]For the death that He died, He died to sin once for all; but the life that He lives, He lives to God. [11]Even so consider yourselves to be dead to sin, but alive to God in Christ Jesus. Romans 6:3-11

In Galatians Paul writes:

> [16]nevertheless knowing that a man is not justified by the works of the Law but through faith in Christ Jesus, even we have believed in Christ Jesus, so that we may be justified by faith in Christ and not by the works of the Law; since by the works of the Law no flesh will be justified. [17]"But if, while seeking to be justified in Christ, we ourselves have also been found sinners, is Christ then a minister of sin? May it never be! [18]"For if I rebuild what I have once destroyed, I prove myself to be a transgressor. [19]"For through the Law I died to the Law, so that I might live to God. [20]"I have been crucified with Christ; and it is no longer I who live, but Christ lives in me; and the life which I now live in the flesh I live by faith in the Son of God, who loved me and gave Himself up for me. [21]"I do not nullify the grace of God, for if righteousness comes through the Law, then Christ died needlessly." Galatians 2:16-21

In Ephesians we learn:

> [13]In Him, you also, after listening to the message of truth, the gospel of your salvation--having also believed, you were sealed in Him with the Holy Spirit of promise, [14]who is given as a pledge of our inheritance, with a view to the redemption of God's own possession, to the praise of His glory. Ephesians 1:13-14

And:

> [4]But God, being rich in mercy, because of His great love with which He loved us, [5]even when we were dead in our transgressions, made us alive together with Christ (by grace you have been saved), [6]and raised us up with Him, and seated us with Him in the heavenly places in Christ Jesus, [7]so that in the ages to come He might show the surpassing riches of His grace in kindness toward us in Christ Jesus. Ephesians 2:4-7

The amazing reality of this "In Christ" truth is that the unity with Christ is every time said to be by God's doing. All we do is trust (faith, belief) in Jesus. And there is not one single instance of a person being said to be "out of Christ", "thrown out", "un-baptized", "un-united" or "un-identified with Christ. It is a once and for all permanent association with Jesus Christ in His death, burial, resurrection, ascension and seating at the right hand of the Father. And in Christ, the Righteous one, there can be NO condemnation at all! Praise the Lord.

Romans 8:2

For the law of the Spirit of life in Christ Jesus has set you free from the law of sin and of death.

The Explanation

The explanation of this reality and our freedom is simple. When we were placed in Christ Jesus, and His Spirit was placed in us we were given a new "natural law" to follow. This is not talking about the "Set of rules or standard" type of law, this is regarding the second kind of law, the "natural law" type of law. The way that this type of law was illustrated in Romans 7 was: "Every time I try to obey the law I wind up with my sin nature calling the shots." Just like gravity. If you like, Christ didn't give us new strength to fight the old gravity (the law) He gave us a new gravitational center and force to be naturally drawn to (Himself).

Freedom!

As you walk in the Spirit, and rest in Christ Jesus you are also walking in the fact that you have already been set free from the law of sin and death. We are no longer under obligation to try to impress God, or try not to offend God, we simply need to rest with our eyes fixed on our Savior and trusting in His Spirit within us. We have been set free from this natural law that every time we try to resist our Sin Nature we are defeated.

Romans 8:3-4

3For what the Law could not do, weak as it was through the flesh, God did:
sending His own Son in the likeness of sinful flesh and as an offering for
sin, He condemned sin in the flesh, 4so that the requirement of the Law
might be fulfilled in us, who do not walk according to the flesh but
according to the Spirit.

What the Law Couldn't Do

The Law is shown to be unable to conform the saint to the image of Christ. The weakness, as was established, is not in the law but in the Sin Nature. We saw the inability of the Law to save a person in terms of justification in chapters 2-3 and we saw the law's inability to sanctify a person in chapters 6-7. In both cases, the problem was not the law. The law in each case was righteous, but the sin nature was too complete and toxic a force to be tamed by a list of commands.

God did

What the Law couldn't do. What I couldn't do of my own best efforts: GOD DID! This is the great message of the gospel. The reality that we cannot sanctify ourselves proves the reality that God did it. The truth of the gospel for justification is just as necessary for our growth in Christ. And just as we will never be saved apart from trusting wholly in Jesus, we will never be sanctified until we trust wholly in Jesus for that process as well.

How God did it

God did this by sending His son. The Sacrifice of Christ on the cross wasn't just a "get out of hell free card" it is what we need to be trusting in and resting in every single day of our lives as believers. Two things occurred:

1) *Christ was an offering*: This is a sin offering. It speaks of how all sin was paid for at the cross. Our past, present and future sins were all paid in full at the cross of Jesus Christ.

2) *Condemned Sin (nature) in the Flesh* – He not only appeased God's righteousness at the cross. Jesus also condemned the sin nature in our flesh. We know that our sin nature will one day be removed from us when we leave this earth by death or the rapture.

The Cross of Christ dealt with both the sins and the sin nature. Every need for sinful man was met at the cross.

Mission Accomplished

The righteousness that we could never achieve by obeying the Law becomes ours in Christ and in Him alone. The righteousness of the Law here is said to be fulfilled in us. This is a righteousness that is much fuller than anything the world has known. It is in a passive voice, that is to say, it is not something that we are doing, it is something that Christ has done and we trust in. This is the only righteousness that fallen man can have. This is the only righteousness that will satisfy God. This is real righteousness.

Get ready to walk

The word "walk" was a typical metaphor for the conduct of daily life. This final phrase gets at the very core of the Christian experience. How are we to conduct our lives if it is not by a set of rules? How will we know what to do? The answer here is repeated in Galatians 5:16:

But I say, walk by the Spirit, and you will not carry out the desire of the flesh.

Our eyes are not to be fixed on ourselves, nor on any set of rules, but on the person and character of Christ. As we grow in our ability to walk trusting in Him, resting in His completed work, by beholding Him through His word (2 Corinthians 3:18), we grow in our daily condition to be more and more like what we already are in our permanent heavenly position. In other words:

Law says: What you do makes you what you are.

Grace says: What you are will dictate what you do.

ROMANS 8:5-8

The Big Picture

Sometimes a good chart can illustrate clearly what could take pages and pages of written text. The following chart is helpful for understanding graphically what Paul is describing in words.

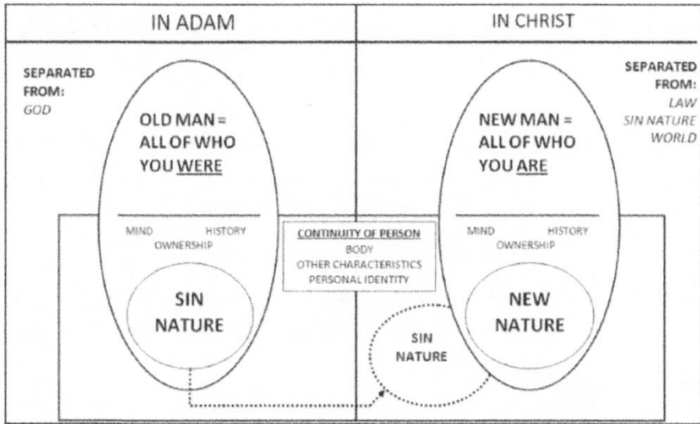

<u>Romans 8:5</u>

[5]For those who are according to the flesh set their minds on the things of the flesh, but those who are according to the Spirit, the things of the Spirit.

Walking Accordingly

Paul is now contrasting the two ways that a believer can walk at any given time. Not shockingly the two different walks have wildly different results. The two different choices a believer is free to make at any time are described in extreme terms in these verses: Life and Death. It is the difference between a life of constant growth and fellowship with God in the relationship which He has freely given us in Christ, or a life that is devoid of that grace, love and fellowship described here simply as: Death. This shows us clearly that someone can be a genuine believer their entire lives and never "get it"! A believer may never understand what is needed to grow and thus spend an entire life out of fellowship with God and trying to make it on his or her own steam. This is a great tragedy that must be understood at all costs if we are to become what the Lord longs to make us to be. So Paul here sets up the two options for believers:

The Flesh – This is a synonym for the Sin Nature (*the Sin*). And harkens back to Paul's statement in Romans 7:

For while we were in the flesh, the sinful passions, which were aroused by the Law, were at work in the members of our body to bear fruit for death. Romans 7:5

But sin, taking opportunity through the commandment, produced in me coveting of every kind; for apart from the Law sin is dead. Romans 7:8

For I know that nothing good dwells in me, that is, in my flesh; for the willing is present in me, but the doing of the good is not. Romans 7:18

but I see a different law in the members of my body, waging war against the law of my mind and making me a prisoner of the law of sin which is in my members. Romans 7:23

So one option available to every believer is to live a life that is focused on (and thus controlled by) the Flesh, or the Sin Nature. This can take either of two guises:

> 1) Living in overt sin which brings about the functional death described in Rom. 6:23: "For the wages of sin is death, but the free gift of God is eternal life in Christ Jesus our Lord."
>
> 2) Attempting to be perfect ourselves by some outside law or standard ending in the death and frustration described in Romans 7 and culminating in 7:24: "Wretched man that I am! Who will set me free from the body of this death?"

Notice that either "ditch" that the believer may fall into is self-focused. Whether focused on "my own personal lusts" or "my own persona desires" the focus is on the same person: *me*. The opposite of being focused on the self, is to be focused on Christ.

Do you Mind?

This verse also mentions the "mind" which is here set either on the flesh or on the Spirit. The word translated "set their minds" is a Greek word that means their entire mindset. It has the idea of the entire mentality being controlled by one principle or the other. It is not just one conscious decision but rather a mental state of being that is controlled either by the flesh or the Spirit. This, again, is the vital choice that each believer makes on a day-by-day, moment-by-moment basis. Our mindset will be, at any given time, either carnal (set on self) or Spiritual (set on the Spirit). Each choice has consequences.

Get Spiritual

The world has great misunderstandings about the idea of "spirituality". Even Christians mistake and use this term unbiblically quite commonly. A person who is involved in eastern mysticism may be called "spiritual" as could someone who is an aesthetic, absorbing themselves with their petty abstinence from whatever worldly evils they view as destructive. A person may be called "spiritual" because they are particularly charismatic and interesting in a group. However, none of these things are Biblical spirituality. To be spiritual from the biblical perspective is to be in fellowship with God. That is, to have one's mindset controlled by the Spirit in the context of relationship and trusting in what God has done for us (and is doing in us) through the life and work of Jesus Christ.

Romans 8:6

6"For the mind set on the flesh is death, but the mind set on the Spirit is life and peace,"

Cause and Effect

Having a "fleshly (or carnal) mindset" has certain effects on the life of the believer. The result of having this mind set is "death". As has been made plain by the study of the use of the word "death" throughout the book of Romans (and the greater context of the Bible itself going back to the first occurrence in Genesis) "death" is separation and spiritual death is separation from fellowship with God. A person who has placed their faith (trust, belief and faith) in Jesus Christ has been saved from "eternal death" (hell and eternal damnation) but can still experience a temporary, functional "death" of lost fellowship with God.

Life and Peace

"Life and peace" are two wonderful words! Just mentioning them can bring a pleasant reaction in our mentalities. We all long to enjoy what Christ promised in Himself:

"The thief comes only to steal and kill and destroy; I came that they may have life, and have it abundantly." John 10:10

"Peace I leave with you; My peace I give to you; not as the world gives do I give to you. Do not let your heart be troubled, nor let it be fearful." John 14:27

"Life" here is abundant flowing Spiritual life that comes from connectedness to the source of life – the God who created life, and is Himself life. Jesus illustrated this reality in John 15:4: "Abide in Me, and I in you. As the branch cannot bear fruit of itself unless it abides in the vine, so neither can you unless you abide in Me." Just as a branch cannot continue to live when severed from the vine, so we dry up quickly when we are not connected to the life giving sap source of the True Vine Jesus Christ.

"Peace" in the biblical context is far more than simply absence of conflict. This has the idea of a wholeness, a completeness that knows no want. This is why Paul was able to say: "I know how to get along with humble means, and I also know how to live in prosperity; in any and every circumstance I have learned the secret of being filled and going hungry, both of having abundance and suffering need." (Philippians 4:12) Paul is able to endure every situation because he has found the wholeness, completeness (that is peace) that is in Christ alone.

<u>Romans 8:7-8</u>

[7]because the mind set on the flesh is hostile toward God; for it does not subject itself to the law of God, for it is not even able to do so, [8]and those who are in the flesh cannot please God.

WHY?

Children have a wonderful way of asking why? When they don't understand something they simply keep asking "why" until they do understand. Paul is catering to this demand of the human mind because when we understand why something is the case it should better prepare us to make correct choices. The "carnal mind" is said to be hostile towards God. "Hostile" here is a strong word that invokes the emotion of hatred. The fleshly mindset is at odds with God by its very disposition. Whether that hostility expresses itself as the desire to do horrible, ugly, disgusting or hateful things, or it seeks to earn righteousness by its own power, the end reality is that it rejects man's essential need for Christ's righteousness in all things.

Not Subject

Even when we try to attain righteousness through the flesh and the law we find that our sin nature is not subject to the Law. The Sin Nature doesn't WANT to be subject to the Law of God, even for the purposes of self-righteousness. This is why every legalist is, at core, a hypocrite. Even if they can fool others into believing that they never violate God's standard of perfection we find that they (or we) do so inadvertently. Then Paul gives the reason why. Not only is the flesh (the sin nature) simply unwilling to subject itself to God's righteous standard it is UNABLE to do so. Even if the desire is there (as it very much was for Paul in Romans 7) the ability (literally – potential power) is simply not there. The flesh is not "reformable"; it must be left at the cross where God dealt with it by identifying us with Jesus Christ.

Those who are in the flesh

Who is "in the flesh"? Clearly every person who has not trusted Jesus Christ is in the flesh, as there is no other place for them to be. However, the context of this chapter isn't talking about believers and unbelievers. The context has believers squarely in view. The believer in Jesus Christ can walk by the flesh or by the Spirit. The consequences of walking in the flesh are plain, and of the UTMOST importance.

cannot please God

This is a statement that could not be understated in importance. Anything we do while abiding in the flesh. Anything that we do for selfish reasons does NOT please God at all. This is quite important as believers are often tempted to try to do the "right thing" to maintain appearances. We may choose a life that we think is the most sure to please God (like a ministry livelihood, missions, or any sort of social justice) yet if it is not done while walking in the Holy Spirit is it WASTED TIME from the perspective of our own personal spiritual growth. A person could spend their entire lives feeding the poor, handing out tracts or doing missions in the most dangerous places and never once do a single thing to please God.

Still about the Relationship

This may start to seem a bit dry, but in the end it is a continuation of everything that Paul has written about so far. Everything revolves around our fellowship and connectedness to Jesus Christ. If a man is in fellowship with his wife she will be blessed just talking to him. If he has been a scoundrel and is not in fellowship with her then no amount of flowers and gifts will win him back into her favor. Similarly, in our relationship with God only what we do with the life He provides will result in spiritual growth. This chart by Vern and Randy Peterman illustrates:

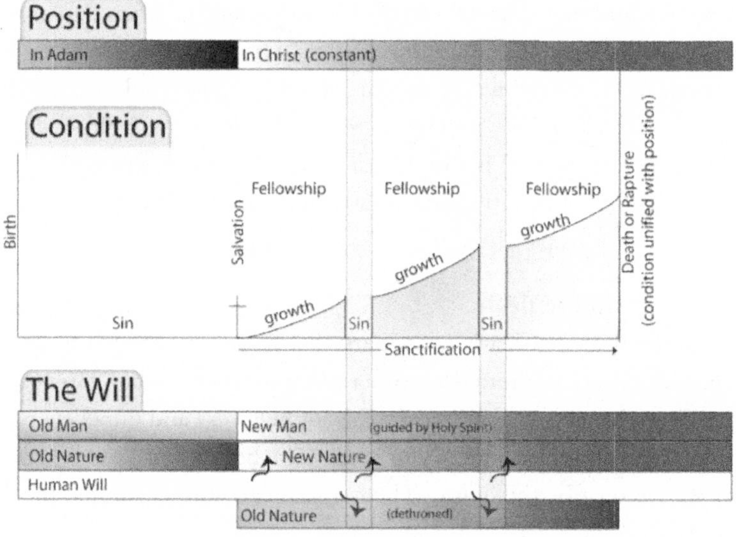

ROMANS 8:9-11

The Holy Spirit

These verses deal with the life source of the believer: the Holy Spirit. There is a great deal of revelation in Scripture about the nature and work of the Holy Spirit, and there is also a great deal of false teaching and misunderstanding about this vital power source in the life of the believer. Some teach that the Spirit is coming and going in the life of the believer and cannot be counted on. Others teach that we can do something to lose the Holy Spirit at one point and then regain it at another point. Both of these false errors are in distinct opposition to the teaching of scripture. These verses focus on the immense power that is available to the believer each and every moment because of the permanent indwelling of the Holy Spirit that has sealed us. These verses need to be understood and applied in the life of every single believer in order for us to grow. This is great news!

Romans 8:9

However, you are not in the flesh but in the Spirit, if indeed the Spirit of God dwells in you. But if anyone does not have the Spirit of Christ, he does not belong to Him.

However

The previous verse revealed a very important spiritual reality. If someone is operating out of the basis of the sin nature they can, by no means, please God. For the unbeliever, this is the only "life-source" that they have to operate from. There is no second choice. The believer however has a choice to make every day. We can operate in fellowship with God with the Holy Spirit as our controlling principle, or we can operate in broken fellowship with God and will fall either into legalism or license. The only option that pleases the Lord is when we are operating in an open and working relationship with Him through the permanently indwelling Holy Spirit.

What you are not in, and what you are in

As believers, we are positioned permanently in Christ. Operating in the flesh (or the sin nature) should be the exception to our usual manner of living. While the believer has only one option (operating in the flesh), the believer is a new creation. The believer is in Christ and now has both his old sin nature and his new nature (The Holy Spirit). As was discussed in the previous lesson the believer is spiritual when he or she operates by the power of the Holy Spirit in fellowship with Him.

Interesting "ifs"

Conditional sentences are interesting. When we make an "if/then" statement in English it nearly always implies the possibility that the "if" statement is either true or false. This has caused a great amount of misunderstanding in reading the Bible. The Greek language has four different classes of conditional sentences. Greek "if" statements can convey the idea that the "if" statement is true, false, probable or possible. This is the first kind of conditional sentence. Thus the "if" is assumed to be true. Translators, in reference to this fact, often translate these sentences (correctly) with the word "since." This is the case here. Paul is not suggesting that the Roman believers who have put their faith in Christ may or may not be indwelt by the Holy Spirit. He is saying that they are, in fact, indwelt with the Holy Spirit. A fuller translation would read: "However, you are not in the flesh but in the Spirit, ***since*** the Spirit of God dwells in you."

Anyone who doesn't have the Spirit

Paul lays it out on the line. Anyone who does not have the Spirit simply is not saved. The Holy Spirit isn't someone that comes and goes. We don't "lose the Spirit" nor do we need to "invite the Spirit in" as some are prone to do. Quite to the contrary, the presence of the Holy Spirit in our lives is something that is permanent and complete. As Paul wrote to the believers in Ephesus:

> [13]*In Him, you also, after listening to the message of truth, the gospel of your salvation--having also believed, you were sealed in Him with the Holy Spirit of promise,* [14]*who is given as a pledge of our inheritance, with a view to the redemption of God's own possession, to the praise of His glory.* Ephesians 1:13-14

Here the reality of the Spirit is confirmed (just as it is clearly stated in Romans 8). Having placed faith in the gospel the saint is then permanently indwelt by the Holy Spirit. Permanence is found in each word here. A seal, in the context of Biblical cultures was a serious affair. No one could break an official seal. In fact, unauthorized tampering with a sealed document or item carried the death penalty depending on the authority of the one who placed the seal. A seal implied ownership, security and destiny. This is what the Holy Spirit is to the believer.

Not Belonging

The person who does not have the Holy Spirit is the person who has not placed faith in Jesus Christ and thus is "none of His." The person who has placed faith in Christ is said to be Christ's possession, property and responsibility. The same idea is conveyed in John 10:

27"My sheep hear My voice, and I know them, and they follow Me; 28and I give eternal life to them, and they will never perish; and no one will snatch them out of My hand. 29" My Father, who has given them to Me, is greater than all; and no one is able to snatch them out of the Father's hand. John 10:27-29

The Greek in this passage is even clearer than the English. The sense of this passage is that the sheep of the Lord cannot perish of their own doing. No person or force can snatch them from His mighty hand. Neither the believers' own failures, nor the powers of darkness, nor any other person can revoke the indwelling Holy Spirit by whom we are Christ's possession and the sheep of His pasture. Praise the Lord!

Romans 8:10

10If Christ is in you, though the body is dead because of sin, yet the spirit is alive because of righteousness.

Hebrew Poetry

Paul often wrote with Hebrew poetry patterns that focus on repetition to make something clear. We might display this poetic repetition as follows:

But if anyone does not have the Spirit of Christ,

he does not belong to Him.

If Christ is in you,

though the body is dead because of sin,

yet the spirit is alive because of righteousness.

The negative is stated and then "rhymed" with the positive. "If the Spirit weren't in you then you wouldn't be His, but since He IS in you (who believe) you are His!"

"If" again
Here again we see a similar construction that can be more clearly translated since. Paul is making the statement to further dispel the idea that the negative statement "were the Spirit NOT in a person (note Paul uses the word "anyone" when talking about the absence of the spirit and "you" – plural- when he talks about the person who IS sealed with the Spirit". Paul's point is clear – If you have placed your faith in Christ, then the Spirit is in you.

The Body
Though our physical body will have an end (either at death or the Rapture), our spirit lives because of righteousness. Going back to Romans 3, Paul wrote:

> *21 But now apart from the Law the righteousness of God has been manifested, being witnessed by the Law and the Prophets, 22 even the righteousness of God through faith in Jesus Christ for all those who believe; for there is no distinction; 23 for all have sinned and fall short of the glory of God, 24 being justified as a gift by His grace through the redemption which is in Christ Jesus; 25 whom God displayed publicly as a propitiation in His blood through faith. This was to demonstrate His righteousness, because in the forbearance of God He passed over the sins previously committed; 26 for the demonstration, I say, of His righteousness at the present time, so that He would be just and the justifier of the one who has faith in Jesus.* Romans 3:21-26

As we see repeated here, the believer is continually dependent on the only true righteousness that is available – Christ's righteousness. There is no point in our lives that we will be able to look to God and say, "Look what great things I have done for you." At every moment the only truly righteous actions that we are able to produce are those that we do while resting in Him. Paul echo's this sentiment in Galatians 2:20-21:

> [20]*"I have been crucified with Christ; and it is no longer I who live, but Christ lives in me; and the life which I now live in the flesh I live by faith in the Son of God, who loved me and gave Himself up for me.* [21]*I do not nullify the grace of God, for if righteousness comes through the Law, then Christ died needlessly."* Galatians 2:20-21

The point is plain – we continually have spiritual life (connection to God in relationship) because of the righteousness of Jesus Christ and our identification with Him. There will never be any other source of life for the believer.

Romans 8:11

But if the Spirit of Him who raised Jesus from the dead dwells in you, He who raised Christ Jesus from the dead will also give life to your mortal bodies through His Spirit who dwells in you.

Note: "if" is again "since" here.

Which Spirit is that?

Note the ways in which the Holy Spirit is referred to. In these verses He is called the Spirit, the Spirit of God, and "the Spirit of Him who raised Jesus" that is the Father. So we see here, a clear demonstration of the Trinity. Jesus and the Father are displayed equally as the source and identification of the Holy Spirit, who is sent forth from both the Father and Christ together.

Identification, Identification, Identification

These chapters are so very clearly about our identification with Christ. It is odd that the truth surrounding our Spiritual birth (by grace through faith in Jesus Christ) is often understood by students of the Bible, yet the understanding of our identification with Jesus Christ is entirely missed, even though our identification with Christ is mentioned as many times in Scripture as the reality of our new birth! These chapters are chiefly concerning our identification with Jesus Christ in His death, burial, resurrection, ascension and seating as the chief means of our sanctification (or our growth in Christ). So it is very important to our development in the Lord.

Raised Jesus from the Dead

Here our spiritual life is again equated with the death, burial and resurrection of the One in whom we placed our faith. In mentioning the historical fact that the Holy Spirit raised Christ from the dead Paul is relating that the same spiritual reality is accomplished in all who have believed. These words echo Paul's words in Romans 6:

> [3]*Or do you not know that all of us who have been baptized into Christ Jesus have been baptized into His death?* [4]*Therefore we have been buried with Him through baptism into death, so that as Christ was raised from the dead through the glory of the Father, so we too might walk in newness of life.* [5]*For if we have become united with Him in the likeness of His death, certainly we shall also be in the likeness of His resurrection,* [6]*knowing this, that our old self was crucified with Him, in order that our body of sin might be done away with, so that we would no longer be slaves to sin;* [7]*for he who has died is freed from sin.*
> Romans 6:3-7

Outsourcing our Labors

While our earthly bodies offered no hope of attaining Eternal Life, and while our Sin Nature could never achieve the approval of God our lives in the body are not a hopeless waste of time. They are not a waste of time because of the provision of the indwelling Holy Spirit. The Holy Spirit is here the conduit of Spiritual Life in the believer. We find that the Holy Spirit is the one who is constantly giving us life, but there is more! We find that here the future promise is equally sure. There is no fear in death for the believer because it is this same Holy Spirit that will resurrect us to our perfect new life, with new bodies that have no indwelling sin nature. This is a wonderful blessing that leaves us with no cause for worry or for fear. We can look forward to a resurrection like the resurrection of Jesus Christ because we are indwelt with that same Spirit. This is a great and powerful comfort to believers in the face of the physical death that is before each of us, unless the rapture comes first!

Conclusion

The Holy Spirit, writing through Paul, very clearly wants us to understand with crystal clarity how our lives are to be lived. At any given moment we can find out what we are to be doing. We are to be beholding Christ, through the Spirit that indwells us. If we are walking in the flesh we need to agree with Him that we are not walking in the right source, and continue in fellowship with the Holy Spirit. Paul stated this clearly in Ephesians 1:18-21:

18 I pray that the eyes of your heart may be enlightened, so that you will know what is the hope of His calling, what are the riches of the glory of His inheritance in the saints, 19 and what is the surpassing greatness of His power toward us who believe. These are in accordance with the working of the strength of His might 20 which He brought about in Christ, when He raised Him from the dead and seated Him at His right hand in the heavenly places, 21 far above all rule and authority and power and dominion, and every name that is named, not only in this age but also in the one to come.

Paul repeatedly states that this powerful Holy Spirit that has indwelt us, and identified us with Jesus Christ in His death, burial, resurrection, ascension and seating, is our life source. We are to be in constant communication and fellowship with Him. And the only reason that this need can be fulfilled in our lives is because Christ died on a cross for us. Paying for our sins, separating us from our sin nature, and giving us life.

ROMANS 8:12-17

Daddy!
These verses deal with one of the most pivotal elements in understanding our Salvation. It is the understanding of the fact of our actual relationship to God as His children. For some people even the mention of the word "father" can be painful; wrapped up in memories and experiences of pain and hurt. Here we see the believer has God as his or her true Father. We find that only God will satisfy that longing, or need, of all of us to be known and deeply loved by the One who made us. These verses continue the amazing description of what is true of the believer based wholly and entirely on God's amazing grace.

Romans 8:12-13
12So then, brethren, we are under obligation, not to the flesh, to live
according to the flesh-- 13for if you are living according to the flesh, you
must die; but if by the Spirit you are putting to death the deeds of the body,
you will live.

Great! More logic!
Paul continues with his use of logical connectives. This argument continues to build increasingly on what the Lord Jesus Christ has done for us. This is rooted in the verses before in which the Spirit of God was seen to permanently indwell every single believer in Jesus Christ. The indwelling Holy Spirit was seen there to be a mark of ownership and was equally attributed as being both the Spirit of Christ and the Spirit of God, again clearly alluding to the entire Trinity being at work in the amazing miracle of our salvation. Building upon this Paul continues this out to say that not only are we assured of Christ's ultimate victory in our lives, it is even more personal than that!

What do I owe you?
When we break off a relationship with a landlord we may yet owe them a security deposit. When a prisoner is released from jail they may have some

remaining obligation to meet with a parole officer. In the previous verses we found that we have been released completely from the demands of the flesh. Here we see that there is no debt that we have left to pay to the flesh. We don't owe the sin nature anything, and are never again going to be in a relationship where we must obey the sin nature. Even when the only option in the world seems to walk according to the sin nature, nothing could be further from the truth.

Live according to the flesh

The way this is described is with the phrase "live according to the flesh". The idea going back to the reality that the believer has two life-sources from which we can operate: the sin nature (flesh) or the Spirit. When we are operating according to the flesh it can look like overt sinful actions, or like legalism. When we are walking according to the Spirit we experience nothing but life, righteousness and peace. The fact that we are never again obligated to walk in the flesh teaches us a couple of important facts:

1) When we live according to the sin nature it is because we chose to.

2) We never need to choose to do so again (we don't have to).

Death

Here, again we see death in the Bible as separation. Many translations give the sense that this is a future death, but in the text here "you will die" are present tense and indicative mode. This is to say that "when you walk in the flesh, you die." This is a simple statement of fact. When we walk in the flesh we are separated in our fellowship with God. The believer who is walking according to the flesh (and every believer will do so at some time or another) is instantly in broken fellowship with God. The answer? To live by the Spirit!

Experiencing Death, or Putting to Death

Here we have the two different modes of existence categorized. Either we are separated in our fellowship from God, or we are reckoning ourselves dead to our sin nature and are in fellowship with God. This idea of "putting to death the deeds of the body" may sound abstract, or even mystical. But once again, a consistent understanding of the word "death" makes it far less confusing. Very seldom are we tempted to walk in the sin nature by someone coming up and saying, "Take your eyes of Christ! Get really angry at me instead!" Often the situation that arises tempts us and takes our eyes off of Christ. How do we respond?

Do we respond by taking ourselves out of situations where we may be tempted? This may be wise to a point (an ex-alcoholic would do well to avoid bars). However, even if we were to confine ourselves to a small cell with nothing but a bed and a chair we would find that we brought our flesh in with us; every instance offering us the temptation to take our eyes off of Jesus.

We find the answer is to recognize the desires and temptations for what they are and remembering that we truly are dead to our sin nature, and that we are not obliged in any way to hand control over to the sin nature, at any time. By this we "put to death" the deeds of the body. We agree with the Lord that His work on the cross with which we were identified was effective. We are, indeed separated from the sin nature and no longer are under any obligation to obey it.

Live

The result of this mindset is great! LIFE! This is the life and life to the fullest that Christ promised. It is life in a moment by moment fellowship with the God of the Universe through His wonderful Son, Jesus Christ. This is what we are all longing for, and the only thing that stands in our way, is our own trembling will. We so often fall, look away, hand the reigns over to the Sin Nature. The results never change: fear, hopelessness, pain, despair. Yet we do it again and again. God's grace is sufficient for each loss and we are to respond by getting up, confessing again and getting back into fellowship with Him, each time being willing to trust Him to do what He has told us He will do.

Romans 8:15

15For you have not received a spirit of slavery leading to fear again, but you have received a spirit of adoption as sons by which we cry out, "Abba! Father!"

What you don't have

Here Paul draws a sharp distinction. So much of manmade religion is fear based. "Do this or else!", "Give this much or else!", "Obey me, or else!"

Many Christians have wrongly assumed that fear must still be used to threaten people into obedience, or to give. Nothing could be more disgustingly unbiblical! We see that when we place our faith in Christ, God makes us into a new creature and this new creature is not to be motivated by fear any longer! That is not the relationship that the Lord longs to have with us. This is great news. Jesus Christ said: "No longer do I call you slaves, for the slave does not know what his master is doing; but I have called you friends, for all things that I have heard from My Father I have made known to you." This verse draws the circle of intimacy even closer yet!

A spirit of adoption

Roman adoption was far different from our modern idea of adoption. People were generally not adopted as infants like we see in our culture. Adoption was a complex legal procedure by which a person was permanently placed in a new family. Their legal connection to their old family was done away with completely. All of their debts were wiped out completely. They were given full access to all of the family accounts as an adult son. The adopted could not be supplanted, or replaced, even by a natural son. The new adopted son was placed permanently in the new family. When Paul used this term he could not have found a more permanent cultural symbol for our new relationship to God through Jesus Christ. Whether we are in fellowship with our Heavenly Father or not, we are His permanently adopted children. Placed in Him once and for all, never to be released or cast away!

Daddy!

The Jews would never have the audacity to call the God "my Father." They would call him "*our* Father" but to claim that God was "my Father" was a statement that constituted blasphemy and the Jews sought to stone Jesus for making it. Yet, Jesus is the true Son of the Father, and it is in Him that we are placed. Thus we can go to God with the most intimate expression – *Abba*! Abba was an intimate form of the word for Father. Most like our English "Daddy" or "Papa". This is a position of unparalleled honor and blessing, and it is ours EVERY MOMENT OF EVERY DAY IN CHRIST! At any time, any moment, we can climb onto the lap of our Heavenly Father and say, "Daddy, I need you. I love you. I am so thankful for you!" He hears us! How often do we get confused by our fleshly view of "religion" and not live in accordance with this wonderful relationship that we have been given in Jesus Christ? How would our relationship with God, and our lives, look if we lived constantly in awareness of this amazing relationship that is ours?

Romans 8:16-17

16The Spirit Himself testifies with our spirit that we are children of God,
17and if children, heirs also, heirs of God and fellow heirs with Christ, if
indeed we suffer with Him so that we may also be glorified with Him.

A good testimony

Here we see the Holy Spirit portrayed as what He is – a personality. As the third member of the Trinity, He indwells us and bears a constant witness to the reality that we are children of God. In the previous verses we saw the magnificent reality of the permanent indwelling Holy Spirit and how He is the constant seal on us, telling ourselves, the world and the powers of darkness that we are the property and possession of God. Not just property, but the very children of God. We are now related to God not on the basis of what we do, but on the basis of who we are in Jesus Christ!

Children

This word for "children" here means literally – "born ones" we are truly born anew of God, just as John 1:12-13 says: "But as many as received Him, to them He gave the right to become children of God, even to those who believe in His name, who were born, not of blood nor of the will of the flesh nor of the will of man, but of God." Birth is a permanent process. When a child is born there is no process by which it can be "un-born". This new life that we are born into is eternal, and therefore cannot be broken or damaged. If it could then it could not be described as "eternal". It is the durable full reality of God's new redemptive creative act in Christ! But there is MORE GREAT NEWS!

Inheritance

In our culture we often think of an inheritance being something that happens at the time of a person's death. However, in the context of the cultures of the New Testament a Father would prepare an inheritance for his children when they became legally accepted as sons. Our new inheritance is found in Christ, in whom we have been given every spiritual blessing in heavenly places. This inheritance includes the fact that we will be united to Christ permanently into all of eternity! This is very exciting: One day, Christ will inherit the whole earth and we will be with Him, ruling and reigning with Him as His Bride. This inheritance is the eternal fullness, wholeness, peace of being united to Jesus forever!

Suffering and Glory

Here we see the impending reality of our earthly condition. We will, indeed, suffer for our faith in Him. Whether the persecution of the world, or from our flesh, we are promised suffering on this planet (Romans 3:5; James 1:2-3) however, along with that suffering now comes the promise that God will also glorify us with Jesus Christ. The next section outlines the reality of our suffering and the glory that is ours in Christ, all by His grace, through His work!

ROMANS 8:18-22

Ah! Suffering!

Paul is dealing with one of the major issues that believers have to deal with. What is our relationship to suffering? Why do we suffer? How should we view suffering? It is easy to get caught thinking about suffering in overly simplistic terms. Many of us hide many wrong thoughts about suffering such as:

- Legalistic - "All suffering happens because I did something wrong."
- Atheistic/Agnostic – "Suffering is proof that God doesn't care, exist, or isn't able."
- Victim – "It is always someone else's fault."

More unbiblical attitudes about suffering could surely be added to this but Paul doesn't waste time with that. Rather, the Holy Spirit gives us a clear understanding of where trials come from, what purpose they are serving and how the believer is to respond to them.

<u>Romans 8:18</u>

For I consider that the sufferings of this present time are not worthy to be compared with the glory that is to be revealed to us.

Reason it out…

In the previous verse Paul noted an important point about suffering. We are positioned in Christ, thus He identifies with US in our suffering. This is difficult for us to imagine, however, it is the biblical truth. And just as He shares in our suffering we are both sharing now in His glory as we are transformed (2 Corinthians 3:18) and will ultimately be conformed to that glory when we behold Him face to face (either at the time of our death or at the rapture when Christ will return for His Church). Paul then continues with the idea of logical argument.

"For I consider" here was the same word translated "consider" in Romans 6:11: "Even so consider yourselves to be dead to sin, but alive to God in Christ Jesus." This word means to put something down as true. It was used in accounting for placing the correct figures in the book and including them in all of the sums to follow. This word also has the sense of a "fully reasoned out conclusion." So the idea is that Paul considers this a good and reasonable fact. It only makes sense to rely on a fact and incorporate it in your understanding and reaction to all relevant circumstances.

Suffering in the Now

The present world offers no shortage of suffering. Relationships that don't work out the way we had hoped, work troubles, food shortages, disasters and catastrophes all make us say, "It shouldn't be this way!" Yet, the word is all inclusive here, all of the sufferings are in view here. Paul had experienced a great amount of personal pain and suffering. When he placed his faith in Christ he left a great deal behind him. Undoubtedly he had a number of friends, likely he even had admirers and those who would talk about how great he was around the dinner tahle. All of these relationships fell away when he became a Christian. Those very people who applauded him before were now persecuting him with equal vigor. Not only that, we know that Paul struggled with health problems, physical persecutions and imprisonments. We have sufferings of our own and now Paul gives us some superb advice as to how to consider those difficulties.

Holding it up to the Light

When you need to get a good look at something you hold it up to the light and make sure that you are getting a clear view. The believer is to hold all of their struggles up to the light of God's revelation to us in the Bible. When we look at what has been promised to everyone who enters into a relationship with Christ through faith we get to see things in perspective. And that makes all of the difference.

Very often we look at our situations and get bent out of shape about a detail, or an offhanded comment, or some minor incident. Looking at it a day later we find that the thing that had our feathers so very ruffled was really nothing of any great importance when considered in perspective. This is what happens to EVERY struggle when we truly understand the magnitude of the glory that the Lord has shared, and will share, with us in the person of Jesus Christ.

Placing Prepositions
Glory has been well described as the "Radiant essence of who God is." It was this glory that Moses could not look upon and live. It is this glory that caused Isaiah to say "I am undone!" The glory of God is a reality that we cannot fully comprehend. Yet, this is our present as we rest in Jesus Christ and our position in Him. Our future is tied up in the glory of God. This is something that needs some time to soak in. Essentially the future that lies before us will be characterized by a perfection and a wonder that we know very little of from our day to day experience. This is fantastic news.

Some translations have this phrase brought across that the glory will be revealed "to" us, and others have the glory being revealed "in" us. The Greek word properly has the idea of "into". But here is the reality: God's glory will be revealed both in and through us. We will behold His glory and we will reflect His glory. At that time we will be perfect instruments of His glory. This is our future. This is what our earthly struggles cannot even compare to.

The Point: It is perfectly logical, and spiritually appropriate when dealing with struggles, to turn your mind to the glory that will be yours when you are face to face with Christ.

Romans 8:19
For the anxious longing of the creation waits eagerly for the revealing of the sons of God.

You are not the only one!
Often times suffering brings a sense of loneliness and isolation. A person can easily be tempted to feel as if they are the only one suffering or struggling in the way that they are at any given moment. Yet in these verses we see that it is not just the believer who is suffering…the very earth itself is not as it was intended to be! Paul starts a poetic personification of the physical world (ascribing to the universe, earth, animal and plant kingdoms human emotions and personality). But here is the point: Suffering was never God's idea. God did not invent death, neither did He invent

suffering. These verses look at the objective reality of the hard parts of life in light of our loving, perfect, savior God.

Leaning In

You know when someone is really paying attention to you. When you are telling an interesting story, or giving someone information they need, they lean in, they make and maintain eye contact. They make noises that confirm that they are listening ("Yes…Uh-huh…right"). This is the word picture attached to word translated here "anxious longing." Paul is saying that the world is paying rapt attention awaiting the moment. Much like a cat stalking a mouse hole this is the focal point of the creation.

Well, what are you waiting for?

The whole creation is waiting for the "revealing of the sons of God." Believers in the Church are repeatedly told to look forward to the coming of Christ for His Church (commonly called "the Rapture"). This is, in fact, the next future event in unfulfilled prophecy. This is what Paul was looking forward to and expected that it may well be in his lifetime. While this wonderful promise is mentioned constantly in the New Testament the most specific teaching about it is found in 1 Corinthians 15:35-50; 1 Thessalonians 1:10, 2:19-20, 5:1-11; 2 Thessalonians 2:1-17. This is where believers are removed from the earth before the period in which the Lord will pour out judgment and wrath upon those who remain.

Romans 8:20-21

[20]For the creation was subjected to futility, not willingly, but because of
Him who subjected it, in hope [21]that the creation itself also will be set free
from its slavery to corruption into the freedom of the glory of the children
of God.

Subjection

Here some very important points about the state of the world are made clear. The entire creation was affected by the results of Adam's sin. However, we see that the "subjection" of the creation was passive in nature. This is something that was done to the earth. Whenever we see an earthquake, a flood, a tornado, a hurricane, a tsunami or a volcano eruption we often hear people asking: "Why would God allow this?" It is important that we understand that these things come about not because God wanted pain and death and destruction but because it was necessary for the process of redemption. So when we look at the principles of death and decay, horrible events in the world and the difficulties of life on this planet and think that it shouldn't have to be this way, we are correct. God never intended the world to be a place of difficulty and cruelty that it is. It was sin that brought about these conditions and the earth itself is longing for the end of the futility that it now experiences as the victim.

Agency

Notice what caused this state of futility in the physical creation. It wasn't directly Adam, and it wasn't Satan. Neither are mentioned here. This verse says that it is God that subjected the creation to futility. This is referring to the curse recorded in Genesis 3 and the results of that time. Notice, however, the situation about which Paul is talking. God created this beautiful universe and planet that existed without death or decay. It was gorgeous and glorious and God regularly pronounces the judgment "It is good" upon His beloved creation. Then He creates mankind in His own image. He makes man to be, like Him, relational and spiritual while also having a physical body. Then mankind sins, and is no longer fit for the perfect creation and garden which He had made.

Logically, the answer would be simple: Destroy/remove the broken piece (mankind) from the equation of perfection, joy and beauty. God, however, chose to do the opposite. God chose to allow the sin of Adam to effect everything else. Subjecting everything to the principles of death, decay and catastrophe all because He loves you and I. God has allowed the death and dishonor to His name to continue while rebellious man has continued to defy and reject Him for six thousand years because He knew every person whom He had set up to be created in Adam and Eve (that includes us!) and He loves us. He would rather destroy His beautiful creation, and sacrifice His own Son than be separated from humanity and be glorified by us for His wonderful grace, mercy and love.

In Hope

However, the destruction and futility of the earth is by no means the end of the story. Just as God sent Jesus Christ to earth to provide the opportunity to all who receive Him to be redeemed, so He will also redeem and restore His creation. This is a legitimate hope for us as well! Hope, in the Biblical sense, does not convey the idea of contingency (as in, "This may happen…and I *hope* that it does!) it has the idea of certainty. We can go through and face all of the difficulties knowing that we will get to see the earth in its restored form, and that is very exciting!

Freedom!

We can see and perceive that the world is not as it's meant to be. Dramatic language is used: It was made futile, subjected, enslaved. We see in earth still much of the beauty and glory of its Creator. However, we also see the reality that it is a harsh, cruel and dangerous world in which countless beings perish in a seemingly cold and uncaring atmosphere. Yet, one day (as soon as seven years from today) the earth will be set free from its bondage and corruption. We will see the earth as it was meant to be. The freedom that it was designed for and that it "longs for" is the freedom of serving and meeting the needs of those who long to love and glorify God. God created the original Garden of Eden to be a place of comfort, pleasure and productivity for humanity and anyone who has placed faith in Christ will see the earth restored to its original function.

Romans 8:22

For we know that the whole creation groans and suffers the pains of childbirth together until now.

What do we know now?

Knowledge is very important. What we know, and apply, affects the way we live our lives at every turn. Paul is appealing both to their theological understanding (in the case of the Jews and God-fearers there) as well as to their senses. This word for "knowledge" focuses on "knowledge by perception". They know this because they have seen it. They have seen the explanation of it in the Bible, they see the effects of it every day. Whenever a natural disaster occurs, or a pestilence sweeps across the land we are shown the reality of Paul's statements.

Having a Baby

Pregnancy is an amazing process. Because of the fall, it is a process that involves a great deal of discomfort and pain. The mother finds herself often sick and unable to keep food down, then she finds her body changing in very uncomfortable ways to accommodate this little life within her. As the baby gets bigger she gets bigger, and less and less comfortable. As the time for the birth approaches she very often begins to feel different pains and contractions leading up to the "active labor period." The birth process itself is very dramatic and incredibly uncomfortable. But at the end of that process (if all goes well) she holds her beautiful child and will often say, "It was worth every moment of pain and discomfort."

This is the picture to which Paul is appealing. The one "in labor" is the whole physical creation. Pain, turbulence, decay and difficulty are all common on earth. After the Lord comes for His Church (John 14) then the seven year "active-labor" process will begin. This is the final seven week period predicted by Daniel in Daniel 9:20-27. That same seven year period is described in great detail in Revelation 4-19. This period (The Tribulation, The Great Tribulation, The Day of the Lord, The Day of Jacob's Trouble) will be the darkest hour of the cosmos, and all of creation will be affected. However, just as in the illustration of a human birth, this time of greatest pain will "give birth" to a new and glorious day: The Millennial Reign of Christ.

The details of the millennial reign of Christ are given throughout the Prophetic word. While the details of life in the Kingdom of God are truly exciting to study and well worthy of the believer's time as they are exactly the encouragement the Lord means for the believer to have in difficulty, we will focus on the centerpiece of the Millennial Kingdom: The King. In this Kingdom Jesus Christ will rule from Zion in perfect wisdom, justice, understanding and love. The creation itself will cease to be subjected to the principles of decay and will be redeemed and life on earth will be more like it was supposed to be than it has been since Adam fell. After this thousand years Satan will be allowed to lead one final rebellion which will be quelled, the Great White Throne Judgment of unbelievers will take place and the New Heavens and the New Earth will begin.

ROMANS 8:23-27

Hope and Help

The previous verses described the world subjected to futility. It was noted that while the futility of the world systems was not part of God's original creation, it was something that God did in order to save fallen man. These verses make sense of suffering in the world. All of the horrific events of reality are found to be the result of Sin, and will ultimately be removed from the physical creation. The believer has special assurance in spite of all of these difficulties. The one who is in a relationship with Christ looks forward to the glory of the Lord being revealed both in and through him. The believer in Christ can also look forward, in faith, to the time when the physical creation will be restored and made right. This is an exciting thing for the believer, as we will behold with our very eyes what the world was meant to look like during the millennial reign of Christ. This is an exciting thing indeed. The following verses talk about that hope that we have been given in Christ and our help in the Holy Spirit, with Whom we are indwelt.

Romans 8:23

And not only this, but also we ourselves, having the first fruits of the Spirit, even we ourselves groan within ourselves, waiting eagerly for our adoption as sons, the redemption of our body

Continuing the thought…

It is important to remember that, while it is quite profitable to look at Scripture one verse at a time it was written as a letter. It is a constant tension that we must keep both looking carefully, but understanding that each of the verses flow together into larger themes and purpose. Paul's purpose in chapter 8 of Romans is still to display the life of the Christ in the believer for whom there is now no condemnation in Christ Jesus (Romans 8:1). This verse starts with a logical connection that says that Paul is adding to the train of thought that he was already working with. In previous verses Paul had the believer looking forward to his or her glorious future in Christ.

We, not just "you"

Paul takes these believers shoulder to shoulder with him here. He tells them that this is something that every believer shares. So many man-made religions are riddled with a sense of hierarchy in which people have differing positions before God based on how much money they have, or what they have done or given up "for God." There is none of this in the Biblical faith. Every believer comes to God through Faith alone, by Grace alone, in Christ alone. Paul is very clear that every believer shares this same destiny, and he is pleased to include himself in this same fact and expectation.

First fruits of the Spirit

Paul has already written about some of the ministries of the Holy Spirit in this chapter. He has established firmly that the sealing of the Holy Spirit is not an "up and down – Now you see Him now you don't" ministry.

However, you are not in the flesh but in the Spirit, if indeed the Spirit of God dwells in you. But if anyone does not have the Spirit of Christ, he does not belong to Him. If Christ is in you, though the body is dead because of sin, yet the spirit is alive because of righteousness. But if the Spirit of Him who raised Jesus from the dead dwells in you, He who raised Christ Jesus from the dead will also give life to your mortal bodies through His Spirit who dwells in you. Romans 8:9-11

The Spirit Himself testifies with our spirit that we are children of God, and if children, heirs also, heirs of God and fellow heirs with Christ, if indeed we suffer with Him so that we may also be glorified with Him. Romans 8:16-17

The indwelling Holy Spirit is the chief resource for living the Christian life. A fear that He would be constantly abandoning us or "coming and going" is a destructive idea that will keep us from our full potential of joy, peace and love in Christ.

But there is more to this exciting story. This indwelling Holy Spirit that is the provision for our day by day moment by moment existence is here called the "first fruits". The Jewish system of harvest was in three broad stages. The "first fruits" were the first element of the harvest, after the first fruits came the bulk of the harvesting season, finally the gleanings were gathered as the final phase in the harvest season. Notice, that the indwelling Spirit, while a greater blessing than we can comprehend, is only the beginning of what the Lord is doing in our lives. In Ephesians 1:13-14 describe it this way:

In Him, you also, after listening to the message of truth, the gospel of your salvation--having also believed, you were sealed in Him with the Holy Spirit of promise, who is given as a pledge of our inheritance, with a view to the redemption of God's own possession, to the praise of His glory. Ephesians 1:13-14

Here the Holy Spirit is called a "pledge" or a down-payment. The Holy Spirit is the beginning (and WHAT a beginning!) of what the Lord is doing in us. There is yet more ahead for the believer and our final conformation to the image and character of Jesus Christ. Believers have much to look forward to in every situation, along with the constant assurance that the Lord is not done with us yet. Praise the Lord for His great and wonderful gift!

Groaning

Paul is not talking about whining here. What Paul is writing about here is the experience of most believers who understand the Lord's great love for them and all that is ahead for them. In the last verse the world was "groaning" but here the believers are groaning as well. A deep groan is sometimes the only way to express what we are feeling, often at the times that words won't do. It is important to understand for what we are groaning, as believers. Note, that Paul includes himself in this groaning as well. It is common, you may even say normal, for a believer who understands the Lord's love to feel "out of place" here on earth. We look around and wish for the time when we are no longer plagued by our sin nature, when the world system is ruled by the one legitimate ruler: Jesus Christ.

More than anything else this sensation is akin to homesickness. We may have experienced the desire to be back with family, or friends when we've moved, or when we first left home to go to school, or on a long trip of some sort. The desire for familiar things burdens us and we are emotionally effected. The strange thing about this homesickness is that it is a desire for a place that we have never yet been. However, it is looking forward to unbroken fellowship with Jesus Christ that makes it perfect, that increases our longing. He is the one with whom we will always be thereafter, never to depart from Him. It is important to realize that those feelings (and desires) are entirely godly and acceptable. Everyone who is walking with the Lord Jesus Christ by grace through faith longs to know Him better. The longing actually draws us closer to Him!

Longing for what?

The thing looked forward to here is translated "adoption as sons". In our context we talk about adoption chiefly in terms of a child, or a baby, who is brought into a new family. While this is a beautiful picture, this was not what Paul is saying that the believer is waiting for. This Greek word combines the word for "son" with the word for "to place, or position". So this is really a "son positioning". This was not a process that was done to a child or to a baby. Up until a child was "son-positioned" his father could kill him, or disown him at any moment. However, when a person was "son-positioned" a few radical things occurred:

1) Once "placed" a person could never be eliminated or abrogated. If the "placed" person was not of the biological family of the one doing the "placing" even a biological son couldn't take his place.

2) All former identifications were severed permanently – no longer considered a part of their previous family, and all debts against the person were wiped out completely

3) The "placed son" was given access to all of the family accounts, riches and resources.

This idea of being "son-placed" by God was something that is shocking, and amazing. Truly we have in this simple word a promise of our security, a deeper understanding of our position in Christ, and a fuller appreciation for all that God has done for us in Jesus Christ.

Interestingly, there are other scriptures that say that we have already received this "son-placing" (Ephesians 1:3-14), yet it appears that there is an experience of this that is yet future. We will have fully come into our inheritance at the return of Jesus Christ for His Church (the Rapture). And we are longing for that time with our deepest desire.

Romans 8:24-25

[24]For in hope we have been saved, but hope that is seen is not hope; for who hopes for what he already sees? [25]But if we hope for what we do not see, with perseverance we wait eagerly for it.

Hope worth Hoping for

Here true biblical hope is again explained. It is important to notice that "hope" in the Bible is never an "I hope so" type of hope. Hope, in the biblical sense, is something that you know is ahead. In considering what the believer looks forward to there is not any doubt whatsoever about what the believer is looking forward to. That is why biblical hope is such an enduring encouragement. It is the absolute assurance about what is ahead for us. When the Holy Spirit, writing through Paul, says "in hope we have been saved" it is telling us that it was daring to believe in the promise that God has given that saved us.

Have been

The word translated "has been saved" is in the passive voice. Paul places into the very grammar the fact that we did not save ourselves, nor do we maintain this salvation ourselves. God had to act upon us, on our behalf, in order for us to be saved. Yet while we are in these bodies we look forward to "the redemption of the body" which was mentioned at the end of the last verse. The thing that we are looking forward to "our Hope" is the return of the Lord Jesus Christ for us.

Encouragement

Paul then talks about the nature of hope. Our relationship with Christ is beyond anything that we could ever imagine. Our day by day moment by moment communion with the Lord Jesus Christ through His indwelling Spirit is beyond understanding. Our access to Him through His word (the Bible) and the illumination that we receive through the Spirit is also beyond compare, and an endless source of encouragement for us. Not only this, believers are gifted to be a part of the Body of Christ. We have our brothers and sisters in Christ as relationships that constantly point us towards Him. Of all of these blessings and the Lord's constant provision for us what we look ahead to is greater still. These beautiful blessings are only a shadow of what is to come. We aren't hoping for something that is qualitatively much like this "only a little bit better." We aren't looking forward to "Life 2.0" we are looking to an existence in the future, the greatness of which is only alluded to by the best moments and aspects of our current existence.

Perseverance

So, what is ahead for us remains yet to be seen. Because our eyes are fixed upon these amazing promises of God we wait with perseverance. This word for "perseverance" has been called "the manliest of the Christian virtues." It is a patience that stands firm under the most adverse circumstances. It has a sense of courage to it, it is the same kind of courageous perseverance that stirs our hearts when watching movies like Braveheart, Rocky, or Rudy. This perseverance, however, is not rooted in the essential and inherent strength of the person, but in the greatness of the promises that have been given to us in Christ. In order for the believer to withstand the world with this kind of courage his eyes must be fixed on the Lord and His promises. Most centrally the greatest promise that we will be with Christ in all things. That is the defining feature of our future: with Christ always. That is worth waiting for eagerly!

<u>Romans 8:26-27</u>

[26]In the same way the Spirit also helps our weakness; for we do not know
how to pray as we should, but the Spirit Himself intercedes for us with
groanings too deep for words; [27]and He who searches the hearts knows
what the mind of the Spirit is, because He intercedes for the saints
according to the will of God.

More Groans…

In verse 22 the whole creation is described as groaning, in verse 23 the saints are groaning and now in verse 26 the Holy Spirit is groaning. The idea is clear that it is quite plain that things are not yet as they should be, though they will be someday, yet until then everything that longs for everything to glorify God as it was designed to groans in anticipation of that day. These verses give yet more vital information about the Holy Spirit, who is the life source and essential resource for the believer to rely upon in living life with Christ.

Helps our Weakness

The word "weakness" is translating a word that means "feebleness or infirmity." The idea is that we are spiritually incapable. We notice this "feebleness" when we attempt to run our own lives. As limited, finite, humans we simply don't know what must be done in most situations. Because we are unable to control all the factors our ideas and our plans are frequently completely the wrong way around.

Our limitations also disable us from praying with all wisdom. We may pray for the Lord to take a trial away from ourselves, or a loved one, when His desire is for us to go through that trial and grow in the way that He intends us to. We may pray that the Lord spare us from one situation, when His plan is actually for us to go through it so that we might avoid another difficulty later down the road. The reality of the matter is that we are fully incapable of saying what will happen, what should happen or what would have happened if something had gone differently. However, that does not mean that we are not to pray! Prayer is not centrally concerned with what the Lord will or won't do. It is not twisting God's arm to give us blessing. These worldly views of prayer also suggest that God doesn't already long to give us what is absolutely the best for our lives and relationships – which He does. Prayer is concerning relationship. It is us, talking to the Papa who loves us, and who cares for us.

Prayer Partner

We may occasionally have a relationship that is dedicated to prayer (a "prayer partner"). This verse is about the ultimate Prayer Partner – the Holy Spirit. Here Paul makes clear the fact that the Holy Spirit is actually interceding for us in prayer. Think of the advantages of this! Does the Holy Spirit know exactly what we need? Of course! He sees every believer all the way to the core. The Holy Spirit knows right down to the very bottom of a person's spirit what they are in need of, what their greatest struggle is and what their greatest need. So the perfect Holy Spirit is then guaranteed to be praying for the believer perfectly. But that is not all! The Holy Spirit, as the third person of the Trinity, will never be denied His request of intercession by the Father. It is amazing to think that every believer has within them the Holy Spirit, Who knows everything about that believer, and knows exactly what he or she needs most in the world and then requests the Father for those things on the believer's behalf. Can a believer resist the "prescription" of the Holy Spirit? Of course. However, for the believer who is in fellowship with the Holy Spirit there is a 100% chance of growth each and every day and each and every situation. This if phenomenal news! But there is more!

Groaning

Not only does the personality of the Holy Spirit do His work in the believer perfectly, He is also a personality. He even groans, mourns, and longs to see the burden of sin wiped away. He intercedes with us with a groaning of his own. One that is "too deep for words" (Literally – "unutterable, unspeakable"). So while we may groan on a physical "surface level" the Holy Spirit groans in a deeper way still, both seeing and understanding the full effect of Sin and embodying the full glory of God which sin offends. No one understands the suffering that Sin brought about more than God.

As a special note, many have wrongfully equated this verse with weird ecstatic experiences such as "prayer languages" and "prayer groaning." There are two major problems with this interpretation. Firstly, it is the Holy Spirit who is groaning here, not the believer. This is not something that we are doing (as the believer was groaning in verse 23). Secondly, the text specifically said that this groaning is "unutterable" thus it could not be communicated with the human lips tongue and vocal chords. The third problem (which is less a textual problem as an exegetical problem) is that this interpretation seeks to take a human experience (carnal psychological phenomenon) and read it into the text of scripture anywhere it looks possible. This, however, is very much not the thrust of the passage.

The Father…

Yet, the Father is involved with our Spiritual growth, maturity and experience of suffering as well. The Father is the one who searches the hearts and minds of men. It may be terrifying for the unbeliever to think of a God who knows every unspoken thought, every hateful intention. However, for the saint this is nothing to fear at all. Not because we have no sinful thoughts, but because we know that God is now able to view our thoughts with a desire to forgive and renew us. Now the fact that our thoughts are known is a relief because in Christ alone is the only forgiveness and restoration that we could ever hope for.

Working together

Verse 27 tells us that there is no sense in which the Holy Spirit is pleading for us before an unwilling Father. Far from it! The reality is that the Father, Son and Spirit are all in total agreement about the goals for the believer, and God will not fail! We see the Father being pleased to grant the requests of the Spirit regarding the believer because He knows just as well as the Spirit what is needed in every moment in the believer's life. The words "will of" in the last phrase were added by the translators. The true sense is that the requests of the Spirit are fully in accord with the character, nature and desire of God the Father. This is a "cannot fail" situation. When we understand what an amazing amount of power is being exercised on our behalf we realize that we are able to rest in what God is doing in our lives. We can rest in the life and character of Jesus Christ. Then we will be equipped to see what He will do!

ROMANS 8:28-30

Missing the Point

Sometimes when discussing the Bible people are prone to "miss the point." In looking at verses like these it is very easy to get sidetracked into an argument which is generally unprofitable. Most often these arguments are fraught with false dichotomies and adding liberally to the clear statements of scripture by supplying new information from some extra-biblical "system" of theology (Examples of these are Calvinism-Reformed, Armenianism, and Open Theism). Each of these systems attempts to "fill in the gaps" on what we are not told in scripture to produce some harmonization where the Lord has clearly left a tension in what has been revealed. So this study will not waste time arguing what "goes in the gaps" left by these positive statements. We will NOT miss the point!

So, what *IS* the Point?

Remember what Paul is getting at here: Paul wants these believers to know that they are in the eternal plan of God. That they can trust in their salvation in Jesus Christ. He is telling them about the amazing Salvation that the Lord Jesus Christ has won for them. Each of these three phases are by God's grace and in each of them man brings nothing to the table, they are God's doing:

> 1) **Justification** – This was the chief subject of the first 5 chapters. The word "justification" translates a word meaning: "To be declared righteous." We are justified by faith in Christ alone. As Paul wrote in Philippians: "…and may be found in Him, not having a righteousness of my own derived from the Law, but that which is through faith in Christ, the righteousness which comes from God on the basis of faith," (Philippians 3:9 NASB) Paul comes to the finale of this revelation in Romans 5:1: "Therefore, ***having been justified*** by faith, we have peace with God through our Lord Jesus Christ."
>
> 2) **Sanctification** – Chapters 6-7 go through the realities of our

Sanctification (the process by which we are conformed, in our day to day lives, to the image of Jesus Christ. In Romans 6:1-11 Paul laid out the means for our conformation to Christ. Romans 6:6-10 focus on the importance of the believer knowing how complete our identification with Christ in His death burial and resurrection. The next step stated in Romans 6:11 is to count on that reality, in faith. Trusting in the accomplished fact of what Christ did at the cross. The balance of chapter 6 concerned the believer who decided to continue to live in sin anyway. The result of this choice is loss of fellowship with the Lord, making the sinning believer the most miserable person on earth. Chapter 7 illustrates what happened to Paul when he tried to go back and 'earn righteousness' by living according to the Law, rather than live by faith in what Christ had done. The result was loss, death and despair.

3) **Glorification** - Chapter 8 concerns our glorification. In previous studies we have seen that the Lord WILL complete this work in us. In this final phase we will be given new bodies, we will be redeemed and continue on free from the pain and trials of our Sin Nature. This is a wonderful thing indeed!

So this is "the Point"! Paul meant this book to be taken personally. Not to be used as a killing floor to argue abstract theological points about who is and isn't chosen. So as we examine these powerful verses we want to be taking them intensely personally, realizing that these are the promises that we cling to, and look forward to as we go through every moment of every day.

Romans 8:28
And we know that God causes all things to work together for good to those who love God, to those who are called according to His purpose.

We KNOW
The grammar behind this "knowing" is very strong and secure. This is a very assured knowledge. The Greek word here means "to know by perception." Having the sense that this is something that is seen and observed. Where could this reality have been observed? This is seen

throughout the Scripture. God repeatedly uses the very darkest and most difficult situations as a platform to show His own power, grace, love and wisdom. This was seen when Joseph was sold into slavery by his brothers. His brothers meant to harm him because they were jealous, yet God used that terrible and difficult event to save the whole fledgling nation of Israel. God worked through dark situations in the lives of Moses, Joshua, David and Elijah. It seems that God majors in taking dark, difficult sinful situations that either man or Satan have ruined and turning it into a display of His wondrous love and provision.

Notice who has this knowledge: we. Paul includes himself and his readers. For Paul the Lord worked through his various trials and difficulties for the progress of the Gospel. Many of us can look back on the challenges and difficulties of our life and see how God used them for our better good. This is something that every believer has claim to.

God causes all things

First of all: God is the one doing this. It is important to recognize what is and isn't said here. The Spirit here does NOT say that God makes the bad things happen. The most dark and difficult situations of human history, or our personal history, are not a result of God's doing, they are a result of sin. God is able, however, to work with every set of circumstances, every set of human choices and work it together for our good and His glory. Something else to note:

ALL MEANS ALL. This is difficult for us as believers. There are situations in our lives that seem good and easy to see how the Lord is working through them for our good and His glory. Other situations seem far more difficult to understand how He could ever use them. There is an element of trust involved in the Christian life. Trust that even though we cannot understand things, we CAN trust Him. He is able to work these things together for good, not just the good, not just the bad: everything!

For whom?

The reality that the Lord WILL work ALL things together for good is a comforting thought, however, there is an important limitation to this. This promise only applies to those who *love Him.* If we don't understand this we miss everything. This promise is meaningless to an unbeliever. For those of us who are in a relationship with Jesus Christ our difficulties and trials make sense. The Lord is using them to conform us to the image of Jesus Christ. The only thing the trials and difficulties of the unsaved produce is to (hopefully) incline their hearts towards placing their faith and trust in Jesus Christ.

Calling

Every believer here is said to be called. This verse does not say that anyone is NOT called, but only that we have all been welcomed according to His purpose. What His purpose is will be laid out in the following verses.

<u>Romans 8:29</u>

For those whom He foreknew, He also predestined to become conformed to the image of His Son, so that He would be the firstborn among many brethren;

Foreknowledge

The Lord is all knowing. Before He created Adam and Eve He knew every person whom He created in them. For the Lord, being outside of time, all of time is a single unit. He is able to view it all as a completed picture, which is distinct from our view of things, being stuck in the "time tunnel". The Lord knew, before He created anything, who would accept Him and who would reject Him. Paul's purpose here is not to make everyone out to be robots, far from it! Foreknowledge is NOT dictation. Just because the Lord knew who would make what choice does not by any means imply that He made them make that choice. That suggestion would, by implication, clearly mean that God MADE Adam and Eve sin, which is impossible (Jas. 1:13). This is intensely personal. The Lord knew you, even before you existed. He created you and can be trusted with your future: your short term future as well as your eternal future!

A Great Destiny

These whom He knew would place their faith in Christ He gave a destiny. The word translated "predestined" here combines the words for "before" and "set a boundary" the Lord planned out beforehand that any who would place their faith in Jesus Christ would be given this destiny. This is something that He declared by His power, His might, His authority. It is important, because as we examine this destiny that we have been given we must realize that just as our salvation is totally by HIS doing, so our ultimate glorification will be HIS doing as well. This is all by grace, through faith in Jesus Christ!

Being a Conformist

The destiny that you have been given is to be conformed to the image of Jesus Christ. The Greek word here is the root of the English word "morph". The idea is that the Lord will ultimately have us completely transformed into the complete and perfect image of our Lord, Jesus Christ. Once again, this destiny is not something that can be earned, and it is not something that can be lost. This is something that is given entirely by His grace, and completed entirely by His power!

Firstborn

This is a tremendous reality that we can only understand and receive through faith. As we look at our daily lives and experiences this becomes more and more astounding! We see our shortcomings, our challenges, our difficulties, and our struggles and think that it would be impossible for anyone to change us into more than what we are. However, this brings into sharp relief the importance of our continued faith in Jesus Christ. Every moment that we say, "I can never do it!" We come to a greater realization of the truth: We could never conform ourselves to His image, we always had to trust in His power, His ability, and His grace to complete this. When we look forward to our glorification we see that it is just as much to His glory as the first phase of our salvation!

Romans 8:30

and these whom He predestined, He also called; and these whom He called, He also justified; and these whom He justified, He also glorified.

Called

Here those for whom God has set out this destiny in Christ were also called. Note that Paul does NOT say who is NOT called. That is not Paul's purpose here, the only thing that is being clearly stated here is that everyone who places their faith in Christ has responded to the call and received this destiny in Christ (which is conformity to His image). However, the ones whom He foreknew (that is every believer) DID respond! And in this response of faith every believer was justified.

Justified

Here Paul goes back to the concept he explained in chapters 1-5. The word "Justify" means: "To be declared righteous." However, we know that this declaration of righteousness was no work of our own. The righteousness that is being spoken of is Christ's righteousness. We were justified by our identification with Christ wherein our sin was imputed on Christ at the cross and His righteousness was imputed upon us. God did this because He is infinitely just, and everything in His equation must be balanced out. The infinite sacrifice of the perfect Son of God was enough to pay for every sin every person on earth has ever committed (1 John 2:2). However, it is only applied to those who accept it in faith. Anyone who chooses to reject Christ's payment for their sin chooses to pay for their sin on their own, for all of eternity.

Glorified

This is an amazing statement! Not only justified (declared righteous) but GLORIFIED! Glory is the radiant essence of Who God IS! This is the most noteworthy portion of His character. It was God's glory that would have destroyed Moses if He had seen it directly. It was God's glory that rendered Paul blind. And He has chosen to glorify US with that same glory! This is beyond understanding! But let's attempt to look at a distant shadow:

Imagine a poor girl who is growing up in a poor country town. She grows up each year of her life exchanging one tattered old hand-me-down dress for the next. Her whole life she has never worn a pair of shoes. Then a wealthy woman comes and invites the girl to join her for a few days. When they get to the city, the woman picks out dress upon beautiful dress for the girl who had never worn anything but tattered rags. The girl looks in the mirror and can hardly recognize herself with her shining shoes, done-up hair and beautiful dress and beams a priceless smile at the woman who shared her wealth (glory) with the child.

This is a wholly imperfect illustration, but it gives us a glimpse of what is going to be revealed in us. Here is the cool part: this glorification that was set to be a future event in verse 18 is here said to be a past tense event. The glorification of the believer is such a sure thing, such a complete certainty that it can be described as an accomplished fact. Christ (in whom you are positioned) is glorified, and when our position and condition are united we cannot but be glorified as well. This is a tremendous promise for every believer to take hold of and trust in every single day.

Taking it personally

Again, these verses have been twisted, perverted and poisoned to back any and every theological error imaginable. The worst thing that happens when this is done is that what the Lord is ACTUALLY saying often gets "lost in the mix" of some "high-minded" theological debate. Here is what the Holy Spirit wants EVERY believer to know:

- *Before God created anything He knew YOU, personally and specifically.*
- *Knowing that you would trust Him, He gave you a destiny. That destiny is to be conformed to the image of Jesus Christ. HE will be the one to conform you to the image of Christ.*
- *In the context of time He called you, and you responded.*
- *Though you were sinful, helpless and broken He placed you in His Son and declared your sins paid for, and declared you righteous as a permanent state of affairs.*
- *As certain as anything else in the world (or beyond) the Lord will also glorify you, totally by His grace, through the work of Jesus Christ and your identification with Him.*

This is WHO and WHAT you are in Christ. All that is left for the believer to do is to trust in what God has done, and is going to do in his life. This is tremendous news that every believer needs to know and appropriate (take personally). Not to win an argument, but so that we can face tomorrow as the Lord intends us to.

ROMANS 8:31-34

Position of Power

Paul continues to parade this amazing salvation before his audience. Having just spelled out, again, the completeness of our salvation, there is more wonderful news ahead. We found that our salvation is rooted in eternity and that each and every believer was known by the eternal God even before He said, "Let there be light…" The last verses highlighted how believers are foreknown, given a destiny (to be conformed to the image of Christ), Called, Justified, and that our glorification with Christ is equally as certain a fact. Notice again, that this is about what God is doing and not what we do. But Paul drives this point home throughout this chapter and hasn't finished letting us know what an amazing thing it is to be "in Christ."

Romans 8:31

What then shall we say to these things? If God is for us, who is against us?

What to say?

These verses continue the argument by evaluating what our reaction should be. As the argument here gets more and more passionate, rhetorical questions are used. The rhetorical question is Paul's way of involving the reader in the discussion. He is asking the reader to engage with what he is saying, trying to get each of us to actually accept and apply this important truth. Having just told them how amazing their present and future in Christ is, Paul wants them to think it over. Many of us will easily assent when we hear something said, or read anything, but Paul wants engagement because we can often nod our head and say "Yes, yes" and not realize that we held some other belief that conflicts with the new belief.

Paul knows that grace is scary to those who long to achieve something, or wish to show off in one way or another. Paul has dealt with every objection to God's grace. He dealt with the "If we are under grace we can sin all we want" in chapter 6. In chapter 7 he dealt with, "Can't we just earn righteousness through the law?" In chapter 8 he dealt with our constant, moment by moment need for Jesus Christ, for the Holy Spirit.

If God is for us…

"If" here may seem like Paul is not sure. However, the context supplies the nature of this "if". The fact that "God is for us" has already been proven in the verses before this. This was proven in the fact that God is the author of every phase of our salvation. Our salvation is of God! It is His doing, not ours!

Wait! God is FOR us?!

This is too big to miss. So often we fall back into the pagan mindset that God is either against us, or at least impartial. How often do we have a view of God as being seated on the Heavenly throne, looking down and waiting for us to mess up? When we sin, stumble, goof up, or make mistakes we very commonly view God as changing in His attitude towards us and now trying to destroy us. Get this…it is huge. GOD IS FOR YOU.

God is on your side. He won this salvation for you, He has given you everything that you need for life and godliness. You are not going to succeed in your walk with Christ because of what you do, but because of what HE has done and is doing and is yet to do. You can go into each day with the confidence unmatched by anything because the God who has ultimate and final control over all situations and final outcomes is FOR YOU! He is on your side. Grab onto this promise with both hands. You will need it, because the world is not for us. It is against us. We will likely see many difficulties and disappointments that lead us to believe that God has abandoned us, but this is never the case. God is, and always will be, for you.

Who can be against us?

The answer to Paul's rhetorical question is clear. However, it should be examined. What other force might we think could draw this amazing promise and work of God into question? We may sight our flesh, or trembling will, the world system, the Devil and those demons who fell with him. All of these forces ARE working against us and against our sanctification and glorification. If they had only to defeat us in order to rob us of our salvation not one person could be saved. These forces are far beyond our ability to stand against. We cannot defeat the world on our own. We certainly do not have the power in ourselves to defeat the devil (once among the most powerful of created beings). However, we need not even go that far. As Romans 6-7 show even our flesh defeats us and gets the better of us when we attempt to deal with them on our own. Fortunately, those forces are not working against us, they are working against God. We feel loss and frustration when we try to do God's part and fight those battles on our own. While they may deceive us, they will NEVER defeat God. This is a question of absolute and final power and authority, and no person (whether ourselves, or any angelic power) can compare, or compete, with the power of our God.

Romans 8:32
He who did not spare His own Son, but delivered Him over for us all, how will He not also with Him freely give us all things?

All too often misquoted
We often here politicians complaining "I was misquoted." However, no single source in the history of the world could have been repeatedly misquoted as the Bible. This verse is among the more common misquotes. This verse is often said to mean, "God gave up His Son for us, so He will also provide for all of your physical needs." This perversion sometimes goes so far as to say "God is going to give you whatever you WANT." Neither of which is a true statement, biblically speaking. As we look at this verse we have to remember the context: our salvation and spiritual growth.

Not Spare
When it came to creating this salvation it is noticeable that God gave EVERYTHING He had, used His very best resource to create it for us. He didn't just speak it into existence. He actually sent His own Son. This is remarkable. When we think of a child of a rich father we can imagine the child making tons of messes and the father using his wealth to clean up after him. However, the child may actually be affected if his father were to personally interfere in the situation. Jesus Christ personally came down and put on flesh and became as one of us. There is no fuller expression of God's love and character than the person of Jesus Christ.

This may recall Abraham to our minds. In Genesis 22 God tells Abraham to sacrifice his only son Isaac. Isaac was a miracle baby, born to two people who were well past the age of fertility. Yet the Lord had been faithful to His promise and given them this child. Then God tells Abraham to sacrifice Isaac. As Abraham prepares to make this sacrifice he collects Isaac and tells him to come along. When they approach the site Isaac asked, "Where is the lamb for the sacrifice?" Abraham says, "God will provide the lamb." God interfered, and spared Abraham's son, Isaac. Then they found a ram whose horns were caught in a thicket. God didn't provide the Lamb for thousands of years, until Christ was crucified for our sins.

What has been done, and what will be done…

Paul explained how God delivered Christ up for our sake. There is nothing of value equal to Christ. When we think of the immeasurable value of Jesus Christ, the Son of God that is the price that God paid for our salvation. Having paid all of this for salvation will God let that salvation fail? Of course not! He has provided for us fully in every phase of salvation. This is not a promise of physical things, or even basic physical necessities. A believer may die of starvation, martyrdom or any other horrible death, however, we never lack a single spiritual resource. As Paul put this in Ephesians 1:3 God has "blessed us with every spiritual blessing in the heavenlies with Christ."

God giving us everything we need for our salvation isn't all that is said here: the way that it was given is also explained. God won't give us everything we need for our growth in Christ begrudgingly, but rather "freely"! God isn't saying, "I gave my Son for you and now you figure the rest out." Paul describes God's attitude as saying, "I am pouring EVERYTHING into this. I gave you my son, and now I have given you the word, the Holy Spirit, I am working through your trials and all of your circumstances. I am hearing your prayers and My hand is not off of you for a single moment. I will succeed. And I do it gladly, freely, because I love you and want to see you conformed to the image of My Son. Failure is not a possibility."

<u>Romans 8:33-34</u>

33Who will bring a charge against God's elect? God is the one who justifies;
34who is the one who condemns? Christ Jesus is He who died, yes, rather
who was raised, who is at the right hand of God, who also intercedes for us.

More Questions
Paul continues with His method of asking rhetorical questions. This is meant to challenge the reader to answer the question and interact with what Paul is writing, and find that the statement is absolutely true!

Who will bring a charge?
Paul is not talking about an electrical charge. Paul is using legal language to describe a spiritual situation. Who will bring the believer before the court on charges? Who could do this? Satan? He is the "accuser of the brethren". Other people? They may think that they have an argument or evidence against a believer. The only logical person who could bring up a charge that would stick would be God Himself! Yet He is the One Who gave His Son to pay the penalty for sin! Satan has no reasonable accusation of the believer because Christ always returns with the same response: "Perhaps my child did sin, but I paid for that at the Cross." The one who paid the price constantly stands before the Father "interceding" for us. This is our amazing salvation! This is what we are given in the person and work of Jesus Christ our Lord.

Identification
It is worth mentioning that anyone who has placed their faith in Jesus Christ for salvation has also been included with Jesus Christ by God in every one of these processes! Both in Romans 6:4-6 and Ephesians 2:4-6 clearly state that every believer has been identified with Christ in His death, burial, resurrection, ascension and seating. Having been placed in Christ and imputed His righteousness we are united with Him in His glory. This is a tremendous reality for us to understand!

> [4]*Therefore we have been buried with Him through baptism into death, so that as Christ was raised from the dead through the glory of the Father, so we too might walk in newness of life.* [5]*For if we have become united with Him in the likeness of His death, certainly we shall also be in the likeness of His resurrection,* [6]*knowing this, that our old self was crucified with Him, in order that our body of sin might be done away with, so that we would no longer be slaves to sin;* [7]*for he who has died is freed from sin.*
> Romans 6:4-7 NASB

> [4]*But God, being rich in mercy, because of His great love with which He loved us,* [5]*even when we were dead in our transgressions, made us alive together with*

Christ (by grace you have been saved), [6]and raised us up with Him, and seated us with Him in the heavenly places in Christ Jesus, [7]so that in the ages to come He might show the surpassing riches of His grace in kindness toward us in Christ Jesus.
Ephesians 2:4-7 NASB

ROMANS 8:35-39

More Questions

The questions just keep on coming. Paul is not asking these questions so that we would doubt our salvation. He is asking them rhetorically in order to get the point across. In these final verses of chapter 8 Paul drives the point all the way in to the hilt. The Holy Spirit wouldn't have any believer doubting for one moment who gave us our salvation, and how it will be drawn to completion.

Romans 8:35

Who will separate us from the love of Christ? Will tribulation, or distress, or persecution, or famine, or nakedness, or peril, or sword?

Who?

Based on the previous verses and the nature of this question the obvious answer is "nobody". Far from the many man-made religions that place one person over everyone else's salvation. There is no earthly source that can separate, nor any ability of any man to excommunicate a believer from salvation. No earthly ruler or authority has any say at all in the issue of a believer's position, identity and destiny in Christ Jesus. This is GREAT news! Because there is another "who" that is, of necessity a part of this statement: "ME! MYSELF!" If the word is true a person who has trusted Jesus cannot even separate themselves from His powerful and redeeming love and future. This is something that is beyond our full comprehension, but should bring us endless joy!

The Love of Christ

The question of separation is from something very special: The Love of Christ. The Greek word here is *agape* – it is the Greek word that describes God's love. This kind of love is unconditional, selfless and perfect. This love has well been defined: *The unconditional love of God that always looks out for the greatest good of the loved one, regardless of the cost.* This statement is saying that there is no being, in heaven or on earth, that can separate the believer from this magnificent love that Christ displayed on the Cross (Romans 5:8).

What about these things?
In continuing this description of Christ's amazing love from which we cannot be separated Paul adds a handful of difficult circumstances. Let's look at some of these words:

- *Tribulation* – Crushing pressure, painful difficult circumstances.
- *Distress* – Being in a tight spot, passing through a narrow path that squeezes in on us.
- *Persecution* – Being Pursued by enemies – either literally or metaphorically
- *Famine* – failure, or lack of, certain physical necessities.
- *Nakedness* – Want of clothing or basic coverings
- *Peril* – Danger, fearful or frightening situations
- *Sword* – The specific sword of the Roman Legions. It was a precise weapon of slaughter. Metaphorically for a violent death.

Paul runs off a list of nearly every negative, terrible, horrible situation of which he can think. From internal pressure to external, from emotional and political to physical want. The idea that he is getting across is that our position is secure no matter what may happen in our circumstances. This is the only genuine outlook of each believer that makes any sense whatsoever! Things truly may come to the very worst in this sin-scarred life. However, what waits for us is not threatened by any of these situations. This is tremendous news!

Romans 8:36-37
36Just as it is written, "FOR YOUR SAKE WE ARE BEING PUT TO DEATH ALL DAY LONG; WE WERE CONSIDERED AS SHEEP TO BE SLAUGHTERED." 37But in all these things we overwhelmingly conquer through Him who loved us.

Expectations
Often we see people trying to "sell Christianity" with highly charged stories

about how bad and difficult their life was until they became a Christian and now everything is better. Paul seems to predict the opposite for the believer. Quoting Psalm 44:22, Paul sets for the principle that the saints of the Lord can expect to experience difficulty, trial and challenge. Many believers struggle to understand how God can allow calamity and difficulty to enter their life. The reality of Scripture is that believers are NOT promised an easy ride. We are NOT promised that we won't starve to death, or that we will not lose loved ones. We are promised that no matter what happens God will work things together for our ultimate good (conformity to the image of Jesus Christ). We are given every spiritual blessing in every situation (Ephesians 1:3-14). Many believers are disappointed in their expectations because they hold unbiblical expectations!

Hebrew Poetry Patterns

Being a quote of the Psalms (Hebrew Poetry) this quote comes to us in the form of Hebrew Poetry. Hebrew Poetry differs from western poetry. Rather than rhyming phonetic patterns, Hebrew poetry rhymes meaning. This can be done in a handful of different ways but here the effect is to repeat the sentiment in different terms. The first clause has the duration of the martyrdom (all day long) and the second describes the value of their lives (as sheep). Those who are faithful to God have undergone repeated persecution, and it is common for those who do not fear God to put a very low value on believers' lives. This should not surprise us. As believers in this world we occupy enemy territory. Both human and satanic powers have killed countless of the faithful. Yet, that is not a shame to them, rather it is glory to their account! The true believer in Christ can look at the very worst that the world can dish out and say, "You cannot touch what is really valuable."

More than Conquerors

The "But" that opens this verse is a strong contrasting connective. Paul encourages believers not to look at their trials and difficulties and despair. Rather, in sharp contrast to the idea of despair, they are to see themselves as God sees them. But how does God see them? This is a fun Greek word. It combines the word related to Nike (the winged God of victory) with the word that transliterates as SUPER! Everyone in Christ is a "SUPER-WINNER"! Not because of what we did or do, but because of what Christ has done! John described this reality similarly:

> *"For whatever is born of God overcomes the world; and this is the victory that has overcome the world--our faith. Who is the one who overcomes the world, but he who believes that Jesus is the Son of God?"* 1 John 5:4-5

We are considered conquerors because of what Christ has done on our behalf. No matter what the world, the flesh or the devil do the believer will be finally victorious. Christ and His word on our behalf is the source of the victory. If we ever think that we have won the victory ourselves we have already been drawn away from the truth. The truth is that we must rest in Christ's sufficiency at every moment and in every situation. This is a great privilege, honor and blessing!

Through Him

It certainly bears repeating: This victory is available to us only in resting in Christ and what HE HAS DONE! Any works based salvation, or sanctification is bound to fail. Any other view of reality falls woefully short of the wonderful reality of what is ours in Christ. This is not made available by the works of our hands, this is not some level of spiritual prowess that only the "high level" believer attains. This is the reality for every single believer through Christ. Here, again, we see Christ's love being the motivating factor. It is not because He "had to" or because someone "talked Him into it" His love is why He came, and His love will carry our salvation to completion. Were it based in anything less we would have no hope at all!

<u>Romans 8:38-39</u>

38For I am convinced that neither death, nor life, nor angels, nor
principalities, nor things present, nor things to come, nor powers, 39nor
height, nor depth, nor any other created thing, will be able to separate us
from the love of God, which is in Christ Jesus our Lord.

Convinced

This word means "convinced, confident, and persuaded fully". There is not the slightest doubt in Paul's mind as he writes these words through the Holy Spirit. Clearly understanding these simple verses is vital to our understanding of the relationship that we have in Christ. Our security cannot be doubted in this chapter. Every believer is saved, not by what we do, but by what God has done. But looking at what Paul is convinced of is very exciting indeed!

- *Death* – Nothing in physical death
- *Life* – Nothing that we can do or will happen to us in our life
- *Angels* – These are God's messengers who brought messages and did miracles far beyond human abilities.
- *Principalities* – This has the idea of "authority" it can be used to include either spiritual or physical authorities.
- *Present* – Nothing in the present moment.
- *Things to Come* – Nothing in all of the future moments
- *Powers* – That is no created thing's natural capacity, might or ability (including our own)
- *Height* – Looking all the way up, even further than the Hubble telescope can see.
- *Depth* – No matter how deep down we were to dig there is nothing to challenge God there
- *Nor any other created thing* – Think this over – there are two types of things – Uncreated (God alone– existing eternally in the three persons of the Trinity) and Created (EVERYTHING ELSE). Nothing will separate us from the love of God. Even our own weak and trembling wills.

The Love of God

Remember verse 35? There it was the love of Christ that was at issue; here it is the love of God. This shows us a couple of important facts. Firstly, that Christ is God and that there is no part of Him that exists in opposition or exclusion from the other two Members of the Trinity. But also, again we see the entire Trinity at work in saving, sanctifying and glorifying the believer. There is no part of the Godhead that loves humanity less. Our Salvation was the design of the entire Trinity, which is the reason why it is fully reliable.

In Christ Jesus

Here again we see that this unbreakable love of God is expressed where we are positioned in Christ Jesus. This is our permanent and eternal placement. When God looks at a believer He sees the righteousness of His Son. It is of vital importance to note that while the phrase "in Christ" is used constantly by Paul to describe the placement, mode and manner of the believer's life, the phrase "out of Christ" or "moved out of Christ" never once occurs. This is a permanent state of affairs. Our relationship with God is not something that is coming and going, or something that goes up for renewal every 5 years. It is always and eternal, just like His unchanging love. And THAT is why and how a believer is to succeed.

ROMANS 9

ROMANS 9:1-5

A Whole New Section

Paul now opens up a whole new section in this description of our salvation in Jesus Christ. Paul has told us what place everyone was in – sinful, fallen, and helpless (Chapters 1-3). Paul told them what God did and how we are declared righteous by faith in Jesus Christ in Chapters 4-5. He told them about how our faith in Christ will be the source and method of our sanctification, rather than rule keeping (Chapter 6-7). Finally, we saw how our salvation cannot fail, because it is the work of the omniscient and omnipotent God of the Universe in chapter 8. This is great news! But it may have left another lingering question in his reader's mind. Many of the people that Paul was writing to were Jews and they would have had a question: "What about all of the unconditional promises that God made to us?" The next logical question would be, "If God just got tired of Israel and decided to abandon them for some new program how can I trust Him to do all of the things described in Romans 1-8?" Paul's response: "God is NOT done with Israel!" You can trust in what God has promised in your life because God is always faithful, and He will YET be faithful to all of His promises made to Isreal. That's what the next three chapters are about

Telling the Truth

Paul assures these Roman believers that he is giving an honest account of his feelings and emotions. Paul is very real with his raw feelings and emotions and recognizes these feelings as being right in line with the longings of the Holy Spirit. The relationship between emotions and our faith is an important one to get right. While the world often relies on feelings and emotions to make decisions this is not what we see as the Biblical model for decision making. Emotions are to follow our faith in the revealed facts of God's wonderful word. This is the way in which we are to understand reality. We may be tempted to understand our reality through the lens of our feelings, but that will usually lead us away from the truth of God's word. Our emotions show their true value when they are following our faith in the facts of God's word. Regarding these feelings Paul wants his readers to know that he isn't just saying this because he feels like he should, these are really His feelings. He tells us that the Holy Spirit is accordingly evidencing this godly emotional response.

Why so glum, chum?

When looking at the emotional response it is clear that these are quite extreme feelings. Paul tells us that he is experiencing "great sorrow". Sorrow, or sadness can gnaw at the very core of our being, keeping us from appreciating even the most wonderful circumstances. The other description that Paul uses is "unceasing grief in my heart." Grief is an emotional response to loss, or some sort of unfulfilled desire. Can a person experience both the joy of knowing the facts in Romans 8 and the grief that Paul describes in Romans 9? Clearly the answer is "Yes." It is difficult for us to synthesize our emotions, thoughts and feelings as we can only feel or experience so much at one given time. However, there is a reality that even while we are not attending to a given emotional response it is still there. Paul is filled with continual grief and great sorrow over Israel's rejection of Christ.

It is important to note what hasn't caused Paul sorrow. He has been personally rejected time and time again. The book of Acts records his constant difficulty and pains for the gospel, yet it is not physical discomfort that brings him this level of grief and sorrow. Paul is made sorrowful because the people he loves reject the Lord. This is the heart of Christ that wept over lost Jerusalem. This is the heart of the believer. If we truly understand what life and eternity apart from Christ mean then we can do nothing but weep over those in our lives that do not know the love, joy and peace provided by God.

Wishful Thinking

Verse 3 is shocking! Paul (still under his statement that "this is the truth") would wish himself accursed for the sake of the Jewish people. Paul says that if he could somehow lose his salvation to see them saved he would do it! This is an amazing love. This love is rooted in the love of Christ that went to a cross to save us, even though we were His enemies! Paul's love for Israel (his people) is such that he would give up his own eternal life with Christ in order to see them come to Him. Paul knows that this is an impossibility, and that even if he were to offer this trade to God, it is not His way to over-ride free will. Yet, it shows the passionate love and desire that Paul feels for his fellow Hebrews. It is interesting to see that Paul did not abandon his earthly association completely when he was placed in Christ. He still identifies with his fellow Israelites and hopes with everything in him that they would come to see and accept their Messiah.

Who are you?

For Americans "our people" becomes a slightly more complicated idea. Many Americans have no idea what their heritage is, and may not care if they do know. Hopefully, we will feel some sense of this desire that everyone in our respective nation will come to know Christ. Perhaps we feel more strongly connected to some social group or perhaps our professional environment. As we rest in the Lord and understand how wonderful this salvation is we will begin to feel this sorrow (because it is of the Lord). It is heart-breaking that anyone at our schools, workplaces or social clubs would be living without the love and life of Jesus Christ.

According to the flesh

Paul recognizes that the fellowship that he shares with the Jews is that he shares their ethnic identity, it is according to his physical birth, not according to his spiritual re-birth in Jesus Christ. This is an important distinction (difference) between the Church and Israel. In order to be a full-fledged member of the nation of Israel means that you had to be born a Jew. However, in the Church we find that physical birth (or linage) doesn't matter one bit!

Israelites

The Israelites are God's chosen earthly people. Abraham was the beginning of the line and the recipient of God's covenant to his physical descendants. However, interestingly, not every descendant of Abraham qualifies! Only those who were offspring of Isaac. However, not everyone descended from Isaac counts because those who were born of Esau weren't included, only those born of Jacob (who was re-named "Israel"). So, this very special group of people have been given a very special series of promises to their children and the children of their children. Looking at what they have been given:

> *The Adoption as Sons* – We saw in Romans 8:15 and 23 that the Church has an adoption. However, here we see that Israel also has been given an adoption as sons (literally, a "son-placing"). Just as was the case in the church we see unconditional promises being made to the physical descendants of Abraham, Isaac and Jacob. God called Israel the apple of His eye (Zechariah 2:8). God has a plan for Israel that cannot be changed, defeated or destroyed.
>
> *Glory* – The Israelites alone were given the glory of a national relationship with God. Reading the Old Testament shows the immense love and care with which He looks after Israel. He is ever faithful to Her and always draws her back to Himself. He repeatedly acted miraculously in Israel's history and no other nation has known the Lord so intimately.
>
> *Covenants* – A covenant is an agreement. Israel was the recipient of a handful of different covenants with God. Both conditional and unconditional. We won't look at all of the covenants in the Bible here, but we will look at a few of the major ones:
>
> *Abrahamic Covenant* (Genesis 15:18; 17:4-8, 19-21) – This was an *unconditional* covenant between God and Abraham's physical descendants through Isaac. God Promised to Bless Abraham, to make his name great, to give him countless descendants, to make him a father of many nations, to give him the land of Canaan (from Egypt to the Euphrates) for an everlasting possession, to bless those who would bless him and curse whoever would curse him. He also promised the sign of this covenant would be the sign of

circumcision.

Mosaic Covenant (Exodus 19-24) – This is a *conditional* covenant that set up the relationship of physical blessing by God in exchange for their obedience to the Law of Moses. If the Israelites were faithful then they would be blessed and have freedom, abundance and prosperity. However, if they were disobedient they would receive curses from the hand of the Lord. This covenant does not annul the Abrahamic Covenant, but rather dictated how God would deal with Israel. If Israel had been able to live up to her part of this covenant then she would have fulfilled the role of mediator between the world and God.

The Palestinian Covenant (Deuteronomy 29-30) – The Palestinian Covenant is an unconditional covenant going back to promising the land, seed and blessing in the same unconditional manner as the in the Abrahamic covenant. This Covenant, therefore, is saying, "Israel, you will fail, and I know that, and I will bring you back because I am faithful."

Davidic Covenant (2 Samuel 7:8-19) – This is another unconditional covenant with David promising that David's line would endure forever, and that the people of Israel would not ever be eliminated. It also dictated that David's kingdom will be established forever, into eternity. David would have understood this rightly to mean that someone would rule on his throne on into eternity. David's throne will be established forever. This covenant will be fulfilled during the millennial reign of Christ (who is in David's line – according to both Joseph and Mary's lineage).

The New Covenant (Jeremiah 31:31-34) – This is the final expansion to the Abrahamic covenant and includes the fullest descriptions of the millennial reign of the Messiah. It is detailed throughout the Prophets and is described in Ezekiel 36-37 as well. This final covenant describes the blessed life under the millennial reign of Christ when He returns to reign for a 1,000 years on earth leading to continuation in the New Heavens and the New Earth that follows thereafter.

Law, Temple, Promises – These three things are also signs and symbols of God's amazing grace and love towards Israel. They were special. God repeatedly reminded them that this was not because of how great they were, but because of how amazing His love is. They were chosen as a people who were to represent Him to the world and given special signs and promises that simply cannot go away. Paul knows that it is not in the character of God to give up, as He CANNOT fail.

From whom is the Christ, according to the flesh
"The Christ" is an official term. It is a title meaning "anointed one". *Christos* is the Greek word for *h'amashiah* or Messiah. The messiah was the promised One who would come. Jesus Christ came through the Hebrew people as far as His earthly lineage was concerned and that, alone, should be enough for us to share sympathies with them (but there are many other reasons). This Christ is over all, and will ultimately be the vehicle through which every other covenant promise will be fulfilled. He will bless the earth. He will reign forever from David's throne. He will be ruling the earth during the most blessed 1,000 year period that it has ever seen. He will be faithful to every promise that God made to the Jews. That is great news!

God is faithful
Paul is going to spend the next chapters explaining God's amazing faithfulness. Because of God's faithfulness to the Hebrew people we can also be assured that He will be faithful to carry through our salvation, even when things seem to be most difficult and at their very darkest. Furthermore, we see the heart of Jesus shining through this passage in the great passionate desire that "none should perish." With whom has the Lord burdened your heart?

ROMANS 9:6-18

God is Faithful

The previous five verses highlighted the fact that Paul was distressed about Israel's continuing rejection of Jesus Christ. He even highlighted the importance of the Biblical covenants (unconditional promises) that God had made. This section is a defense of God's faithfulness to Israel and to the promises that He made to Israel. His reason for this seems to be two fold. First: Paul cares about his people, and still regards them as his nation in the sense of his personal lineage. The second reason is perhaps the more important: He needs believers to know that they can trust God's promises to them. Believers need to know that God didn't just "Change his mind" when it comes to the clear promises that He made to Israel and He will not do this for believers now in the church age either. Thus: Chapter 9 is a description of Israel's history, chapter 10 is a description of Israel's present, and chapter 11 talks about the future that lies ahead for Israel.

<u>**Romans 9:6-9**</u>

6But it is not as though the word of God has failed. For they are not all
Israel who are descended from Israel; 7nor are they all children because they
are Abraham's descendants, but: "THROUGH ISAAC YOUR
DESCENDANTS WILL BE NAMED." 8That is, it is not the children of
the flesh who are children of God, but the children of the promise are
regarded as descendants. 9For this is the word of promise: "AT THIS
TIME I WILL COME, AND SARAH SHALL HAVE A SON."

God's word can't fail

Paul reminds them that the promises of God will not fail. God's faithfulness and truthfulness are two of His most pronounced characteristics. Paul is repeating the idea that the Lord is faithful to all of His promises and we must not assume for a second that He will change His mind.

Getting to the point

Here a very core idea behind some Jewish mythology is challenged. There were those who believed and taught that every Hebrew child who was circumcised was, in a sense "safe" and it didn't matter what happened thereafter. Paul points out here that bloodlines alone never saved anyone. Not one single person was given a relationship with God based on who their parents were. Paul begins by describing how the nation of Israel came about. He points out that just being descended from Abraham was not enough. Abraham had two sons and descendants (Isaac and Ishmael), and only those who were through Isaac could be so.

Children of the Promise

This is an important point in the history of Israel. Obviously, the Messiah could only be brought through one descendent and Isaac was the child of Promise. Ishmael was conceived because of Abraham and Sarah's attempts to utilize social customs to fulfill the plan of God. This was their deliberate attempt to "do God's work for Him". It was, of course, a disaster. God intended to provide for Abraham a legitimate heir from his and Sarah's union, miraculously, which He did in Isaac. It was to Isaac that the Abrahamic covenant was repeated, and through Isaac that the Messiah would come.

Romans 9:10-13

[10]And not only this, but there was Rebekah also, when she had conceived
twins by one man, our father Isaac; [11]for though the twins were not yet
born and had not done anything good or bad, so that God's purpose
according to His choice would stand, not because of works but because of
Him who calls, [12]it was said to her, "THE OLDER WILL SERVE THE
YOUNGER." [13]Just as it is written, "JACOB I LOVED, BUT ESAU I
HATED."

More Selection

However, the selection between Isaac and Ishmael isn't the only selection that God made. He also made a selection between the two sons of Isaac and Rebekah! She conceived twins and it was prophesied that even before they were born that each would have a destiny. Note, that in the drama of redemption God reserved the right, according to His purposes to choose through which lines the Messiah would finally come. Note also the nature of what is being chosen here. God is not overpowering people's wills. Nor is He choosing who will and who won't be saved (as the Calvinists often contend). He is only making selections having to do with fulfilling His promise to Abraham. The final point at which Scripture arrives is that even among those of the "chosen" bloodlines many would reject God and not trust in Him, which is exactly what he lamented in verses 1 through 5. It is very easy to read these verses out of context to make them say what they were never meant to say, and these verses outlining the history of Israel are not there to make a theological point about the nature of salvation, but rather about the history of the Jewish people.

The Choice

Paul especially makes the point that God's choice of Jacob over Esau was not in relationship to anything that they had done. This is an important reality about God's plan of redemption. There was nothing left to chance. God didn't say, "Let them battle it out and see who is fit to be the inheritor of the promise." Neither did God take the cultural norm and simply give it to the first born (which was Esau). He challenged the cultural norm in making His choice of Jacob over Esau, but did it with full confidence. Interestingly all of the troubles of Jacob's personal life came because, like Abraham, he tried to "do God's job for Him."

God hates this guy!

Verse 8 is a quote from Malachi 1:2-3. This has often been misunderstood as God arbitrarily hating one of the sons Isaac even before he was born. There are some who become absolutely drawn to the idea. However, we find that the Hebrew conception of hate is not quite like our own. We think of hatred as a burning emotion that longs for nothing but the final and ultimate destruction of the hated thing. This is not even close to the Biblical context for the word "Hate" in this context. How could God who "So loved the world (i.e. the people in the world)" and, who Himself IS love, arbitrarily hate a baby who had not yet been born. The reality of this language pattern is that a common way to say "I chose one over the other" is with the expression "I loved this one and hated that one." So the purpose here is to say that God chose Jacob over Esau as a part of His plan of redemption to be recipient of the Abrahamic promises of land, seed and blessing.

Romans 9:14-18

14What shall we say then? There is no injustice with God, is there? May it
never be! 15For He says to Moses, "I WILL HAVE MERCY ON WHOM I
HAVE MERCY, AND I WILL HAVE COMPASSION ON WHOM I
HAVE COMPASSION." 16So then it does not depend on the man who
wills or the man who runs, but on God who has mercy. 17For the Scripture
says to Pharaoh, "FOR THIS VERY PURPOSE I RAISED YOU UP, TO
DEMONSTRATE MY POWER IN YOU, AND THAT MY NAME
MIGHT BE PROCLAIMED THROUGHOUT THE WHOLE EARTH."
18So then He has mercy on whom He desires, and He hardens whom He
desires.

NO FAIR!

Then Paul brings up the obvious question: Is God playing favorites? The answer of course is a resounding "May it never be!" It is easy to see how someone may say that it was unfair for God to choose one line of people over another, however that is an incorrect view of justice. Mankind can never be said to have "earned" God's interference on our behalf. Furthermore, we must confess that we don't have the perspective that God has. God has a specific purpose in the drama of redemption. He showed us through Israel the truth of His character, the consistency of His faithfulness, and the reality that the only way a person can ever be right with God is through the work of the Messiah. As Paul points out, we are looking to Him for mercy and compassion. The Israelites were given specific command to be a nation that represents and shares the One True God with all of the world. It was their failures here that brought them the critique of God in Ezekiel 37.

Pharaoh, Pharaoh!

Paul then draws on the example of Pharaoh in the Exodus. The Lord used Pharaoh's hard-heartedness to demonstrate His greatness and endorse the testimony of the Hebrew nation in following Him. News of these miracles reached as far as Jericho in the ancient world, and likely elsewhere, causing at least Rahab to turn and honor God. It is important to note that Pharaoh hardened *his own* heart no less than six times before the Lord finally hardened his heart (Exodus 7:13,22; 8:15, 19, 32; 9:7), so even this was not a complete control over the will of Pharaoh, but seemingly enforcing the will that was already there.

God's Will

This can be difficult to understand, and the fortunate reality is that we are not challenged to understand it. Paul goes on to let us know that going to the trouble of asking God "Why did you choose Isaac and Jacob?" Or "Why did you do it this way instead of just plopping the Messiah down in front of everyone?" is asking questions that are out of our pay-grade. It is important to remember what is not in view here: Paul is not making any statements about God's controlling anyone's will in regards to their personal choices to trust in Him for salvation or not. Paul is simply outlining the plan by which God brought about and chose Israel, pointing to the fact that choosing Israel was totally rooted in God's gracious plan and not in any sense of man's justice

ROMANS 9:19-33

Fault finding mission

Paul continues in his pattern of anticipating the potential logical questions and objections that his readers may have. Having discussed the reality that Israel is currently in unbelief he explained how much personal distress their rejection brings him. He also explained why it was so very important that we understand that God would ultimately be faithful to all of His promises to the nation of Israel. Following the mention of all of the promises that have been laid out for Israel Paul described the history of those promises as they were handed down from Abraham to Isaac (and not to his half-brother, Ishmael), and then to Jacob (and not to his twin brother Esau). Having established that this is about God's sovereign plan and His ultimate faithfulness he answers the next logical question: If God is ultimately in control how can anyone be condemned? If He is the one in charge how could we say that anyone defied His will? This is an interesting and important study. However, it is important to remember that in all of this discussion of God and His faithfulness to Israel, personal salvation is never specifically in view. The people of Israel were not saved by being born Jewish, just as people today are by no means saved because their parents or grandparents were Christians. And while God interacts with human history divinely, thus far the text has said still nothing about predestining an individual to or away from personal salvation.

<u>Romans 9:19-24</u>

19You will say to me then, "Why does He still find fault? For who resists
His will?" 20On the contrary, who are you, O man, who answers back to
God? The thing molded will not say to the molder, "Why did you make me
like this," will it? 21Or does not the potter have a right over the clay, to
make from the same lump one vessel for honorable use and another for
common use? 22What if God, although willing to demonstrate His wrath
and to make His power known, endured with much patience vessels of
wrath prepared for destruction? 23And He did so to make known the riches
of His glory upon vessels of mercy, which He prepared beforehand for
glory, 24even us, whom He also called, not from among Jews only, but also

from among Gentiles.

Asking the Question

Paul is addressing a question that bothers many people even to this very day. "If God is God, why didn't He just prevent evil?" or "If God is all powerful isn't it ultimately HIS fault if someone rejects Him? Isn't it a shortcoming in His sovereignty that causes the problem here?" From people who struggle with the idea of a holy, just and righteous God we often hear statements like, "I just can't believe God would send people to Hell just because they didn't choose to believe in Him on earth." These can be difficult questions to answer, some may even trouble us as believers from time to time. The Holy Spirit, writing through Paul here, has the perfect response, even if those who reject God may not find it fully satisfying.

Who are you, again?

Often sports spectators believe they have a corner on what is going on in the course of a game. They loudly yell at their TV screen and criticize coaches, managers and owners of teams confident that they could do better, were the chance presented to them. However, when faced with such criticisms most professional coaches are not in the slightest bit phased. This is because they have ALL of the facts. They have a greater perspective on the team, players and the sport that is being played than those who would watch at home and faithfully read their sports page. This is sort of what is going on here, but to an infinitely greater degree.

Paul responds to this question by drawing us back into perspective. C.S. Lewis wrote a marvelous essay entitled "God in the Dock". This is referring to the British court system where a person who is being questioned in court sits in the "dock" to defend themselves. The great change that he says occurred in recent years is that when people in generations passed would discuss whether God exists they did so with a reverent fear, because if this all-powerful, all-knowing being does in-fact exist then each one of us is ultimately responsible to Him. However, the change has occurred and when people now ask the question does God exist they assume that if God exists He may be somehow responsible to US! Paul wants to cut this error off before it even gets started. Paul is bringing our vision into focus. God exists, as such He does not owe any single person an answer, or an explanation. This, in great part, was God's response to Job. Job, upon being straightened out retracted all of his complaints, even though he really had suffered terribly.

APOLOGETIC HINT: When speaking to non-believers do not accept their presupposition that somehow people have the privilege of standing in judgment over God. Gently and lovingly remind them that if God does exist (and He does) we are responsible to Him, not He to us.

Pictures and Illustrations

Paul then begins employing illustrations that begin to give us an idea of our place before the Lord. The first illustration is of an artist making a sculpture. Of course, the artist doesn't sit down and say to a lump of clay, "What would you like to be, lump of clay?" It would be ridiculous. Rather the artist starts with a specific goal in mind and will achieve that goal with the piece of clay. While the clay may resist being shaped for one physical reason or another the "will" of the clay isn't what is important, the will of the sculptor is what matters. This is the ultimate reality for human history. We can look at the dark and horrid parts, and look at the horrors that are yet ahead for humanity and planet earth and wonder if it is fully necessary, but ultimately this is God's creative act and He will see it to its ultimate end.

Similarly, the image of a potter makes pots for whatever needs he may have. He makes the beautiful vase knowing the lovely flowers with which it will be filled, he makes the humble water pot knowing the work that it will endure. God is able to do this because He is ultimately the one in charge. And again, while we are free to ask Him anything as His children (as displayed in the previous chapter) we must always realize that what He chooses to reveal to us is His business entirely and we are owed absolutely none of it!

Why did you do that?

The next question is also a logical one, but the answer is the same. If God knows who will choose Him and who doesn't why not just not allow that person ever to exist? Wouldn't it be easier simply to cut them off before they have a chance to reject Him? God has chosen to be glorified in His infinite and gracious character. He is gracious in spite of man's rejection. Rather than saying, "I won't suffer any to reject me, I UNMAKE YOU!"

Even though God knows who will reject them He still allows them to be created, and will yet be glorified even in their rejection of Him, and even more so (by contrast) in the lives of those who trust Him.

That's us

Paul brings about some important distinctions. He has been speaking about the Jews and now references "us". Here "us" cannot possibly mean Israel it has to be a new body. This "us" is referring to the new body that Paul is a part of: The church. Paul gives the ethnic makeup of this new body which is not made up simply of Jews, or any other single group. Rather this call was given to all Jews and all gentiles alike.

Romans 9:25-29

25 As He says also in Hosea, "I WILL CALL THOSE WHO WERE NOT
MY PEOPLE, 'MY PEOPLE,' AND HER WHO WAS NOT BELOVED,
'BELOVED.'" 26 "AND IT SHALL BE THAT IN THE PLACE WHERE
IT WAS SAID TO THEM, 'YOU ARE NOT MY PEOPLE,' THERE
THEY SHALL BE CALLED SONS OF THE LIVING GOD." 27 Isaiah
cries out concerning Israel, "THOUGH THE NUMBER OF THE SONS
OF ISRAEL BE LIKE THE SAND OF THE SEA, IT IS THE
REMNANT THAT WILL BE SAVED; 28 FOR THE LORD WILL
EXECUTE HIS WORD ON THE EARTH, THOROUGHLY AND
QUICKLY." 29 And just as Isaiah foretold, "UNLESS THE LORD OF
SABAOTH HAD LEFT TO US A POSTERITY, WE WOULD HAVE
BECOME LIKE SODOM, AND WOULD HAVE RESEMBLED
GOMORRAH."

Getting the Quotes

Paul brings about some important teaching from the Old Testament. God had told the Israelites repeatedly about the ramifications of their rejection of Him. God also told them that He knew that they would rebel against Him and reject Him. This brings about a very important teaching in scripture: the doctrine of the Remnant. In every trial, in every difficulty God always preserves for Himself a remnant among the Jews. In each age, in each time, and in each trial of Israel, God always preserved a remnant, a group of faithful and believing Jews to whom and through whom He will fulfill His promises. These quotes make clear the reality that it is God's will to see His plan completed. If the salvation of Israel had been left to hinge on Israel's faithfulness then Israel would have been destroyed long ago. However, as we saw in our study of Romans 9:1-5, God made unconditional promises on the basis of His amazing unlimited Grace.

Romans 9:30-33

30What shall we say then? That Gentiles, who did not pursue righteousness,
attained righteousness, even the righteousness which is by faith; 31but Israel,
pursuing a law of righteousness, did not arrive at that law. 32Why? Because
they did not pursue it by faith, but as though it were by works. They
stumbled over the stumbling stone, 33just as it is written, "BEHOLD, I
LAY IN ZION A STONE OF STUMBLING AND A ROCK OF
OFFENSE, AND HE WHO BELIEVES IN HIM WILL NOT BE
DISAPPOINTED."

More questions

Paul then draws on a deep and saddening irony in response to this, however, he sums up the state of affairs perfectly. Note that previously the focus has been God's hand and plan throughout the large swath of human history. Now getting into this specific generation their failure has nothing to do with fatalism, nor anything to do with God willing them to do something or believe in him. Their shortcoming is clear.

What the Gentiles got…

The Gentiles who were completely alienated from God were not pursuing God in any way. They were not trying to keep the Law of Moses, they didn't even have the Law of Moses! Yet they attained to the kind of righteousness that was explained in Romans 3-5. This is an amazing display of God's grace, and is deeply ironic. It should have been very difficult for the Gentiles to recognize that they needed Christ's righteousness by faith, they had not had the opportunity to try to attain righteousness by the Law. Where the Jews could look back at their own national and personal failures at keeping the Law of God the Gentiles had to take this on faith. This is amazing, especially in counter-distinction to the Jews.

But Israel…

On the other hand Israel having the Law, and revelation about the character and nature of the one true God missed the mark. Even though they had every reason to understand and turn to accept the Messiah they did not. It must be noted that Paul is not saying that NO Israelites had turned. Far from it! There were thousands of Jewish believers at this time, however the majority, and most importantly the Jewish leadership, were still in rejection of Jesus Christ as their Messiah.

Why?

Paul then asks the million dollar question! Why did they reject the Messiah? The reason is that they did not pursue God in faith. Their eyes were set on earthly things. They longed to have God stand up and applaud them for what they were doing, rather than look and glorify Him for what HE is doing. They began to think that it was all about them and their righteousness rather than about God and His faithfulness. This is the ready message of the Old Testament. God longs to be in a relationship with Israel. This great passionate pursuit of Israel by God is echoed by the words of Jesus Christ Himself: "Jerusalem, Jerusalem, who kills the prophets and stones those who are sent to her! How often I wanted to gather your children together, the way a hen gathers her chicks under her wings, and you were unwilling." Matthew 23:37

The Same Old Problem…Legalism

The problem that they fell victim too is summed up in one simple word: legalism. They wanted to have their own righteousness before God. Therefore, the idea that they would have to rely on the love and grace of Jesus Christ is offensive to them. It causes them to stumble. It yet causes many to stumble. They are offended that they cannot impress God with their righteousness. They are frustrated that God would ever tell them that the very best they can provide are no more than "sewage" ('rubbish' in Philippians 3:8) and filthy (menstrual) rags (Isaiah 64:6). Then just as now people are offended by the fact that we are fully incapable and that keeps them from beholding Christ. However, now (just as always) all who trust in Him will NOT be disappointed.

ROMANS 10

ROMANS 10:1-13

A Whole New Chapter

Paul is not done with this discussion of what God is doing in Israel. In addressing the issue the question is still the same. "If God has made unconditional promises to Israel that are yet unfulfilled, and Israel is not currently walking with the Lord, then how can believers in the Church trust in His promises to them?" Paul began addressing this question in Romans 9:1-5. For gentile believers we may be tempted to ask why the Holy Spirit would allow three chapters to answer this relatively straight-forward question. Couldn't Paul just say, "Don't worry, He's getting to it."? While that answer may be true it does not seem to satisfy the need of the moment. For Hebrew Christians (of whom Paul was one) this question hits far closer to home. They were raised on these promises of God. There are at least three reasons why this long explanation is necessary:

> 1 - God's character is in view - Unlike the pagan gods and goddesses the God of Scripture is unlimited in His righteousness, holiness, perfection and truth. If there can be any shadow of God being unfaithful then our entire concept of God is forfeit. This issue is too important to God, to Paul, and it should be so to us.
>
> 2 - Israel is a BIG deal - Many believers want to downplay the

relationship that God has with Israel as being more or less the same as His relationship with the Church. However, we see that nothing could be further from the truth. God has dealt with Israel differently, and has made promises to them that were not made to the Church. Any attempt to make the glory and blessing of the Church eclipse (or assume) Israel's place will lead us to a misunderstanding of God.

3 - The Weight of Scripture - The vast portion of Scripture is addressed to, and directly regards the nation of Israel (Genesis through John plus the bulk of Revelation). It is all God's inspired word and is all useful for teaching, rebuking, correcting and training in righteousness (2 Timothy 3:16) yet so much of Scripture concerns God's interactions with Israel that it merits a fuller discussion in this amazing epistle.

So, given the level of importance involved it makes perfect sense for the Holy Spirit writing through Paul to fully explain the entire issue in three logical sections:

Romans 9 - Israel's Past

Romans 10 - Israel's Present

Romans 11 - Israel's Future

Romans 10:1-4

Brethren, my heart's desire and my prayer to God for them is for their salvation. For I testify about them that they have a zeal for God, but not in accordance with knowledge. For not knowing about God's righteousness and seeking to establish their own, they did not subject themselves to the righteousness of God. For Christ is the end of the law for righteousness to everyone who believes.

An Important Reminder

Paul reminds his readers that this is not simply an intellectual issue to him. This is something that he thinks about regularly, something that consumes his emotional energy. The term "heart" does not mean the beating organ that moves blood, it is a term encompassing the thought, will and emotions. Paul desires with his heart and commits time in prayer to God for them.

Us and Them

Once again it is important to realize that Paul is using "us" and "them" language here. Without getting overly technical it is the very clear reading that "us" must refer to the Church (current believers in Jesus Christ). Were he meaning to exclude himself he would have said "you", were he meaning to exclude his readers he could not have said "us". The only natural referent for them, then, is Israel - the physical descendants of Abraham, through Isaac and finally through Jacob.

The Desire and the Prayer

Paul's desire and prayer for Israel is that they would come to know salvation. He is going to demonstrate very clearly how Israel will ultimately be saved in the future. However, his desire is that more would be saved now and be incorporated into the church.

Good Testimony

Paul then tells the good side. Unbelieving Israel then (just as now) has a zeal for God. They pursue and protect His word. Paul did not doubt their passion and their effort. This brings about an important point. It is easy to get confused between intentions and reality. Some of the worst things that have ever been done on earth have been done with the best intentions. It is important to realize that many can very hardily, honestly, and genuinely be trying to earn their salvation, however, they will not achieve their goal. Paul draws the distinction:

Knowledge

This is a sobering thought. It seems that all of man's efforts in the wrong direction equals nothing. It doesn't matter how zealous a person is in seeking after God, if they are not seeking Him according to the knowledge of His revealed word, and the willingness to submit ourselves to the message found therein then zeal will only distance them from the Lord. Imagine a road trip where a person takes a wrong turn and is headed in the opposite direction of their destination. No matter how fast they drive they will never reach their destination until they learn where they are and what direction they SHOULD be going.

What they don't know

The key knowledge that they are missing is the knowledge of the righteousness of God. God's righteousness is perfect and infinite. What legalists of all stripe do in their attempts to earn righteousness and salvation before the Righteous God is drag the idea of God's infinite righteousness down to a level that feels more attainable. The Israelites here are said to be looking for their own righteousness. These acts being unacceptable in relationship to God's perfect and full righteousness they cheapen Him in order to feel like they could make up the balance. This is why legalistic churches often work to attain a feeling of reverence and holiness, they believe that by being more righteousness they can earn God's approval. Not being able to do so (and not being able to fool themselves for long) they live in fear of the Living God.

Un Submitted

Paul gives the reason - They are unwilling to place themselves under God's righteousness which He provided in Christ. Like frustrated children they try again and again and again thinking, "I will do it this time!" and they never finally succeed, far worse for them if they think that they have. It is the righteousness of God found in Christ that is necessary, and no other smaller measure will suffice.

Christ is...

Christ is said to be the end of something here. Christ is the end of going to the law to try to attain the human kind of righteousness. The opportunity to attain righteousness by way of the law is not long since passed. For Israel, before Christ came, keeping the law was the way that they were to honor Him (though even then, law-keeping did not provide spiritual salvation). That time is now gone, ended and finished. The Christian's only righteousness will always be only the righteousness which he has received from Jesus. Whether the righteousness that we receive in the judicial sense (justification) or the righteous life that comes only from relying upon Jesus Christ and His life within us, faith in Christ is the only righteousness available to mankind.

<u>Romans 10:5-10</u>

[5] For Moses writes that the man who practices the righteousness which is
based on law shall live by that righteousness. [6] But the righteousness based
on faith speaks as follows: "DO NOT SAY IN YOUR HEART, 'WHO
WILL ASCEND INTO HEAVEN?' (that is, to bring Christ down), [7]or
'WHO WILL DESCEND INTO THE ABYSS?' (that is, to bring Christ up

from the dead)." [8]But what does it say? "THE WORD IS NEAR YOU, IN YOUR MOUTH AND IN YOUR HEART" --that is, the word of faith which we are preaching, [9]that if you confess with your mouth Jesus as Lord, and believe in your heart that God raised Him from the dead, you will be saved; [10]for with the heart a person believes, resulting in righteousness, and with the mouth he confesses, resulting in salvation.

Moses says...

The Law that God gave Moses was a full life system. There were very few questions left to a person after they finished answering the question: "What does the law require of me?" The one who practices this law lives based on the righteousness that he achieves. Under the Law a person could expect blessing for obedience and curses for disobedience. That would mean that, under the administration of Law, a person would quite literally live or die based on their personal performance (righteousness).

Contrasts

Paul then contrasts the righteousness that comes by faith with the righteousness that is based on the Law. The character of this contrast is not simply the quantity of man's righteousness (which can only be finite and temporary) and God's eternal righteousness, but also the quality of man's righteousness which differs from God's righteousness. This has to do with the central message of the Gospel. We did not have to climb up to heaven to get it, nor claw our way down to the grave. Christ came to us, as a human like us. Not only that, but He is now near. The message of His death for us is now available to everyone who will hear it and believe it.

Salvation available to all

Far from the idea that God is choosing some to salvation and others to damnation, here the Gospel is available to all who would as a matter of will believe in the message. Some have tried to make this "confess with the mouth" some sort of condition to salvation, however, that is not consistent with the message of the context, nor does it harmonize with the rest of Scripture. Faith (belief) is what is in view here. It is a logical consequence that our faith will be displayed by agreeing before men what we believe and that is how others will know that they are believers. Note that this is not a public confession. It is perfectly natural to think that if someone places their faith in Jesus Christ then they will quite naturally say it out loud, even if only to an empty room. A confession alone is not sufficient (though many make them). The reality is that genuine trust, from the heart is needed. We aren't able to judge that in each other, we can only know if we have trusted in Christ.

Translation Issues

It is worth noting that there is a heretical teaching present in Christianity today which is sometimes called "Lordship Salvation." This false teaching about salvation suggests that you aren't REALLY saved until you *make* Jesus the Lord of your Life, which is different from trusting in Him for salvation (accepting His free gift). This is a works based salvation that suggests, against the manifest message of Salvation by Grace through Faith that there is some unspoken level of submission that must be attained or given over before a person can be saved. This is deep and vile error that has many believers terrified because they don't understand the information in Romans 6-8 regarding the Sin Nature of the believer and salvation by grace through faith. The distinction Paul makes here is that there may be a professing believer who has not believed in his heart, that man is not saved. He is not saying that there is a person who has believed in Jesus, but not submitted to Him fully as a matter of salvation. Translations like that found in this verse are often used (though not intended by the translators) to back this heresy. The Greek, however, could just as well be translated "confess the Lord Jesus" as we see in the King James Version and the New King James Version. It is Jesus that saves, we only receive this gift by faith. It really is that simple.

The Hebrew Poetry Patterns

Hebrew poetry differs from western poetry greatly. While we focus on rhymed word sounds Hebrew poetry focuses on rhymed meanings. Sometimes rhyming by saying the same thing again in different words, other times by saying the opposite. Another form that was used was the literary form of chiasm which is a mirror image in writing. Among other things this structure is used to put the most important point (or the central theme) at the "center" of the mirror image. These verses are a Hebrew Poetry pattern. The advantage of these patterns is that we are able to interpret the statements in light of one another. Here is what this pattern looks like when spelled out in its structure:

A - That if you confess with your mouth the Lord Jesus,

B - And believe in our heart that God raised him from the dead,

C - You will be saved;

B' - For with the heart a person believes, resulting in righteousness,

A' - And with the mouth he confesses, resulting in salvation

This is all part of the same moment when a person enters into a relationship with the Lord Jesus Christ based on His work for us on the Cross. In the center: You will be saved. This is in the passive voice: the believer is saved by God. It is in the future tense, in this case the person is an unbeliever, until they believe, then they will be saved. This is a statement of fact. This isn't a "maybe", and it doesn't give the idea that it is contingent upon anything else. Salvation is a completed fact because of what Jesus has done for us. Notice, believe and confess are paired as are righteousness and salvation. There could be no salvation apart from this righteousness, nor any salvation for one who had not been made righteous. This is a clear poetic statement of our need for Jesus Christ.

Romans 10:11-13
11For the Scripture says, "WHOEVER BELIEVES IN HIM WILL NOT
BE DISAPPOINTED." 12For there is no distinction between Jew and
Greek; for the same Lord is Lord of all, abounding in riches for all who call
on Him; 13for "WHOEVER WILL CALL ON THE NAME OF THE
LORD WILL BE SAVED."

Back to Belief
Paul, again uses the Old Testament (Isaiah 28:16 and Joel 2:32) to state an eternal principle that applies to ages and time periods. Spiritual salvation has always been by trusting in the Lord. The Lord designed humanity to believe and trust in Him. Here more than ever we see the reality that when it comes to placing faith in Christ in the current time there are no Jews nor Gentiles. In this special time (remember the focus of this chapter is on Israel's present) sometimes called the church age everyone who believes becomes one new body. This is the chief message of Ephesians 2 as well.

Paul's prayer is that the Israelites would turn, see their error in rejecting Jesus Christ and be made a part of the Church. As we will see in chapter 11 this would not change or negate the promises that the Lord has made to Israel.

It's a faith thing

Again we want to note that faith is what the Lord is looking for. He has made this wonderful salvation available to anyone who would be willing to trust in Him for salvation. Faith is trusting in the clearly revealed facts of scripture. The question is not whether the reality explained is reasonable: it IS reasonable; the question is whether a person chooses to trust in the Savior, the Messiah, Jesus Christ.

ROMANS 10:14-21

On Purpose

In this section of the book of Romans Paul begins to be very clear about what is going on in the current age. Paul gives some essential reasons for and functions of the Church in relationship to Israel. It is noteworthy that Paul is still using that same "us and them" language between these two bodies. Never once is the indication made that the church has replaced Israel, nor assumed her blessings. In fact, one of the major functions of the Church is to be a tool in bringing Israel back into belief and faith in her God and in the Messiah Whom He has sent!

<u>**Romans 10:14-17**</u>

14How then will they call on Him in whom they have not believed? How
will they believe in Him whom they have not heard? And how will they hear
without a preacher? 15How will they preach unless they are sent? Just as it is
written, "HOW BEAUTIFUL ARE THE FEET OF THOSE WHO
BRING GOOD NEWS OF GOOD THINGS!" 16However, they did not
all heed the good news; for Isaiah says, "LORD, WHO HAS BELIEVED
OUR REPORT?" 17So faith comes from hearing, and hearing by the word
of Christ.

Remember?

The previous study looked at Israel's current situation. The Israelites rejected the Messiah because they preferred to try to make up, or create, a righteousness of their own. Their desire for self-righteousness caused them to miss the righteousness that is given by God in Jesus Christ. Thus, this new body (known forever to God, but hidden in the Old Testament revelation) called the church began. In it there is no distinction between Jew or Gentile. Verse 13 ended the previous section with the assurance that anyone who calls on the name of the Lord will be saved. There is something here that is not to be missed.

Who are you going to call?

The Jews before Christ came could simply call on Yahweh, the Lord. They were not responsible to the full revelation of Jesus Christ. However, now that Jesus has come one cannot just call on the limited revelation of the Old Testament without calling upon God in the form of His Self-revelation in the person of Jesus Christ. We find that Jesus Christ is the visible image of the invisible God (Colossians 1:15), that in Him the fullness of Deity dwells (John 1:14, Hebrews 1:2). One cannot reject Jesus and yet call upon the name of God. To reject Jesus is to reject God. (John 8)

Zeal without Knowledge

This is another valuable point. As the first verses of this chapter revealed, zeal without knowledge is useless. Here we find out that calling on the name of the Lord but rejecting the revelation of the Lord in the Person of Jesus Christ is also useless. This brings Paul's series of questions to a clear point. They could be arranged as follows:

> How then will they call on Him in whom they have not **believed**?
>
> How will they **believe** in Him whom they have not *heard*?
>
> And How will *hear* without a *preacher*?
>
> How will they *preach* unless they are ->sent<-?

Each rhetorical question begins with the answer to the previous rhetorical question so we could add in the assumed answer as follows:

> How then will they call on Him in whom they have not believed?
>
> (*They must hear about Him*)
>
> How will they believe in Him whom they have not heard?
>
> (*Someone must tell them*)
>
> And how will hear without a preacher?
>
> (*Someone must preach)*
>
> How will they preach unless they are sent?

(*Someone must be sent*)

It seems Paul is getting to the point of finding an answer to the problem. They just need to be told. Surely a clear explanation will fix everything!

Support from the Old Testament

This thinking makes even more sense because it is backed by principles from the Old Testament. Paul quotes from Isaiah 52:7 and Nahum 1:15 to prove that good news should be well received. It is easy to get confused by the world's rejection of the Gospel. As the Musicians of DC Talk once quipped we are made to feel like: "We are spreading some kind of disease." However, we find that Gospel is still the greatest news ever given to mankind. For starters we have: forgiveness of sins, restoration to fellowship with God and total freedom in Christ. All by God's grace through faith! Philip Yancey put it very well in his book What's So Amazing About Grace when he said that the only reason not to believe in Jesus is because it is TOO GOOD to be true.

Problem Solved? Not quite…

While the reasoning above may be flawless we find that it doesn't match up with reality for some reason. Many a new believer charges out into the world with fresh excitement overjoyed to share the good news of Jesus Christ with everyone they meet, only to find that everyone that they talk to (or nearly everyone) refuses to believe in Him. Martin Luther purportedly had a great heart for the Jewish people early in his ministry. However, once he experienced what Paul experiences here he fell into the trap of Romans 11 and became coldly anti-Semitic just as the Catholic Church was and most churches still are today.

Not new…

This is sadly not new for humanity, and also not new in the story of the God's interactions with the Jewish people. Isaiah was one of the chief prophetic sources of information about the Messiah more than 700 years before He came. Yet even then we find Isaiah coming with the good news of the Messiah starting of Isaiah 53 bewailing the fact that no one will listen to the good news of God.

Faith comes from Hearing

Next comes a very important point for every believer. This point has an impact on the personal faith as well as upon how the gospel is shared. Here we find out where faith comes from: the hearing. This "faith" here has the definite article ("the") in the Greek. This is the specific things that are believed. We know what we believe, and others can know what we believed based on the word of God.

The word of God

The "word" here is not *logos* as it is in John 1:1. This "word" focuses on the idea, not so much on the message, but on the spoken word. The idea in our evangelism is that we are to be speaking the word of God to others. This does not mean that we need to come into every situation armed with a dozen verse references (though that isn't a bad idea) it means that we need to be soaked thoroughly in the word so that we can speak and accurately represent what is contained in the Bible. The old saying is particularly true here: "You are the only Bible that some people will ever read." In general just throwing Bibles at people is not always an effective way to spread the gospel. Just handing out tracts has proved to be monumentally ineffective. However, the speaking to the people in our lives is how they can know what the Bible teaches, and they may only choose to believe (place their faith) in what they know, as no one can believe something before they know it. That is a part of our function as believers.

<u>Romans 10:18-21</u>

18But I say, surely they have never heard, have they? Indeed they have;
"THEIR VOICE HAS GONE OUT INTO ALL THE EARTH, AND
THEIR WORDS TO THE ENDS OF THE WORLD." 19But I say, surely
Israel did not know, did they? First Moses says, "I WILL MAKE YOU
JEALOUS BY THAT WHICH IS NOT A NATION, BY A NATION
WITHOUT UNDERSTANDING WILL I ANGER YOU." 20And Isaiah
is very bold and says, "I WAS FOUND BY THOSE WHO DID NOT
SEEK ME, I BECAME MANIFEST TO THOSE WHO DID NOT ASK
FOR ME." 21But as for Israel He says, "ALL THE DAY LONG I HAVE
STRETCHED OUT MY HANDS TO A DISOBEDIENT AND
OBSTINATE PEOPLE."

Never Heard?

Paul then asks if they have ever heard? Clearly the Israelites were well aware of this group of people who had popped up. If nothing else, because they remember with great lucidity the ministry of Jesus. Many were present, and many more informed later about the mock trials and the crucifixion of Jesus Christ. Furthermore, it was important enough to the Jewish leadership to use their sway to post official Roman guards at the tomb. However, that wasn't the end. They continued to hear through Peter, John and the other Apostles, whom they were repeatedly dealing with severely throughout the first chapters of Acts.

Spreading Message

The book of Acts also records the progression of the gospel out to the very ends of the Roman Empire. Paul, Barnabas and others were actively taking the gospel everywhere they were taken or driven. It made sense that they would tend to follow Paul's pattern of going "first to the Jews and then to the Gentiles…" as Paul did throughout his ministry in Acts. The point? They have heard. Much more so, Paul's journeys would soon bring him, in bondage, into Rome and give him the opportunity to share the gospel with the very households and praetorian guards that were central to Caesar himself.

Told you so

As we have seen, Israel had been provided ample reason and opportunity to repent (change their minds) about the Messiah, Jesus. However, Israel at large chose to reject the Messiah. God, knowing that this would be the case told them what He would do, and this gives us part of the purpose for the church: to provoke Israel to jealousy. This is not something that the church is to be doing, this is one of God's purposes in the Church that He will see done. As He freely displays His love and grace for all humanity through the church Israel would think: "What claim do they have on the Messiah? What are they doing with MY Messiah?" and finally realize that He came to be their Messiah first.

God's Heart

God's heart in the matter is not neutral. God is portrayed in the Old Testament as a loving Father who longs to gather the nation of Israel to Him in spite of their endless betrayal and failure. Hosea's life was made to be a living parable to God's heart for Israel when he was commanded to take an unfaithful bride. She continually left him, and God told Hosea to take her (Gomer) back, forgive and restore her. This is a powerful picture to the Lord's amazing love for Israel. While they are (as all sinful humanity is) disobedient and obstinate, they are still His beloved and chosen people. Here again, we see that the character of God's love is not conditional and changing like man's love. God's love is permanent and undefeatable, and He will be faithful to His every promise.

ROMANS 11

ROMANS 11:1-16

On to the Future!

Having covered the past of Israel in chapter 9 and the present situation of Israel in chapter 10 Paul marches onto the future of the nation of Israel. It is important to understand that through every challenge and unbelief that the Lord is still faithful to Israel. The reasoning behind this is not because of Israel's greatness but because they are the object of the promise of God. The reason why Israel will not be forsaken is because of the promises which God has made to them through Abraham, Issac, Jacob, Joseph, Moses and David. It is not a matter of man's goodness, only a matter of God's amazing faithfulness.

Romans 11:1-6

1I say then, God has not rejected His people, has He? May it never be! For I
too am an Israelite, a descendant of Abraham, of the tribe of Benjamin.
2God has not rejected His people whom He foreknew. Or do you not know
what the Scripture says in the passage about Elijah, how he pleads with
God against Israel? 3"Lord, THEY HAVE KILLED YOUR PROPHETS,
THEY HAVE TORN DOWN YOUR ALTARS, AND I ALONE AM
LEFT, AND THEY ARE SEEKING MY LIFE." 4But what is the divine
response to him? "I HAVE KEPT for Myself SEVEN THOUSAND

MEN WHO HAVE NOT BOWED THE KNEE TO BAAL." [5]In the
same way then, there has also come to be at the present time a remnant
according to God's gracious choice. [6]But if it is by grace, it is no longer on
the basis of works, otherwise grace is no longer grace.

Negative Responses

Opening this chapter we get another rhetorical question. This time the question is based on the fact that Israel had at the time rejected God's Messiah Jesus Christ. The obvious logic would be that the Jews rejected God so God would then reject them. On a human level we may find this logic very appealing. If you owe someone some money and they reject your attempts to give it to them you may feel justified in just keeping the money. This is similar to what is happening with Israel and God. He promised a Messiah who will be King of kings and Lord of lords. He provided that Messiah and the Jews rejected Him. Who could blame God if He were to say that He tried His best? This is one of the major differences between God and man. While man can often talk himself into "letting himself off" for various reasons, God will always be faithful to His word. Thus Paul's usual extreme response: "MAY IT NEVER BE!" This phrase, again, means: "Don't even conceive of such an idea!"

Now it's personal!

Paul uses himself as his first line of evidence that the Lord has not simply given up on Israel. The very fact that Paul (and much of the early church) was made up of Jewish believers was evidence that the Lord had not forgotten His promises and special relationship with Israel. In fact, we find that throughout western history there have been Jewish Christians who were, in part, acting as the saved remnant of Israel. Even though these people become part of the Church there is a reality that the Lord has preserved the Jewish people and still has a great desire to see them (as individuals and as a nation) turn to Him.

How many of the world's ancient religions are still functioning today. There are those who have attempted to revive faith in the pagan systems of the Norse, Greek or Roman gods and goddesses, but never with any substantial success. While the new age movement may have latched on to some of the practices and attitudes of Native American religious ideas and practices we find that they are a far cry from the faith practiced by the ancients. Judaism is the only faith that goes back to the dawn of time and has never been replaced or outmoded. This is because of God's faithfulness to do just what He says He is going to do.

Feeling Lonely

The focus then moves to an example from History. The prophet Elijah was in a horrible life and death struggle with Ahab and Jezebel who were then king and queen of the Northern Kingdom of Israel. Elijah was representing God while Jezebel was spearheading the effort to keep the Israelites worshipping the false God Baal (and Ahab was following her unquestioningly). Elijah felt totally alone, like he was the only one who still believed in God enough to face death rather than worship Baal. This is something most believers can identify with. Standing up for what is right, often means we will stand alone. However, there is more to the story. The Lord assures Elijah with the great message that Elijah is actually NOT alone at all! In fact, God has preserved seven thousand men who had never worshipped this false god. This is another important lesson about walking with the Lord: You never know who may be inspired by one person's faithfulness.

All of Grace

This is a great moment. After the reminder of God's faithfulness in Elijah's day is brought up, the main point is brought back! This, even this, is all by God's grace. God is always gracious, always much more gracious than we could ever imagine. God longs for people to be in a relationship with Him, thus He gives every single opportunity. The distinction is made yet again, that "if it were by works it would not be grace." This highlights the reality that God's grace cannot be earned. Not even in the slightest degree. God's love and plan must be accepted based on trust in Him, His character and ability.

<u>Romans 11:7-12</u>

7What then? What Israel is seeking, it has not obtained, but those who were
chosen obtained it, and the rest were hardened; 8just as it is written, "GOD
GAVE THEM A SPIRIT OF STUPOR, EYES TO SEE NOT AND
EARS TO HEAR NOT, DOWN TO THIS VERY DAY." 9And David
says, "LET THEIR TABLE BECOME A SNARE AND A TRAP, AND
A STUMBLING BLOCK AND A RETRIBUTION TO THEM. 10"LET

THEIR EYES BE DARKENED TO SEE NOT, AND BEND THEIR
BACKS FOREVER." 11I say then, they did not stumble so as to fall, did
they? May it never be! But by their transgression salvation has come to the
Gentiles, to make them jealous. 12Now if their transgression is riches for the
world and their failure is riches for the Gentiles, how much more will their
fulfillment be!

What then?

Paul's next question is regarding this idea of the faithful remnant. Even though the bulk of the chosen people (Israel) were not attaining to salvation there are those within that group that respond to the call of Jesus Christ and are chosen to be a part of the church. The rest are said to be "hardened". This describes exactly the mind and the attitude of the unbeliever. They are hardened, like soil that has been packed down. Neither water nor seeds can get through their hardened shell. As we have seen before this hardening happens by their own repeated rejection of God, it happens through the world system and it happens because of the work of Satan. Those who reject the free and full offer of eternal life in Jesus Christ are left with no other choice but to continue to harden themselves and be hardened by their circumstances.

Not New

This is not a new pattern in the book of Romans. The first chapter spent a substantial amount of time (Romans 1:18 and following) which described the role of the person who rejects God. The result of rejecting God is moving further and further from Him. The result of being pushed away from Him is a decreased ability to ever correct their thinking. This ultimately ends in spiritual blindness, deafness and inability to escape from what has drawn such a person away from the Lord.

Is this for always?

Paul then asks the big question. Did the nation of Israel make a permanent stumble? The answer: Of course not! However, the Lord, who alone is able to work all things together for good for those who love Him, is using their rejection to bring salvation to the gentiles. This is the first time since Moses in History that gentiles have access to God without first becoming Jews. That is a remarkable reality indeed! However, this doesn't mean God has given up on Israel, they have stumbled by their faithlessness, but they will not ultimately fall.

Riches for you and I

This is a powerful moment in the narrative. Israel's loss in rejecting the Messiah was a great gain for the rest of the world. The Lord was able to use a very dark situation and turn it into a new kind of success that had never been seen before on the earth: People of all tribes, tongues and nations now having access to the God of the Universe through the person and work of Jesus Christ! This is a BIG deal. The next question, however, if this is what comes when the children of promise reject the Messiah what will it be like when they accept Him and are restored! This event, is the millennial kingdom! This time, when Israel is back in relationship (nationally) with God will mark the most wonderful and prosperous time in all of earth's history. This is something to get excited about. We should long for Israel to come to know Jesus, not because it will speed up His coming (the Father has already set that date) but because they need to know THEIR Messiah!

Romans 11:13-16

[13]But I am speaking to you who are Gentiles. Inasmuch then as I am an
apostle of Gentiles, I magnify my ministry, [14]if somehow I might move to
jealousy my fellow countrymen and save some of them. [15]For if their
rejection is the reconciliation of the world, what will their acceptance be but
life from the dead? [16]If the first piece of dough is holy, the lump is also; and
if the root is holy, the branches are too.

Conclusions and Applications

Paul then addresses his Gentile readers directly. Paul reminds them of his identification with them as he (Paul) was God's especially sent messenger to the Gentiles. Paul gives us an interesting conclusion and purpose statement for His ministry: To move Israel to jealousy so that they would come to know and accept Jesus Christ, *their* Messiah! Please note: Paul here gives an interesting tension. While the great portion of Israel has rejected Jesus Christ there are those who have come to salvation by trusting in Jesus. Paul doesn't seem to be even slightly fatalistic (i.e., reducing the individual's option to place their faith in Christ) as He thinks it worthwhile to try to induce them to look to Jesus by means of jealousy. If they had no choice in the matter then this would be a silly idea indeed.

A Call to Action

Paul brings about an important point for every believer today. The nation of Israel is precious indeed to the Lord. The Jews are beloved of Him. As believers today we have every reason to love, pray for and share the gospel freely with Jews as much as we possibly can. Not because this will in any way haste the day of the Lord's return, but because this will mean an increased blessing for the church. We as believers are to adopt the Lord's heart and viewpoint about everything. This means adopting His great love for the Jewish people as well. We should thank and respect them for being God's chosen line through which to bring the Messiah. Believers ought to be loving respecting and helping Israel and the Jews at every opportunity because of the place they have in the heart of our loving Savior!

ROMANS 11:17-29

Who is who?
Paul now begins to use imagery of branches and a root. Whenever symbolic language begins to be used people get confused, mostly because of not reading clearly. The symbols that are being used are very clear and involve all of the same people whom have been spoken of for the last three chapters. Here are the symbols:

> **The branches of the cultivated tree** – The people of Israel. Physically descended from Abraham and heirs of the unconditional promises of Scripture. The people of Israel had been "cultivated" by God's continual involvement with them, their history and their access to the Lord's word.
>
> **The branches of the wild olive tree** – These are the Gentiles. Not having the advantage of having been raised up with the same exposure to the Truth and the promises of God. They are wild, but they are here grafted into "the root"
>
> **The rich root of the olive tree** – This is the symbol for Christ – the root of blessing, and the source of all salvation.

Understanding the identity of these symbols is the key to understanding the passage. Many have mistaken the Root with Israel (who is the branch) to argue that Israel has been replaced by the church, however, that is just bad reading.

<u>Romans 11:17-24</u>
17But if some of the branches were broken off, and you, being a wild olive,
were grafted in among them and became partaker with them of the rich
root of the olive tree, 18do not be arrogant toward the branches; but if you
are arrogant, remember that it is not you who supports the root, but the
root supports you. 19You will say then, "Branches were broken off so that I
might be grafted in." 20Quite right, they were broken off for their unbelief,
but you stand by your faith. Do not be conceited, but fear; 21for if God did

not spare the natural branches, He will not spare you, either. [22]Behold then
the kindness and severity of God; to those who fell, severity, but to you,
God's kindness, if you continue in His kindness; otherwise you also will be
cut off. [23]And they also, if they do not continue in their unbelief, will be
grafted in, for God is able to graft them in again. [24]For if you were cut off
from what is by nature a wild olive tree, and were grafted contrary to nature
into a cultivated olive tree, how much more will these who are the natural
branches be grafted into their own olive tree?

Some were broken off…

Paul continues with his warning to the gentile believers. It would be the worst thing possible for gentile believers to get arrogant and forget God's eternal and loving heart and unconditional promises towards the nation of Israel. Yet, in reading this passage we can see that this is exactly what has happened. The church has grown to be peopled mostly by gentiles and the gentiles throughout History have turned on their spiritual forebears. Rather than loving, and supporting Israel the church has turned on Israel and snubbed her. False teachings of "replacement theology" have fallen into this trap causing years of satanic anti-Semitism throughout the history of the Church. This passage is very much for the church today, though many still ignore it.

It is also valuable to note that not "all" of these natural branches have been broken off. As was noted in the previous verses, the Lord always preserves for Himself a remnant of Israel and so it is in the Church today that there are large and growing faithful messianic Jews who are deeply in love with Jesus Christ, trusting in Him for salvation.

The Wild Ones

Then Paul addresses the gentile believers as "wild olive branches" that were grafted in after Israel rejected the Messiah and was removed from the root (temporarily). Grafting branches onto other plants was a fairly common practice in keeping an ancient olive plant. However, it was not considered to be particularly valuable to graft a wild olive branch in. The cultivated branch would be the one that would bear the most fruit year after year. The cultivated branch has every advantage of having been selected, bred and cared for correctly for its entire existence. However, as a matter of God's mercy and grace He has grafted the gentiles into Christ in response to Israel's rejection of the Messiah.

Access "with them"

Notice, the language of distinction continues. There is no intimation that the gentile's access to the Lord replaces that of Israel, nor that the church assumes the name, promises or position of Israel. Only that we have access together through Jesus Christ. The gentile believer today must never become arrogant towards the Jewish believers today. We must never look at the rebellion and rejection of Israel and suggest that we are here because we are somehow better, smarter or faster. Far from it, gentile believers should rather be overjoyed at the opportunity to share the wonderful news of the Messiah with those Jews who still reject Him. Even that with respectful reverence for the place that they hold in the plan of God. This is the attitude that comes only from a full recognition that it is God's work that saves, not ours. It is God who has grafted us in, by His grace and mercy, and the gentile believer must never forget it!

Watch what you say…

Paul sees the temptation of the gentile believer to observe that branches were broken off so that they may come. This is a sort of "spin" that we must notice. The incorrect assumption of this way of thinking is that God discarded the Jews to make room for the gentiles. This is exactly the arrogance that many Christians throughout history have viewed God's relationship with Israel. In sharp contrast with this way of thinking Scripture demands a humble viewpoint.

The Problem

The Holy Spirit reminds the believers that the Jews weren't cast away by the will of God, but by their own unbelief and unwillingness to recognize the Messiah. We must never lose this valuable and important perspective. Regardless of all other factors Salvation is always, and will always be, by grace through faith alone in Christ alone. Israel is disconnected from Christ because of their unbelief, not any action or inaction on the part of the Lord. The believer today stands by that faith alone and we must never forget that, lest we fall into the same trap as Israel in trying to earn their salvation. Or teach others either by statement or implication that they must earn their salvation. This is of the utmost importance.

Fear

Here the Holy Spirit brings into view the appropriate attitude: one of humble and reverent exultation. We must continually remember that we were saved by no work of our own, but by the work of Christ alone. It was God working on our behalf that brought about our salvation. We must not think that it is because of anything special or unique in us that we might take credit for. Our salvation exists for the glory of God, just as the nation of Israel does. "Fear" here is different from terror or phobia. However, there is a reason why the same word that can mean terror-fear is used here for reverent-fear. When we see how amazing and powerful, how wonderful and amazing is our God, we are moved to an emotional experience that is not totally dissimilar from what we would ordinary call a feeling of fear. A revelation of the holiness, or the "other-ness", of God is more than the human creature can process or understand. Much like we may experience a thrill as we look at a great blue whale, or at the power of the ocean, even when it does not bear us any threat, so we must have this reverent and awe-filled respect for God. This correct perspective will safeguard us from a great deal of error on our behalf.

The Big "IF"

There seems to be an insinuation here that the Lord may take a person's salvation, however given the repeated instruction of Romans chapters five through eight that cannot be possible. The Holy Spirit is still talking about people groups here rather than the salvation of individuals. We see that the world will see a time when "the fullness of the gentiles has come in." At that time the Lord will return for His Church and God's focus will again return to the Jews during the tribulation period. We notice that in the Church, just as in Israel, God has no grandchildren. Each person is responsible for their own relationship with the Lord and just because someone was "raised Christian" has nothing to say about whether or not that individual is in a relationship with Jesus Christ by grace through faith.

Also "If"

Paul then alludes to the coming time in the future when Israel will no longer continue in her unbelief. God is able to "graft" them back into the root. This will, in fact, be far easier for them than for those of us who were grafted in apart from the promises and History that the Jews have. There is no question that the character of God is displayed clearly throughout the

Old Testament. In fact, there is not one attribute of God that is not just as clearly displayed in the Old Testament as it is in the New Testament (and vice versa!). God is unchanging and without any confusion of character. Thus, when the Jews return to the Lord and come to understand His revelation of Himself in the person of Jesus Christ it becomes very natural for them to move into life in Christ because God's character is completely unchanging.

Romans 11:25-29

[25]For I do not want you, brethren, to be uninformed of this mystery--so that you will not be wise in your own estimation--that a partial hardening has happened to Israel until the fullness of the Gentiles has come in; [26]and so all Israel will be saved; just as it is written, "THE DELIVERER WILL COME FROM ZION, HE WILL REMOVE UNGODLINESS FROM JACOB." [27]"THIS IS MY COVENANT WITH THEM, WHEN I TAKE AWAY THEIR SINS." [28]From the standpoint of the gospel they are enemies for your sake, but from the standpoint of God's choice they are beloved for the sake of the fathers; [29]for the gifts and the calling of God are irrevocable.

Shhhh! It's a mystery!

In Paul's day there were mystery religions that thrived on the idea that a person must have secret knowledge in order to be saved. These were often multi-level secret societies and orders in which a person had to be sworn up to greater levels of mystery and secrecy, and each secret must be kept on pain of death. These secret knowledge cults were very common in the ancient world, yet Paul has another idea. He doesn't want ANYONE to miss out on the things that God has revealed. He is declaring it from the rooftops, and no less this mystery than the other amazing revelations that God has made through His Son, Jesus Christ.

Be not wise in your own eyes.

Again, humility is in view. Gentile believers must maintain the strictest humility and gratitude for our salvation and should be deeply grateful to the Hebrew people for their contribution to our faith, and for God's ultimate faithfulness towards them. In order to remind every believer of the humility that we must logically maintain Paul reveals an important reality:

God is allowing this hardening of Israel for the purpose of saving the Gentiles, not as a final state of affairs. We must recognize that we have placed our faith in Jesus Christ not because we are smarter, wiser or in some way better, but because of the work of the Holy Spirit and a positive response to Him. Our salvation is never a reason to feel good about ourselves, or glorify yourselves for our good choice. The only logical response to our salvation is the humble adoration and praise of the wonderful God who saved us!

Partial Hardening

Two important things:

> 1 – This is only partial. There have continued to be Jewish people who trusted Jesus Christ from the Disciples through to the present day.
>
> 2 – God allows this partial hardening (or blindness) to continue until He has gathered in the "fullness of the gentiles". When He has completed His purpose He will awaken the hearts of all Jewish peoples in the time that we refer to as the Tribulation Period. The purpose of that seven year period (Recorded in Daniel 9:24-27) will be to soften the hearts of the Jewish people. At the end of that period there will only be believing peoples left on earth to repopulate after the terrible judgments that will occur.

A Difference of Perspective

For the believer in the first century many of the major difficulties and persecutions were coming at the hands of the Jews. Paul himself was among these Jews who were persecuting the faith with great zeal and energy. However, Paul wants to remind believers that even though they may be working to destroy the faith even THAT does not annul the promises that God made to them. Thus, the Jewish people are still God's beloved and chosen people because His calling of them is irrevocable. It cannot be destroyed, removed or disassembled.

GREAT APPLICATION!

So we see that God's great love and faithfulness to the Jews is not about how great they are, but rather, HOW GREAT HE IS! It is not about our strength or faithfulness, it is about His great faithfulness in spite of our inability and faithlessness. This is great news for us in the Church as well. It tells us that what God has purposed to do in us will be completed because it is He Himself that will do it! We need not fear that our salvation will fail, or that even our own faithlessness will cause Him to leave us, because He will never be proved faithless by one of His creatures. In many ways this verse parallels Romans 8:38-39 very well:

> *For I am convinced that neither death, nor life, nor angels, nor principalities, nor things present, nor things to come, nor powers, nor height, nor depth, nor any other created thing, will be able to separate us from the love of God, which is in Christ Jesus our Lord.*

ROMANS 11:30-36

Us and Them to the End

This section closes the section of the book of Romans regarding God's guarantee of faithfulness to the nation of Israel. Even with this explicit warning in Scripture the church as a whole has often fallen into the ridiculous idea that the Church has somehow replaced Israel or become the "New Israel." The Holy Spirit here hits the primary reason that believers in the Church Age will attempt to read themselves into Israel's promises and blessings: pride. It is a spiritual arrogance of the highest order to assume that the Church has somehow replaced Israel in the plan of God. It is of paramount importance to understand God's faithfulness in regards to Israel because that also established His character and trustworthy nature regarding our salvation and relationship with Him in the church.

<u>**Romans 11:30-32**</u>

30For just as you once were disobedient to God, but now have been shown
mercy because of their disobedience, 31so these also now have been
disobedient, that because of the mercy shown to you they also may now be
shown mercy. 32For God has shut up all in disobedience so that He may
show mercy to all.

You Who?

Who is the "you" in this verse? This plural "you" is referring to the Gentile believers. Gentile believers, in the previous verses, are commanded to remember with humility that the Lord has not abandoned his promises to Israel and He will be faithful to them. The Gentile believers are given a reminder here. Paul tells them what they were. Paul often does this (see Ephesians 2:1-5 and 1 Corinthians 6:8-11) to remind believers that the only thing that separates them from the unbelieving world is the person and work of Jesus Christ. The arrogant, self-righteous believer is an absolute contradiction in terms. If what the Bible has to say is true, then the believer should come into every situation with the greatest humility and love in being able to share the good news about Jesus Christ to every person, knowing that: "But for the grace of God, there go I."

Then and Now

This is an exciting couple of verses because it contrasts two different things. Interestingly, the Spirit, writing through Paul here, does not contrast disobedience with obedience as one would expect. The contrast is between disobedience and *mercy*. In the simplest terms possible mercy is not giving someone "what they deserve." This is very important because we often think of ourselves as stepping into obedience, or being obedient as believers, but the effective force here is not *our* obedience, but *God's mercy*. That is quite a change of perspective indeed. At every turn our salvation is seen to be of God, by God, to God and for God, which we will see more of as we move forward.

Heavenly Economics

When we consider the flow of wealth and power in the world there is a distinct sense of limited resources. "Either I have it or you have it" encapsulates this idea that if something is going well for one person someone else must be suffering lack or loss as a result of that. While this is often the case in earthly matters, it is never the case from the perspective of heavenly matters. God is not ever in a case of limited resources. There is not a limited amount of mercy that was afforded to Him at the cross to give out as He sees fit. In fact, God uses every opportunity to offer more mercy than before. So even those who reject His grace and His mercy seem to open up new opportunities for His grace and His mercy to shine out even more! This is a wonderful and amazing facet of our walk with Christ. Whenever we see a brother growing in Christ, or a sister who is truly conformed to the image of Jesus we need never wonder if there is enough grace left that we may be yet more transformed as well. There is always more grace, always more mercy found in Jesus Christ.

Shut up!

The word behind this translation "shut up" is the idea of being "hemmed in" or "concluded". The essence of this statement is found in the repetition of what was concluded about the state of all mankind in Romans 1:18-Romans 3: Man (corporately and individually) is hopelessly, completely trapped in Sin. In his position and his actions, every single man is a sinner and he proves it. This is the case for every single person without any exceptions. This is what God has allowed to happen to all of humanity.

SO THAT…

Then the great news! God allowed all of humanity to fall to the logical conclusion of their sinfulness so that mercy can be shown to all. There is not one person living that is not able to receive His mercy and grace. It is available to every single individual on the planet. There is not one person for whom Christ does not have the grace, mercy and power to save. Which then demands the question: "Why isn't everyone saved?" The answer to which is plain. Though God has offered His mercy to every single person without exception, not every single person will accept it. For some it will be because they are too proud to admit that they cannot save themselves. For others it is because they don't believe God is powerful enough to save. Most of these shortcomings are issues of belief. Either bringing God down, or bringing man up to God's level. Wishing to earn one's salvation is saying, "By my hard work I can become like God – and therefore free from destruction." Believing that God cannot, or will not, save is to bring Him down to either human power levels or human level of inability to show grace and mercy.

<u>Romans 11:33-36</u>

33Oh, the depth of the riches both of the wisdom and knowledge of God!
How unsearchable are His judgments and unfathomable His ways! 34For
WHO HAS KNOWN THE MIND OF THE LORD, OR WHO
BECAME HIS COUNSELOR? 35Or WHO HAS FIRST GIVEN TO
HIM THAT IT MIGHT BE PAID BACK TO HIM AGAIN? 36For from
Him and through Him and to Him are all things. To Him be the glory
forever. Amen.

The Nature and Character of God

The crux of the whole issue is perfectly distilled in this simple passage. The question remains: Who is God. If we don't believe what the Bible has to say about Who God is and His nature as being completely other than us, completely outside of nature then we are left with nothing worth believing. If God isn't who Scripture says that He is, then no other argument really matters. This is of the deepest importance in understanding reality. Whether we attempt to elevate ourselves to God's level or bring God down to our level we are left with the same ultimate result: a complete destruction of reason, and a skewed understanding of biblical truth.

Depth…unsearchable…unfathomable

When speaking of God's attributes the most extreme words must be employed. There is a reason for this. It is very easy for humans to fall into the trap of thinking that God is just like a really big human. This thinking works along the lines that God differs from man, but only in degree. If man is smart, God is a little bit smarter (or even just a lot smarter). This is the same error that Satan fell into when He began to think that HE could sit in the place of God, and in some way take over God's work and position. We must realize that God's knowledge is not like our knowledge "only more" it is a full and complete knowledge of such a character that we *could never* possess it. If a person could expand their mind to contain all of the facts in the universe he still would not *know* everything as God *knows.*

What is so deep?

These attributes that are described in terms of God's unlimited perfection are all important to this section of scripture. First we will look at them individually, then apply these characteristics of God to each situation.

> *Wisdom* – This is the attribute of knowing something and applying that knowledge well. The Lord is never waiting for "all of the facts" to come in, nor does He ever have to stop and see how He is going to work all of these different bits of information together. In every situation, and in every way we see that God is going to make the very best choice.
>
> *Knowledge* – The word for knowledge here focuses on an in depth working knowledge that is based upon experience. That is a great thing to realize. We very often are in the place of making a decision with limited information. We make our decision and find that we erred because we did not know some key or vital piece of information. This is never the case of God. Again, His knowledge differs in its very nature from our knowledge. He is the ONLY being that ever sees and knows all things as they actually are, not as a matter of perception, but as a matter of fact.
>
> *Judgments* – This has the idea of a decision arrived at, or a decree.

When God makes His decisions, or decrees, they are based on His infinite wisdom (ability to use knowledge correctly) and His complete knowledge. Thus, while His decisions may even seem baffling to us, they are exactly what is necessary in order to achieve His purposes for creation.

Ways – The word translated "ways" can mean "paths" or "patterns." Obviously, physical paths are not in view! However, this is easily understood in the analogy to humans. Each person has a way that they conduct themselves, or a way that they act in certain situations. Similarly, the Lord has ways that are always consistent with His perfect character. While we may grow familiar with a particular person's ways and be able to predict them, such is never the case with God. He regularly shocks and amazes us in His "ways" because He is totally different from us.

This is of vital importance as we consider the question, the issue of following the Lord. We may very often be tempted to question the judgments of the Lord. We often pray as if we were telling Him something that He may have been unaware of, and this misses the point of prayer altogether. God's plan for the ages may seem overly complex to us. It may seem to have too many loose ends, or not be getting there fast enough from our limited perspectives. However, it is never the case. Believers must approach every question and situation with a firm grasp on who God is. Without understanding the limits of our understanding we will surely fall into error and make mistakes of all size based on or lack of information, knowledge or faith in the One who, alone, is the source of those attributes.

Getting Quotes

Paul then quotes from the Old Testament (see Isaiah 40:13; Jeremiah 23:18; Job 36:22, 41:11) and shows that this was always the case. God never once showed himself to be comparable to man in terms of His knowledge, wisdom or power. He, furthermore, never once needed the advice of a human. Moving forward, we see that God has never been in debt to any human person ever. There is no one who could ever say, "God I did this, and now you owe me." God is the possessor of all of the resources, and even more importantly, because He is infinite and eternal He could destroy all of the resources in existence and remake them completely and not be any smallest measure lessened in His nature. As humans we need to maintain the full and believing humility that we do not have all of the information (but God does) and we do not have any resources but the ones that He has given us. We are entirely dependent upon Him for our existence and He is entirely independent of the world which He (in the perfect Trinity) has created. We need Him and He has no need of us (though, by His grace, He uses us!)

THE POINT

This is not just the point of the argument here, it is the point of EVERYTHING! Everything begins, exists and will ultimately be completed for His glory. That is why anything exists, including Satan. God could have snuffed out Satan's candle the minute He rebelled. However, God let him continue because God would be glorified even through Satan's free choice to rebel. The same can be said of every single action, motion, person, institution and being. Everything will ultimately (willingly or unwillingly) glorify God and show some aspect of His perfect, complete, amazing and unlimited character. Praise the Lord!

ROMANS 12

ROMANS 12:1-2

A New Section
Chapter 12 marks a change in section. Having finally and thoroughly dealt with the issue of how very important Israel is in the plan of God, and how the Church has not replaced Israel at all Paul is ready to get to the application section. Romans, like many of Paul's letters, uses the first major part of this letter to explain doctrinal truth. It was in these 11 chapters that Paul brought up the issue of sin, the extent of sin, the need for Justification, the reality that justification comes by Faith alone in Christ alone, the process of sanctification and our growth in Christ, and our assured future of being united with Jesus Christ in glory forever and ever. These however, are all somewhat abstract ideas. They are major fundamental changes in thinking. If we were to ask what the practical application of the fact that "all have sinned" the answer is more complicated. Paul does this for a very important reason:

WHAT WE BELIEVE DETERMINES HOW WE WILL LIVE.

Our faith is not a religion, it is a relationship. Sometimes when the word "practical" is used in connection with spiritual instruction it is related to some small minded command, habit or practice that is then to be adopted. This, however, does not usually amount to real change. What needs to change is our belief. Just changing behaviors doesn't get us even half of the way there. We need to change what we believe and then let our actions flow logically from what we believe. This is the way Paul's epistles work first. The Holy Spirit challenges us to think correctly, and then live consistently with what we believe. If we are not walking in our relationship with the Lord all of the practical applications in the latter section of the book can be made into a simple legalism. ("Don't do this! Do that!" Etc.) Whereas the sort of transformation that God intends to affect through His Son and His Spirit in our lives is a far deeper change than the behavior modification that the world offers.

Romans 12:1

Therefore I urge you, brethren, by the mercies of God, to present your bodies a living and holy sacrifice, acceptable to God, which is your spiritual service of worship.

Moving On

Remember: This book is a logical argument. No section is "out of left field" and the Holy Spirit did not have Paul heading down any rabbit trails here. The focus has been the focus. Paul has been explaining the faith. That is why he begins this new section with another "therefore". This "therefore" could rightly encapsulate every bit of information before it, and in a sense it likely does. However; it seems that the logical argument and flow from the previous verses makes the most sense. Romans 11 ended with the words:

Oh, the depth of the riches both of the wisdom and knowledge of God! How unsearchable are His judgments and unfathomable His ways! For WHO HAS KNOWN THE MIND OF THE LORD, OR WHO BECAME HIS COUNSELOR? Or WHO HAS FIRST GIVEN TO HIM THAT IT MIGHT BE PAID BACK TO HIM AGAIN? For from Him and through Him and to Him are all things. To Him be the glory forever. Amen. Romans 11:33-36

This statement of God's completeness and limitless perfection in everything brings the argument naturally to the question of how are we to correctly respond to this great and amazing, wholly powerful, entirely perfect God, who loved us and saved us? Obviously, we have nothing that He needs. There is nothing that we could give Him or do for Him without which He would be in any way impoverished. How do we respond to His wholeness, completeness and perfection?

URGING CARE!

Paul then urges them. This is a very special verb. Paul had the authority to command them to do something. He could use a simple imperative and say: "Do this!" However, this is not the verb that Paul uses. What Paul does here is to "urge" believers. This word, in the original language, is made up of the words for "alongside" and "to call". The image here is of a person calling another alongside them, or in certain cases a person coming alongside another to help or comfort. The point? Paul is not bossy, he is not asking believers to do anything that he himself is not already doing. There is a sense in this choice of words that Paul is saying "Based on what we believe (stated in chapters 1-8) it only makes sense for me to do this, and we should all respond in this way.

By the Mercies of God

There is a very important sense of reason here. Paul has already stated that he is calling them alongside himself. Then he gives them the motivation for this response. Mercy is sparing someone from their just deserts. As we have seen, man deserves nothing but death and Hell, yet God saved us through the person and work of Jesus Christ and gave us what we did not deserve (eternal life). Furthermore, He did not just save us from death (the penalty of our sin) He is saving us from the power of our sin (Romans 6-7) and it is by faith in Christ alone that we grow. Finally, He will also raise us up and glorify us with Jesus Christ, also by grace through faith. This is not just to be our salvation, it is also to be our motivator. This salvation cannot be earned, nor can it be paid back. We will never be in a place where we are independent of God, we will be reliant upon Him, His grace, His mercy for all of eternity. This should motivate us, not by fear or guilt, but by love and gratitude, which is the only just motivation to live the Christian life.

LOVE AND GRATITUDE FOR WHAT GOD HAS DONE ON OUR BEHALF IS THE ONLY PROPER MOTIVATION FOR THE BELIEVER.

The Command

Finally, the command comes. The tense of this command is controlled by the previous verb, "urge", which is in the present tense. So this is something that is to be an everyday, moment by moment response of the believer to grace. The only logical way for a believer to respond to God's amazing love and grace is to present his body a living sacrifice. Before looking at the idea of a living sacrifice the presentation is important. This is the same word found in Romans 6:19:

I am speaking in human terms because of the weakness of your flesh. For just as you presented your members as slaves to impurity and to lawlessness, resulting in further lawlessness, so now present your members as slaves to righteousness, resulting in sanctification

The idea of "yield" is found in this verb, as well as the idea of presenting one's self for military service. The idea is to make one's self wholly available and at the behest of the one who is in charge. There is a full exchange going on here. While we have been raised up to live our life with Christ in the Heavenly places He is going to live our life down here. Us in Christ, and Christ in us. This is a daily, moment by moment choice.

Living Sacrifice

Someone once said, "The problem with a living sacrifice is that it keeps crawling off the altar." We may ask why it is our body that is to be presented rather than the soul or the spirit of the believer. A person's body is the way that he interacts with the world around him, and it may be presented either to the Lord or to the Sin Nature. It is our choice whether we will make our body available to our sin nature to control, or whether we yield ourselves to the Lord. If we live in an active and vital relationship with Christ, the Lord sees this as a sacrifice. Sacrifice in the Old Testament consisted of something dying, either to thank God for His provision, worship God, or to pay for sin. Yet the sacrifice that took away Sin was Christ. This sacrifice of our self-will, and submitting to God's will is a thank offering. This living sacrifice is also said to be "holy". The word "holy" has gotten the idea of something being sinless. However, that is not the full definition. The real sense behind the word "holy" is that something is set apart. God is "holy, holy, holy" and completely set apart from and independent of His creation and His creatures. We are, by the work of

Christ also set apart for His purpose. Yielding our bodies to Him by believing what He has done for us is the process by which our daily condition is conformed to our eternal position in Christ.

Acceptable to God

This sacrifice of presenting ourselves to Him in a day by day, moment by moment relationship, is the acceptable response. This also makes sense. God saved us, not because He needed us, but because He loves us. It is well pleasing to Him when His children trust Him and seek His face.

Spiritual Service of Worship

"Serving God" or giving one's life to "serve the Lord" is often used as a figure of speech for entering vocational ministry. Or whatever ministry activity of which a person may give some of their time, energy and effort. This however, is not truly what it means to serve the Lord. Every believer is to have this act of service to the Lord as a moment by moment definition of his or her reality. This is important to many of our definitions. We often think of service and worship as being that we go. Worst of all we say things like "I am going to the main service, to worship." These secondary uses of terms are not necessarily bad, they must simply be recognized for what they are. We serve God and Worship God by first and foremost remaining in moment by moment communion and fellowship with Him. This is the primary directive, everything else is derivative of this great reality!

A Word on Worship

We may think that we worship when we sing in a group with other believers. We may be worshipping, but much church singing is just singing with a group, and has nothing to do with biblical worship whatsoever. Corporate worship is important, but if a person is not in daily fellowship and communion with the Lord, then those words in a Sunday morning service mean very little if anything at all. Worshipping God is something the believer does every moment of every day as he rests in the provision of Jesus Christ.

Romans 12:2

And do not be conformed to this world, but be transformed by the renewing of your mind, so that you may prove what the will of God is, that which is good and acceptable and perfect.

More commands:
These logical imperatives continue. It is amazing how many of these logical imperatives exist in Scripture. The imperatives under law differ wildly from the imperatives under grace. Under law the imperative is: "Do (or don't do) this or else you will be punished." Under Grace our imperatives say, "God has already done this, and this is the only rational way to respond!" The imperatives under grace don't come with sticks and carrots. Believers are already blessed with every spiritual blessing in heavenly places. All that is left is for the believer to act like the person he has already been made in Christ.

Non-conformists
The natural thing for the believer to avoid is being conformed to things that differ from Christ. This is a graphic word that has the idea of being formed, or shaped from outside pressures into the form of something else. What we see is that the believer is not to be conformed by the pressures and influences of the world. But this also gives us some key insight: the World system IS going to be trying to conform us to what it desires us to be, yet we are not to allow it to do so. The very fact that this imperative is there suggests that we are not ever to think of ourselves as victims of these outside pressures. Far from it! This passive "do not" is matched by a passive "do" in the following verse.

Transformist!
So the believer is not to be passively conformed to the world, however, the answer to that is not to try to actively conform oneself to another image. The positive command is given in stark contrast to the negative command: transformation! Note that Paul does not say "transform yourself" he says, "be transformed." This is an outside force operating on the believer who is passive in the process. This is an interesting point. We are left with only two options and both are passive options. Either the believer will be conformed to the model of the world, or the believer will be transformed by the power of the Lord and His word. Man is not able to shape himself, only chose whom he will be shaped by. While the world wants to mash everybody into the same mold, the same shape, the same few acceptable forms. The Lord longs to transform a person into a wholly new, entirely

original creation of His love.

This transformation is to occur by some very important processes. The believer will be transformed by "the renewing of the mind."

Renewing you Mind

The word translated "renew" here means to "renovate completely" or to "completely change for the better." One commentator likened it to completely reformatting a disc on the computer. It is a complete removal of all worldly information (the original messed up formatting) and replace it with the proper operating system. The question is: How is the mind to be renewed? Is that something that is just requested? Can we get a mind make over? This renewal of mind comes from regular time in the Bible and fellowship with the Spirit. The Bible gives us the new operating information that we need. While the world will continue to try to conform us, we are to be changed into a different form altogether by constantly beholding the Lord Jesus Christ through His word.

Good Results

There are good results to this. Complete, repeated exposure to the word of God with the illumination of the Holy Spirit enables a person to test and approve the will of God. The word "prove" here is a word used for testing the qualities of metal. It has the sense of examining everything and finding out exactly what the character of it is. The only way that the believer is going to be capable of spotting worldly thinking or the deceptions of the enemy is by testing them against the standard and measure of the word. This is what every believer needs, this is how the will of God is discovered in the life of the believer: in light of the character of God. The chart on the next page may be helpful in understanding what this means to the believer:

Briefly, however, we see that a person's position in Christ is a part of God's sovereign will which is why our salvation can never fail. God's moral will is the same for every person and involves us walking by means of the Spirit (Galatians 5:16), abiding in Christ (John 15:1-5), and remaining in fellowship with Him and with one another (1 John 1). This is what God is primarily concerned about in the life of the believer. A believer's choice of spouse, job, car, clothing, education and the like are all secondary to the central question, "Will this draw me closer to my Lord." If a person is presented with an opportunity to take a job where they will regularly be expected to lie, cheat or steal then it would be foolish to take that job (no matter how well it pays) rather than disrupt their fellowship with God. If a person has "fallen in love" with a non-believer it would be foolishness to marry that unbeliever because that person will not help them grow towards Jesus Christ. These daily choices are made based on our beliefs and understanding of the centrality of Jesus Christ to our lives.

Brief Recap

Present yourself to Him -> Resist conformity to the world -> be transformed by exposure to the Bible and the Holy Spirit - > examine EVERYTHING by the standard of His life and word.

ROMANS 12:3-13

Be yourself, as you are in Christ

In any part or portion in life there is always the temptation to look over your shoulder and see what someone else is doing. Sometimes this is called "Keeping up with the Jones"". The idea is that we very frequently want to look to others and believe that we are somehow better than them, by comparison. This same sickness can go the other way and lead to hero worship, wherein we assign the real work of following Christ to some individual (or set) "super-Christian". Either disease gets us thoroughly off track. This strange habit of humans should be completely foreign to us in our walk with Christ. There should be no looking over at the other believers to compare what the Lord is doing through us with what the Lord is doing through them. Interestingly, entire churches are founded on this attitude of "spiritual one-upmanship". This usually looks like "us" being the best Christians while all of the other churches are the worst. In extreme cases this view can turn into the cultic view that "we" are the only true believers. This must be resisted at every turn. It must be resisted because it is a great temptation for man to want to feel special for all of the wrong reasons.

Romans 12:3-5

3For through the grace given to me I say to everyone among you not to
think more highly of himself than he ought to think; but to think so as to
have sound judgment, as God has allotted to each a measure of faith. 4For
just as we have many members in one body and all the members do not
have the same function, 5so we, who are many, are one body in Christ, and
individually members one of another.

The Body

Verses 3-5 concern the nature of the Body of Christ. This is an incredibly important metaphor in understanding what we are to be doing and how we are to interact with other believers. This picture of a body is a fantastic organic image of what the universal church (everyone who has placed faith in Christ for salvation) is like. Our human bodies have an amazing number of processes and parts that all work together to keep us alive. Medical Science finds more and more each year how much the body depends upon itself, and one small dysfunction in the smallest body part can cause massive destruction and even death within the entire body.

Speaking though Grace

Grace is a no strings attached gift. Here Paul mentions a special grace, a gift that was given to him and not to every believer in general. Paul's specific gift, by which he is enabled to write scripture, is the gift of Apostleship. An apostle was distinct from a messenger in that an apostle was given a message and the authority to see the message through to its completion. Thus the Apostles were a limited group of believers in the first century to establish the Church and give revelation. As Ephesians 2:20 states, once the scripture was given and the early church established this gift ceased to be given along with the other sign gifts. The point here, however, is plain: Paul is speaking on the basis and authority of his divine appointment as an apostle.

Arrogance, Self-Esteem, and other BIG problems

The Holy Spirit then brings a simple logical encouragement that applies to every believer, all of the time. It is so easy for humans to start to think that we are indispensable. That God somehow NEEDS us individually. Nothing could be further from the truth. God has no need of any of His creatures. It is by His grace and His love that He has redeemed us, saved us and uses us for His glory. However, believers who are especially gifted or capable (either spiritually gifted or naturally gifted) may easily fall into the trap of thinking that they are in some way above or beyond other believers in some capacity. This is sternly warned against. We must not ever come to an inflated sense of self-importance for a very serious reason: to do so would be silly, stupid and insane.

A Sane View of Self

What has the Holy Spirit revealed about who we are in the book of Romans? We are creatures of God. We were hopelessly stuck in Sin with no chance of working our way out. We are rebels, hateful, and enemies of God. Yet God by His amazing grace and mercy saved us through the life and work of His Son, Jesus Christ. This is the only sane starting point: "I am nothing, Christ is everything." Moving forward we see that our natural talents, gifts, and abilities are all, also given only by the grace of God. Being proud of our intelligence, physical strength or special abilities makes no more sense than being proud of our eye or hair color. They came to us only by the grace of God. This is even more the case for Spiritual gifts, as we are going to see. But the point is plain: God and His glory are the important factor here. This is the view of ourselves that gives us sound judgment (lit. "wise-mindedness") and it is in stark contrast with the world's view of what makes a person valuable, important or worthwhile.

Body Life

How often do you look around in a church service and make the firm realization that these people are a part of you? That you rely upon them on a deeper level than you are likely to understand during your life on this planet? Most believers, particularly in the individualistic west, have a tendency to downplay the incredible importance of being connected to the body of Christ. Yet, this is the illustration that the Lord gives here through Paul. Just as your whole body reacts to being cut with a knife or a saw blade, so we react when our brothers and sisters in Christ are hurting. When we see a fellow believer walking in sin, or struggling with some situation we should react in the same way that we would react if we were simply caring for ourselves.

Most important

Getting a little deeper into this picture that the Lord has given here, it is clear to see that many believers will have a tendency to have some sort of prejudice or bias in favor of whatever gift they have. A gifted evangelist may say, "Without my gift, nobody would be here." A gifted teacher may say, "Without my gift there would be no reason for them to be here." And someone with the gift of mercy may say, "Without my gift no one could stand to be around either of you two!" As believers we are to have a high view of one another, and each one's contribution to the body of Christ. While this theme will be made more obvious in the coming verses it is beneficial to think of the ministries, or people, in our local church body that we have henceforth written off as "extra" or "less important" or even "secondary" and adjust our attitude regarding what the Lord is doing in the body of Christ.

Romans 12:6-8

[6]Since we have gifts that differ according to the grace given to us, each of us is to exercise them accordingly: if prophecy, according to the proportion of his faith; [7]if service, in his serving; or he who teaches, in his teaching; [8]or he who exhorts, in his exhortation; he who gives, with liberality; he who leads, with diligence; he who shows mercy, with cheerfulness.

Spiritual Gifts

Romans 12 is one of the three major passages on Spiritual Gifts (the others being Ephesians 4 and 1 Corinthians 12-14). There are some very important notations to make regarding the Spiritual Gifts:

1) They are Spiritual – They are only had by believers and they are only functional when a believer is walking in fellowship with the Spirit.

2) They are Gifts – They are no strings attached gifts to the body of Christ based upon His grace and work in our lives.

3) Every believer has at least one – And to the believer who only has one gift it is exactly the gift that is needed in the local body of which he or she is a part.

4) They are for the edification of the body – The spiritual gifts are not to make the one who has the gift feel good about himself. They are for the purpose of building up the body of Christ in love (Ephesians 4:12).

5) They are all necessary.

6) Exercising our spiritual gift (or gifts) is one of the ways that we are going to grow in the grace and the knowledge of the Lord Jesus Christ.

Prophecy – These were those in the first century who received direct revelation from God. As the Apostles were not yet done writing Scripture the early church needed revelation whereby they would grow. Upon the completion of the New Testament this gift (along with Apostleship) ceased to function (1 Corinthians 13:8; Ephesians 2:20), having been replaced with the full council of God.

Service – This is the spiritual gift of caring for and waiting upon others. Service, when not done by reliance on the Lord, can bring great bitterness. "No one ever thanks me!" and other attitudes can overtake the servant. This is why it is so important that the gifted servant rely upon the Lord for His strength and direction.

Teaching – This gift is the gift of explaining and helping other believers understand and apply the Message of God's word. This (like many of the others) is a gift that needs to be developed. A teacher must first be taught, which brings to light the importance of discipleship in the Church.

Exhortation – This is the word that Paul used in Romans 12:1 that was translated "urge". It has the idea of one who comes alongside another and says: "Let's do this together." It has a sense of counseling, caring, and drawing believers into keeping with the revealed word.

Giving – There is a tendency to err on either side with this gift. First of all, it is important to realize that giving is first of a person's self and then of financial resources. Yet it is also of financial resources. There are those in the body who are blessed with an ability to give far beyond the normal human capacity. Of their time, of their resources and of their wisdom. This gift can be over-estimated and those who give financially may be doted upon unnecessarily, or under-estimated when people are told not to give for one reason or another. 2 Corinthians 9 and Philippians 1 & 4 give a good picture of what grace giving is all about.

Leads – These are those people who are gifted in the body who humbly know where the local body needs to be going and what the local body needs to be spending their time and resources on. This is an important gift for an Elder to have in some measure.

Mercy – These people are of the utmost importance in the body. Mercy longs to protect people from what they have "earned for themselves." This is a vital gift for the body to have because it protects us from factious personalities and any form of legalism. This mercy is to be given cheerfully!

It is easy to look at how the Lord is using someone else and either deride it or worship it. Neither of these, however, is appropriate for the believer. We must strive to be content with how the Lord is using us right now, in

His infinite wisdom. We can name all of our problems or trust in what the Lord is doing in us. Both individually and as a local church body, there is a constant need for us to trust in the Lord and in what He has provided.

Romans 12:9-13
9Let love be without hypocrisy. Abhor what is evil; cling to what is good.
10Be devoted to one another in brotherly love; give preference to one
another in honor; 11not lagging behind in diligence, fervent in spirit, serving
the Lord; 12rejoicing in hope, persevering in tribulation, devoted to prayer,
13contributing to the needs of the saints, practicing hospitality.

Participle Party!
Verses 9-13 (and continuing on) all sound like orders (or commands). Paul is not, however, using imperatives, but rather participles. In English this means using the "-ing" ending after a word. So each of these statements could be brought across as such: "Abhorring what is evil, Clinging to what is good." In other words, Paul is describing what the life of Christ within us is going to look like. He could have used commands, but rather than do that he chose to soften this sense and write, "doing this, and not doing that".

Abhorring Evil - As we grow in Christ we will grow in our abhorrence of evil. The word "abhor" here literally means "to shudder". Most people have experienced what it like to dislike a person or thing so much that it brings about a physical reaction. We will know that we are growing in Christ because we will be increasingly sensitive to those things that conflict with His character and not want to be near them.

Clinging to Good - The word "clinging" has the sense of something that is glued to something else. We may even say, "Being cemented to good." This is a preoccupation with things that are good, right or holy. There is an increased attachment to anything that is reminiscent of God.

Being Devoted - The mature believer will have an increasing natural affection for other believers and a desire to care for them. The idea behind this word is the type of love that parents naturally feel for their children. This is a love that wants to care, protect and help in all things. This is enhanced by the "brotherly love" that is the focus of the verb. Our love for one another should be as our love for our family. Any time my brother is blessed, I have been blessed. Any time my brother struggles, I struggle. There can be no competition, nor envy. It makes no sense for believers in Christ.

Giving Preference to one another in honor - The ESV translates this verse very well: "Outdo one another in showing honor." We are to be honoring and lifting one another up as much as we can. This is an important mark of a mature believer. Immature believers look for praise and laud, the mature believer is free to honor others and put the needs of others before himself.

Diligence - A mature believer is diligent, caring, and trustworthy. There is a sense of earnestness and zeal to be who we are in Christ and have the opportunity to let Christ's life shine through us.

Fervent in spirit - The word fervent means boiling over. The idea is that the mature believer is excited for the Lord. He is bubbling over with excitement and the wonderful good news of all that the Lord has done for us.

Serving the Lord - While there is a gift of service that focuses on helping and serving the body, this is the reality that every believer is to be living their life in the service of the Lord. There is not one class of believers that is to be serving the Lord and another class of believer who is to be sitting back and watching. Every believer is useful to the Lord because it is all about His using us and His glory!

Rejoicing in Hope - The mature believer is always rejoicing in the Lord. Completely independent of earthly circumstances. We can do this because our hope is not tied into the affairs of this world. And nothing can touch the complete and full hope that is ours in Christ Jesus our Lord.

Persevering in Tribulation – The mature believer is courageous in dealing with dangerous, difficult and even life threatening times.

Devoted to Prayer – The mature believer is in constant and ready communication with the Lord.

Contributing – The mature believer is connected to the body so as to know what is needed and ready to fill that need.

Hospitable – The mature believer is ready to entertain other believers. Having them into his home and his life.

THIS is the character of Christ in the believer. He is the only source of this life, and it is never the believer's hard work that brings it about. It is always what flows naturally from the life of Christ in the believer.

ROMANS 12:14-21

One more time
Here again we must fix our eyes on what Paul has written before. This is all based upon the changes affected in the believer by God in Romans 1-8. Paul is now describing exactly what maturity in Christ will look like as it is lived out in the life of the believer. This understanding is clearer in the Greek where we see that Paul is not using commands here, they would all be translated in this present tense descriptive "Blessing those who persecute…" and "Rejoicing with those…" This is a powerful and important section of scripture because it can help us identify very quickly, and in no uncertain terms, whether or not we are in fellowship with the Lord. Not every behavior or question is addressed, however there are some big principles here that will help to point us towards Christ. It should also point us to our need for Jesus Christ. Perhaps as much or more than anything else the honest believer will look at these commands and say, "That's not me!" This character is found nowhere in our flesh, that is the character of Christ.

Romans 12:14-16
14Bless those who persecute you; bless and do not curse. 15Rejoice with
those who rejoice, and weep with those who weep. 16Be of the same mind
toward one another; do not be haughty in mind, but associate with the
lowly. Do not be wise in your own estimation.

Bless those who persecute you
This one is easy, right? Persecute means to put to flight, to abuse, or to molest. This is interesting because the Christian pop culture today has a tendency to reject this advice plainly. Yet Paul did not say "Make fun of those who persecute you." Nor did he say "Take legal action against those who persecute you. " No, the word of God says very plainly that the life of Christ within us will bless those who persecute. Paul must have known how difficult this would be and with a Hebrew poetry pattern he clarifies, that we ought not to be cursing our persecutors, which would be the natural reaction. Christ Himself laid this principle down as one for all ages:

> "Blessed are you when people insult you and persecute you, and falsely say all kinds of evil against you because of Me. Rejoice and be glad, for your reward in heaven is great; for in the same way they persecuted the prophets who were before you."
> Matthew 5:11-12

God always regards the persecution and tribulation of His saints as valuable. Thus, we can bless others as they persecute us as they are providing us with an opportunity for blessing!

Rejoicing and Weeping

It is interesting that at any given time either side of this command may be unnatural to our flesh. Sometimes it seems easy to rejoice with those who rejoice. However, we cannot if we are trapped in our fleshly jealousy. If we are walking in our sin nature we will find it impossible to do either of these things. We will begrudge those who rejoice and wonder, "Why didn't I get that, don't I deserve that more?" and with those who weep we will say, "Ha! I see he finally got his! He was blind if he didn't see this one coming!" Notice that the exhortation is not to judge, not to fix, just to rejoice and weep with those who do so. There is empathy, feeling that comes with a love and a knowledge that can only be found in the character of Christ Jesus.

Having the Same Mind

Like-mindedness is an important theme in Scripture. Interestingly, when we walk after the flesh we find that we want to disagree with everything, We want to flaunt how much smarter or more esoteric our faith is than the masses of superficial Christians or the like. In Romans 8 we found that God is for us. That every believer is indwelt with the Holy Spirit and the Lord is working upon each and every believer and will ultimately complete His stated goal of conforming every believer to the image of Christ. Thus we can strive to find unity with everyone who has placed their faith in Jesus Christ. We do not need to think of ourselves as the better Christians, or the smarter Christians, the most active Christians, or the most devout Christians. Far from it, the life in Christ in us will cause us to have a realistic understanding of our own limitations as well as a realistic understanding of His limitless power and grace, and that is a very good thing.

Romans 12:17-19

[17]Never pay back evil for evil to anyone. Respect what is right in the sight of all men. [18]If possible, so far as it depends on you, be at peace with all men. [19]Never take your own revenge, beloved, but leave room for the wrath of God, for it is written, "VENGEANCE IS MINE, I WILL REPAY," says the Lord. [20]"BUT IF YOUR ENEMY IS HUNGRY, FEED HIM, AND IF HE IS THIRSTY, GIVE HIM A DRINK; FOR IN SO DOING YOU WILL HEAP BURNING COALS ON HIS HEAD." [21]Do not be overcome by evil, but overcome evil with good.

Don't get mad…get forgiving!

Perhaps the above is a bit over the top, but the sentiment isn't far from the truth. The world has a steady belief in revenge, in paying someone back for their actions, or even their mistakes. The believer, as he is in Christ, never needs to do this. Amazingly, just as Christ cried out on the Cross "Forgive them Father for they do not know what they are doing." And Stephen, the first martyr died with a similar cry upon his lips. We find that this response is completely unavailable to the flesh, and incomprehensible from the worlds standards. Times wherein believers are experiencing evil, difficulty and persecution are some of the most powerful and poignant times for us to display the life of Christ to the world.

So far as it depends on you

Paul qualifies this statement very strongly because it will not always depend on believers. This is clearly not peace at any cost. The world will hate and revile all that we are in Christ. This is a promise and an assured fact. We are not to surrender to the world when it demands that we betray or refuse to proclaim the Truth of Jesus Christ. However, our attitude is to be one of peace, and the desire to live at peace with all those who do not accept the truth. Christians are not supposed to be taking over the world system, nor are we ever to be using violence to accomplish the goals of our faith. We believe that Christ will see His will done upon this earth. The commands given to us are to rest in Him, and focus on offering His love and grace to the sin-darkened world.

How can you do that?

While it is fully clear that only the life of Christ can manifest these qualities, characteristics and reactions in our lives, God has also given us some of the reasoning why this is an appropriate reaction. It is the Lord's job to balance out the accounts, and He will do so. God, in His justice and righteousness, cannot see a sin unpunished. And all sin will be paid for in one of three places. On earth, on the Cross or in the Lake of Fire for all of eternity. There is not one sin, or act of unrighteousness that will not be dealt with. This is why it is so important that we not try to avenge ourselves. God is the only righteous judge. He alone can settle the accounts properly. But there is more to our situation than this. Our debt was paid for, eternally at the cross. We must realize that for everyone whose sins are not covered by the righteous blood of Jesus Christ they will spend eternity apart from God in Hell. This is not something that we could wish on anyone. As we grow in the grace and knowledge of the Lord Jesus Christ we will manifest His attitude towards sin (reviling, recoiling, hating it) and His attitude towards those who are enslaved to it (He is not willing that any should perish but that all should come to salvation through Jesus Christ. (See 2 Peter 3:9)

Overcoming Evil with Good

We have an image of the hero as the one who takes up his weapon and goes to war, destroying his enemies with force (and possibly the fact that "right is on his side"). However, in the Church our prototype of a hero is Jesus Christ. He who suffered and died at the hands of sinful men that He may save them at His own expense.

ROMANS 13

ROMANS 13:1-7

God's Word and Government
Human government is God's invention. This is something important to keep in mind when we think about government because it can be quite easy

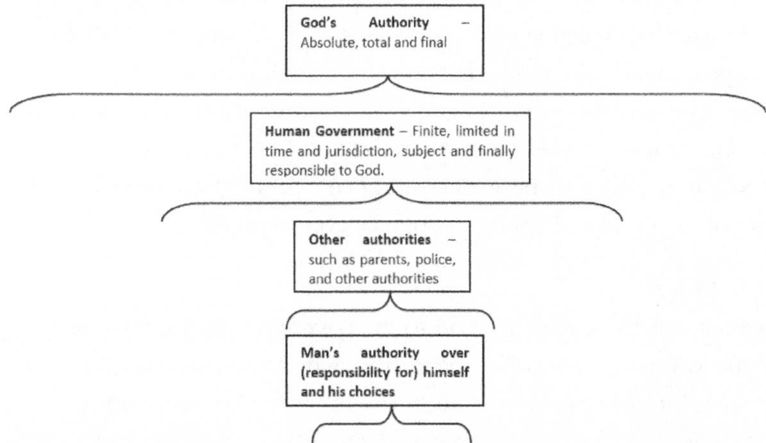

to say, "It's all just a mess and a waste of time!" However, we find that human government is a tool in the hand of God through which He will ultimately see His will done. The first issue that we want to look at in understanding government is authority. We could view authority like this:

God's authority is the top and unquestionable final authority. However, rather than micromanage everything He delegates tasks and responsibilities to different creatures in order to see His will finally played out. Each of these delegates has authority over their own domain, but each one is ultimately responsible to God, and will be held accountable.

Government Begins

Obviously in the Garden of Eden the Lord was the only authority source. As families developed fathers and mothers became temporary authority sources but each person made their own decisions and there was no force or standard by which one person would/could govern another. This finally climaxed in the earth being "filled with violence" which brought about the flood recorded in Genesis 6-9. Once the flood is over God makes a covenant (unconditional agreement) with Noah:

"Surely I will require your lifeblood; from every beast I will require it. And from every man, from every man's brother I will require the life of man. Whoever sheds man's blood, By man his blood shall be shed, For in the image of God He made man."
Genesis 9:5-6 NASB

This passage records the institution of human government, and its central purpose. The original intent and creation of human government was to punish murderers by taking their lives. This, of necessity, means that there must be people who judge whether a person is innocent or guilty. The purpose? To maintain order. This is not a promise that government will always behave as it should; it is a statement that God created government to keep order in society lest the society simply be run by those who have the most physical power and ability to oppress everyone else.

Romans 13:1-2

1Every person is to be in subjection to the governing authorities. For there
is no authority except from God, and those which exist are established by
God. 2Therefore whoever resists authority has opposed the ordinance of
God; and they who have opposed will receive condemnation upon
themselves.

Every Person

Every person means every person. There is not one single person who is in a nation that is not to be subject to the governing authorities of that nation. This is interesting because we often times are amazed that God would have us be subject to so much ungodliness. Remember, however, that Paul wrote this passage, by the power of the Holy Spirit, when the Roman emperors actually believed themselves to be gods and insisted that everyone else do the same! Our subjection to human government is not based on how "good" the government is by our mark. Our subjection to government is based on the next statement:

There is No Authority

This is what the chart above is meant to display. As long as a government holds authority it is because God is still allowing them to hold authority. God is not limited by anything in His ability to draw to an end the most horrifying regime or the most brutal tyrant. If He allows them we must trust in His purpose and remain subject to those authorities because He has either decreed or allowed them to have authority for that time. Every believer would do well to remember that the same God who saved us completely and fully by His perfect and complete work of Jesus Christ on the cross will also consummate this earthly existence, and is now arranging all things for the seven year tribulation followed by the glorious millennial reign of Christ on Earth.

"I have a problem with authority"

Our culture worships this statement. We have heroes in television and movie that repeat this like their anthem, as if having a problem with authority was something to be proud of. It is a sort of American ideal. The idea of moving to the American west was, for many, rooted in the desire to "Do what I want to do and not let anyone say anything about it!" Why is this such a popular attitude? Because it appeals to our flesh. It is a sinful and carnal attitude and it is not in keeping with spiritual maturity at all. The spiritually mature person submits to the authorities that God has allowed or dictated to rule over him (or her).

Civil Disobedience

Are there times to disobey government? Yes. Those times are when (and only when) the government takes steps to hinder the practice of the Biblical faith. If the government outlaws Bible reading, believers are forced to disobey and read their Bibles anyway. If the government demands that a Christian woman have an abortion it is her responsibility (if possible) to flee and save the life of that child. If the government were to make it illegal to share our faith (in contrast with the Great Commission) then Christians would be forced to disregard those laws. This is what we see in the life of Shadrach, Meshach, Abednego and Daniel in the Book of Daniel.

NOT Times for Civil Disobedience

Our Sin nature provides more reasons for us to disobey governing authorities BUT THEY ARE SINFUL (wrong). Here are some incorrect reasons to disobey governments:

- "Because I don't like that rule."
- "Because I don't agree with what they are doing."
- "Because I don't support this leader or that leader."
- "Because I didn't get a say in this."
- "Because I don't agree with what they are saying."
- "Because I hate it when people tell me what to do or what not to do."
- "Because it just isn't fair."

This list is a very small sampling of the many ways that we justify breaking speed limits, or violating different laws or mandates of our government. They are sin. They come from our flesh and our flesh alone.

Romans 13:3-5

3For rulers are not a cause of fear for good behavior, but for evil. Do you
want to have no fear of authority? Do what is good and you will have praise
from the same; 4for it is a minister of God to you for good. But if you do
what is evil, be afraid; for it does not bear the sword for nothing; for it is a
minister of God, an avenger who brings wrath on the one who practices
evil. 5Therefore it is necessary to be in subjection, not only because of
wrath, but also for conscience' sake.

Are you afraid?

A wise woman once told me the secret of not ever getting a speeding ticket. My mind raced quickly to the possibilities of radar detectors, or even ways to know if police were around the corner. While my mind was spinning about all the ways I could get away with speeding she cut right to the heart of the issue: "Just don't ever drive faster than the speed limit." That is brilliant! If we don't break the law we have very little to fear from those who are appointed to minister to us by enforcing the law. Often times we harbor feelings of malcontent and frustration with law enforcement officers, and no police force is perfect. Yet these feelings of resentment are often rooted in our feelings of guiltiness or our desire not to be subjected to God's appointed authorities. When we see police officers we should be happy to wave at them and thank them, if we don't we can ask ourselves very seriously what is keeping us from doing so!

Condemnation or Commendation?

Think about most of the regular, ordinary, day-to-day laws that ordinary governments put in place. Most of them have to do with maintaining safety and health for the nation. Laws against theft, laws protecting people from dishonest business practices, laws preventing people from driving dangerously and hurting themselves or others. There are also laws that restrict or control violence to the appropriate places (like a boxing ring, or a football field). Most of the basic laws that make up a society are there for our help and our protection. Just as we saw, from the very beginning of government it was given by God as a servant to the people.

Be afraid…be very afraid

Paul tells us that if we are not keeping the law then we can rightly be afraid. The phrase that the government "bears the sword" is talking about the governments' God-given right to punish with the death penalty. Under the Law of Moses (which believers today are NOT under) God gave the guidelines for the role and standards of the government of the nation of Israel. In these guidelines there were many offenses that were to be punished with death penalty. That is a part of the authority that human government has been given.

Romans 13:6-7

6For because of this you also pay taxes, for rulers are servants of God, devoting themselves to this very thing. [7]Render to all what is due them: tax to whom tax is due; custom to whom custom; fear to whom fear; honor to whom honor.

Death and Taxes

Since Paul just talked about death it seems natural that he would move on to taxes! The government is meant to be paid for by the people. There has, of course, been much corruption regarding money in government however, that doesn't change the reality: it is right that everyone pay taxes to support the government. It is important to realize that the government is not meant, biblically, to fix our problems, but simply to maintain order and defend the nation. We do well in our thinking about government to realize this reality. Government is not a replacement for God, as many want it to be. In this sense government has become another Tower of Babel by which man seeks to replace the need to trust in the Lord and work.

Render to all

The simple reality is that we are to give to each one exactly what is due them. Pay our taxes, respect our leaders and pray for all of them. Because when the government fails at its role it interferes with the movement and work of the church on earth.

ROMANS 13:8-14

Picking up where we left off...
Remember the most important rule in understanding your Bible is context. This section is preceded by a picture of the spiritually mature attitude towards government and ruling authority. The attitude that Paul demands of the believer is quite shocking to our western, individualistic culture, yet it places for us a great opportunity to submit to what the Bible has to say, even when it is not comfortable. It must be remembered that at the time the Bible was written the government was fully amoral and mostly (and at times completely) antagonistic towards the faith. Yet this submission is exactly what is demanded of the believer who focuses upon Jesus Christ.

<u>Romans 13:8-10</u>
8Owe no one anything except to love one another, for he who loves
another has fulfilled the law. 9For the commandments, "You shall not
commit adultery," "You shall not murder," "You shall not steal," "You shall
not bear false witness," "You shall not covet," and if there is any other
commandment, are all summed up in this saying, namely, "You shall love
your neighbor as yourself." 10Love does no harm to a neighbor; therefore
love is the fulfillment of the law.

Owe no one anything...
This verse has often been interpreted to mean that a Christian should never take on debt. While the uniform warning of Scripture is that debt can be a very dangerous thing, however, it is nowhere specifically forbidden. There can be situations where taking on some debt is the only, or even the best investment. For instance when a person takes on a reasonable level of student debt in order to increase their earning potential (presuming that the cost benefit analysis shows that to be a good investment).

If this verse is not forbidding the borrowing of money, what is it about? Given the context that preceded the most reasonable interpretation is that Paul is talking specifically about giving to the government what it asks (so long as what it asks does not insist that we violate the Word of the Lord) Paul then moves towards the relationships between believers. When we come to the idea of "owing" someone something we get the idea of a legal situation in which a person can say to the other: "You owe me this kind of treatment." or "You owe me your respect." However, what Paul describes when he talks about life in Christ he gives an entirely different view of what our relationships ought to look like.

Grace based relationships

Under the Law of Moses most interactions would be well defined. People knew who was legally due their honor and respect, they knew also who they could shun or treat as outcasts. However, there is a better way offered in Christ: Love. This type of love can be defined as "always desiring what is best for the beloved, regardless of the cost."

Were everyone on the planet to love one another with this manner of love (this is also the word used for God's love - agape) there would never again be a need for any kind of legal or governing system. However, this kind of love is well out of the grasp of fallen humanity. This quality of love is available to us in Christ and in Christ alone.

Better than the Law

In Romans 6-8 we saw how the Grace governed life is an immeasurably better motivator to a truly changed life, so this love based fellowship is immeasurably better than any legalistic view of relationships. If we love one another with the Love of Christ there will be no instance wherein we have to pull out the rule book. More of what this love looks like will be shown in greater depth throughout the coming verses and chapters, however, it is important that we take a good look at our relationships with other believers.

Taking a moment to apply

Think about your relationships with your church family. What characterizes your view of them. We often fall into old patterns of letting our sin nature run the show and what comes from that? Only carnal sinful attitudes and behavior. As we rest in Christ we will love our fellow believers. As we walk in fellowship with Him we will truly want what is the very best for every fellow believer. Love does no harm to others. In this way we need not worry about any law system. If we are always looking out for the best for our brothers and sisters we won't have to ask "What should I do in this situation." In some cases this may look like adjusting our manner of communicating, in others it may look like refraining from certain activities. What does it mean in your situation to love the brethren? Are there places that you need to come before the Lord, admitting that you aren't loving them with His love and change your mind about the way you are thinking, feeling or acting? The answer, of course, is yes. For all of us. We must realize that we are still a work in progress, but our progress will be made by our continual reliance upon the Lord Jesus Christ and what He has done for us and not being entangled in sinful attitudes, thoughts, words or actions towards our brothers and sisters in the Lord.

Romans 13:11-14

11 And do this, knowing the time, that now it is high time to awake out of
sleep; for now our salvation is nearer than when we first believed. 12 the
night is far spent, the day is at hand. Therefore let us cast off the works of
darkness, and let us put on the armor of light. 13 Let us walk properly, as in
the day, not in revelry and drunkenness, not in lewdness and lust, not in
strife and envy. 14 But put on the Lord Jesus Christ, and make no provision
for the flesh, to fulfill its lusts.

When was that, again?

It is easy to get sucked into the world's view of time. The world offers a view that every day will follow yet another day. Yet this is simply untrue. Not one of us knows the hour of our death, nor the hour of anyone else's death. We may be tempted to say, "I will reconcile with that person next week." Or, "I have a long time to work this out, I will just avoid that person." However, the reality is that each day counts tremendously before the Lord for a number of reasons:

1) Each day is honored because it is another opportunity to trust in the Lord and grow in the grace and the knowledge of the Lord Jesus Christ

2) Each day is honored because it is one day closer to the day when we will behold Jesus Christ face to face, whether at death or at the time of the rapture

3) Each day is honored because it bears in it one more opportunity in which an unbeliever may hear the gospel, or see the love and the life of Christ in a believer's life before the Lord comes back for His Church.

There is a sense of urgency to the Christian life. Not in a guilt-ridden, fear-driven way.

But rather in a way that loves, glorifies and honors the Lord and is thankful for all that He has done for us in Christ Jesus. It is an honor to have been left here. Were we not useful to the Lord He could take us home. We have been left here with a very specific purpose of sharing His love and His life. Glorifying Him in the context of the Church and lifting His name before the world. Every believer has been made an emissary, an ambassador of Heaven. The Lord can do this through us.

Sleepers Wake!

The illusion of sleeping is a neat one. What do we tend to think of someone who sleeps when there is work to be done? In the ancient world this practice was even more abhorred because sleeping when the harvest needs to be brought in would mean a winter without food. Thus, this lazy person truly brings upon themselves their own destruction. While our culture still advocates and even idolizes laziness this is not who we are in Christ. Note: this is NOT works based salvation, this is simply a natural, logical response to the work of Jesus Christ. Spiritual laziness, however, can be more deceptive than physical laziness. The Spiritually Lazy person may be very industrious when it comes to his working life. Yet when it comes to spending time in the Bible and in prayer, he is too tired. The spiritually lazy person may choose not to be involved with a church body because they had a bad experience with other believers and they were too lazy (or too cowardly) to work out their differences in a biblical manner.

Closer than ever

Then Paul gives this striking phrase that our salvation is nearer than when we first believed. Wait a minute!? Weren't we saved when we placed our faith in Christ? Doesn't Ephesians 2:8-9 place our salvation as a permanent past tense completed action that nothing can undo or destroy? The Bible teaches very clearly that our Salvation in Christ is more than simply a one-time salvation from the penalty of sin...far from it! The salvation package that the Lord has given us as three distinct phases:

> **Phase 1** - Salvation from the Penalty of Sin - Justification - Past tense for the believer.
>
> **Phase 2** - Salvation from the Power of Sin - Sanctification - Present process in the life of the believer
>
> **Phase 3** - Salvation from the Presence of Sin - Glorification - The sin nature is removed, we are given new bodies and we are finally glorified with Jesus Christ.

This verse is talking about the third phase of our salvation, the wrapping up and completion of the full salvation package. And this day, indeed is closer and closer with each passing day. Either at the moment of our physical death or at the moment of the of the Lord's coming to take us away to be with Him forever we will inherit the full and final reality of our salvation, and that is great news, because either of those events are entirely imminent. There is nothing that must occur prophetically before the Lord returns for His saints, additionally a person may be called home at a moment's notice.

The impetus is upon us to make each moment count. How to make each moment count? By focusing upon Jesus Christ constantly. Believers are to rest in Christ and what He has done, fix our eyes upon Him through His word. Sometimes the Lord may use us for very active things, other times the Lord may have a season of rest in our lives where there is less visible service going on. In every situation our need to be in fellowship with the Lord is vital.

Casting Off, Putting On

It is in light of this fact that the believer is to conduct himself. First, the works of darkness are to be cast off. Unbelievers should not be surprised to find out that we are believers. The selfishness, hatred and pride that characterize life outside of Christ will not characterize the one who is walking in Christ. Let's look at the structure of this statement:

> A - Therefore let us cast off the works of darkness,

B - and let us put on the armor of light.

C - Let us walk properly, as in the day,

not in revelry and drunkenness,

not in lewdness and lust, not in strife and envy.

B' - But put on the Lord Jesus Christ,

A' - and make no provision for the flesh, to fulfill its lusts.

This structure highlights the logical result of what it means to walk in Christ. First of all it involves not being identified with darkness, however, the complementary statement to that is that we would put on the armor of light. When does a person put on armor?

When they are going to war. The reality is that we are in a spiritual war. There can be no doubt. Ephesians 6 gives the posture of the Christian. The Christians stands, by the power of Christ on the completed work of Christ. It is a defensive posture, and there will be attackers. This battle will be fought in the realm of our simple actions and words and attitudes. The Romans had a very labor intensive system for defending their land against invaders. They would stand in a line all across the border. Each soldier depended upon the other soldiers to "hold the line". This is much like our relationship with other believers. When I walk in faith and grow in Christ the believers who deal with me are benefitted. When I walk in sin my brothers and sisters in Christ are the poorer. We depend upon one another, in the spiritual battle, as we are inextricably connected and interdependent in Christ.

What does that armor look like?

We know how a soldier dresses now when he heads into battle. We know, also, how many other soldiers headed into battle throughout history. Good armor technology is based largely upon what sort of weapons are going to be used. A suit of full medieval armor was a very effective protective measure against the glancing blows of a sword, but would be terribly ineffective against a Patriot Missile. Fortunately, in the spiritual war that rages on around us the best defensive technology has already been discovered, and He has been given to us. This armor is the Christ. Jesus

Christ who is "the way, the truth and the life" is also our defense in the Spiritual war. Just as the believer is to rest in Him in order to grow, so the believer must trust in His sure defense throughout the spiritual battle.

Make no provision

When it comes to the nature of how we fall into Sin it draws us back to Romans 6.

There, the sin nature was viewed as a deposed monarch. When we choose to obey the Sin Nature we are just acting crazy. Paul's solution for this is simple: Don't even give your sin nature a chance. Making no provision for the flesh could mean a number of things. Sometimes it will be keeping ourselves out of situations that we know cause us to fall repeatedly. In other instances it will be evaluating an upcoming situation and not giving any credence at all to the voice that says: "I wish I could deal with it this way."

In Conclusion

- Love one another with Christ's unconditional love

- Live and behave in a manner consistent with the spiritual reality of Christ's soon coming

- Maintain your fellowship with Christ, first and foremost and above all things, as your Way, your Direction, your Hope, your Defense and your LIFE!

ROMANS 14

ROMANS 14:1-9

Issues of Conscience

This passage, along with its parallel – 1 Corinthians 8, are the key passages that deal with Christian liberty. This has been a great difficulty for the church, and were these simple chapters heeded the body would get along as it should. It seems quite often that something new comes along. And with each new development we have to ask the question that the world never asks: Should I do that? This question should be governed by the revealed will of God and the abiding desire to glorify and honor the Lord in all things. Romans 12:1-2 tells us how we can "test and approve" the will of God. However, that won't always solve things objectively. For one person overeating may be the greatest struggle of their lives, for others it may be struggles with bitterness or lust. For one person going to a certain movie may insight them to lustful thoughts and to walk in the flesh, for another it may just cause them to have a laugh and move on. This is the issue at hand.

Throughout church history believers have been trying to identify what is going to make people stumble and then eliminate it, or make some law prohibiting it for Christians. Some of the things that have made this list in the past have been alcohol, tobacco, playing cards, gambling, role playing games, video games, dancing, music of various styles, coffee, theater, movies, television, certain foods, and likely countless others. The real question that we have to answer is: What ARE we to do when we know something continually causes us to walk according to our flesh? How are we to respond to others who are tempted to walk in sin by our exercise of our liberties?

A Brief Note

There are a number of moral imperatives revealed in Scripture; things like stealing, lying, cheating, using abusive language, harboring bitterness, drunkenness and the like are all readily laid out in Scripture as being in stark contrast to the word and character of God. These are **NOT** areas of Christian Liberty. When the believer walks in sin it is his brother's place to lovingly restore him (Galatians 6:1-5). These are the things not directly addressed by the Bible.

It's a Life

Why don't we go the simple route? It is one of the marks of all of the major Christian cults (Mormons, Jehovah's Witnesses, Seventh Day Adventists) that they have to keep "updating" their legalism to include all of the new prohibitions and commands. Why didn't God do this for believers? Why don't we get our "updated edition" of commandments from the Lord every year in order to know what is a sin and what isn't?

The answer lies very strongly in what the Lord is creating in us. We are not being conformed to the Law, nor is the Lord making us into robots. The Lord means to conform us fully and freely to the image of Jesus Christ. This is far deeper than just finding out what the new rules are. When the believer walks in the Spirit there will be little struggle to see when something draws him away from the Lord and when something draws Him towards the Lord, this becomes a simple decision that each believer needs to make in their own life as they are conformed to the image of Jesus Christ.

Romans 14:1-4

1Now accept the one who is weak in faith, but not for the purpose of
passing judgment on his opinions. 2One person has faith that he may eat all
things, but he who is weak eats vegetables only. 3The one who eats is not to
regard with contempt the one who does not eat, and the one who does not

eat is not to judge the one who eats, for God has accepted him. [4]Who are you to judge the servant of another? To his own master he stands or falls; and he will stand, for the Lord is able to make him stand.

Getting our Orders

The imperative (command) starts this section simply: Accept. The goal is to accept other believers, as long as it is possible. There are going to be times when a brother cannot be accepted such as when they are teaching something that goes against the Word of God, or when they are living in sin. These brothers are not to be accepted, but rather dealt with in the Biblical manner. However, the hope is that we can accept them, and issues may have to be seriously considered to find out if we have found a sin issue or if this is an area of Christian liberty.

Weak and Strong

Paul now begins to invoke the imagery of weakness and strength. This weakness is in the sense of faith. However, other uses of the word "weak" will help us understand. Someone may choose not to eat spicy Buffalo wings because they have "a weak stomach." Their stomach is not of a strong enough digestive ability to be able to handle this more abrasive food. Another person may refuse to run a marathon because they are too "weak" at that point to do so. This is exactly the picture of the believer here who is not able to partake in all things (specifically here, food and drink). Some cultural insight may be valuable.

Cultural Insight

In this culture, there were many pagan temples. These pagan temples served many purposes. They were the center of worship to a certain idol, they were most like our modern restaurants, they were a source of inexpensive meat (anything that didn't get consumed at the sacrifice could be sold cheap!), and finally they were nearly all places of ritual prostitution. This could cause a number of problems. A person may have made it their practice for many years before meeting the Lord to have dinner at the temple and then go visit the temple prostitutes. It may be that for the rest of his life he cannot divorce the idea of eating at the temple (or even eating meat) from the idea of visiting the prostitutes. Thus, because he has not understood his complete identification with Christ, because He is not yet grown to a place of maturity, he may need to place a hedge around himself and choose not to go by the temple restaurant anymore.

Why else might you be weak?

Outside of the response a person may be weak in their faith because they remember vividly what their life was like when they were in slavery to idols. Simply the knowledge that the meat was butchered by someone who butchered it in dedication to the idol may be too much for them to bear. This may be more understandable when we think of naming babies. "Adolf" was a fairly popular German name. However, after the atrocities of the Nazi party and its ruthless dictator, Adolf Hitler, people stopped using that name any more. A similar thing happened to the name "Ebenezer" after Charles Dickens wrote The Christmas Carol. So a person may not be able to dissociate the product from the source and thus be too weak in faith to partake.

How do I deal with this?

Now we are in the situation where one brother is partaking of a particular issue of Christian liberty while another brother is not. How can they share fellowship when they are divided by an experience with this certain issue? The answer is simple and easy and is wrapped up in the idea of Christ's love. Paul gives a command to each person in the situation.

Weak Brother – Do not regard your brother with contempt-

This shows the obvious temptation of anyone who chooses to abstain from something. The temptation is to think that we are better, or stronger, or more pure, for not partaking of this or that physical pleasure. Legalists have been thinking this way for nearly 2,000 years; pretending that they are somehow better than other Christians because they forgo the simple pleasures and blessings of God. The fact that they forgo these pleasures is fine; however, the attitude that "everyone should do this" or "I am better than other believers because I do this" is sin.

Strong brother – Do not Judge

Once again, this is not talking about a sin issue, this is an issue of Christian liberty. The brother who is not hampered by his weak faith should not judge the brother who cannot enjoy the liberty that is his in Christ. This fellow very often arrogantly looks down upon the one who abstains from something, perhaps accusing him of being a legalist simply for the act of abstaining. Neither attitude is acceptable!

Realize, that you will nearly undoubtedly be on both ends of this spectrum at one point in your life or the other. So both sets of advice apply to every believer at any given point in time. Not realizing this often leads believers to be viewed as hypocrites harshly judging one area of conscience in others while taking advantage of another and calling everyone else legalistic. This is not the ideal for the believer, and it is not the life of Christ within us.

Accepted, Serving and Standing

Now comes the point. The believer is to view his brothers and sisters in the Lord with the greatest sensitivity and understanding. This is based on the fact that the Lord has taken ultimate responsibility for both the believer and his brother. In Christ both are accepted. In Christ both are useful to the Lord and ideally will be walking in the Lord and serving Him. Finally, we get to the idea of standing. Not the fact that the eternal security of believer is in view here again. Every believer will ultimately be made to stand. Not by his or her own works, but because the Lord will make Him stand. This is of the utmost importance. When we get across the table from a brother or sister in the Lord we must understand that they are the Lord's servant and ultimately HE will be the one to establish them, just as He has established us.

<u>Romans 14:5-9</u>

5One person regards one day above another, another regards every day
alike. Each person must be fully convinced in his own mind. 6He who
observes the day, observes it for the Lord, and he who eats, does so for the
Lord, for he gives thanks to God; and he who eats not, for the Lord he
does not eat, and gives thanks to God. 7For not one of us lives for himself,
and not one dies for himself; 8for if we live, we live for the Lord, or if we
die, we die for the Lord; therefore whether we live or die, we are the Lord's.
9For to this end Christ died and lived again, that He might be Lord both of
the dead and of the living.

Watching the Days

Some have wrongly understood this to mean the observation of holidays in general. The context, however, forbids that altogether. The Romans church would have understood this in terms of the demands of the Jewish law. The Jews had special days and season that were given by God to feast and fast, and when they should work and not work. The idea of Sabbath was one that the early Jewish Christians likely continued to observe in some circumstances. Paul is telling these believers that it is not any more pleasing to the Lord to observe the Jewish Sabbath (which goes from sundown Friday night to sundown Saturday night) or whether believers meet together on Sunday (often times wrongly called "the Christian Sabbath", it is not.) Believers could meet together any day of the week at any time of the week, there is no dictate handed down in Scripture. The weak brother sets aside a day, the strong brother observes every day as the Lord's and each one is thankful and is growing towards the Lord.

The "Thank You" test

We can be tempted to try to always be the "strong" one. After all, who wants to be "weak"? And thus force ourselves to partake in certain activities that draw us away from the Lord. On a personal note I have fallen to this. There are certain movies and television shows that I have always enjoyed that I have found contribute to my walking in the sin nature. Those same shows cause no such stumbling in the lives of many of my friends (including my wife!). What I have found? It is okay for me to admit when I am weak. It is good for the believer to abstain from those things which draw him or her away from Jesus. However, I am NEVER to impose my weakness on another.

The thank you test is a simple way to find out if you are actually dealing with some spiritual weakness. If you finish being involved in some activity of Christian Conscience (reading a certain type of book, watching a movie of some kind, enjoying a beverage of some kind) and you can say, "Thank you Lord for that thing. Thank you for the aspect of Your excellence and Your love that I saw there! I praise you for that!" If you can say that in all honesty then chances are this is not something that is a threat to your walk with the Lord at this time. If you cannot give thanks honestly then it may be time to consider distancing yourself from that thing.

Live or Die

Paul brings this issue down to the final importance: it is about the believer's relationship with the Lord. If we live, we live by Christ's life, and by His power. When we die we go home to be with Him. If we are wholly motivated by His grace and His love we may find ourselves participating (or not participating) in a whole number of things that we may not have planned on. A believer, living for the Lord, may find themselves bringing the gospel to places that they would not otherwise go because of some interest that falls into the area of Christian liberty.

Jesus Christ is the life, the hope, and the salvation of the believer. As our eyes are fixed on Him we will be able to avoid the things that draw us away from Him and love others even if they are stronger than we are and not affected by those things. We will also, at times limit our use of Christian liberty because we love a brother or sister enough not to want to tempt them into something that may cause them to struggle or cease to grow in the Lord.

ROMANS 14:10-23

From Liberty to Love

In the previous study issues of Christian conscience was discussed. Once again, this is NOT talking about areas of the Lord's specific moral revelation. There are a number of things that squarely contradict with the Lord's character and command. Lying is not an issue of Christian conscience, neither is sexual immorality. However, other issues like the choice to drink alcohol or coffee, or whether or not the believer will go and see a certain movie (or movies at all) are issues where the individual believer's conscience are involved. To one believer to enjoy a cup of coffee may cause him to praise the Lord. To another believer the act of drinking coffee may make them feel as if they are enslaved to an addictive substance (caffeine) and therefore they cannot drink in faith, with thanksgiving. The command was clear: The brother who abstains is not to distain his brother, and the brother who partakes is not to judge his brother who does not. These verses now build upon the issues of Christian conscience by adding the issue of Christ's love in the life of the believer.

<u>Romans 14:10-15</u>

[10]But you, why do you judge your brother? Or you again, why do you regard your brother with contempt? For we will all stand before the judgment seat of God. [11]For it is written, "AS I LIVE, SAYS THE LORD, EVERY KNEE SHALL BOW TO ME, AND EVERY TONGUE SHALL GIVE PRAISE TO GOD." [12]So then each one of us will give an account of himself to God. [13]Therefore let us not judge one another anymore, but rather determine this--not to put an obstacle or a stumbling block in a brother's way. [14]I know and am convinced in the Lord Jesus that nothing is unclean in itself; but to him who thinks anything to be unclean, to him it is unclean. [15]For if because of food your brother is hurt, you are no longer walking according to love. Do not destroy with your food him for whom Christ died.

Perspective
The previous verses brought us a correct perspective on how we ought to view our brothers and sisters in the Lord. They are servants and possessions of God, saved by grace through faith, and God will make them stand. When it comes to issues of conscience of which we are not able to be involved we are not to judge others for their ability to be involved in that thing at no risk to their fellowship with the Lord. Paul then echoes this thinking by making sure that we understand what it means to judge another brother or sister in Christ. We must keep in mind that the Lord has taken ultimate responsibility for EVERY believer, not just for us! Thus when we judge, or distain, our brothers for issues that are not expressly addressed in the Word or by the character of God we really put ourselves in the place of God over their souls. This is never appropriate.

Judgment Seat
The word "judgment seat" here is the Greek word *bema.* This judgment seat of Christ is distinct from the Great White Throne Judgment of unbelievers recorded in Revelation 20. The Bema seat was a local tribunal where the elders would sit, usually near the gates of the city and judge issues among the city. The bema seat is most clearly described in 1 Corinthians 3.

10According to the grace of God which was given to me, like a wise master
builder I laid a foundation, and another is building on it. But each man
must be careful how he builds on it. 11For no man can lay a foundation
other than the one which is laid, which is Jesus Christ. 12Now if any man
builds on the foundation with gold, silver, precious stones, wood, hay,
straw, 13each man's work will become evident; for the day will show it
because it is to be revealed with fire, and the fire itself will test the quality of
each man's work. 14If any man's work which he has built on it remains, he
will receive a reward. 15If any man's work is burned up, he will suffer loss;
but he himself will be saved, yet so as through fire.

Unrighteous works will be "burned up" but the believer will be saved. It is implied that a believer may not have grown substantially during his entire earthly life, and he will be saved, but his life will have been wasted. Every believer will appear before this seat of Christ wherein the works that we have done as we rested in Christ will be rewarded, while our works done in the flesh will be destroyed, and viewed as wasted time.

Give and Account

As believers, this is an honest way to look at our conduct and our lives. Is what we are doing of eternal value? This doesn't mean that everything we do must be expressly "church activity" making music for the glory of God in one's own room could be every bit as profitable as any other activity if it is done while the saint is in fellowship with the Lord. When we realize that God is longing to reward us for the works that we do when we rest in Him (Ephesians 2:10) we realize the true direction of our lives. Dishes can be done in praise of the Lord. Lawns can be mowed to the glory of the God of the universe. It is we who are to determine in our lives if something is drawing us closer to Christ or away. We are not to be substantially concerned with the areas of conscience that our brothers are involved in, but more concerned with our own lives.

Judging Others

Once again the context here is in issues of conscience. This is not to say that there should be no awareness of sin in the lives of our brothers and sisters. Galatians 6:1-3 is a great example of the reality that we need to be aware and lovingly supportive of our brothers and sisters in Christ when they are walking in sin. This does not mean that we should be tolerant of sin, but rather that we should desire that our brothers and sisters in the Lord who are walking in sin should be restored to fellowship with the Lord Jesus.

Nothing is unclean

This an important issue of understanding the Biblical worldview. Ever since the dawn of Christianity heretics have been attempting to create a false dichotomy between the physical world (as evil) and the spiritual world (as good) however there is no such dichotomy in scripture. A hammer can be very useful for driving a nail, it can also be very useful for murdering someone, the evil of the murder is not found in the hammer but in the person holding the hammer. This is the case with all of the physical substances on earth, as well as many activities. Exercise is not evil, in fact it is good, however a believer may turn exercise into an idol and let that goal of fitness (or the personal vanity associated with being fit) and then it may cause them to walk in sin.

Walking according to Love

Now comes the big standard in the life of the believer: Love. It is the love of Christ by which believers are to be recognized and love should be the ultimate standard of life between believers. This would be impossible to overstate. Thus the question becomes not only: "What am I free to do?" but more importantly, "How will this affect my brother or sister, whom I love with Christ's love?"

Marriage gives us a wonderful illustration of this important point. A husband may like to put the toilet paper roll on with the sheet hanging under the roll, the wife may prefer to have the sheet hanging over the roll. Neither of these two ways of doing this could be said to be "morally right" Thus, we have an issue of Christian freedom. The husband should not be asking, "Why is she so mad about the silly roll of toilet paper." But rather, "I am happy to adjust to your way of doing this, not because it is morally right, but because I love you. It is the same with the believer who is moving to real maturity. Thinking about others before ourselves is what Christ's life looks like in the mature believer.

For whom Christ has died

Remember how much Christ has valued your brothers and sisters in Christ. Just as He died for you, so He died for them. He loves them, values them and cherishes them. When we use our liberty and another is caused to look away from Christ then we must admit that the pleasure that we received from whatever it is pales in comparison to the value of what was lost when another believer took their eyes off of Jesus Christ, even for a moment. This is a radical new standard for us as believers, yet this is the life of Christ in us.

<u>Romans 14:16-23</u>

16Therefore do not let what is for you a good thing be spoken of as evil;
17for the kingdom of God is not eating and drinking, but righteousness and
peace and joy in the Holy Spirit. 18For he who in this way serves Christ is
acceptable to God and approved by men. 19So then we pursue the things
which make for peace and the building up of one another. 20Do not tear
down the work of God for the sake of food. All things indeed are clean, but
they are evil for the man who eats and gives offense. 21It is good not to eat
meat or to drink wine, or to do anything by which your brother stumbles.

22The faith which you have, have as your own conviction before God.
Happy is he who does not condemn himself in what he approves. 23But he
who doubts is condemned if he eats, because his eating is not from faith;
and whatever is not from faith is sin.

Getting the Point

Correct perspective will lead to correct thoughts, attitudes and actions. When we look upon our brother we need to see one for whom Christ has died. Thus, when we have something that is good and yet it causes our brother to take his eyes off of Jesus Christ we could only want to keep that brother from stumbling. When we realize that the thing that we are doing, eating or drinking is of infinitely less value than our brother growing in Christ we will not begrudge not partaking of that in their presence. It will come naturally.

God Approves this Message

The believer who places the need of his brother before his own desires is demonstrating the type of life that God approves: Christ. This is exactly the example that Christ gave us in stepping down to earth, emptying Himself of His self-will, and gave Himself as the payment for our sin. His life will always regard others in this way. And that is what the believer's life in Christ looks like.

Faith and Doubt

Faith and doubt are here. That which is of faith is not sin, yet that which is not of faith is sin. It is amazing to think that there can be perfectly subjective sins. A person who is violating their conscience is actually walking in sin. Just like a child can do something that their parents would approve of thinking that they have to hide it. Even though what they are doing is fine the fact that they were trying to be devious or sneaky in it causes the action to bring trouble between the parent and the child. This is the same issue with us as believers.

Make it personal

Seek to spur your brothers and sisters on towards Christ, even when that means abstaining from something that you know is okay for you to do.

Be true to your own understanding of what Christ has for you, and continue to hold your understanding up to the Bible and check it against the word of God.

Be faithful to what you know will draw you towards Christ and what will push you away from Christ. Live in the realization that it is okay to be where you are at, so long as you are growing in the grace and knowledge of the Lord Jesus Christ.

ROMANS 15

ROMANS 15:1-7

Love
Paul is still outlining what the faith of the believer looks like when it is lived out. This is the practical display of the life of Christ in the believer. It is important to realize that Paul is not making a new law, or a new set of commands, far from it…he is simply laying out the simple reality of what life in Christ looks like. This is the discernment that flows quite naturally out of the character and life of Christ within us, and we see that each of the things discussed has been evidenced first and foremost in the life of Christ.

In Romans 12 Paul wrote about the believer using whatever gifts God gives for the building up of the body. This is what Christ does, and continues to do by indwelling the Church with His Spirit, giving her His Spiritual gifts, and guiding her with His word and Spirit as well as history.

In Romans 13 Paul wrote about being obedient to governing authorities. This was absolutely and amazingly displayed by Jesus Christ when he submitted to the wrongful arrest, trial and persecution of Him for His true claim to be the Christ.

Romans 14 talked about how believers should deal with each other in grace and love regardless of where they stand on certain issues of conscience.

This gracious and loving attitude extends to loving one another based on our mutual and shared position in Christ. Thus, this too is the life of Christ.

<u>Romans 15:1-7</u> (NASB)
[1]Now we who are strong ought to bear the weaknesses of those without
strength and not just please ourselves. [2]Each of us is to please his neighbor
for his good, to his edification. [3]For even Christ did not please Himself; but
as it is written, "THE REPROACHES OF THOSE WHO
REPROACHED YOU FELL ON ME." [4]For whatever was written in
earlier times was written for our instruction, so that through perseverance
and the encouragement of the Scriptures we might have hope. [5]Now may
the God who gives perseverance and encouragement grant you to be of the
same mind with one another according to Christ Jesus, [6]so that with one
accord you may with one voice glorify the God and Father of our Lord
Jesus Christ. [7]Therefore, accept one another, just as Christ also accepted us
to the glory of God.

The Weak and the Strong

Paul is continuing with this idea of the "weak" verses the "strong" believers. In this context the "weak" believer is the believer who cannot, as a matter of conscience, partake of some non-moral issue because it draws him away from Christ. The "strong" brother is the one who is not fettered to any sort of obligations or fears associated with a given issue of conscience.

The weak were told not to disdain those who do something that they themselves are unable to do, the strong believers are commanded not to judge those who cannot partake of something even though it does not affect them. Then Paul progressed to the greater standard of love. It should be the desire of every believer to see his brothers and sisters in Christ built up in everything. As we rest in Christ we will have His desires for our fellow believers and rather forgo our liberties than cause our brothers and sisters in Christ to stumble.

The Purpose of Strength

In the movie Braveheart, William Wallace says to the squabbling nobles of Scotland, "You think these people exist to provide you with position. I think that your position exists to provide them with freedom, and I go to see that they have it!" The purpose of strength in the life of the believer is to build up other believers, not simply to please ourselves. It would be easy to get so enamored with our Christian liberties that we overlook our real calling and purpose of growing in Christ and glorifying Him, exercising our gifts and sharing the gospel. Paul is encouraging believers here to have an eternal mindset.

Putting others first

Each of us is to desire the best good of our brothers and sisters in Christ. We are to desire that the other be built up. Often our sin nature can stand in the way of this. We can be overcome by jealousy or frustration with a person and not desire their best. Other times we may be wanting to use our freedom at their expense, or to their detriment. Neither attitude is concordant with the life of Christ within us, and when we find ourselves wanting less than the very best for other believers (by God's standard, of course) we can be certain that we are no longer walking by means of the Spirit, but are rather walking according to our sin nature.

Just like Jesus

Paul then quotes Psalm 69:9 pointing to that verse's ultimate fulfillment in Jesus Christ. This is in keeping with the reality that this is the amazing and overwhelming life of Christ in the believer. We cannot fake this love. We cannot be deluded into thinking that we could pull this off in any way other than looking directly at Jesus and saying: "I have been crucified with Christ, and I no longer live, but Christ lives in me. The life which I now live, I live by faith in the Son of God, Who loved me and gave Himself up for me." Galatians 2:20. It is only by Christ's amazing life and love that these attitudes and actions will ever be our own.

Whatever was written

Here again, the Old Testament is defended for its inestimable value. For sure we are never to go to the Old Testament looking to come back under the legal system of the Law of Moses, however, in the Old Testament we see the Character of God clearly and completely displayed. We know so much about Jesus from the amazing prophetic writings about him in Genesis 3:15, Psalm 22 &23, Psalm 110, Isaiah 53, Daniel 9 and Zechariah 14-16. We cannot but escape the constant witness of the Old Testament to the character and life of Christ, to man's need for God's gracious provision for man in the person and work of His Son and God's ultimate fulfillment of every promise in the Millennial Reign of Christ on this Earth!

Perseverance and Encouragement

Here the reading of the Bible is linked to the believer growing in both perseverance and endurance. The word "perseverance" here translates an amazing word. The word means to suffer under something and has a specific view to suffering under a serious trial or difficulty. But not just as one who lies down and gives in, far from it, perseverance has a sense of courageously standing up against the trial and weathering it. How could this quality be related to the faithful, believing, and reading of the word of God? For several obvious reasons. The person who reads the word of God regularly and trusts in it knows who the author and perfector of their salvation is (Jesus Christ), they know (and believe) that He who has called them is faithful. As we read and believe the word we see that God called the world out of nothing in six short days' time, and the God who is able to do that is trustworthy in every situation. However, that isn't all the faithful reading of the word is linked to here. It is also linked to encouragement.

The KJV translates this word as "comfort" which is another way to translate this word that would literally translate as "calling alongside." The image is that of one person calling another person alongside (or coming alongside another) and encouraging, comforting, exhorting or strengthening them. The Bible is one of the ways that we encounter the Lord and through the Bible we are transformed from Glory to Glory (2 Corinthians 3:18).

The final thing that Bible reading is linked to is "hope." Biblical "hope" is not "I hope so" hope! Biblical hope is something that we can be certain of. Like the child who knows that summer vacation is coming and thus endures faithfully the final weeks of the semester, our hope is assured for us in Christ. We gain this hope in a number of ways as we read the word. We learn about the amazing character of God. We read of the many stories of His faithfulness and His might and we are reminded that we are in His hands. We are reminded that He will return for us to take His church home to be with Him and await the time when the Tribulation is over and we will reign with Jesus Christ on the restored earth! This is the sure hope that we have been given and that every believer is meant to grow in and rely upon moment-by-moment and day-by-day.

Real, Live, God-made Unity

Another reality of studying the word of God is that believers also grow closer together. Like spokes on a bike tire, as they move closer towards the center they also move towards one another. It is important to note that our unity is a function of what God has done, not a function of something that we do. We are united in the body of Christ not because we have the hobbies, socio-economic class or because we just like each other. We are united based on the person and work of Jesus Christ. This is a wonderful and marvelous thing. And a blessed thing as well. However, if we try to fake or contrive this unity rather than rely on Christ for it we will get nothing but another social club that is of little or no real value to our faith.

One Mind…One Voice

The idea given here is that believers who are united in fellowship will share one mind and one voice. We will not agree about everything, as we are all growing, however, every believer must agree that the Word of God is the ultimate standard and authority. God is not pleased with a variety of different teachings and "opinions" floating around about his word. Many have fallen prey to the epithet: "Unity in the essentials, liberty in the nonessentials, and charity over all." While this slogan seems attractive it is most often used as an excuse for people to refuse to submit themselves to the word of God. Then comes the great challenging question: What is essential? There is little agreement as to where the essentials and the so called "non-essentials" are in the revealed word of God because if God thought it was important enough to communicate with us it would be hard to call something that HE has to say "non-essential". Rather than that flawed way of thinking, believers ought to adopt the truly biblical practice of regularly being in Bible study, readily challenging our understanding and correcting ourselves (and each other) to conform more fully in our thinking, words and actions to the revealed word of God. Such that we are able to honestly say that we are thinking and saying the same thing, or as Paul puts it "having one mind…having one voice."

Charity over all

The one acceptable part of the ridiculous slogan quoted above is the final clause. We are to be longing to accept and encourage one another. Like beloved brothers and sisters we should be patient with one another, knowing that sometimes it takes a long time for a person to change a core way of thinking. This is especially true when the incorrect idea has been imparted and enforced by a long personal history. Thus, our unity is based upon the person and work of Christ and will grow as we continue to grow and progress towards him. There is never any need or cause for belligerent, rude disagreements between believers. We should be able to discuss every issue in honesty and in honest love. Until a person is discovered to be a heretic (standing in opposition to the truth of God) or revealed to be divisive (someone who just delights in arguing or making factions and picking fights), they are to be led forward in grace and love, with all patience, on towards a clear understanding of the word of God.

ROMANS 15:8-21

Romans 15:8-12

[8]For I say that Christ has become a servant to the circumcision on behalf of
the truth of God to confirm the promises given to the fathers, [9]and for the
Gentiles to glorify God for His mercy; as it is written, "THEREFORE I
WILL GIVE PRAISE TO YOU AMONG THE GENTILES, AND I
WILL SING TO YOUR NAME." [10]Again he says, "REJOICE, O
GENTILES, WITH HIS PEOPLE." [11]And again, "PRAISE THE LORD
ALL YOU GENTILES, AND LET ALL THE PEOPLES PRAISE HIM."
[12]Again Isaiah says, "THERE SHALL COME THE ROOT OF JESSE,
AND HE WHO ARISES TO RULE OVER THE GENTILES, IN HIM
SHALL THE GENTILES HOPE."

A Good Servant

The servant in view is Jesus Christ. Paul is appealing to the believers in Rome to maintain the unity that God has won for them on the basis of Christ-centeredness. This is of the utmost importance to understand: THE UNITY OF BELIEVERS IS BASED ON THE PERSON AND WORK OF JESUS CHRIST. If we base it on anything else we will have a local church body that is fractured by the things of this world: by economic status, by ethnicity or descent, by preferences, or by traditions. This is unacceptable.

What Christ Did

Paul then points out that, while the church was never revealed (or seen) in the Old Testament the fact that God loves the gentiles and has a plan for those Gentiles to know glorify and honor Him was never a secret. The reality is (as we saw earlier in this letter) Israel was to be a missionary nation in many regards – pointing the world towards the one true God.

What is the point?

In this wonderful age of the Church (who is the body of Christ as well as the Bride of Christ consisting of all who place their faith in Jesus Christ as described in the first 8 chapters) there is "no Jew, nor Gentile…" thus it makes no sense for us to split up the body of Christ, or depart company from other believers based on that. This was a particularly important issue during the first century as there was open animosity between Jews and gentiles and it was difficult for everyone to reconcile their upbringing to this wonderful amazing thing that God has done for us in Christ Jesus.

Romans 15:13-14
13Now may the God of hope fill you with all joy and peace in believing, so
that you will abound in hope by the power of the Holy Spirit. 14And
concerning you, my brethren, I myself also am convinced that you
yourselves are full of goodness, filled with all knowledge and able also to
admonish one another.

Father May I?

The word "may" here suggests that there is a possibility that this will not happen. Why is that? There is a reality that is of primary importance: This is Paul's wish for the believers in Rome. The next question is that is God the problem when a believer does not experience the joy and peace that is found in Him? The answer: NEVER! God always makes the fruit of the spirit available to every believer who will but abide in Him. God is not the "variable" in the spiritual equation – the believer is.

God of Hope

Hope is something that we look forward to. Man is actually built to have hope, without it we become "hopeless" and this often leads to depression. We were built to rely on God and trust in what He has done and is going to do. This is a remarkable title for God! The God of the Bible is a God who provides hope – something sure that every believer can look forward to. We put all of our hopes in Him, because He is the God of Hope.

Filling

Two ministries of the Holy Spirit that very commonly get confused are the ministries of *indwelling* (the Spirit having taken up permanent residence in the life of the believer) and the *filling* (or control of the believer). While the indwelling of the Holy Spirit is permanent and can never be lost the believer can experience a life *filled* with (a word meaning under the control, or influence of) the Holy Spirit. The believer who is in fellowship with God is filled/controlled by the Spirit, the one who is walking by means of the flesh (or according to *the* Sin Nature) does not.

Joy…peace

Paul is consistent. Galatians 5:22-23 reads: "But the fruit of the Spirit is love, joy, peace, patience, kindness, goodness, faithfulness, gentleness, self-control; against such things there is no law." The reason why Paul is consistent when talking about the characteristics of the Spirit filled life? The Spirit is consistent. When the believer is in fellowship with the Lord these characteristics display themselves *regardless of external circumstances.* This Life is available to every believer at all times because the Lord is so GOOD!

The Power!

By what capacity is this life possible? There are those who work their entire lives to achieve an enduring peace or a joyful attitude. There are many who will look anywhere that even the smallest amount of hope is promised. Even believers accept worldly methods of achieving these ends, however, this is because our sin nature is always unwilling to look to God. However, the Bible never changes the story: this is by the provision of God through the Power of the Holy Spirit. This word for power focus on innate ability. The reality of this statement is that the Holy Spirit is perfectly able to provide this in the life of any and every believer who rests and abides in Him!

Romans 15:15-21

15But I have written very boldly to you on some points so as to remind you
again, because of the grace that was given me from God, 16to be a minister
of Christ Jesus to the Gentiles, ministering as a priest the gospel of God, so
that my offering of the Gentiles may become acceptable, sanctified by the
Holy Spirit. 17Therefore in Christ Jesus I have found reason for boasting in
things pertaining to God. 18For I will not presume to speak of anything
except what Christ has accomplished through me, resulting in the
obedience of the Gentiles by word and deed, 19in the power of signs and
wonders, in the power of the Spirit; so that from Jerusalem and round
about as far as Illyricum I have fully preached the gospel of Christ. 20And
thus I aspired to preach the gospel, not where Christ was already named, so
that I would not build on another man's foundation; 21but as it is written,

"THEY WHO HAD NO NEWS OF HIM SHALL SEE, AND THEY WHO HAVE NOT HEARD SHALL UNDERSTAND." - Rom 15:8-21 NASB

Paul Wrote

These verses enforce what Paul repeated: These letters were sourced in his role and gifting as an Apostle of Jesus Christ. While Paul knew his own limitations and sinfulness, he also knew that these letters weren't just ordinary letters. He knew, very clearly, that he was writing the very words and message of God. Thus he wrote very boldly – because he was certain that what he was writing was no mere "best guess" it was the absolute truth of God. He characterized this reality because of "the grace given me" this specifically refers to his apostolic office (part of which was that the Apostles were used by God to write Scripture). Paul knew his place in Church History was special and that there would be no more apostles after the first generation of believers died away.

The Gospel

Paul highlights his essential role as the "apostle to the Gentiles." As we have seen, Paul didn't ONLY minister to gentiles, but he always went to the gentiles after offering the gospel to the Jews in a new city. Paul's work was to bring the truth of the Gospel into every person's life who would place their faith in Jesus Christ.

The Gospel:

> [3]For I delivered to you as of first importance what I also received, that Christ died for our sins according to the Scriptures, [4]and that He was buried, and that He was raised on the third day according to the Scriptures, [5]and that He appeared to Cephas, then to the twelve." 1 Corinthians 15:3-5 NASB

Then two very special realities about the effects of the gospel are brought forth:

> *Made Acceptable* – All of humanity has been clearly declared to be entirely unacceptable to God. Because God is entirely perfect He cannot accept anything less than perfect. While an earthly

professor may "accept" 70% or 80% as a decent mark, God can accept only 100% righteousness and perfection. How could sinful man hope to be acceptable to God? Only through Christ!

Sanctified – This is a word that we don't often use. The word itself means "to be set apart". So the believer in Jesus Christ has been set apart for Him and for His purposes. This is also related to the word "holiness". We are holy because Christ is holy, and we are positioned in Christ!

When it is Okay to Boast

Boasting is generally abhorred the world over. No one likes to hear another person bragging about their accomplishments or character traits, it is painful and embarrassing. Listening to people talk about their children or their hobbies can be the most painful experience ever because of the horrid nature of boasting. Why? Earthly bragging or boasting comes about when something (or someone) is too central to the believer's self-image. It then becomes disgusting in the sight of everyone else because no matter how good a musician a person is, no matter how wonderful a person's children or grandchildren are, no matter how good at sports a person is, it is not important enough to be worthy of a person's identity. There is NO kind of boasting that is more disgusting than *religious* boasting. A person who is too proud of their grandchildren is far less disgusting than the person who is proud of everything that *they* did for God. However, there is a kind of boasting that is completely appropriate: Boasting *IN* Christ! There are two great reasons for this:

1 Christ (and Christ alone) IS worth finding your identity and self-image in. Every believer should see themselves as a beloved child of God before anything else.
2 Christ IS the only one who can be identified by Himself. When God talks to Moses He says, "I am that I am" God alone is self-existent. We depend upon Him for our existence and thus we can only find a true sense of identity in HIM!

Paul makes it clear that every remarkable and worthwhile thing that he has done has actually been Christ's work in Paul. This is when it's okay to boast: when it is giving glory to Christ alone.

ROMANS 15:22-33

Closing the Letter

Paul is closing up the main portion of his message to the Roman believers, and in so doing we come to the end of the most complete description of Biblical Christianity. Paul closes this Epistle as he started it: by highlighting his desire to be with them. This final section goes over some closing wishes before he takes chapter 16 to give his closing greetings to all of the individuals with whom he has a personal connection.

Romans 15:22-25

22For this reason I have often been prevented from coming to you; 23but
now, with no further place for me in these regions, and since I have had for
many years a longing to come to you 24whenever I go to Spain--for I hope
to see you in passing, and to be helped on my way there by you, when I
have first enjoyed your company for a while-- 25but now, I am going to
Jerusalem serving the saints.

Prevented

Paul's continual commitment to bring the gospel to new places has henceforth prevented him from visiting Rome. He has a longing to go to Rome for quite a number of reasons. As the center of the world at that time it would only make strategic sense to have a church in the hub of the empire. Secondly, it makes the most sense for Paul to be the first apostle to represent Christianity there as it is the center of the Gentile world and Paul is the apostle to the gentiles. Additionally it would be very much the case for Paul to want to make sure that the believers there had not heard some aberrant view of the faith from some unreliable source, as was very often the case in ancient Christianity as well as today.

Getting there…Eventually

Paul had a plan to go back to Jerusalem and then wanted to take a mission trip to Spain which would leave him the perfect opportunity to stop off in Rome for a period of time and strengthen and encourage believers there.

This was a good plan, but God had another plan.

Paul would visit Rome (probably twice). The first time would be in chains. After being arrested in Jerusalem, and being unable to get a fair trial he appealed to Caesar, according to his rights as a Roman citizen. The book of Acts leaves Paul under house arrest in Rome. From this imprisonment he would write the books of Philippians, Ephesians, Colossians and Philemon. Extra-biblical history tells us that Paul was released after his trial and undertook a final mission trip to Spain before He was finally executed by the Roman Emperor Nero.

Paul's round-about path to Rome shows us that the Lord can do amazing things even when what He has in mind doesn't match up with our plans, or how we think things ought to be going.

Romans 15:26-28

26For Macedonia and Achaia have been pleased to make a contribution for
the poor among the saints in Jerusalem. 27Yes, they were pleased to do so,
and they are indebted to them. For if the Gentiles have shared in their
spiritual things, they are indebted to minister to them also in material
things. 28Therefore, when I have finished this, and have put my seal on this
fruit of theirs, I will go on by way of you to Spain.

Making a Contribution

The Jerusalem church had fallen in some very difficult times. Some factors may have been general economic factors. It seems very likely that their initial attempts at communal living had collapsed on itself. This was an understandable situation. The disciples expected Jesus to return any day, so things were sold from time to time when money was needed. However, that pattern could not continue forever and the Jerusalem church was left in a sorry way by this time when they had to allow for the possibility that Christ's return *could* be at any moment but could also be a ways off. However, the Lord met their needs through the generous giving of the other churches that had been planted after the Jerusalem Christians were scattered.

Spiritual and Material Thing

The Church has had a turbulent history when it comes to finances. There have been all sorts of problems in figuring out what the relationship of the church should be to money. Through the millennia institutional churches have been very poor and very rich. Paul himself spoke of the reality that Christians should be giving out of their gratitude for the spiritual blessings that they have been given in Christ, however, whenever the validity of his message was in question Paul would take no money simply because he didn't want anyone else to think that he was sharing the gospel for financial gain. The central thrust of Scripture is plain. We are meant to share physically with those who bless us spiritually, out of gratitude. We can't imagine anyone saying, "I shared this $20 with you and all you gave me was knowledge of the living God!? What a rip off!" It is appropriate and correct for believers to share of their material goods with those who provide spiritual feeding and instruction, however, that feeding and instruction should never come with any fee or charge.

Romans 15:29-33

29 I know that when I come to you, I will come in the fullness of the blessing
of Christ. 30 Now I urge you, brethren, by our Lord Jesus Christ and by the
love of the Spirit, to strive together with me in your prayers to God for me,
31 that I may be rescued from those who are disobedient in Judea, and that
my service for Jerusalem may prove acceptable to the saints; 32 so that I may
come to you in joy by the will of God and find refreshing rest in your
company. 33 Now the God of peace be with you all. Amen.

Fullness of the Blessing of Christ

As we have seen, Paul did not know the conditions under which he would visit Rome. While his situation was not what he had expected, he did come to them in the fullness of the blessing of Christ. Had Paul's plans come through he would have likely had a wonderful time building up and encouraging the saints in Christ Jesus who lived in Rome. However, when he came in bondage he did not see that inconvenience as a curse, but rather as an additional opportunity because he used that opportunity to share the Gospel with the entire guard and many who were involved in the Roman military got a chance to hear the gospel, who may not have otherwise. It behooves every believer to be constantly aware of the wonderful blessings that can take place when God upsets our plans and replaces them with His own best plans.

Urgent Urging

This word for "urge" is the same word that Paul used in Romans 12:1. It has the idea of calling them alongside himself in doing these things. The content of the encouragement is based in the person and life of Christ and the love of the Spirit. What is this urgent urging about? That they would be united. The idea of "striving together" was something that the Romans would understand well. In the Roman military soldiers would back together very closely and form a tortoise shell around them with their shields, thus protecting them from any outward attack of arrows spears or lobbed stones. In order for them to do this they had to be working together, stepping on the same foot at the same time and making sure they wouldn't jostle one another and knock each other over. Believers are meant to share this same unity of thought, direction and purpose. Unity is meant to be the business of a local church body. But not unity around the simple idea of unity, but unity around the revealed word of God and message of the Gospel. The specific endeavor that Paul wants them to be united in is in prayer for him and his ministry.

Prayer Counts

Paul is passionate about prayer. Mentions his prayers for local bodies in every epistle and asks them for their prayer support as well. In fact, he clearly desires this united prayer front even more than he desires physical contribution. The reality is that the Lord wants us to be praying, and the Lord does answer prayer. It is a part of the effective Christian life, and should be a part of our life and growth as a local expression of the universal body of Christ.

Peace

Peace in the Biblical sense (wholeness, completeness) comes only from Jesus Christ and that is Paul's wish for the Roman believers – that they would know Christ's peace. Amen, so be it!

ROMANS 16

Paul does not hate long goodbyes!

The final chapter of this amazing epistle is chiefly concerning Paul's closing salutation, much of which is concerning mentioning individuals whom Paul wishes to greet in Rome. There are undoubtedly a number of reasons for this. First, without our modern convenience of communication a person would try to "kill as many birds with one stone" as possible. So mentioning those relationships in a letter to a distant city simply makes sense. However, there is more. Because Paul had not ever been to Rome it would make sense that he wanted to substantiate his claim by showing the connections between the saints that they already knew and trusted and his own gospel and message. This was, in effect giving him some "street credit" with the believers who had not met Paul face to face. This also established some people they could trust when questions about the faith arose. Then, as now, there were many people longing to pervert the gospel of grace by one means or the other. Paul was mentioning some people whose understanding they could trust.

How to study this section?

While many of these people can be traced throughout Scripture and their names are mentioned in the book of Acts as well as the other writings of Paul; in this study we will focus on some highlights of the things that the Lord finds noteworthy and admirable.

A servant and a helper
Phoebe is mentioned as both a servant and a helper. It was Christ who first was a living example of servant leadership. Mark 10:45 reads: "For even the Son of Man did not come to be served, but to serve, and to give His life a ransom for many." Thus, humble and loving acts of service and helps are wonderful and worthy of recognition before the Lord. It is noteworthy that we have a tendency to make a strange hierarchy of spiritual gifts as well as which jobs are "most important" to the local church body. We find that in God's eyes there is no such hierarchy. Believers must learn to esteem the acts of service that seem simple, easy and humble with the same regard and admiration as the more public "up front" types of gifts. To do so is to see things from God's perspective.

Risked Lives
Pricilla and Aquilla were co-workers with Paul. They were active in evangelism and discipleship. They loved the Lord greatly and even risked their own lives for the gospel. If we understand the gravity of the gospel and how amazing what Christ has done (and what awaits us) we will not value our lives and comfort above what the Lord is doing for us. This does not mean having a death wish, nor does it legitimize reckless behavior, it simply means having an eternal perspective regarding the importance of living out our faith and focusing on Christ regardless of what the world thinks, or what it may cost us (and, throughout history, it has cost many believers their lives).

Position Eyes
Paul's eyes seem to see everyone based upon their position in Christ. The phrases "in the Lord", "beloved", "accepted", "approved", and "workers in the Lord" all speak to the eternal position that each of these believers have in Christ. It is a powerful reality to understand that every believer shares this amazing eternal position in Christ before God. God does not look down and see our frailty and sin, He sees us as we already are in Christ Jesus. It behooves us to do the same thing. This isn't just "putting on a happy face" and pretending that our brothers and sisters in the Lord don't have the same faults that we do, it goes far deeper than that. This is about the tremendous thing that Christ has done in your fellow believers. Recognizing that is the basis for all Christian fellowship, and it is the only appropriate view of your brothers and sisters in Christ.

Romans 16:17-20 (NASB)

[17]Now I urge you, brethren, keep your eye on those who cause dissensions
and hindrances contrary to the teaching which you learned, and turn away
from them. [18]For such men are slaves, not of our Lord Christ but of their
own appetites; and by their smooth and flattering speech they deceive the
hearts of the unsuspecting. [19]For the report of your obedience has reached
to all; therefore I am rejoicing over you, but I want you to be wise in what is
good and innocent in what is evil. [20]The God of peace will soon crush Satan
under your feet. The grace of our Lord Jesus be with you.

TROUBLE MAKERS!

So, rightly does Paul encourage these believers to keep an eye out for trouble-makers. These are people who long to bring about divisive and factious behavior. These are the people who love to argue and love to contradict. Sometimes their motivation is desire for control or power, other times it is an insecurity and a need to be viewed as "right" or "smart" or some other such value; whatever the motivation, Paul warns repeatedly about those who would be argumentative and divisive. In fact, such a man is to be expelled from fellowship if, after two warnings, he does not repent (Titus 3:10).

The Teaching…

Their ability to discern these contradicting and divisive people is found in their adherence to the teaching that they have. For believers today this means knowing what the Bible says. It may seem obvious, but people are open to any and all kinds of deception if minds and hearts are not constantly being set apart and renewed by time spent both in personal Bible reading and in a good teaching situation. This is a stern and serious warning.

Slaves!

Paul reveals these people for what they really are: Slaves! Whether they are slaves to their own physical pleasures, or they are slaves to the desire to be self-righteous and judgmental, they are slaves to their sin nature. The simple reality is that we can often point this out miles before the actual false teaching comes up. A person who is not walking in the Spirit is not going to have the ability to speak on spiritual things. Their minds will constantly be in a state of sin delusion and this will cause them to make factions and splits in the body. Paul warns that believers must keep an eye on people who seem to be on a wrong path.

Still Grace

It is worth mentioning that the word never gets far from this wonderful concept of grace. Even in the verses exhorting believers to be very discerning when it comes to those who would contradict the word of God (or seek to pervert it), there is a reality that what they are to be defending so staunchly is the understanding of grace which Paul has put forth in this epistle. It is the air that they breathe! And Christians who try to live under law or license are like fish out of water – gasping for spiritual air.

Romans 16:21-27 (NASB)

21Timothy my fellow worker greets you, and so do Lucius and Jason and
Sosipater, my kinsmen. 22I, Tertius, who write this letter, greet you in the
Lord. 23Gaius, host to me and to the whole church, greets you. Erastus, the
city treasurer greets you, and Quartus, the brother. 24The grace of our Lord
Jesus Christ be with you all. Amen.

25Now to Him who is able to establish you according to my gospel and the
preaching of Jesus Christ, according to the revelation of the mystery which
has been kept secret for long ages past, 26but now is manifested, and by the
Scriptures of the prophets, according to the commandment of the eternal
God, has been made known to all the nations, leading to obedience of faith;
27to the only wise God, through Jesus Christ, be the glory forever. Amen.

The Mystery

Paul uses a special word to describe his message here: Mystery. A mystery in the biblical sense differs from our common conceptions about a "mystery". While the word mystery may bring images of sleuths and detectives that is almost the opposite of what Paul means by mystery. A "mystery" in the Bible is something that was not revealed in the Old Testament, but has now been made known and made clear. The Church is a mystery that cannot be found anywhere in the pages of the Old Testament. Paul uses the same language in Ephesians 5:32: "This is a great mystery, but I speak concerning Christ and the church." The fact that God would make of Jews and Gentiles a new people distinct from the Jews and the Gentiles (the existing people groups at that time in scripture) was something that was not revealed until the Apostolic time.

To all Nations

In the past God spoke primarily to (and through) Israel. They were His chosen particular people, and in order to truly know and understand God a person had to draw near to the Jews. This, however, is not the case in the Church. In the Church any and every person has access to God. This is of the utmost importance when we understand what God is doing right now in His program for the Church. In this special time we can freely share the gospel with anyone, from anywhere in the world. This is a joy and a pleasure indeed! People do not need to become Jews to be saved, neither do they need to become Americans, or westernized. This is a marvelous blessing for every believer to know and trust in what Christ has done and is doing in making this gospel available to everyone before returning to His program for Israel after the Rapture.

To God be the Glory. Amen.

The purpose of all this? God's glory. God is glorified in His plan for Israel, He is shown to be faithful, righteous, gracious and just. God is glorified through His plan for us in the church. His grace and complete righteousness that were purchased for us entirely at His expense will leave every believer at the end of their lives saying, "Not I, but Christ lives in me!" And giving Jesus glory for everything that He did in each individual believer. Any perversion of this true and wonderful gospel replaces God's glory with man. If man can earn His salvation, then it is to man's glory, but such can never be the case. Additionally, were a person to be able to lose their salvation then keeping it would be, to some degree, the keeping work of the believer for which the believer would deserve glory. However, God's glory is the only glory that is in sight. He will glorify Himself in us, which is a wonderful thing!

ABOUT THE AUTHOR

Bradley W. Maston is the husband of April Maston and the father of four beautiful children. He has walked with Jesus for 20 years and served Him as a missionary, music pastor, youth minister and he is currently the Pastor of Fort Collins Bible Church (www.fortcollinsbiblechurch.com) in beautiful Fort Collins, Colorado. Bradley has a passion for the study and exposition of the Bible and his published works seek to make Jesus Christ known.

Made in United States
Orlando, FL
29 May 2024